ON THE HIGHWAY OF MASS COMMUNICATION STUDIES

The Hampton Press Communication Series
Communication Alternatives
Brenda Dervin, supervisory editor

ON THE HIGHWAY OF MASS COMMUNICATION STUDIES

VEIKKO PIETILÄ

UNIVERSITY OF TAMPERE, FINLAND

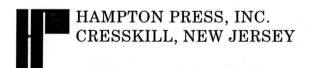

HAMPTON PRESS, INC.
CRESSKILL, NEW JERSEY

Library of Congress Cataloging-in-Publication Data

Pietilä, Veikko.
   On the highway of mass communication studies / Veikko Pietilä
      p. cm. -- (The Hampton Press communication series)
   Includes bibliographic references and index.
   ISBN 1-57273-526-0 -- ISBN 1-57273-527-9
   1. Mass media--History. 2. Mass media--Research--History.
   I. Title. II. Series

   P90.P475 2004
   3'02.23'09--dc22

                               2004040590

Hampton Press, Inc.
23 Broadway
Cresskill, NJ 07626

CONTENTS

PREFACE

This book is a historical overview of theory and research in the field of mass communication studies. It is an account of the major (and some of the minor) scholarly discourses that have been concerned with mass communication within a period that extends from the early days of the press in the 17th century to the time of the Internet and other advanced communication and information technologies at the turn of the new millennium. A preference has been given to scholarly discourses that focus on the relationships of the media and media technology to society, which look on mass communication as consisting of cultural-discursive processes and which analyze the behavior or action of individuals and groups taking part in these processes. The discourses are described with regard to their essential points, and they are contextualized in the social and intellectual settings of their times.

As the aim of this volume is to serve as a textbook, the history of mass communication studies is outlined not for history's sake but for providing the reader with a meaningful entry to this scholarly field. The book is written with the conviction that a historical approach teaches students the importance of looking at the field not only synchronically but also diachronically, as a constellation of discourses that is continually in a process of evolution. What is important to realize is that progress within mass communication studies—as in social sciences more generally—is not linear, but circular. Past discourses and their problematics are constantly reappearing and informing the new discourses, although often in different guises. Therefore, it is essential to know the past in order to be able to assess and analyze the present.

One of the book's starting points is the view that mass communication studies has never lost its nature as a crossroads where influences coming from many different directions meet. Despite being taught as a separate academic subject in many universities, mass communication has not emerged as a unified discipline but has evolved from an incoherent set of approaches into a multiple field of different, often conflicting, discourses. In such a situation, there is a danger that the writer lets his or her penchants and/or dislikes for discourses intermingle with the subject so that the presentation legitimizes the symphatized discourses by putting up so-called "straw men" of the less liked ones. This book has tried to minimize this risk by describing the basic assumptions, main tenets, and research findings of the various discourses as much as possible within their own terms. Of course, the critical debates around them are also discussed, thus not painting them in overly rosy colors.

It is almost commonplace to state that historical accounts of the same subject can be quite different depending on the perspectives from which they are written. Often there is no agreement even on the highways and byways of the development. As shown in chapter 1, there are at least three different "grand narratives" told about the vicissitudes that thinking and research on mass communication have gone through. Of these three, the story outlined within the cultural approach to communication displays a more conscious and less ideologically inclined concern for history than the other two. Consequently, the general outlining of the field's development in this book is informed by that version of history. Within this "grand schema," the focus here is directed on discourses that approach mass communication particularly as a sociocultural phenomenon. Therefore, matters typical of speech communication, rhetorics, linguistics, and other neighboring fields are taken up only in so far as they are articulated in the discourses to be considered, or are indispensable for their illumination. The same applies to normative-political, economic, legal, and historical aspects of mass communication.

The considerations of this book concentrate on North America and western Europe. This may raise charges of myopia, because there is also noticeable work done outside that region in mass communication theory and research. It is, however, indisputable that the work done in North America and western Europe has decisively steered the field's development—even if this may be less due to the ingenuity of thinking than to the fact that English, in particular, but also German and French have enjoyed a hegemonic position as scholarly languages. Whatever the reason, the scholarly world is divided geographically into a privileged center and an unprivileged margin—a fact that one cannot escape when writing an account of a field's development.

The attempt to tell the phases of a scholarly field in a single book is, of course, a risky business. What is presented in the following pages is a result of numerous choices that at many points could have gone in other directions. What is an appropriate way of dividing the field into discourses? From what perspective should the story of the field's development be narrated? On what discourses should one focus when wanting to tell the story from the chosen point of view? What are the major aspects of the chosen discourses that absolutely must be taken into the narration, and what are such minor issues that can be omitted without distorting the description? Every question involves a choice between several alternatives, and each choice unavoidably reduces the richness of the field. But then, this is the way to tell a story. Of course, it remains for the reader to decide how well the story narrated here succeeds in illuminating the field and its fortunes.

This book is based partly on my earlier monograph on the subject, published in Finnish in 1997 by Vastapaino, Tampere. Chapter 1 includes material from my article "Perspectives on Our Past" that was published in Critical Studies in Mass Communication, 11(4), 1994.

It is mostly thanks to the insistence of my colleague Kaarle Nordenstreng that I took the job of writing a book in English on the subject. During the preparation of the manuscript, I benefitted enormously from Seija Ridell's supportive criticism and her ability to find pertinent linguistic expressions at intricate points. I owe further debt to Benjamin Bates who, when visiting Tampere as a Fulbright professor, kindly took the duty of polishing the language, as well as to Brenda Dervin and two anonymous referees whose comments forced me to rethink issues that I had considered already settled. I hope I have been able to meet their critical remarks. It is also thanks to Brenda that the manuscript found its way to the Hampton Press. I am grateful to Barbara Bernstein for accepting the book to be published in the Hampton Press series. Last but not least, my warm thanks go to all my colleagues at the Institute of Journalism and Mass Communication, University of Tampere, who have had, through their extensive comments on the earlier Finnish version, a valuable impact on this English version, too.

—Veikko Pietilä

1

RUSTLING LEAVES
OF HISTORY

Perspectives on the Field's Past

In 1992, Hardt assessed reviews of the development of mass communication studies with the following, not so complimentary words:

> In general, the result of historical inquiry into the field has been fragmentary, mostly episodical or autobiographical in its accounts of the dominant empirical perspectives of communication research and contributes more to the reinforcement of specific theoretical positions than to answers about communication research in the context of social theories. (p. 4)

Although there are quite comprehensive histories of the field—Groth (1948), Hardt (1979, 1992), Lowery and DeFleur (1983, 1988, 1995), Delia (1987), Rogers (1994), Dennis and Wartella (1996), D. Schiller (1996), Schramm (1997) and Mattelart and Mattelart (1998) are relevant examples—Hardt's assessment is, in my view, still largely valid. There are various reasons for this state of affairs, one of them being that the history of writing has been caught in complex ways in the field's inner developments and paradigm struggles. Because of this, it now appears that there are several "histories" of the subject, depending on which particular current ideological position is read back into the past. Not even the "events" that would constitute such a history are agreed upon, as diffuse schools of though and specific lines of inquiry vie for inclusion in the basic narrative (Jowett, 1991, p. 240).

In previous histories of mass communication studies, the ideologies that have guided this writing and led to divergent histories seem to have been furnished above all by the theoretical traditions within which each writer has made his or her contribution. Three traditions, in particular, are pre-eminent (i.e., the classical behavioral tradition, Marxism, and the cultural approach). Each of these traditions has created its own specific story of the vicissitudes that thinking and research on mass communication have gone through. These three perspectives underlie most of the histories of the field written so far.

THE VERSION OF THE BEHAVIORAL TRADITION

In its heyday, from the 1930s to the 1960s, the behavioral tradition was the field's dominant paradigm in the United States and elsewhere. The first U.S. reviews of the field's past were written within this tradition. The actual architects of the tradition's history version were Katz and Lazarsfeld (1955). Their account was the received view that was repeated, with minor alterations, in numerous later reviews. DeFleur's (1966) influential textbook played a major role in disseminating this version.

Research within the behavioral tradition was focused predominantly on the effects of mass communication. No wonder, then, that Katz and Lazarsfeld started with the argument that "all of communications research aims at the study of effect," from "the earliest theorizing on this subject to the most contemporary empirical research" (p. 18). They divided the field's development into two phases, the first consisting of scholarship predating the behavioralist tradition and the second the work of the behavioral tradition itself.

Katz and Lazarsfeld anchored their outline of the first phase in Shils' (1951) view that the so-called theory of mass society was the dominant paradigm of sociological thinking from the late 19th century to the first decades of the 20th century. For them, this theory provided the basis for early theorizing on mass communication, one that included both optimistic and pessimistic views. Although the optimists expected the mass media to create an "informed public opinion," the pessimists looked at them "as agents of evil aiming at the total destruction of democratic society" through their capacity "to rubberstamp ideas upon the minds of defenseless readers and listeners" (Katz & Lazarsfeld, 1955, pp. 15–16).

Nevertheless, the two views had, for Katz and Lazarsfeld, a common root in a conception of modern society as a mass of atomized people largely detached from interpersonal relations and subordinated directly to the media's influence. Katz and Lazarsfeld summarized their view of the early theorizing by saying that the image of its proponents,

> first of all, was an atomistic mass of millions of readers, listeners and moviegoers prepared to receive the Message; and secondly, they pictured every Message as a direct and powerful stimulus to action which would elicit an immediate response. In short, the media of communication were looked upon as a new kind of unifying force—a simple kind of nervous system—reaching out of every eye and ear, in a society characterized by an amorphous social organization and a paucity of interpersonal relations. (p. 16)

The second period, that of the behavioral tradition itself, was described by Katz and Lazarsfeld as an era of empirical research that worked to upset the views they had ascribed to the early theorizing, afterward labeled the hypodermic needle model or the magic bullet theory. This research, they said, showed the relation between the media and the audience to be not direct but mediated by such intervening factors as media exposure or the audience's predispositions. For them, "each time a new intervening factor is found to be applicable, the complex workings of the mass persuasion process are illuminated somewhat better, revealing how many different factors have to be attuned in order for a mass communication message to be effective" (pp. 24–25).

The view of the audience as an amorphous mass—another conception allegedly cherished by the early theorizing—was falsified by sociological small-group research showing that people were by no means short of interpersonal relations (pp. 36–42). The tradition's own studies indicated that the reception of media messages greatly depended on these relations (pp. 25–30). Consequently, interpersonal relations were added as an important variable in the list of intervening factors. In summary, Katz and Lazarsfeld's argument was that due to the intervening variables the mass media were far from the omnipotent force that early theorists supposedly had trumpeted.

Katz and Lazarsfeld's two-phase model of the field's development was tremendously influential. Especially their outline of the first phase was accepted by many as an article of faith (see, e.g.,

Bauer & Bauer, 1960; Bramson, 1961, pp. 96–118; Brown, 1970; DeFleur, 1966, pp. 97–140; Giner, 1976, pp. 231–241; Naschold, 1973; Schramm, 1971). Thus, DeFleur (1966), who is responsible for most popular extensions of Katz and Lazarsfeld's initial view, focused particularly on the second phase. Besides the work of the behavioral tradition, he also paid attention to the co-existent functionalist thinking (pp. 141–158). Moreover, he supplemented the list of intervening variables with sociocultural factors (pp. 133–138). Thus, his picture of the second phase is more nuanced than that of Katz and Lazarsfeld.

One conspicuous feature in the behavioralists' history writing is the almost complete absence of primary sources in building up a conception of early theorizing. For example, when claiming that the early theorists assumed "the omnipotent media, on one hand, sending forth the message, and the atomized masses, on the other, waiting to receive it—and nothing in-between," Katz and Lazarsfeld (1955, p. 20) did not document this claim by any source representing such an assumption. Bramson (1961) and DeFleur (1966), too, scantily documented a corresponding claim, although they, unlike many others, demonstrated that classical sociology contained thoughts inclining toward the theory of mass society.

As is shown later, there have been views coming close to the hypodermic needle model, but on the scholarly arena they formed only a minor trend. For K. Lang (1996), for one, "this frequently cited theory never really had any followers among persons we could consider social scientists" (p. 6). Therefore, the behavioralists' claim that these views constituted the early theorizing in toto implies that they utilized Shils' view as a means for creating a past against which they could give the prestige of scientific truths to their own achievements. In this way, the behavioral tradition, so to say, crowned itself with laurels of science that had driven away a dark superstition. Thus, the tradition's history version functions, above all, as a narrative legitimizing the tradition itself.

THE MARXIST VERSION

In the late 1960s, the behavioral tradition became subjected to escalating criticism. It was argued that the findings, which the tradition had celebrated as scientific achievements, were actually grounded in narrow and questionable premises and that the tradition's preoccupation with individual-level variables had bypassed the broader problems bearing on the media's structural relations to social power and inequality (cf. Gitlin, 1981; Hall, 1982; McQuail, 1977). The critics, mostly Marxists, called for research that would direct its main attention to the dependency of the media on the economic, political, and ideological forces of society.

The critics divided the field's development into three phases instead of two. For them, the first phase was characterized by a belief in the omnipotence of the media; the second, again, by a belief in their ineffectiveness, a belief launched particularly by the behavioralism. The third phase, represented by the critics themselves, was characterized by a tendency to look at the phenomena from a structural point of view. This three-phase model soon gained the status of the received view among Marxists and other critics of the behavioral tradition (see Blumler & Gurevitch, 1982; Curran, Gurevitch, & Woollacott, 1982; Curran & Seaton, 1985, pp. 253–283; Hall, 1982; McQuail, 1977; Philo, 1990; V. Pietilä, 1977).

Although the critics vehemently attacked various aspects of the behavioral tradition, they seemed to have no objection to the tradition's picture of the early theorizing on mass communication. Curran et al. (1982, pp. 11–12), for example, endorsed it fully while writing that the early theorists had "a relatively uncomplicated view of the media as all-powerful propaganda agencies brainwashing a susceptible and defenseless public. The media propelled 'word bullets' that penetrated deep into its inert and passive victims" (pp. 11–12).

On the other hand, the picture drawn by the Marxist version of the second phase of the field's development differed in some respects from that of the behavioral version. Most notably, the Marxist version paid attention to the Frankfurt School, which the behavioral version had disregarded. For Curran et al., the theory of culture industry created by the Frankfurt School during its exile in the United States represents a Marxist mass society theory. They imply, thus, that the School continued the line of thinking typical of the first phase at the same time as the behavioral current was already busy creating "a new academic orthodoxy" to replace it (p. 12; see also Bennett, 1982, pp. 41–47; Curran & Seaton, 1985, pp. 253–261; Hall, 1982, p. 58).

In their appraisal of the behavioral tradition, the critics sought to strip it of the laurels with which it had crowned itself. They did not write a new history of the tradition as much as they judged its history differently: whereas the tradition saw that its work had banished a superstition, the critics argued that it only had replaced a superstition with another—with the doctrine of the minimal effects of the media. Here the critics' allegation was strongly polemical, however (Katz, 1987; see also C. Wright, 1986, pp. 29–31). Their view of the second period was one-eyed also in the sense that, with the exception of the Frankfurt School, it neglected other strains of thinking also appearing in this period (cf. K. Lang, 1980).

According to the Marxist version, the third phase of the field's development was opened through the critique of the behavioral tradition. For Curran et al. (1982, pp. 13–14), the critique came from two directions: the pluralist and critical schools. Both represented already the third phase. Focusing their attention on the critical school, Curran et al. (pp. 23–28) distinguished, with special reference to the British situation, three strains: a structuralist one (the so-called Screen theory), a political economist one, and a culturalist one (represented by Birmingham critical culture scholars). This is one outline of the third phase; another is put forth by Hall (1982, 1989) for whom the third phase is simply tantamount to the rise of a critical paradigm.

The naivete with which the Marxists and other critics of the behavioral tradition took the behaviorists' view of the early theorizing is exhibited by the fact that they did not trouble to go into primary sources. Asp (1986) aptly wondered why "the reviews almost never include explicit reference to mass communication scholars who represented the unreflected ideas" (p. 33) ascribed to early thinking. Although subsequent schools and traditions are more substantially documented by the Marxists, one gets the impression that their version of history is not motivated by an ardent interest in the past as much as creating a weapon in the struggle for hegemony in the field in the late 1970s and early 1980s.

THE VERSION OF THE CULTURAL APPROACH

As we have seen, both behavioralists and Marxists considered the first phase of the field's development as characterized by a blind belief in the omnipotence of the media. On the other hand, the cultural approach, gaining momentum in the 1980s, dismissed this view of history right from the beginning. As a matter of fact, the cultural version paid specific attention to the thinking on mass communication prior to the rise of the behavioral tradition. There are several reasons for this.

Carey (1975, p. 10), a central figure of the U.S. culturalism, once asked where one should turn "for the resources with which to get a fresh perspective on communication," and replied that one ought to go backward to what such theorists as Goffman, Geertz, Duncan, Burke, Park, Dewey, and, still earlier classical sociologists have said about the issue. The field's beginning phase was regarded as an important source for a cultural theory of communication. Maybe J. Peters (1986) had this in mind when he said that without an awareness of the thinking of its ancestors, "mass communication theory will never be able to take its place as an articulated citizen in the republic of social theory" (p. 1).

Parallel with those promoting cultural theory, some others in the early 1980s began to consider the received view of the early theorizing as "almost a cliché" (V. Pietilä, 1982, p. 34). Among others, Wartella and Reeves (1987) concluded from their review of the research on the relationship between media and children that the hypodermic needle model was just as atypical of the research prior to the behavioral tradition as the model of minimal effects was of research in the era of behavioralism's domination. Chaffee and Hochheimer (1985; see also Rowland, 1983) argued that the "'hypodermic needle' and 'magic bullet' images represent misinterpretations of metaphors drawn from medicine, and appear to have been 'straw men' created . . . as a naive conception against which the limited effects model could be contrasted" (pp. 289–290)

Czitrom (1982), representing the cultural approach, said that mass society theory, on which the hypodermic needle model was erected, was "an artificial and spurious construct, an intellectual straw man created by its opponents" (p. 136). On the other hand, Bineham (1988) emphasized that what one sees in history depends on one's point of view. Those seeing the early phase as determined by the "hypodermic needle model" can support their stand with certain primary sources while their opponents can resort to others. The culturalists, then, in their rough treatment of the behavioralists' conception of early theorizing, are not writing "objective" history; they are writing their own version of it.

In the cultural version, the field's development is divided into two or three phases, with the period of the behavioral tradition's domination serving as a structuring principle. The first phase, extending from the late 19th century to the late 1930s, consists of thinking prior to the behavioralists' rule. The second phase covers the growth and bloom of behavioralism from the late 1930s to the late 1960s. The few formulations of the cultural history version that come nearer to the present time pay attention to the critique of the behavioralism and to the rise of cultural voices since the late 1960s as a prelude for a new, third phase of the field's development (e.g., Hardt, 1992, pp. 173–216; Rowland, 1988; Sproule, 1989).

Delia (1987, pp. 20–24) has characterized the first phase as an era of scattered openings. He sorted them into the following thematic strings: communication and politics (including theorizing on propaganda and public opinion), communication and social life, social psychological analyses of communication, communication and education, and commercially focused communication research (pp. 25–54).

History writing from the cultural perspective has paid most attention to the first two strings. Both strings had a common root in progressivism, a social movement that blossomed in the United States from the late 19th century to the 1930s. Nonetheless, the thinking within these two strings took different courses. For example, Lippmann, representing the former string, has been thought to herald behavioralism, whereas Dewey, a representative of the latter string, has been regarded as a starting point for the development leading through symbolic interactionism and dramaturgic analysis to U.S. culturalism as it is represented in recent times by Carey and others (see, e.g., Carey, 1989; J. Peters, 1989a).

Of the second phase, dominated by the behavioral tradition, the culturalist version paints a more plentiful picture than the other versions. Czitrom (1982, pp. 122–146), for example, paid notice not only to behavioralism and the Frankfurt School but also to film studies and cultural anthropology, as well as to criticisms launched by Lynd and Mills against empiricism. He also included Innis and McLuhan, who are often ignored in the field's histories (pp. 147–182). An even more fulsome picture is provided by Hardt (1992, pp. 77–172). When considering the behavioral tradition, the cultural version does not so much criticize it than to focus, for example, on its aspirations to turn itself into an institutionalized scientific discipline (cf. Delia, 1987, pp. 56–73; Hardt, 1992, pp. 84–113; Rowland, 1982, pp. 52–86).

Among the culturalists, the most comprehensive attention to the third phase has so far been paid by Hardt (1992, pp. 173–216). For Hardt, the shift to this phase took place with the arrival of consolidated British cultural studies in the United States in a situation where the various openings of the 1970s had already driven the field into a ferment and where the Frankfurt School, after a long time in the margins, had already begun to attract the attention of communication scholars. Hardt crystallized his point by saying that the third phase took shape "when the American exponents of British Cultural Studies popularized and revitalized the idea of culture as a necessary context for the study of communication and society" (p. 172).

Although the culturalist version of the field's development has, like its predecessors, been shaped by the premises and viewpoints of its own, it nevertheless displays a more conscious concern for history than the earlier versions. For example, its view of the first phase, mythologized by the earlier versions, is firmly built on primary sources. Of course, it is important to keep in mind that primary sources can be chosen and interpreted to support the picture one wants to develop. This also applies—perhaps most particularly—to the history of disciplines.

THE PLOT OF THIS BOOK

The narrative of the field's development told in this book owes much to the culturalist history version. The protagonists of this narrative are not so much individual scholars than the scholarly discourses that are shaped and reproduced through the scholars' work. In other words, the field is seen as a multitude of criss-crossing discourses, and its development is approached through the changes in the constellation of these discourses, that is, through the description of what kind of discourses there has been in the field at each point of time. In more exact terms, the description is focused, in particular, on the way mass communication has customarily been approached and contextualized in the discourses.

The discourses do not exist as such in the scholarly world but rather are created by the analysts of this world on the basis of what kind of similarities and dissimilarities they perceive in the scholarly work. On the other hand, what counts as similar and dissimilar may vary from one analyst to another, as also may vary the pictures they draw of the field's discourses. Moreover, the traditions and discourses seen by some analysts as highways in the field's development, may represent byways to others. It is, thus, a messy and contested terrain on which I have ventured by writing this book.

What I have regarded as highways are discourses articulating, first and foremost, the social, cultural, and/or behavioral aspects of the mass media and mass communication. In other words, I have given preference here to approaches that focus on the relationship of the media and media technology to society, that look on mass communication as a cultural process, and/or that analyze the behavior or action of individuals or groups taking part in this process. Matters that belong to neighboring fields or that concern normative-political considerations or media economy, media law, or media history come to purview only in so far as they are integral parts of the discourses to be taken up. These discourses are not described in their fullness because that would surpass all reasonable limits of a book, but they are illuminated with respect to what I regard as their essential points.

Most reviews of the field's past start from the turn of the 20th century. I, however, have located the starting point of the narrative in the 17th century—in the literature on the press that began to emerge soon after the establishment of the newspaper. Because it was European scholars who first "found the press as problematic institution," worthy to be reflected on (Carey, 1979, p. 11), my story starts from Europe. Americans' belief that a free press would quite automatically function as "an invisible hand leading the will of individuals to the maximation of the social good" (p. 12), began to crumble first around the turn of the 20th century, with the consequence that mass communication was subjected to greater reflection. This moved the field's point of gravity beyond the Atlantic Ocean. My narrative follows the banner, even if I return occasionally to the European scene. First, since the 1970s, when the field began to grow into a truly international undertaking, my narrative, too, takes a more international flavor.

I have divided the field's development into three phases, rather similar to culturalist history version, except that I have put the starting point of the first phase, that of scattered openings, in the 17th century. The second phase, that of consolidation, covers the rise and heyday of the behavioral mass communication research from the late 1930s to the late 1960s. The third phase, termed the period of multiplication, extends from the late 1960s to the threshold of the new millennium. The field's journey through these phases is illuminated with scholarly discourses, judged as most typical of each particular phase.

The most important discourses of the phase of scattered openings were not so much discourses on the press and other mass media as discourses on society that happened to pay notice to the mass media as a specific social institution. This holds true especially in regard to the discourses prior to the turn of the 20th century. Actually, this era forms something like a prehistory of the field. After the turn of the century, the attention of those regarded as the field's representatives began to turn more exclusively to the press and other media even though their discourses did not as yet constitute any disciplinary structure, with the exception of German newspaper science.

In the U.S. context, where mass communication research grew most rapidly at that time, the field began to take form as a distinct scholarly domain first in the second phase, mostly through the work of those representing the behavioral tendency. This is why I call this phase, following Delia (1987, pp. 54–73), the era of consolidation. In this phase, mass communication studies came to age. In fact, what the behavioralists pursued was a discipline properly grounded on principles that they considered scientific. Yet, behind the consensual facade they erected the field was full of contradictions that eventually disrupted the seeming consensus and led to a prolonged "ferment in the field" in the 1970s and early 1980s.

So far, the field had included only a handful of discourses. The ferment changed this by sparking new discourses in such a quantity that the third phase, heralded by the ferment, can well be termed the era of multiplication. Behind this multitude of discourses, one can discern two very broad currents: Marxism blossoming from the 1970s to the early 1980s and the cultural studies approach that took the leading position in the field during the 1980s. These currents are, however, not uniform but both consist of different, even partly conflicting discourses. In concert with the field's multiplication, it also began to break out of its former parochialisms and to grow into a genuine international enterprise.

With these lines as our travel guide, we are now ready to start our journey.

I

SCATTERED OPENINGS FROM THE LATE 17TH CENTURY TO THE 1930S

Carey (1997, p.14) dismissed the "motley collection" of publications on the press, which appeared before the turn of the 20th century, as not relevant for the history of mass communication studies. Here, I disagree with him, because in my view that "motley collection" is important in illuminating the beginnings, however humble, of scholarly work in the field of mass communication. On the other hand, Carey's view gives reasons to divide the long trajectory from the 17th century to the 1930s into the field's prehistory and the beginning of its history proper, with the turn of the 20th century as the dividing point.

The most important context shaping the early discourses considering the press was the coming of what is termed as modernity (Giddens, 1990; J. Thompson, 1995). Modernity did not come into being automatically but rather was brought into existence through a political project carried out by bourgeoisie or, more precisely, by circles that regarded the prevailing social structures as obstacles in the way of the expansion of the (capitalist) economy. The press was involved in complex ways in the political struggles—in fact, it was at that time markedly political press (Groth, 1928, pp. 579–693; K. Pietilä, 1980, pp. 209–279). For this reason, it comes as no surprise that in those days newspapers were considered, first and foremost, from a political perspective.

The breakthrough of modernity enhanced the discourses considering the press with new points of view—the press began to attract attention, among other things, as a vehicle connecting people, as an economic institution, and as a symptom of the commercialization of culture. But there did not arise discourses of the press per se but mostly discourses on society, on economy, or on culture that paid notice also to the press. After the turn of the 20th century, the situation began to change. This change was very conspicuous in Germany—there emerged in the last years of the 1910s a brand new academic discipline, German newspaper science, which concentrated expressly on the periodic press per se.

In the United States, the change was more imperceptible. There, signs of a disappointment at traditional democratic ideals began to appear among observers of political life during World War I, at the latest. Also the press, seen previously simply as a precondition for the realization of those ideals, attracted thereby critical attention. The diagnoses of the situation, and of the mass media's function therein, differed markedly from one another, those presented by Dewey and Lippmann representing the opposite extremes. Park offered sociological perspectives on the matters. It was largely due to their discourses that mass communication became placed firmly on the U.S. scholarly agenda, albeit not yet as an object of a self-sustaining field of research.

The first steps in this direction were the early empirical studies of mass media effects. There are different factors that contributed to the rise of the scholarly interest in this subject. A very important one was that the rapid spread of the then new media, the moving pictures in particular, caused much public concern of their possibly harmful effects on their audiences. Soon after World War I there began to pour public charges that the movies were dangerous to the mental health of children and youth. The Payne Fund project, inspired by these worries, was the first large-scale empirical inquiry into the possible effects of the media. It anticipated the main route taken by mass communication studies in the second phase.

2

PREHISTORY OF THE FIELD

Early Perspectives on the Press

As the talk of modernity in the prologue implies, the press is a phenomenon of modern society. This form of society matured gradually from the dawn of the modern times in the 15th century to the times of the Industrial Revolution in the 18th century. What was at stake was a radical social transformation in which an industrial society founded on capitalist commodity production and market economics displaced traditional agricultural communities.

Already in its process, this transformation began to intrigue persons of letters. The resulting discourse on modern society reached its peak in the classical sociology in the latter part of the 19th century. There, the transformation was customarily described with the aid of two contrasting models of society, the most known labels of which are Tönnies' (1887/1935) Gemeinschaft and Gesellschaft, community and society. The view was that an "old" form of society had been replaced with a fundamentally "new" one.

What separated the "old" and "new" society was especially social organization, that is, the kind of connections between people. The organization of the Gemeinschaft was based on blood relationship, common language and tradition, feeling of togetherness, and so on. People's relations were personal, and everyone had a definite place and status in the community. For these reasons people were "essentially united despite all factors separating them" (Tönnies, p. 40).

The social organization of the Gesellschaft is based on the market. By prompting competition and conflicts of interest, the market undermined the Gemeinschaft's "inherent" unity and induced people to become self-governing individuals detached from each other. Personal relations no longer constituted the basis of organization, but were replaced with impersonal, businesslike relations mediated through the market and its elements: commodities, money, and contracts. This has made people in the Gesellschaft "essentially separate despite all factors uniting them" (Tönnies, p. 40).

The press was born, in the beginning of the 17th century, in a close connection to the "new," Gesellschaft-like forms of organization that were maturing deep in the bowels of the "old" society (see K. Pietilä, 1980, pp. 164–346). The early exposés on the press were either polemical or enlightening and educating—advising people, as did Stieler in his in 1695 published book Zeitungs Lust und Nutz, to use the newspaper usefully (Conter, 1999; Groth, 1948, pp. 14–61)—but after the breakthrough of the Gesellschaft the press was considered particularly within the discourse on modern society. There it was approached from diverse perspectives that I have compressed here into sociological, political, press economic, crowd psychological, and (mass) culture critical ones.

THE SOCIOLOGICAL PERSPECTIVE

Compared to traditional communities, modern societies are far more complex. They are, inter alia, territorially vast, and have a high division of labor and a heterogenous population. An intriguing question was how such complexes manage to survive—for example, how was a continental nation like the United States "to be held together, to function effectively, to avoid declension into faction or tyranny or chaos" (Carey, 1989, p. 5).

In principle, the answer was that modern society's ability to cohere and to function coordinately required its parts to be connected with one another. This fixed the attention to the channels making the contacts between the parts possible. For instance, conditions for the cohesion of the 19th-century United States were "sought in the word and the wheel, in transportation and transmission, in the power of printing and civil engineering to bind a vast distance and a large population into cultural unity" (Carey, p. 5). "In this fragile society technology and communication, then, created the hope of economic, political, and cultural unity" (p. 8).

The Press as a Social Bond

Given the problem of modern society's scope and complexity, it was not hard to envisage the press as a connecting link helping society to cohere. In Germany, Fr. Becher wrote in 1817 that the ads in the newspapers, particularly, will help "our tribe, being now dispersed in principalities, cities, towns and villages, to close the ranks and to form a community" (cited in Groth, 1948, p. 82). Karl Knies (1821–1898) developed this view in a specific direction by envisaging, in his book Der Telegraph als Verkehrsmittel, the press as a vehicle that carries "information through time and over vast distances" (Hardt, 1979, p. 79). This transportation served an integrating function: As carriers of information the newspapers were "the means by which individuals share in the life process of society" (p. 91).

In contrast to Knies, Albert Schäffle (1831–1903) put more emphasis on the meaning of Verkehr as intercourse than as transportation. For him, the press helped "the intercourse of people detached from each other by space and time" (Schäffle, 1867, cited in Groth, 1948, p. 258). This intercourse consists of communication which transmits from one space or time to another "symbolic (ideal) goods" (Schäffle, cited in Groth, p. 259)—that is, words and other symbols carrying information, thoughts, feelings, and so on.

In his magnum opus, Bau und Leben des socialen Körpers (1875–1879) Schäffle viewed society as an organism where the means of communication function as its nerve system (Groth, pp. 264–269; Hardt, pp. 44–57). As society develops, everybody becomes a nodal point where many threads of communication intersect; everybody has "innumerable connections with other active elements of the society's spiritual life" (Schäffle, cited in Groth, p. 266). "Every new book one reads, every newspaper one subscribes, every assembly one steps into—all this increases one's participation in spiritual linkages tenfold or hundred times even in a single day" (cited in Groth, p. 266).

The third grand old man of the early German press theory, Karl Bücher (1847–1930), followed Knies and Schäffle when he stated that "the newspaper is one link in the chain of modern means of transportation/intercourse, that is, of institutions which mediate the exchange of mental and material goods in society" (Bücher 1892/1981, p. 118). The decisive prerequisite for its birth was that society, or parts of it, began to extend beyond the narrow confines of

Gemeinschaft. This prerequisite was fulfilled not until the dawn of the modern times—before that time there was no such "economic interest that would have transcended the tight town walls or manor boundaries and bound people in contact with one another" (pp. 122–123). Only during the 15th century did news begin to be gathered in some systematic manner:

> News from all over the world piled up especially in great seats of transportation and commerce, in nodal points of message flows and in centers of higher learning. There they were combined and sent as letters or appendages to flow in all directions. These handwritten news were already titled as "Zeitungen" or "neue Zeitungen." (p. 125)

Mass communication was viewed as a social bond also in the early U.S. sociology. Charles Horton Cooley (1864–1929), for one, saw it as connecting individual minds so that the public consciousness, which earlier had been limited to local settings, "extends by even steps with that give-and-take suggestions that the new intercourse makes possible, until wide nations, and finally the world itself, may be included in one lively mental whole" (Cooley, 1909/1967, p. 81).

> In the United States, for instance, at the close of the eighteenth century, public consciousness of any active kind was confined to small localities. . . . The isolation of even large towns from the rest of the world, was something we hardly can conceive. . . . The change to present régime of railroads, telegraphs, daily papers, telephones and the rest has involved a revolution in every phase of life; in commerce, in politics, in education, even in mere sociability and gossip—this revolution always consisting in enlargement and quickening of the kind of life in question. (pp. 82–83)

For Cooley, the expansion of communication paved the way for an organic and human social organization in contrast to "mechanical and arbitrary forms of organization" (p. 90). Before that expansion, a human organization was possible only in primary groups. Namely, "as the web of relations extends," the requirements of structure "become more and more difficult to meet without sacrificing human nature; so that, other things equal, the freedom and real unity of the system is likely to vary inversely with its extent" (p. 54). Therefore, only "a rapid improvement in the means of communication . . . supplies the basis for a larger and freer society" (p. 55).

Newspapers and Public Associations

In his famous book, De la démocratie en América (1835, 1840/1990), the Frenchman Alexis de Tocqueville (1805–1859) compared the American democracy with the then French aristocracy in order to find out political democracy's strengths and weaknesses. One of the peculiar things in the United States to which he paid attention were public associations, and he considered the press, in distinction from the theorists just mentioned, in relation to the associations rather than to society as a whole. On the other hand, he also found that the newspapers functioned as connecting bonds; they linked the members of the associations together. Namely, when "men are no longer united among themselves by firm and lasting ties," as in an aristocracy, some other connecting link must be found if there are people wanting to unite (Tocqueville, 1840/1990, p. 111). The means for this is the newspaper.

As a matter of fact, newspapers "become more necessary as men become more equal" (p. 111). In an aristocracy, newspapers are not so indispensable because its principal citizens "discern each other from afar; and if they want to unite their forces, they move toward each other, drawing a multitude of men after them" (p. 111). In a democracy, on the contrary,

> it frequently happens that a great number of men who want to combine cannot accomplish it because as they are very insignificant and lost amid the crowd, they cannot see and do not know where to find one another. A newspaper then takes up the notion of the feeling that had occurred simultaneously, but singly, to each of them. All are then immediately guided towards this beacon; and these wandering minds, which had long sought each other in darkness, at length meet and unite. The newspaper brought them together, and the newspaper is still necessary to keep then united. (pp. 111–112)

Hopes—But Also Fears

From the sociological perspective, the press was seen, in short, as a means of public intercourse in different contexts from associations to society as a whole. As such, it formed one precondition for the social organization of modern society. The newspapers enabled the organization to expand while preserving at the same time its integration. They realized this integrating function in a "natural historical" way—

that is, they were not established purposefully to care for it. Although their role as connecting links was seen mostly in a positive light, it stimulated also fear. Carey (1989, p. 8) has condensed the 19th-century discussion about this issue in the United States as follows:

> The entire experiment could descend into a factionalism or, worse, contagions of demagogic enthusiasm. The lines of communication that transmitted common culture and connected the union could be run backward: a nervous system in reverse might collect anti-democratic energies, mass movements, and primitive enthusiasms in the provinces and concentrate them in the capitals. The hope and the fear are the systolic and diastolic beats of the culture.

THE POLITICAL PERSPECTIVE

The political perspective is the most varied of those considered here. Common to its different themes is a focus on the relationship of the press to democracy and to the public sphere as its precondition. Therefore, I survey first shortly the development of the public sphere using Jürgen Habermas' (1929–) The Structural Transformation of the Public Sphere (1962/1989) as my guide.

Habermas considered the most focal form of the modern society's publicness—the bourgeois public sphere. It began to take form along with the division of society, from the 17th century on, into civil society as the realm of private affairs and public authority or bourgeois state as the realm of public affairs. This division arose from the expansion of the capitalist commodity production and market economy (Habermas, pp. 14–26).

The public sphere grew into an interface connecting the two realms with one another. It was first an extension of the state into the civil society. In this phase, the state authorities used "the press for the purposes of state administration" promulgating through it their "instructions and ordinances" (p. 21). Through this activity, "the addressees of the authorities' announcements became 'the public' in the proper sense" (p. 21). The public sphere began to take bourgeois form when private people came together as an acting public and began to claim "the public sphere regulated from above against the public authorities themselves" (p. 27). Public discussion and use of reason should inform and control the wielding of power. What was actually at stake was the effort of the third estate, the bourgeoisie, to influence the exercise of power and to advocate social reforms that would speed up the capitalist economic development.

Ideally, the bourgeois public sphere was viewed as a site for public discussion and critical use of reason "that do not rest on economic or political power relations but on the convincingness of arguments" (Koivisto & Väliverronen, 1987, p. 20). Those championing this publicness demanded that public opinion, ensuing from the public discussions, ought to be "the only legitimate source" for the legislation (Habermas, p. 54). And, according to Habermas (pp. 79–88), public opinion eventually acquired this status, at least in part. On the other hand, critics of Habermas have argued that public discussion and public opinion have never functioned quite in the way Habermas has insisted, not even during the era of classical liberalism (Koivisto & Väliverronen, pp. 37–53).

A Free Press

Even though the bourgeois public sphere would have deviated from Habermas' ideal picture, it nevertheless was the arena for bourgeois political activity "from below." To be successful, this activity required specific means such as a press free from the censorship of the authorities. Only a free press could function as "a genuinely critical organ of a public engaged in critical political debate" (Habermas, p. 60). No surprise, then, that the question of the freedom of the press—or, more broadly, free speech—had already aroused discussion at the time when the public sphere began to take form. A precursor of this discussion was Areopagitiga, a pamphlet published by the English poet John Milton (1608–1674) in 1644 (see, e.g., Altschull, 1990, pp. 36–42). There he formulated the thesis that when truth and lie get into a race, truth will at last win. But this to happen, speech must be free.

Instead of the scattered remarks on the subject in the 18th century (about them, see Altschull, pp. 43–141), I take up here two views from the 19th century. The first originates from the Englishman James Mill (1773–1836) and the second from Tocqueville.

In his essay Liberty of the Press, Mill (1825) argued that the only kinds of press content that could legitimately be restricted was that which exhorts people "to obstruct the operations of government in detail" such as proceedings "of a court of justice" or of the "administrative functionaries, in the execution of the duties with which they are charged" (Mill, 1825/1992, p. 111). On the other hand, the press should have an unrestricted freedom to exhort people to act against the government itself. Mill's (p. 112) argument for this radical view was that such an exhortation "can have no effects which is worth regarding," unless there exists a wide consent of the necessity of overthrowing the government, in which case "nothing can prevent the exhortation; and forbidding it is useless."

For Mill, only a press independent of the authorities is able to function as a watchdog and to raise people's dissatisfaction with a vicious government that sacrifices "the interests of the many to the interests of the few" (p. 116). Without a check, the government's misdemeanor is inevitable, and there cannot be an "adequate check without the freedom of the press" (p. 116). Mill rejected the claim that freedom of the press is unnecessary because people can rectify the misconduct through the choice of their rulers. How can people know about the misconduct so that they might choose next time wiser, he asked, and the answer was self-evident: in no other way than through the information disseminated by the free press.

> If any set of men are chosen to wield the powers of government, while the people have not the means of knowing in what manner they discharge their duties, they will have the means of serving themselves at the expence of the people; and all the miseries of evil government are the certain consequence. . . . Without the knowledge then, of what is done by their representatives, in the use of the powers entrusted to them, the people cannot profit by the power of choosing them, and the advantages of good government are unattainable. It will not surely cost many words to satisfy all classes of readers that, without the free and unrestrained use of the press, the requisite knowledge cannot be obtained. (pp. 118–119)

According to Pope (1986), Tocqueville also emphasized the significance of "free public opinion and its associated institutions, such as a free press," above all because they act as watchdogs subjecting "the government to the glare of publicity." In contrast to a censored press, a free press functions as an independent intermediary between the government and the people. It "helps the government to increase its responsiveness and effectiveness" by informing it of its failures "to meet the people's needs" and by mobilizing "support for legitimate government action." On the other hand, a free press can pressure "the government to meet the people's needs" and mobilize "opposition to use its force" (p. 66).

In practice, however, Tocqueville viewed with mixed feelings the consequences of a free press in the United States in the first part of the 19th century. He thought, on the one hand, that in democracies "the censorship of the press is not only dangerous, but absurd" (Tocqueville, 1835/1990, p. 183). The right of every citizen to share in the government of society is based on the presumption that they are able to appreciate different facts and to choose between different opinions. "The sovereignty of the people and the liberty of the press may therefore be regarded as correlative, just as the censorship of the press and universal suffrage are two things which are irreconcilably opposed," Tocqueville wrote.

A free press had also an unpleasant side, though. To illustrate it, Tocqueville compared the U.S. press with that of France:

> In France the space allotted to commercial advertisements is very limited, and the news intelligence is not considerable, but the essential part of the journal is the discussion of the politics of the day. In America three quarters of the enormous sheet are filled with the advertisements, and the remainder is frequently occupied by political intelligence or trivial anecdotes; it is only from time to time that one finds a corner devoted to passionate discussions like those which the journalists of France every day give to their readers. (p. 185)

Furthermore, where the French journalist discusses "in a violent but frequently an eloquent and lofty manner" the political matters, the American journalist appeals coarsely "to the passions of his readers; he abandons principles to assail the characters of individuals, to track them into private life and disclose all their weaknesses and vices" (p. 187).

But these are minor issues compared with the fact that a free press can have an enormous influence on public opinion, precisely thanks to its liberty. Whereas people read censored newspapers with a certain mistrust, they have no reason not to believe a free press. Thus, if "many organs of the press adopt the same line of conduct, their influence in the long run becomes irresistible, and public opinion, perpetually assailed from the same side, eventually yields to the attack" (p. 188). This can lead to the tyranny of public opinion.

The Press and the Public Sphere

The discussion around freedom of press was intimately connected with the differing views of the role played by the press in the public sphere. In Germany, this discussion was exceptionally heated in the first half of the 19th century. The reason for this was that the German press was at that time subordinated under more severe restrictions than the press in England or France, let alone in the United States.

For those championing a free press, the press was "the exponent of the people" in the public sphere (Groth, 1948, p. 106). Because in their view, it expresses the people's opinions and aspirations, restricting the press means that the people are "shorn of the right and opportunity to express its opinion" (p. 148). For instance, Prutz stressed, in his writing Der deutsche Journalismus (1854), that "the soul of journalism" is "the free and creative participation of the people for whom journalism should mirror the folk itself, its needs, wishes and hopes, and not what its kings 'please to ordain'" (cited in Groth, p. 178).

The opponents of a free press saw, on the contrary, the press not representing the opinion of the people but instead that of the publishers and editors. In their view, "public opinion is manufactured by the publicists who simply bring their ideas and pretensions in the masses; thus . . . they and their papers must be kept in check" in order not to allow them "to mislead the people's judgment and sound opinion" (pp. 106–107). For Groth, the dispute around freedom of the press was, in the end, a struggle for "the domination of public opinion" (p. 109). In this struggle, the champions of the liberty represented the ascending bourgeoisie; the opponents of it, again, the "absolutistic governments" (p. 106).

The stand that the press represents "the people's voices" mediating "between the governments and their folks" (p. 110), still echoed the classical view of the public sphere described by Habermas. After the mid-19th century, this view began to be replaced with another one. For instance, Schäffle (1875, cited in Groth, pp. 270–271) defined the public sphere as consisting of information, values and expressions of will, disseminated "through the word, writing and print among the mass of people or at least among specific interested circles." Even though he saw it as an intermediary between the rulers and the ruled (cf. Hardt, 1979, pp. 60–63), he did not share the classical view of it as a site for critical public discussion.

In Schäffle's work, the public also lost its classical critical thrust. A public was for him "an object of outside stimulation rather than an aggressive or giving force" (Hardt, p. 63). He saw there being many such receptive publics. Likewise, public opinion was for Schäffle no longer a critical power, but merely reflecting the public's reactions "to specific ideas, decisions and feelings expressed by the leadership of society" (p. 64; cf. also Groth, p. 271). The function of the press was to disseminate these élite thoughts among the common people, on the one hand, and to inform the élite of the popular reaction, on the other (Hardt, pp. 65–69).

Although Schäffle did not see public opinion as a necessarily genuine outcome of a fair interaction between the élites and lay publics, he considered it quite possible "that public opinions are manufactured through clever use of the press and to the point at which the public believes in what it hears and adopts those ideas as its own creation" (p. 64). As this indicates, he did not view the press through very rosy spectacles; for him, it was quite prone to become corrupt and to falsify issues to benefit the politically and economically powerful circles (p. 67).

For Habermas (1962/1989, p. 240), Schäffle's thought is one example of the process in which public opinion became detached from its classical determinations and transformed into "an object of social-psychological research." Signs of this process were visible also in the thought of Tocqueville and the English philosopher John Stuart Mill (1806–1873). Instead of regarding public opinion as something that is created in the public's rational discussion to influence public affairs, they both viewed it above all as a conforming force.

For Tocqueville (1840/1990, p. 10), people's equality in democracies makes public opinion "more than ever mistress of the world." Because democracies are, unlike aristocracies, devoid of eminent people whose differing opinions could give model for the opinions of common people, individuals in democracies are susceptible to what the surrounding majority thinks. From this perspective, the majority opinion is like a tyrant under which one must submit itself. So public opinion itself, "that until then had been deemed the guarantee of reason against force in general" (Habermas, p. 133), began to be looked at as a force against which there are no guarantees.

> Whenever social conditions are equal, public opinion presses with enormous weight upon the minds of each individual; it surrounds, directs and oppresses him. . . . As men grow more alike, each man feels himself weaker in regard to all the rest; as he discerns nothing by which he is considerably raised above them or distinguished from them, he mistrusts himself as soon as they assail him. Not only does he mistrust his strength, but he even doubts of his right; and he is very near acknowledging that he is in the wrong, when the great number of his countrymen assert that he is so. (Tocqueville, p. 261)

Tocqueville thought that if the press unanimously advocated a certain opinion, it would soon begin to function as a public opinion subsuming individuals under its tyranny. Thus, the press has in democracy both positive and negative points: A positive point is its capacity of effectively assembling public associations; a negative point, again, is its capacity of signaling individuals, lost amid the crowd, what opinions they should uniformly have.

Mill's essay On Liberty is a passionate defense for the freedom of individual opinion from the majority or public opinion. Mill's (1859/1948) basic view ran as follows: "If all mankind minus one were of one opinion, and only one person were of the contrary opinion, mankind would be no more justified in silencing that one person, than he, if he had the power, would be justified in silencing the mankind" (p. 14). The unfortunate thing was, however, that non-conforming minorities were always in danger of being silenced by a mediocre majority.

In fact, for Mill, mediocrity was "the ascendant power of mankind" (p. 58). He saw, like Tocqueville, that "individuals are lost in the crowd. In politics it is almost a triviality to say that public opinion now rules the world" (p. 58). Although "those whose opinion go by the name of public opinion are not always the same sort," they always are a "collective mediocracy" (p. 58). Unlike in earlier times when opinions were adopted from eminent persons, the mediocre persons of today adopt their opinions from "men much like themselves, addressing them or speaking in their name, on the spur of the moment, through the newspapers" (p. 59).

A mediocre public opinion is not the fittest for managing the society. For Mill, a better alternative seems to have been a sort of aristocratic democracy. No government, he said, be it democratic or aristocratic, "ever did or could rise above mediocry, except in so far as the sovereign Many have let themselves be guided . . . by the counsels and influence of a more gifted and instructed One or Few" (p. 59). Therefore, as

> opinions of masses of merely average men are everywhere become or becoming the dominant power, the counterpoise and corrective to that tendency would be the more and more pronounced individuality of those who stand on the eminence of thought. It is in these circumstances most especially that exceptional individuals, instead of being deterred, should be encouraged in acting differently from the mass. . . . In this age, the mere example of nonconformity, the mere refusal to bend the knee to custom, is itself a service. Precise because the tyranny of opinion is such as to make eccentricity a reproach, it is desirable, in order to break that tyranny, that people should be eccentric. (p. 59)

An intriguing question is for what reason the classical view of the public sphere began to be replaced, in the mid-19th century, with views like those of Tocqueville and Mill. The fact that bourgeoisie had already succeeded to get into effect those social reforms it had struggled for, probably has something to do with this change. In this new situation, public opinion could not easily claim the heroic role it had had in the previous century. It should also be noted that the public sphere had extended to include new segments of population. Perhaps also this advanced the view that public opinion had regressed to represent mediocrity.

The Press and Democracy

As Carey (1979, p. 11) has stated, scientific discussion around mass communication got started, in the United States, actually as late as in the beginning of the 20th century. Up to that time it was generally agreed that if conditions of the freedom of expression "were maintained then the consequences of mass communication were relatively automatic—an invisible hand leading the will of individuals to the maximization of the social good" (pp. 11–12). However, at least the role of the press in democracy was a theme discussed lively already before the beginning of the scientific discourse proper of the mass media.

According to Carey (1991), one of the focal questions at the Constitutional Convention in the 1787 ran as follows: "Could a representative democracy—a republic—effectively function if it were continental in size and virtually undefined in population?" (p. 33). For instance, as Cooley (1909/1967) has remarked, political philosophy, "from Plato to Montesquieu," had insisted that democracies "must be small." He had an anecdote that "Frederick the Great is said to have ridiculed the idea of one extending from Maine to Georgia" (p. 86). Carey (1989), for his part, referred to Plato's calculations, according to which "the optimal number of citizens in a democracy [is] 5,040" (p. 4).

Those at the convention, who believed in the possibility of a democracy on a continental scale, based their belief on the assumed connecting capacity of communication channels, among them the press. This sociological point is already familiar to us. There is an interesting difference between Europe and the United States: In Europe the political role of the press was usually approached from a vertical perspective as the interface between the rulers and the ruled, whereas in the United States it often was approached from a horizontal perspective as a means to bind the corners of this vast country together.

This view of communication as a horizontal nexus, enabling the continent-wide democracy to survive, was expressed now and then in 19th-century United States. For instance Samuel Morse, the inventor of the telegraphic code, considered telegraphy vital for democracy (J. Peters, 1986, pp. 46–47). In the 1836, six years before the setting up of the first telegraph line, he said, foreshadowing the McLuhanian view of a global village,

> that it would not be long ere the whole surface of this country would be channeled for those nerves which are to diffuse, with the speed of thought, a knowledge of all that is occurring throughout the land; making, in fact, one neighborhood of the whole country. (cited in Czitrom, 1982, p. 177)

In the 1865, poet James R. Lowell visioned that "the newspapers and telegraph gather the whole nation into vast town-meeting where everyone hears the affairs of the country discussed" (cited in Carey 1989, p. 192). However, if he visioned them as means for a democracy by people, he idealized the situation. For instance, the telegraph, owned by the Western Union, did not serve a citizen democracy but the solvent circles involved in news business and commercial activities of other kind (D. Schiller, 1996, pp. 7–10).

Cooley (1909/1967) also approached the relationship between communication and democracy from a horizontal perspective:

> In politics communication makes possible public opinion, which, when organized, is democracy. The whole growth of this . . . is immediately dependent upon the telegraph, the newspaper and the fast mail, for there can be no popular mind upon questions of the day, over wide areas, except as the people are promptly informed of such questions and are enabled to exchange views regarding them. (p. 85)

Due to its chiefly horizontal perspective, U.S. thought lacked a view of the public sphere as a structural space mediating between public authorities and civil society—a space within which and for which different forces are struggling. Characteristic of that thought seems to have been a sincere belief that communication channels are capable of extending democracy nationwide from its earlier local limits. Quite soon, however, this belief began to raise criticism—and even from different directions as chapters dealing with Dewey and Lippmann show.

THE PRESS-ECONOMIC PERSPECTIVE

Along with the commercialization of the press—a process that got started in the first half of the 19th century—some scholars began to pay attention to the conditions and consequences of press economy (see Groth, 1948, pp. 117–118). There were two broad themes capturing the attention: The first concerned the economic conditions of newspaper business, the second involved the critical question of whether or not a privately owned press is capable of fulfilling those public functions it is expected to attend to.

The Economic Conditions of the Newspaper Business

According to Groth (p. 248), Knies was one of the first press economists. Knies stressed, in particular, that press production had an inborn tendency to grow into mass production on a big industrial scale. He thought this resulted from the fact that fixed expenses do not rise to any appreciable extent even if the quantity of copies of one newspaper issue would increase from 100 to 100,000. Due to this, "every step taken towards the realization of big production brings exceptionally great benefits for the publisher and the editorial staff" (Knies, 1857, cited in Groth, p. 248). Schäffle saw similarly the publisher's costs to reduce in proportion to "the advance of technology and the expansion of demand" (cited in Groth, p. 262).

Knies and Schäffle had, after all, quite a limited view of press economy. Wehle's view, presented in his book Die Zeitung (1878), was richer. He saw, like Knies and Schäffle, that with increasing circulation the expenses per one newspaper copy will fall (Groth, p. 305). Thus, the effort to enlarge the circulation is relatively advantageous, particularly because a wide circulation probably would bring in more advertisements that compose the enterpriser's main source of income. But the argument that the "wider the circulation the greater the profit is valid only up to a certain limit" (Wehle, 1878, cited in Groth, p. 305). This limit is reached when the newspaper copies have become so cheap that the money coming from subscribers does not cover the total production costs of the subscribed copies. In such a situation, the enterpriser must spend a part of the returns on advertising on the production costs and must, consequently, be satisfied with a lower profit. With an expanding circulation the profit diminishes increasingly.

The economic conditions for newspaper business as a big industry were, thus, not so simple as Knies and Schäffle had assumed. This was noted also by Emil Löbl in his book Kultur und Presse (1903). Adding to Wehle he saw that the yield on ads has an upper limit "set by the general market conditions, by the capital resources of industrial and commercial enterprises, and by that part of the entrepreneurial capital which the firms can invest in advertising" (Löbl, p. 165). Beyond that limit, every new subscriber is pure loss so that a superb content increasing the paper's circulation can, paradoxically, lead it into a bankruptcy.

The Dual Nature of the Press

Another question was whether or not the privately owned press could attend to the public service expected from it. In Germany, this question was discussed already in the context of the struggle for freedom of press. As remembered, those championing this liberty regarded the press as the exponent of the people's voice toward the rulers while those opposing it saw the press only to represent the opinion of the publishers and publicists. According to Groth, the opponents supported their stand with a reference to a "glaring contradiction": the champions of the liberty of printing charge the press idealistically with the noble duty of advancing democracy, but in reality the press is dominated by "the publishers' and editors' craving for money." Thus, in the opponents' view, a free press "is ruled not by public opinion but actually by profit" (p. 119).

After the mid-19th century, the dual nature of the press as a source for private profit making and as an institute serving the public good was a permanent theme in the German discussion. In the view of Schäffle, for one, the private side will suppress the public one. The market economy will corrupt the press rendering it prone to be bribed to praise or to blame or, equally well, to remain silent. He did not accuse the publishers or editors for this fault; for him, the prime culprit was "capitalism, the dominating system of national economy which has handed the periodic press over to money tycoons" (p. 278).

Bücher had similar views. "The worst fault of the modern newspaper is its nature as a capitalist enterprise, as a profit source for a publisher who is totally unconcerned with the ideal goals the paper might pursue," Bücher (1915, cited in Groth, p. 289) wrote. For him, the dual nature of the press appeared most clearly in the opposition between the newspaper's advertising and editorial parts. A newspaper is, then, an enterprise "that produces advertising space as a commodity to be sold with the aid of the editorial part" (Bücher, 1922, p. 5).

> The entrepreneur does not aim, as naive people believe, to represent in his or her paper public interest and to disseminate the achievements of culture, but to pursue profit through the sale of advertising space. The editorial content is but a costly means for this end. (Bücher, 1892/1981, p. 146)

The criticism, aroused by the dual nature of the press, led to diverse propositions for press reform. Schäffle, for one, saw that the evils of the press could be cured in no other way than by "overthrowing the capitalist system, by transposing private capitals to the capital of public institutions of production and exchange" (Groth, p. 278). He did not, however, advocate the socialization of the press—state control would be even worse alternative than the prevailing one—but proposed the press to be handed over to "publicly owned corporations" (Hardt, 1979, p. 70).

Bücher proposed a lot of reforms (see Groth, pp. 290–292; Hardt, pp. 112–124). To begin with, he thought that professional training might increase newspapermen's strength against economic pressures. He proposed further the abolition of the anonymity principle in newspaper writing and the establishment of a news agency controlled by the press to offset the hegemony of commercial agencies. His most radical proposal was that advertising should be dissociated from the press and municipalized. "Emancipated from the pressures of the publishers' business interests the editorial staff could begin to represent its own stand and strive for nothing else but to serve the common wealth," Bücher (1922, p. 34) dreamt.

According to Hardt (pp. 187–225), the press was criticized on similar grounds also in the United States. Edward A. Ross (1866–1951), for one, was well aware of the dual nature of the press when stating that the purveyance of news is, as responsible public service, "the corner-stone of liberty and democracy," while the sale of advertising space amounts to the marketing of a ware and is "a convenience of commerce" (Ross, 1912, cited in Hardt, p. 210). The latter has risen into a dominant position for which reason the duty of public service suffers. To improve the situation, Ross proposed "the establishment of endowed newspapers" supervised by public boards with representatives from different "civic and professional groups" (p. 212).

THE PERSPECTIVE OF CROWD PSYCHOLOGY

As was indicated in chapter 1, the reviews of the field's past started quite long with the assumption that the scholars preceding the behavioral tradition were mass society theorists believing in the omnipotence of the mass media. And indeed, there appeared occasional views implying a mass society conception. Tocqueville's and Mill's ideas on the reign of mediocre mass opinion are examples of this (cf. Bramson, 1961, pp. 29–30; Giner, 1976, pp. 43–50). In this regard, both gentlemen anticipated the crowd psychological perspective that is the early tendency coming closest to a mass society theory. According to Moscovici (1985), the crowd psychologists thought that their age was the era of masses and that masses are the outcome of "the media" that standardize opinions and change "individual minds into mass minds" making individuals "always ready to be part of a mass" (p. 25).

> When that actually happens, what we see is the troubling and unforgettable spectacle of a multitude of strangers who, without ever having seen each other, are spontaneously swayed by the same emotion and respond like a single being to a band or a slogan and spontaneously fuse into one collective entity. (pp. 25–26)

The Era of Crowds

Moscovici's description of the role that crowd psychology attributed to mass communication is, however, somewhat exaggerated. Let us look at this on the basis of Gustave Le Bon's (1841–1931) classic The Crowd (1895/1960). In it, Le Bon proclaimed the dawning age "the era of crowds" (p. 14). For him, the motor behind the rise of crowds into power was the social upheaval dissolving society through the destruction of the "religious, political and social beliefs in which all the elements of our civilization are rooted" (p. 14). This corresponds to the view, ascribed to the mass society theory, that the social upheaval atomized the traditional orderly societies into an unstructured chaos of masses (cf. Nye, 1975, pp. 73–78).

The picture painted by Le Bon of the era of crowds was dark. For him, the psychology of crowds deviates from that of individuals: the joining of individuals "into a crowd puts them in possession of a sort of collective mind" (p. 27), the most focal characteristic of which is that it makes hardly any room for reason. Being "far more under

the influence of the spinal cord than of the brain," a crowd is dominated by exaggerated "sentiments" and "unconscious motives" (p. 36).
Since the reason is not in control, crowds are susceptible and easy to
provoke through suggestion and a kind of hypnosis to almost any sort
of action (cf. Nye, 1975, pp. 69–71).

Because Le Bon considered society as a mass of irrational
crowds, one expects that he would have entertained a hypodermic
needle theory of mass communication. At least according to Moscovici
(1985, pp. 89–90), he looked at the means of communication as "a
technique which made it possible to subject individuals to the power
of suggestion and hypnotise them in large numbers." On the other
hand, in The Crowd, the power of the press to influence is not
described as overwhelming. In the era of crowds, the press is no
longer able to direct opinions but "the newspapers only reflect opinion" (Le Bon, p. 150). Yesterday's influential press

> has had, like governments, to humble itself before the power of
> crowds. It wields, no doubt, a considerable influence, but only
> because it is exclusively the reflection of crowds. . . . Becoming a
> mere agency for the supply of information, the press has
> renounced all endeavour to enforce an idea or a doctrine. It follows
> all the changes of public thought, obliged to do so by the necessi-
> ties of competition under pain of losing its readers. (pp. 150–151)

Thus, the press influences only through reflecting changes in
public opinion—and this influence affects not so much crowds as the
élites in power at each time. Namely, in order to remain in power the
élite must adapt itself to public opinion. Even though Le Bon's view
of the reign of the crowds and public opinion through the press represents an aristocratic version of the theory of mass society (see
Kornhauser, 1960, pp. 21–43), it does not correspond particularly
well to the hypodermic needle theory as figured in Katz and
Lazarsfeld (1955, pp. 15–30).

The Crowd and the Public

The view of Gabriel Tarde (1843–1904), another key figure of crowd
psychology, differs in many regards from that of Le Bon. Where Le
Bon saw only crowds, Tarde (1901/1969) made a distinction between
crowds and publics. In crowds, people are physically present; in
publics, they are "physically separated" and their "cohesion is entirely

mental" (p. 277). People scattered separately over vast areas can cohere mentally only through the press or some other common medium. This view of Tarde represents clearly the sociological perspective.

A number of people reading the same newspaper is, however, not yet a public. What is needed is a bond between them. "This bond lies in their simultaneous conviction or passion and in their awareness of sharing at the same time an idea or a wish with a great number of other men." (p. 278) If a newspaper seizes its readers by a certain idea, the readers become fused "into a simple and powerful unison," a communion of that idea, "a public" (pp. 286, 288). Such publics can be quite similar with crowds: "there are crowds and publics which are convinced and fanatic and those which are impassioned or despotic" (p. 289). The difference is that publics are in these respects less extreme but "far more tenacious and chronic" than crowds (p. 289).

Tarde saw that, in their capacity of creating publics, the press and publicists had a tremendous power of influence. Far more than statesmen, important publicists "make opinions and lead the world" (p. 284). According to Moscovici (1985, p. 189), Tarde thought that by playing on the "prejudices and passions" of their readers, publicists turn them "into a mass of obedient automata, exemplified by hypnotic subjects who can be made to believe and do anything." Did Tarde, thus, entertain a hypodermic needle theory of mass communication?

The answer must be in the negative. Most importantly, Tarde did not see the press as influencing directly. The transformation of an individual opinion to public opinion is, admittedly, due "to the press," but also, and most particularly, to "private conversations" between people (Tarde, 1898/1969, p. 300). In other words, the press influences by prompting discussion everywhere of the issues of the day and by giving it material. "If no one conversed, the newspapers would appear to no avail . . . because they would exercise no profound influence on any mind" (p. 307). This view anticipates the two-step flow hypothesis presented by the behavioral tradition decades later (Moscovici, 1985, pp. 190–192). So the view of K. Lang and G. Lang (1993, p. 93) that Tarde did not regard the media as "all-powerful," seems to hold true.

Crowd Psychology and the American Mind

Crowd psychology, quite an European current, exerted some influence also on U.S. thought, although, for Sproule (1989), "the European image of an unwashed, alienated mass was transformed by the characteristic American optimism about democratic life" (p. 228).

Nevertheless, there are glimpses of mass society theory also in the U.S. thinking of mass media. Cooley, who took an almost enthusiastic stand to mass communication as a means enabling society "to organize all phases of life on a larger scale and on a more human basis," could also state critically that nowadays contagion may "work upon a larger scale than ever before, so that a wave of feeling now passes through the people, by the aid of the newspaper, very much as if they were physically a crowd" (Cooley, 1909/1967, pp. 193, 151; see also Czitrom 1982, p. 100).

It is, however, a gross exaggeration to label, like Bramson (1961, pp. 100–101), such U.S. scholars as Robert E. Park, Herbert Blumer, or Louis Wirth as mass society theorists and to imply that they entertained a hypodermic needle theory of mass communication. As observed, not even much more extreme thinkers such as Le Bon or Tarde made themselves guilty of it. Although they believed in the influencing power of the press, they both qualified this belief in important ways—Le Bon by seeing public opinion as the real social force and by degrading the press to its servant, and Tarde by regarding conversation as a necessary complement of the press without which there would be no influence whatsoever.

THE PERSPECTIVE OF (MASS) CULTURE CRITIQUE

The early critique of (mass) culture developed hand in hand with the commodification of culture in modern society. Some attacked directly the fruits of this process, whereas others took an indirect route by defending the traditional high culture as a means to hold up such social developments they saw as problematic. Tocqueville represents the former form of critique while the English critic Matthew Arnold (1822–1888) is a prominent representative of the latter.

Mass Culture as the Decay of Culture

Tocqueville has been regarded as a central figure in the journey of mass culture critique (see Giner, 1976; Kornhauser, 1960; Lowenthal, 1960/1968; Rosenberg & White, 1957; Swingewood, 1977). Although he saw democracy as a good system in many respects, he did not remain silent about its evils. One of the defects was "that so-called superior forms of art do not find a favorable soil in modern capitalist democracies" (Lowenthal, 1960/1968, p. 43).

In his arguments, Tocqueville (1840/1990, pp. 48–50) paid attention to the way goods were produced and marketed in a traditional aristocracy and modern industrial democracy. Although the producer in the former sells the product at a high price to a few, in the latter he or she tries to sell it at a low price to all. The price can be lowered either by inventing "some better, shorter, and more ingenious method" of producing the goods or by manufacturing "a larger quantity of goods, nearly similar, but of less value" (p. 50). For Tocqueville, it quite often happens that the producer debases the product's quality "without rendering it wholly unfit for the use for which it is intended" (p. 50). This holds true also for art in democracies: "In aristocracies a few great pictures are produced; in democratic countries a vast number of insignificant ones. In the former statues are raised of bronze; in the latter, they are modeled in plaster" (p. 51).

When comparing literature he saw typical of democracies with that of aristocracies, Tocqueville (p. 59) stated that, in regard to its form, it

> will ordinarily be slighted, sometimes despised. Style will frequently be fantastic, incorrect, overburdened, and loose, almost always vehement and bold. Authors will aim at rapidity of execution more than perfection of detail. . . . The object of authors will be to astonish rather than to please, and to stir passions more than to charm the taste.

According to Lowenthal, Tocqueville believed "that only mass communications will be successful in modern society, and that they can only be products of popular culture, unrelated to valid intellectual, artistic, or moral criteria" (p. 43). Tocqueville admitted, however, that where aristocratic culture is for a few, democratic culture is for many. For instance, democracy "infuses a taste for letters among the trading classes" (Tocqueville, p. 61). A sad thing is, however, that this "introduces a trading spirit into literature" (p. 61). Thus, in the end, the evils that democracy causes in the realm of the arts weigh more than the benefits it entails.

In the subsequent mass culture critique, one finds many Tocquevillean accents. For instance, in his book Revolt of the Masses (1929), Jose Ortega y Gasset raised these concerns to a higher power, especially because he did not see in democracy any particularly good points—for him, democracy was almost pure decay of civilization. Also the Frankfurt School's critique on mass culture echoes certain Tocquevillean views although it rests on a far more nuanced theory.

Fine Culture as a Guard Against Cultural Decay

Whereas Tocqueville regarded fine culture as almost impossible in the conditions of modern democracies, Arnold trusted to its power and thought, in addition, that it could be brought to everybody. As a matter of fact, he considered people's cultural education very important since, in modern society, entirely new functions have fallen on culture.

According to Williams (1980), Arnold's (1869) central work Culture and Anarchy was prompted by workers' demonstrations in London for universal suffrage. Such happenings were, for Arnold, signs of a social crisis: They indicated that anarchy was drawing closer. Things paving way for this development ranged from the idolatry of machinery, a consequence of industrialism, up to the fact that the disintegration of traditional life-guiding norms had enabled people in all classes to do as they like. Arnold (1869/1965, p. 119) assessed critically that "the anarchical tendency of our worship of freedom in and for itself, of our superstitious faith . . . in machinery, is becoming very manifest." He claimed to have

> found that at the bottom of our present unsettled state, so full of seeds of trouble, lies the notion of its being the prime right and happiness, for each of us, to affirm himself, and his ordinary self; to be doing, and to be doing freely and as he likes. (p. 176)

Because Englishmen have "a very strong belief in freedom and a very weak belief in right reason" (p. 121), they are inclined to act without thinking while the right way would be to think first and act then. This brings us to culture. Namely, Arnold saw it as a counterweight to anarchy, produced by thoughtless action, and as a means to curb the crisis that was threatening society. In a situation where a "profound sense of settled order and security, without which a society like ours cannot live and grow at all," is in danger to disintegrate,

> culture, which simply means trying to perfect oneself, and one's mind as a part of oneself, brings us light, and if light shows us . . . that the really blessed thing is to like what right reason ordains, and to follow her authority, then we have got practical benefit out of culture. (p. 123)

But what is culture, more exactly? With a glance to what ordinary people are offered, in contrast to what they need, Arnold characterized it as follows:

Plenty of people will try to give the masses, as they call them, an intellectual food prepared and adapted in the way they think proper for the actual condition of the masses. The ordinary popular literature is an example of this way of working on the masses. . . . [C]ulture works differently. It does not try to teach down to the level of inferior classes [but] seeks to do away with the classes; to make the best that has been thought and known in the world current everywhere; to make all men live in an atmosphere of sweetness and light, where they may use ideas, as it uses them itself, freely—nourished, and not bound by them. (pp. 112–113)

The bringing up of people within the sweetness and light of culture, the inner perfection of men and women, "is particularly important in our modern world, of which the whole civilization is, to a much greater degree than the civilization of Greece and Rome, mechanical and external, and tends constantly to become more so" (p. 95).

This Arnoldian strand re-emerged in the so called Leavisism in the 1930s. Represented most notably by F.R. Leavis and Denys Thompson, it was a high cultural current resisting especially "the influence of 'civilization,' of which one of the most corrupting manifestations was the mass media" (Masterman, 1985, pp. 38–39). It designed the first program for media education, offering the English teachers "a missionary position: a positive and heroic role as bastions of cultural values in a world of change, change that had destroyed 'organic' rural communities and had replaced them with mass production, standardization and a levelling down in cultural and material life" (p. 39). But this is already another story belonging no longer to the field's prehistory.

3

THE GERMAN NEWSPAPER SCIENCE

As indicated in the previous chapter, one of the main promoters of the early press theory was 19th-century German social thought in which the press was approached as an integral part of modern society. Viewed against this background, it is quite interesting that the German newspaper science, Zeitungswissenschaft, which got started in the last years of the 1910s, did not proceed along these broad societal lines, but concentrated mostly on the newspaper as a phenomenon sui generis. This is related to the fact that, as an academic field, its origin traces back to the lectures on the press arranged at certain universities by scholars of different disciplines. Although receiving incentives from these disciplines, its identity was determined by its subject matter—the newspaper institution.

THE COMING OF THE NEWSPAPER SCIENCE

Lectures on the press had been given at German universities from the late 17th century on (Groth, 1948, pp. 25–26, 39–40; Jaeger, 1926, pp. 3–4), but it was only in the late 19th century that this activity got established on a bit more regular basis (vom Bruch, 1980, 1986;

Maoro, 1987, pp. 23–34). The reason was the transformation of the German press into a mass press (vom Bruch, 1986, p. 2). Press performance suffered because the resulting demand for journalists had to be met with untrained manpower. In this situation, some suggested that a university-level education on the press might provide a remedy.

The publishers' and journalists' organizations disagreed at those times as to what kind of education, if any, was desirable (Neff, 1986; Maoro, 1987, pp. 151–160). Most agreed that to become a journalist requires specific innate talents—talents that cannot be learned. On the other hand, the publishers saw that the talents might be cultivated, whereas the journalists' organizations were not so enthusiastic. More acceptable to both parties was the view that future journalists needed education in economic, political, and other social matters and that there was a need for an all-round education on the press for the lay citizens.

The teaching consisted mainly of dissemination of general knowledge about the press. This kept the field "far away from any systematic discipline" (Klose, 1989, p. 15). The way toward a discipline was first opened with the establishment of a specific institute for the subject, Institut für Zeitungskunde, by Karl Bücher at the University of Leipzig in 1916 (Bücher, 1915/1980; cf. Straetz, 1986). The institute paved the way for an autonomous newspaper science notwithstanding that Bücher himself resisted the idea of such a science and regarded the Zeitungskunde, at the most, as an applied subdiscipline of political economy or political science (Groth, 1948, pp. 284–285; Bohrmann, 1986, pp. 100–101).

Zeitungswissenschaft, the science of newspaper proper, began to take form as institutes like the one in Leipzig were set up at other universities, although they usually remained quite small until the Nazi era. Many were financed to a considerable extent by funds granted by the publishers' and, to a lesser degree, journalists' organizations. The financiers aimed, among other things, at raising the generally low esteem of journalistic work and business through the prestige of an academic science (Bohrmann, pp. 96, 103-104; Maoro, pp. 151–165). This support directed the field's gaze narrowly to the press as isolated from wider social contexts—an unhappy situation regarding the development of of the field's potentials.

The establishment of the institutes was often advocated with the argument that the German press had failed in the World War propaganda battle. Afterward, this argument has proved to be quite suspect (Hachmeister, 1987, p. 25), but immediately after the war it seemed plausible. A good example of how newspaper science was justified with a plea of the World War events is offered by Kleinpaul (1927), one of the field's first representatives:

The experiences of the World War and the times straight afterwards opened the eyes of wide circles to see what a power the
press is, if it is led adequately, and what a danger it is, both in
domestic and foreign political sense, if it is conducted badly. This
gave the first impetus to the scientific study of the press as an
important vehicle of public opinion. (pp. 1–2)

WHAT WAS NEWSPAPER SCIENCE LIKE?

Newspaper science was argued for with the necessity of finding out
how the press influences public opinion; yet, after having secured its
foothold, the field gave up the kind of questions that had "initially
launched its disciplinary development" (Bohrmann, p. 105). Instead
of studying the social functions and effects of the mass media, newspaper science developed into a field that "oscillated quite helplessly"
between practical know-how of press work and "scientificism" being
demonstrated predominantly through "an extensive use of definitions
and classifications" (Hachmeister, 1987, pp. 30, 94). Its "scientific
yield remained scanty" (Bohrmann & Sülzer, 1973, p. 86).

Groth (1948, pp. 332, 333) judged the work of academic newspaper scientists by saying sarcastically that in so far as they "exercised theoretical work at all," it took place in their "popular writings,"
which barely came up to professional journalists' treatises on the
press and which at no point surpassed what their predecessors such
as Bücher or Löbl had said. In one respect, however, their writings
did differ from those of the predecessors: Many of them contained programmatic viewpoints as to what kind of discipline newspaper science
is. In fact, early newspaper scholars put much effort into marketing
the field as an autonomous academic discipline comparable to such
settled disciplines as history, political economy, or political science.

Reasons for the Pursuit of the Status of an Independent Science

The fact that there were university-level institutes of newspaper science did not as such mean that the field would have been favored
with the rights of a full-fledged academic science. There were many
obstacles to overcome. For example, the settled disciplines often
looked askance at the newcomer. It was questioned why should there
be an independent science of newspaper. After all, even if ornithology
is necessary, an independent science of hen or duck is not, as Tönnies

mockingly remarked (Käsler, 1981, p. 234). Moreover, the academic circles felt a deep distrust of commercial dailies that "did show no scientific dignity" (vom Bruch, 1980, p. 580). Not "any object taken from today's everyday life qualifies to constitute a science tomorrow," the critics claimed (Haacke, 1970, p. 29).

The field's dependence on publishers' and journalists' organizations made up a specific problem because these groups wanted to keep it close to the practice. This is one reason that the field became a mixture of practical and scientific ingredients (Hachmeister, Baum, & Schuppe, 1983). One can assume that the field's "practicism" and its dependence on outside interest groups increased the mistrust felt toward it in settled academic circles—perhaps an additional motive for its representatives to discuss its nature in a programmatic vein.

The effort to legitimate the field's independency did not stem from an inferiority complex alone but was prompted also by material considerations. It was important for the field to "secure the institutes financially," because "only in this way their survival could be guaranteed" (Bohrmann, 1986, p. 104). The support from the publishers' and journalists' organizations was always dependent on economic fortunes. Thus, there were reasons for the field to strive for an acknowledgment as an independent science, that is, for equal status with the already settled disciplines.

What were the prerequisites for a field to be accepted as a genuine science in Germany at that time? According to Groth (1948, p. 5), it needed an object of study of its own, studied by no other field, and a specific method to approach that object. In addition, it had to build up a disciplinary system that incorporated the knowledge, obtained by studying the object, into a coherent whole. "The object, the method, and the system of the science determine mutually each other" (p. 5). Yet, the most important is the object because it is the starting point for the rest. Not surprisingly, then, the discussion about the independent nature of the field was concentrated on its object of study.

The Discussion About the Field's Object of Study

The view that the field is, or will be, a science with "its own object and own methods" was for its representatives an unquestionable conviction (Bohrmann, 1986, p. 104). The field merited this status simply because, in proportion to its importance, the press was badly neglected by existing disciplines (Everth, 1927, pp. 1–7). Moreover, other disciplines were incapable of studying the newspaper as it is in itself, as one of the field's father figures, Emil Dovifat (1890–1969), said. For him, other disciplines

> study the newspaper only because it mirrors life on realms in which they are interested. The newspaper science, for its part, is not interested in the mirror images but in the mirror itself and the laws of mirroring. (Dovifat, 1929, p. 10)

For this reason Dovifat rejected the idea that the study of the newspaper should be handed over to "different sciences and their methods" and proclaimed: "Our discipline is as independent as its object of study. Distinct and autonomous. A typical phenomenon sui generis" (p. 11).

Another father figure, Karl d'Ester (1881–1960), said that because other disciplines studied the newspaper from their own points of view, the inquiry had seldom "been focused on the newspaper or magazine as such, with all their conditions and consequences" (d'Ester, 1928, p. 123). On the other hand, because "the newspaper can be studied from different angles," the newspaper science was for d'Ester "a combination of existing disciplines" rather than a brand new one (pp. 124, 129). In his way, d'Ester saw the field as a crossroads of disciplines.

The dogma of the field's independence did not produce any consensus in regard to its object of study. This may sound somewhat curious—for what else might be the object if not the newspaper? However, already quite early some newspaper scientists emphasized that focusing on the newspaper restricts the study unnecessarily. Thus, it should to be extended also to other forms of communication. Jaeger (1926, p. 67) reminded that the field's "central problem is the question of public opinion." He said, if one wants to approach this problem, the study should be focused on the Mitteilung, the message. In other words,

> the study should be extended to all forms that the message can assume, to conversation, letter, document, poster, leaflet, newspaper, magazine, almanac, book. Hence, the object of cognition does not stop at the means of expression of the social consciousness but expands to the message as that means. (p. 67)

On this ground, Jaeger (p. 67) suggested that the field should be renamed publizistische Wissenschaft—science of public communication—because the newspaper science was for him unsuitable regarding the extended object of study. Also Traub (1933) spoke for an extended object that would cover the "anonymous, public, mental intercourse of human beings" (p. 180). On the other hand, because he saw all the media serving this intercourse as newspaper-like, there was no need change the field's name.

Schöne (1928), for his part, criticized Jaeger's suggestion. He found it a mistake to count "conversation, letter or book" in that object—"different message forms" belong to it only provided that "they contain ingredients typical of the newspaper" (p. 25). In a way he left the door open for the object's expansion, but did not himself step through that door. Instead, he said that the discipline studies "the newspaper as a manifestation of social consciousness" (p. 25). Here social consciousness amounts roughly to public opinion.

Also Dovifat (1929) took up initially a cautious stand toward the idea of expansion. For him, "a science of public communication" would necessarily be "a discipline whose subject matter would stretch to infinity" (p. 7). Hence, he looked awry at suggestions of a publizistische Wissenschaft and said that such a science, being still in a purely imaginary state, "would be served best by fixing one's gaze on a very restricted area" (p. 8). The fittest for this purpose is newspaper science—after all, in a newspaper "the whole spectrum of public life assumes forms which can be observed exactly" (p. 8).

During the Nazi era, "the discipline split into two hostile camps" (Hachmeister, 1987, p. 55). On the one side were the defenders of pure newspaper science whereas the other side consisted of those advocating the extension of the field's scope to the radio and film and wanting to turn its name into Publizistikwissenschaft, science of public communication (pp. 54–61; Boguschewsky-Kube, 1990, pp. 53–58; Kutsch, 1984). As the end of World War II drew closer, the Publizistik camp, championed particularly by the younger generation of sworn Nazi scholars, seemed to get the upper hand (Hachmeister, pp. 58–60; Maoro, 1987, pp. 399–410).

In the Nazi era, Dovifat, himself no professed Nazi, had begun support the idea of Publizistik (Hachmeister, pp. 88-106). He did not only speak for the broadening of the field's scope to different media, but wanted specifically to focus the study on the publicists at the cost of the journalists. The German parlance distinguished between a publicist, a political opinion leader in the opinion press (Gesinnungspresse), and a journalist, a news worker in the commercial press (Geschäftspresse) (vom Bruch, 1980, pp. 579–585). For Dovifat, the goal of all public media was "mental education and guidance that leads through the powers of conviction into deed and action" (Dovifat, 1955, cited in Hachmeister, p. 109). Consequently, he put the great publicists and their works at the center of the discipline (Rühl, 1980, pp. 25–41).

After the war, the field was reconstituted predominantly as Publizistikwissenschaft (Bohrmann, pp. 109–112). Dovifat's normative doctrine was one branch of it, but there were also competing variants, such as systematic or functional Publizistik which abstained from normativity (Hachmeister, pp. 106–117, 161–171, 210–217; Boguschensky-Kube, 1990, pp. 62–85). Some, however, continued to prefer the old newspaper science. Groth (1948, pp. 334–335) defended newspaper science by arguing that Publizistik would extend the field to cover, for example, theater and even transport services (!). This would lead the field into total chaos. He suggested that only by starting with the newspaper's true essence (Wesen) was it possible to arrive at "an autonomous and systematic newspaper science with an object of study and a method of its own" (p. 338). A similar view was endorsed also by the so called Munich School (Boguschewsky-Kube, pp. 85-89; Hachmeister, pp. 217-222).

The differences between the newspaper scientists and the adherents of the Publizistik, on the one hand, and the competing approaches within the Publizistik on the other, kept alive a heated debate about the field's nature and object long into the 1960s. At that time, it quieted down simply because the empirical study of communication, stimulated by the U.S. example, pushed the so far dominant approaches aside (Bohrmann & Sülzer, 1973). After that, there has been only incidentally discussion about the nature of the field.

Centerpiece: The Newspaper as a Medium

When Dovifat (1929, p. 9), for example, defined a newspaper company as a site where "mental, technical and economic factors stream in an exceptional way into the same channel and form a unity inside the newspaper," his focus was on the newspaper as a particular medium, not as a part of a wider communication process. This focus was typical of most newspaper scholars who, moreover, emphasized mental factors, as they saw them appear in the form of printed newspaper issues, and paid only minor attention to technical and economic factors.

Even before the field got established, the question of the newspaper's essence (Wesen) preoccupied the minds of those writing treatises of the press. What is characteristic of the newspaper? What separates it from other forms of communication? The attempt to solve questions of this kind led the predecessors and the representatives of the field to "an extensive use of definitions and classifications" (Hachmeister, 1987, p. 30).

The attempt to catch the newspaper's essence with a definition proved so difficult that some were discouraged by the task. Brunhuber (1907, p. 12), said that the newspaper "discloses such a quantity of variations and forms of appearance that it is impossible to stuff this diversity of actual forms into the Procrustean bed of a uniform definition, save by stretching the definition so wide that it becomes practically valueless." Nevertheless, many put forth such definitions. For instance, Löbl (1903, pp. 21–22) defined it as "a publication that is issued in regular intervals, copied mechanically, accessible to all people and having a collective and many-sided content which is generally interesting and drawn from the events and situations of the immediate present."

Bömer (1929, p. 10), although valuing the conceptual sharpness of Löbl's definition, criticized it and corresponding definitions for being "valid always only under specific conditions or with regard to a definite era." Often, the features put forth as essential characteristics of the newspaper—as periodic issuing, public availability or timeliness of the content, and so on—are valid in regard to "the modern daily" (p. 11). Groth (1960, pp. 258–343), for his part, charged the definitions for misconceiving unessential characteristics, such as mechanical copying or general interest of the content, as essential. Groth's analysis of the newspaper's Wesen is considered shortly.

In addition to the effort of specifying the essential characteristics of the newspaper, there were attempts to develop taxonomies capable of bringing the multiplicity of the press into order. The question was, into what types do the publications and the texts included in them split up. The effort to solve this problem produced many classifications, the first ones going back to the 18th century (Groth, 1948, pp. 54, 74). They all remained quite commonplace, though, so that one example suffices to illustrate their nature: in his classification of the newspaper content, Löbl (1903, pp. 44–98) first distinguished ads from editorial content, and categorized the latter into portraying content (consisting mostly of news), opinion material and feuilleton, that is, writings on culture and arts.

There were only a few who viewed the newspaper, and also other media, to be components of a wider communication process. Adopting this position seems to have been connected with a distinct sociological orientation (A. Peters, 1930) and/or a view that the field's scope extends to all public media (Traub, 1933). For Traub, the function of the newspaper and other media is to mediate "between a need to inform and a readiness to receive" (p. 14). This is not a one-way process, however, because senders and receivers influence one another—"the message goes to and fro" (p. 15). This way Traub embedded the media in a net of tensions between sender, message, and receiver.

The reviews of the field's history seldom forget to mention Max Weber's (1864–1920) proposition for an empirical sociological study of the newspaper at the first German congress of sociology in 1910. Weber (1910, cited in Hardt, 1979, pp. 181–182) emphasized the project's empirical nature by saying that it will be started "with scissors and compasses to measure the quantitative changes of newspaper contents during the last generation" and that only after "these quantitative analyses we will proceed to qualitative ones." The project gave impetus to some empirical studies, such as Groth's content analysis of the press of Württenberg, reported in his doctoral thesis in 1915 (see Eberhard, 1965, p. 198; Käsler, 1979, p. 215), but it itself came to nothing, for various reasons (Hardt, pp. 183–184; Kutsch, 1988; Obst, 1986).

At least some newspaper scientists were aware of Weber's proposition, but his proposition was not able to push the newspaper science in the direction of an empirical, social scientific research, again for various reasons (Kutsch, 1988, pp. 21–23). One reason was that most early representatives of newspaper science were not versed in sociology. The majority had come to the field from history, and many had also studied political economy, statistics, or jurisprudence. This accounted for the fact that—as the bibliography compiled by Bömer (1929) showed—press historical themes dominated the field's research, followed by economic, statistic, and legal themes. Sociological and psychological themes were neglected for a long time despite some scholars acknowledging their significance (e.g., Everth, 1927, pp. 19–26).

OTTO GROTH AS REPRESENTATIVE OF NEWSPAPER SCIENCE

In conclusion, I specify the picture of the field by considering Otto Groth's (1875–1965) thoughts of the essence of newspaper. Groth was a notable newspaper scientist despite his failure in his aims at entering on a university career (cf. his biography in Publizistik, 1965, 10:3). This perhaps explained his sarcastic attitude toward the academic newspaper science. He wrote his impressive output—including a work in four volumes on the theory and history of the newspaper, Die Zeitung (1928–1930), and a work of seven volumes on the foundations of the newspaper science, Die unerkannte Kulturmacht (1960–1972)—in addition to his regular job as a journalist, and after his retirement forced by the Nazi authorities in the 1930s.

The following review is based on the Kulturmacht. This magnum opus did not have an altogether happy lot. In the first place, it was never completed. Its last volume, edited with great difficulty by Groth's son, was published long after Groth's death (Groth, 1972, p. iv). In the second place, the scientific circles ignored it almost totally (Hachmeister, 1987, p. 208; H. Wagner, 1993, p. 508). This may have depended both on Groth's outsider position and the fact that the empirical, social scientific approach to communication, which was in the ascendancy when the work came out in the 1960s (Bohrmann & Sülzer, 1973, pp. 89–92), had made newspaper science seem hopelessly out of mode. The fate of obsolescence was, in those days, typical of approaches representing the German cultural science (Geistes- or Kulturwissenschaft). Like many traditional newspaper scientists, Groth had followed its banner.

German Cultural Science

One way of elucidating German cultural science is to start with the so called dispute of Erklären/Verstehen or explaining/understanding in the late 19th century (see Riedel, 1978). What was at issue was the methodological nature of human and social sciences. Do they, or do they not, proceed like the natural sciences that were seen to approach their objects of study "from outside," attempting to explain them causally?

The view that human and social sciences are methodologically similar to natural sciences did not get much support in the turn-of-the-century Germany. The opposite view reigned. It consisted of two basic arguments. The first argument was that the objects studied by human and social sciences exist in fundamentally different way than the objects studied by natural sciences. The second argument stated that, because of this difference, the methodological relationship of the sciences to their objects must be dissimilar.

The difference in the objects' way of existence can be illuminated with the aid of Heinrich Rickert's distinction between natural and cultural objects, as interpreted by Juntunen and Mehtonen (1977, pp. 94–98). The starting point is a view that nature is devoid of human aims or purposes whereas culture is constituted precisely of them and of meanings originating from them. Accordingly, natural objects exist by themselves whereas cultural objects exist intentionally or purposefully and have definite value to us. Yet, in the last instance, the difference depends on how objects are considered. If an object—say, a coin—is considered as a purposeful object, as a means of payment, for example, it is an object of culture, but if it is considered as shorn of all its purposes, it is an object of nature, nothing but metal.

Objects' way of existence determines how they are methodologically approached. Human and social sciences approach their culturally existing objects by way of interpreting in order to understand
what values and purposes they embody, how they are determined by
them, and so on. Natural sciences, again, approach their naturally
existing objects from an explanatory angle wanting to account for the
effects of outer causal forces on them.

Groth's View of the Study of Cultural Objects

For Groth, the newspaper is a cultural object and the newspaper science a cultural science par excellence. He agreed with those who
stressed that an object of culture consists of human values and purposes that determine its meanings—it is an object that "people create
purposefully or construct meaningfully so that it suits or is believed
to be suitable for satisfying their bodily and mental needs" (Groth,
1960, p. 5). For Groth, the study of such an object proceeds along two
different axes, which he named Sein- and Solldisziplin. The former
deals with what the object is in reality, whereas the latter deals with
what it could or should be.

The study of what the object is in reality splits up into what
Groth (p. 9) termed timeless and temporal research. These types of
research correspond to theoretical and empirical research. The former is concerned with the object's essence—that is, with the value
images that have motivated the creation of the object, and with the
thereby generated properties or essential attributes that define the
object's specificity and distinguish it from other objects. The value
images belong to ideal, nonmaterial reality (p. 60), and the essence is
timeless in the sense that it cannot be transformed without the object
being turned into something else. For Groth, what a science studies
is determined by the ideal and timeless essence of its object: The
study covers all things possessing the object's essential attributes.

The essence of an object is realized in material and temporal
things. They constitute the area of empirical study that aims, for
instance, at finding out how the things have developed (pp. 9–18).
For Groth (p. 8), things are "constructed in compliance with a certain value image" but they realize this image always imperfectly,
never completely. This "disagreement between the image and the
reality does not leave the creative mind in peace; human beings are
possessed by an effort to bring their creations closer to a general
'model' or 'ideal'" (p. 8). Here is the starting point for normative
considerations.

The normative study of what the object could or should be was divided by Groth (pp. 19–22) into dogmatics and technology. The purpose of dogmatics is to study and clarify the values that an object could or should realize, and to draw from this conclusions for practical actions. This study must recognize that the object's essence restricts the range of possible values: an attempt to force it to realize values alien to its essence may be disastrous. Finally, the objective of technology is to find out practical means for creating such material-temporal things that serve ever better the realization of those values and purposes allotted by the dogmatic study to the object in question.

Most basic of all is the theoretical study of the object's essence, because it would be impossible even to begin to plan an empirical, dogmatic, or technological study without a clear conception of what the object is and what distinguishes it from other objects. That's why Groth put a special emphasis on the theoretical scrutiny of the newspaper's essence and, through it, on the determination of what newspaper science actually studies.

The Meaning of Newspaper and its Essential Attributes

The scrutiny of the newspaper's essence is based on the view that cultural sciences aim at recognizing, through interpretive understanding, "the meaning [Sinn] of human creations, their purposes and motives, the 'teleological context' of things constructed by human beings" (p. 33). Understanding (Verstehen) is the cultural scientific method of making out the essence of an object. On the other hand, the creation of a cultural object can be motivated by several different value images—or, at least, the object can be put into use for various purposes, even for such ones that initially were not thought of. In this sense, it can have multiple essences.

The newspaper, for example, serves a range of economic, political, and social purposes. Due to this, it belongs to the domain of several cultural sciences. This being so, newspaper science can become an autonomous science only on the condition that it can find such a perspective to the newspaper that is possessed by none of the existing sciences. It must interpret the essence of newspaper from this particular perspective and, in so doing, construct a distinctly newspaper scientific formal object. The object of study of a cultural science, then, is not material found ready in reality, but a formal one, constructed by the science itself via the method of understanding, that is, by interpreting the material object from its own perspective.

Groth (p. 12) started his interpretation of the newspaper's essence with the view that the meaning of the newspaper stems from the basic purpose that is served by it—that is "the 'mediation' of mental products." A problem was, however, that "mediation" or, more precisely, the intercourse mediating between people was already studied by sociology. How could it, then, manifest the specificity of newspaper science? To solve this problem, Groth (p. 54) stressed that "the 'essence' of newspaper is not determined through the mediation of human interaction"—which is what sociology studies—"but through what is mediated and how."

The what does not refer to the actual content of a newspaper but to two general characteristics of it (i.e., to universality and timeliness). Similarly the how does not refer to concrete means of mediation but to two general characteristics of them (i.e., to periodicity and publicness). For Groth, these four essential attributes defined both the specificity of newspaper as a means for realizing the value of the "'mediation' of mental products" (p. 12) and the specificity of newspaper science as an autonomous discipline.

Periodicity. A newspaper must be issued in regular intervals. Of course, the publication frequency can, depending on circumstances, vary even greatly, which is why one cannot say for sure what the interval should be. In any case, a sporadically issued text, such as a leaflet, is not a newspaper. Furthermore, the periodic issuing separates the newspaper from the book, for example. For Groth (p. 119), the significance of periodicity lies especially in the fact that without it the newspaper "could not be realized as a universal and timely phenomenon." Periodicity shapes most forcefully the rhythm of the newspaper work (p. 120).

Universality. A newspaper must convey information universally "about all areas of human life and action" (p. 131). Universality is a limit that is never reached. "Like all phenomena in reality a single newspaper is an individual and, hence, narrow—its content is multiple but not universal," Groth (p. 133) stated. In fact, universality is potential: a newspaper "can take on conveying all what it learns about the issues and events in the world" (p. 160), but many circumstantial factors prevent the realization of this potential. According to Huhtiniemi (1986, p. 53), Groth saw the social significance of the (relative) universality of newspaper content in its capacity "to connect individuals as parts to a totality": by providing many-sided information about the social world, this content "functions as social cement preventing the breaking up of social bonds and the atomization of society."

Timeliness. The material conveyed by a newspaper must be "timely, that is, up-to-date, present, abreast with the times, fresh" (p. 171). The time span between the happening of an event and the newspaper's reporting of it should be the shortest possible. Ideally, they are simultaneous in which case "the span between the moments = 0" (p. 173). Newspapers pursue this so eagerly that they eventually "exceed the present and anticipate the future" (p. 175). Due to their keenness for timeliness, their truth is "today's truth" and, hence, "transient, temporary and subjective" (p. 200). Groth (p. 187) admitted that newspapers also contain nontimely material, but, for him, this did not disprove the fact that timeliness is an essential attribute of the newspaper.

Publicness. A newspaper must be publicly available so that, "in principle, everybody can acquire information from it" (p. 206). The intention of a newspaper is to address all people and to "gather them to its readers" (p. 214). Yet, this is possible only until a certain limit beyond which, for instance, its content cannot be equally up to date for everybody, merely because of transportation problems. Consequently, each newspaper occupies "a certain area of circulation, a certain journalistic space" where it is able to transmit to its readers material that is relatively universal and fresh (pp. 219–220). In this space, the newspaper functions "in a uniting, community-creating way" (p. 251).

In addition to these four attributes, Groth (p. 258) spoke of "so-called traces of essence" including, among others, mechanical copying and general interest of the content. Even if properties of this kind go with the newspaper, they are its external marks, not parts of its essence. In regard to the essential attributes it should be noted that they condition and restrict each others' realization. For instance, publicness and universality may confine each other: when a newspaper intends to increase its circulation "in some area or a certain social stratum, it has to limit the width and many-sidedness of its material accordingly" (p. 250). All in all, the relations between essential attributes are anything but simple.

Because Groth defined the newspaper as the object of newspaper science on the basis of ideal attributes, this object includes all things possessing these attributes "regardless of whether the things are materialized in the form of print on paper, letters on wall or words on radio" (p. 7). Thus, the newspaper science does not limit its study only to things that everyone recognizes as newspapers, but extends it to all things being characterized by periodicity, universality, timeliness and publicness. In order to be included in the formal object studied by newspaper science, a thing must display these attributes at least to some extent and be, in addition, improvable in regard to them.

Evaluating Groth

Groth's ideas have been discussed only occasionally. The critique has focused on his distinction between the ideal, timeless essence of newspaper and the material exemplars consumed by people. For Rühl (1969, p. 30), this was pure Platonic idealism where the material world is conceived as an incomplete incarnation of a complete world of ideas. Because Groth privileged the perfect world of ideas, he was unable to study the newspaper as it mundanely is—as a continually changing institution subjected to diverse pressures from its environment (pp. 29–35). The reduction of the newspaper to some fixed essential attributes—an act regarded in any case as highly suspect by empirical social science—does not do justice to "the complexity of journalism" (Rühl, 1980, p. 320). Moreover, Groth's purely conceptual construction of the newspaper's essence remains "subjective and, thus, quite arbitrary" (p. 172).

Groth's way of expression, in particular, fueled this kind of interpretation. Yet, it is possible to see the essential attributes not as entities that mysteriously pop up from an ideal world to determine material newspapers, but as generalizations of conditions that are peculiar to the newspaper institution (cf. H. Wagner, 1993, pp. 508–510). Without fulfilling the requirements of periodicity, universality, timeliness, and publicness, to some discernible degree at least, one does not produce newspapers and the end product will be something else. So there is necessarily no arbitrariness in the construction of the attributes even if they can be judged as quite trivial (Rühl, 1980, p. 320) and their use by Groth as more or less inconsistent (Merten, 1973).

For Rühl (1969, p. 34), "an unbridgeable gap" separates the Grothian abstract essence and concrete newspapers: they are incommensurable realms. For Huhtiniemi (1986, p. 72), again, the essential attributes invade the mundane newspaper work and define "the specificity of journalistic practice compared to other performances of intellectual work" by staking out "the limits and necessities that confine journalistic work." Groth (1962, pp. 217–242) analyzed interestingly, although very theoretically, the forms the journalistic work takes on within the limits of the essential attributes. For instance, periodicity makes it fragmentary: It continually breaks off and begins anew. Universality makes it wide but superficial. Timeliness determines the work tempo, the style of expression, and the content of journalists' thought.

Groth's effort to lay the foundations for an autonomous newspaper science remained after all half way. He was preoccupied with assigning a specific object of study for this science, but the object alone cannot establish a self-sufficient discipline. This is revealed, for instance, by the fact that in describing the "newspaper-scientific" object Groth had to rely on "results of innumerable subsidiary sciences" (Huhtiniemi, p. 68). In other words, even if Groth's theory did not reside in some ideal world, isolated from the mundane reality, he nevertheless did not succeed to show how this theory might be utilized in empirical research (p. 69).

MARGINALIZATION OF THE NEWSPAPER SCIENCE

In the 1960s, the Zeitungs- or Publizistikwissenschaft began to lose its positions when behaviorally oriented empirical mass communication research started its triumphal march in Germany, too (Hachmeister, 1987, pp. 206–247). Its position was also diminished by the critical or Marxist currents appearing in the late 1960s (Bohrmann & Sülzer, 1973; Robes, 1990, pp. 5–18). Since the 1970s, the science of newspaper/public communication lingered in the field's margins.

Newspaper science was charged by the representatives of the ascending approaches for many sins. It was seen as having remained "at the stage of closet scholarship" (Vehmas, 1964, p. 466). It was characterized as "cumbersome and, for the most part, fruitless" (Vehmas, 1967/1985, p. 1) or "estranged from reality" (Silbermann, 1973, p. 4). It was blamed for nurturing a view that it is "much more 'scientific' to speculate about facts than to investigate them with appropriate methods" (Eberhard, 1961, p. 261). These kinds of judgments probably stem from newspaper science's excessive preoccupation with conceptual definitions and classifications at the cost of empirical research.

Many critics saw the normative orientation of newspaper science as its original sin. Eberhard (p. 264; cf. also 1964) was one of the earliest turning against this and demanding the discipline to be "a value-free science in the sense of Max Weber." He also substituted natural science for cultural science as the ideal to be followed. Similarly, Dröge and Lerg (1965, p. 253) demanded the field to turn "from a normative discipline to a value-free empirical science." For them, the newspaper science was nothing but "ideology concerning either 'the publicist as a personality' or journalistic profession—all this enlivened, at best, with more or less systematic history writing that almost in no case does risk going beyond the epochs of Johannes Gutenberg."

German newspaper science is a peculiarity in its almost monomaniac urge to establish itself as an autonomous science. In no other tradition of the field does one meet a corresponding persistence, although the field's disciplinary status has been discussed quite frequently. The debate has fluctuated along a dimension ranging from those who speak without hesitation of communication studies as a discipline (e.g., DeFleur & Ball-Rokeach, 1975, p. vii; Fischer, 1978, pp. 11–23), to those who reject all its aspirations to be one (e.g. Hall, 1989). Yet, it is unusual to discuss the conditions on which communication studies might become an independent discipline (cf. V. Pietilä, 1978). By tackling this question outright, German newspaper science has provided an example that those occupied with the field's scientific status should take into account.

The preoccupation with the field's scientific status led the culturally driven newspaper science to approach the newspaper from a perspective that is not far from today's views of meaning and genre. Because such views have remained alien to the behavioral current, it is easy to see why newspaper science's conceptual hustle around the newspaper seemed, from the behaviorists' viewpoint, cumbersome, fruitless, and estranged from reality. Although the pursuit of autonomous discipline came, in the end, to nothing, it was not "much ado about nothing" because it ascertained, at least, that the newspaper is communication sui generis—communication that cannot be reduced to something else and that "in its specificity, gives the grounds for its evaluation and criticism" (K. Pietilä, 1985, p. 4).

4

COMMUNICATION IN SOCIAL LIFE

John Dewey and Robert E. Park

At the same time as German newspaper science was born, mass communication also began to gain increasing scholarly attention in the United States. Among the U.S. pathfinders were philosopher John Dewey and sociologist Robert E. Park. Influenced by German 19th-century social thought (but not by newspaper science), both men were concerned especially "with the role of communication in social life" (Delia, 1987, p. 25). Their work represents the way in which communication was approached in the Chicago school of sociology (pp. 30–37; see also Carey, 1997; Hardt, 1992, pp. 31–76). This work established a tradition of thought and research that is, in the form of American interpretive cultural studies, still alive today.

Both Dewey and Park were adherents of progressivism, a tradition of social thought and a social movement influential in the United States from the late 19th century to the 1930s. It was brought forth by the rapid change that transformed the United States from a scattered patchwork quilt of small local communities to a territorially wide, urbanized and industrialized Great Society. The progressives saw that in addition to bringing forth positive consequences, this change undermined democracy and caused other social problems. Consequently, they advocated reforms for curing the ills and adapting people to much changed circumstances. This was the context for them to approach mass communication (see Carey, 1991; Jowett 1991; J. Peters 1989a, 1989b; Sproule, 1987, 1989, 1991).

COMMUNITY AS COMMUNICATION: DEWEY

John Dewey (1859–1952) was a versatile thinker-philosopher and critic of society who is known, in particular, as a spokesman for the "learning-by-doing" principle in education. He was one of the thinkers interested in reflecting philosophically on human practical conduct. In his philosophy, he represented American pragmatism (see e.g., Hardt, 1992, pp. 31–76) which was the chief philosophical current underpinning the reform-driven progressivism.

Characteristic of Dewey's brand of philosophy was that he was planning, together with Park and certain others, the establishment of a newspaper called Thought News. The purpose of the newspaper would have been to represent society by means of scientific, statistic reporting instead of customary news reporting: Changes in different sectors of society were to be monitored as exactly as the changes of exchange rates. Thought News was planned to be a sociological newspaper. The venture, however, came to nothing (see Matthews, 1977, 20–30; Westbrook, 1991, pp. 51–58).

Starting Points of Dewey's Social Philosophy

As a pragmatic philosopher, Dewey stressed that in order to understand and explain the existence and functioning of large collective formations, such as the state, one should start with individuals and their practical activities. In his main work of social philosophy, The Public and Its Problems (1927/1954), Dewey regarded individual actions as the prime force behind all social occurrences: "all deliberate choices and plans are finally the work of single human beings" (p. 21). Resisting the extreme individualism of the liberalism of his time, he looked on individuals as inherently social beings molded by their social habitat. And, for him, individual actions become always interlocked, directly or indirectly, into joint action: "conjoint, combined, associated action is a universal trait of the behavior of things" (p. 34).

Dewey considered human (joint) action above all with respect to its results. Action leads always to consequences of which some may be such as intended, others not. These results begin to condition further action which, again, produces both intended and unintended results. Dewey distinguished two kinds of results: direct "which affect persons directly engaged in a transaction," and indirect "which affect others beyond those immediately concerned" (p. 12). The division of consequences into intended and unintended, on the one hand, and into direct and indirect, on the other, is the philosophical basis of Dewey's views of community, society, and social development.

Community = Communication

For Dewey, one finds "the germ of the distinction between the private and the public" in the distinction between direct and indirect consequences (p. 12). In his view, "a public interest arises whenever there are indirect consequences of individual, private transactions" (Carey, 1991, p. 38). The public begins to form when the actions extend their impact on many people outside of those involved in the actions. It "consists of all those who are affected by the indirect consequences of transactions to such an extent that it is deemed necessary to have those consequences systematically cared for" (Dewey, pp. 15–16). Consequently, the public deals predominantly with those consequences that the actors' actions cause for other people.

For Dewey, the form of the public depends on the form of the ensemble of relations tying people together. In those small self-sufficient local communities, which still predominated in the United States in the middle of the 19th century, the public was a face-to-face phenomenon. Its basis was interpersonal communication. As such, it was almost spontaneously led on democratic tracks (Belman, 1977, pp. 34–35). Its most institutionalized form was the town meeting, where issues needing public treatment were discussed and decided together. In these communities, the influentials were local and "consequently visible," whereas the state, "even when it despotically interfered, was remote, an agency alien to daily life" (Dewey, p. 97).

This view of local publics is perhaps tinted with romantic nostalgia (see Schudson, 1992). Whether or not it resulted from Dewey's small-town background is contested (cf. Westbrook, 1991, pp. 1–2). It brings forth Dewey's basic conception that a community or society exists essentially in discussion, in communication:

> Society not only continues to exist by transmission, by communication, but it may be fairly said to exist in transmission, in communication. . . . Men live in a community by virtue of things they have in common; and communication is the way in which they come to possess things in common. (Dewey, 1916, p. 15)

Communication has been characterized in several ways, but characterizations have often been crystallized to two basic conceptions: In one view, communication consists of technical transmission of messages; in the other, it amounts to a sharing of common sociocultural world together (Carey, 1975; Williams, 1976, pp. 72–73). Despite the word transmission, Dewey conceived communication in the latter way. For him, the fact that "the fruit of communication should be participation, sharing, is a wonder by side of which transsubstantiation pales" (Dewey, 1925, p. 132). As participation, communication is not simply a form for communities to exist but to exist democratically.

"The Eclipse of the Public"

For Dewey, one of the most grave problems caused by the transformation of the United States into a vast modern society was "the eclipse of the public" (Dewey, 1927/1954, p. 110). In this transformation, resulting from "the new technology applied in production and commerce" (p. 98), local communities lost their self-sufficiency. The management of issues, which the local publics had cared for hitherto, was transposed in far-away hands. Thereby "the local communities found their affairs conditioned by remote and invisible organizations" (p. 98). In the new "ways of aggregate activity," generated through the new conditions, the community "is not a conscious partner, and over them it has no direct control" (p. 98). In short:

> The local face-to-face community has been invaded by forces so vast, so remote in initiation, so far-reaching in scope and so complexly indirect in operation, that they are, from the standpoint of the members of local social units, unknown. (p. 133)

In these conditions, the old form of public, functional in small self-sufficient localities, was no longer appropriate. But neither had there emerged a new form of public, adequate for the new conditions. Hence, the public was driven into a state in which "it cannot find itself" or "cannot identify and distinguish itself" (pp. 123, 126).

For Dewey, the problem was not technical but intellectual. He saw that the coming of the Great Society had already called forth those technical channels that connected its parts with one another and enabled the expanding social organization to function:

Railways, travel and transportation, commerce, the mails, telegraph and telephone, newspapers, create enough similarity of
ideas and sentiments to keep the thing going as a whole, for they
create interaction and interdependence. (p. 114)

The critical point was that the technological expansion had
not expanded the intellectual or substantial aspect of the Great
Society correspondingly: There had emerged "no political agencies
worthy to it" and the "democratic public" was "largely inchoate and
unorganized" (p. 109). The available intellectual resources simply did
not suffice "to cope with" the growing mass "of public concern" (p.
126).

Moreover, because public issues had become more complex
and because they were managed increasingly "on an impersonal
rather than a community basis" (p. 126), people felt alienated from
them and became politically apathetic. Along with the issues becoming "too complex and intricate" people felt "that they are caught in
the sweep of forces too vast to understand and master" (pp. 132, 135).
They lacked knowledge, skills, and means to participate in the management of those issues. This was the fault for which Dewey sought
remedy. What remedy he thought might help, is disclosed by the following words that state, again, the discrepancy between technical
and substantive aspects:

Intellectual instrumentalities for the formation of an organized
public are more inadequate than its overt means. . . . We have the
physical tools of communication as never before. The thoughts
and aspirations congruous with them are not communicated, and
hence not common. Without such communication the public will
remain shadowy and formless, seeking spasmodically for itself,
but seizing and holding its shadow rather than its substance. Till
the Great Society is converted into a Great Community, the
Public will remain in eclipse. (p. 142)

Utopia of a Great Community

The restoration of the public requires, thus, the conversion of the
Great Society into a Great Community. Because the "existing political
and legal forms and arrangements are incompetent to deal with the
situation," the need is "that the non-political forces organize themselves to transform existing political structures: that the divided and

troubled publics integrate" (pp. 128-129). For this, the means should be discovered "by which a scattered, mobile and manifold public may so recognize itself as to define and express its interests" (p. 146).

But what means would do? Dewey (p. 142) answered: "Communication can alone create a great community." We meet again his central thesis that the foundation of a community, be it small or large, lies in communication. However, a Great Community cannot, unlike local communities, be founded merely on face-to-face communication. The sine qua non for it is mass communication. Only mass communication is comprehensive enough to start processes through which people, in modern social conditions, can "come to possess things in common," that is, only it can stimulate wide public discussion that would nourish informed public opinion and provide people with skills and means needed for public participation.

Dewey had to observe, however, that the contemporary media did do not much to advance such processes. He noted two impeding factors. The first was the tendency of the media to serve private interests, able "to manipulate social relations for their own advantage" (p. 169). The second was the character of the news work. Dewey (p. 180) criticized especially the way journalists select as news transitory but sensational happenings and present them isolated from their backgrounds, consequences, and other contexts:

> Hence even if we discount the influence of private interests in procuring suppression, secrecy and misrepresentation, we have here an explanation of the triviality and "sensational" quality of so much of what passes as news. The catastrophic, namely, crime, accident, family rows, personal clashes and conflicts, are the most obvious forms of breaches of continuity; they supply the element of shock which is the strictest meaning of sensation; they are the new par excellence, even though only the date of the newspaper could inform us whether they happened last year or this, so completely they are isolated from their connections.

This criticism notwithstanding, Dewey credited the media with the key position in creating, through public debate and cultivation of informed public opinion, a new public in the scale of a Great Community. To do their share, however, the media were in want of relevant material. Like the other progressives, Dewey put his confidence in this respect in the burgeoning field of social research. Precisely it was capable of producing knowledge needed for acting in a complex society. Only continuous inquiry "can provide the material of enduring opinion about public matters" (p. 178).

Yet even the information of highest quality does little before "it is published, shared, socially accessible" (p. 176). Here lay the media's social responsibility. Dewey was aware, of course, of the claims that people might not be ardently interested in information about social matters. For him, however, the attractiveness of an issue did not depend so much on the issue itself but rather on the way it was presented. And he was convinced that the "bare existence" of an issue having a "widespread human bearing" would irresistibly invite to present it in a way "which would have a direct popular appeal" (p. 183). In general, he advised the journalists to take artistic expression as a pattern to follow.

But even if the media would publish high-quality social information in an appealing form and even if people would welcome it, the problem would not be wholly resolved—there would not yet be a living public opinion. It begins to live only "when it is made active in community life" (Carey, 1989, p. 81). The final actuality of social information "is accomplished in face-to-face relationships by means of direct give and take" as its meanings "pass from mouth to mouth" (Dewey, pp. 218–219). "That and that only gives reality to public opinion" (p. 219). Thus, in the Great Community, "the local neighborhood environment would add oral communication to that of the printed word," in which way "the small community and the larger organized intelligence" would "complement one another" (Czitrom, 1982, p. 112).

Assessing Dewey

Dewey's thought has been criticized from many angles. It has been charged, for instance, with being "a congenital optimism, a romance with the small town, a disastrously simple-minded view of technology" (Carey, 1989, p. 83) or for an overvaluation of "scientific information and communication technology as a solvent to social problems" (Carey, 1975, p. 10). Further charges are that Dewey did not notice that mass communication, "no matter how well-researched or well-articulated, may be as likely to promote apathy as engagement" (Simonson, 1996, p. 332), or that he did not even hint "as to just how we might transform privately owned media of communication into truly common carriers" (Czitrom, p. 112). More generally, Dewey has been blamed for "a refusal to address the reality of social and economic conflict in the present" (p. 112, also see D. Schiller, 1996, pp. 29–38).

Dewey's utopian vision of a Great Community has also been criticized. Westbrook (1991, p. 309), for instance, stated that in so far as Dewey attempted to show "how the public could escape its confusion and organize itself for effective political action," he did not succeed "in very compelling fashion" because he did "not address the problems of the political organization of the public, confining himself only to its 'intellectual problem'." Although Dewey specified "the 'infinitely difficult' conditions for the emergence of the Great Community," he offered only "little guidance for overcoming them" (p. 316). This question was left in his argumentation, "at best, an implicit, wholly undeveloped element" (p. 316).

This criticism notwithstanding, Dewey's ideas have been a permanent source of inspiration in mass communication studies. In particular, his insistence on communication as the elixir of life of communities has been important as a counterweight to the more technical transmission view of communication advocated especially by the subsequent behaviorism. For example, Carey (1975, 1989), the leading communication scholar within American interpretive cultural studies and a formidable critic of the behaviorist tradition, sincerely expressed his indebtedness to that aspect in Dewey's thought. Moreover, Dewey's view of the need to reconstitute the public has impressed many scholars from Keane (1984, pp. 146–156) and Carey (1987) to the designers of the public journalism project (Bybee, 1999; Coleman, 1997; Heikkilä & Kunelius, 1996; Rosen, 1994).

COMMUNICATION AS SOCIAL FORCE: PARK

Robert Ezra Park (1864–1944) was a bit of an exceptional scholar in that he began his academic career late, when he was almost 50 years old (Matthews, 1977; Raushenbush, 1979). He graduated from the University of Michigan, where Dewey was one of his teachers. From Dewey, he took "a life-long interest in the role of communication as a force for integrating society" (Matthews, p. 5). After some 10 years as a newspaper reporter, Park continued his studies and defended his doctoral dissertation in Heidelberg, Germany, in 1904. He then held some nonacademic jobs until he was offered a position as lecturer of sociology at the University of Chicago in 1913.

The University of Chicago has a notable place in the history of sociology. Its department of sociology is the oldest in the United States, and it was also the leading department right up to the late 1930s. In the history of sociology, it is customary to speak of the Chicago school of sociology (see e.g., Bulmer, 1984; Harvey, 1987; Smith, 1988). This refers to the unique thought and research of the Chicago sociologists from the days of World War I to the 1930s. Many of the later sociologists recognized themselves as continuers of the school's work. One of the school's most impressive members was Robert Park.

Characteristics of Park's Sociology

Park approached (mass) communication naturally as a sociologist. He thought sociology was concerned not so much with structures of society as with collective behavior and the social movement produced by it (Matthews, 1977, pp. 131–137; Turner, 1967, pp. x–xvii). In contrast to history, sociology was for Park an abstract science that develops generalized conceptual frames of reference capable of ordering and explaining phenomena. Where history seeks to interpret concrete events "in time and space," sociology wants to find "natural laws and generalizations" that hold good for "human nature and society irrespective of time and of place" (Park, 1921/1955, p. 197). If considered from a sociological perspective, history is turned into "natural history" (pp. 202–209).

On the other hand, sociology was no armchair speculation for Park. In order to abstract and generalize, it was in need of empirical observation. Even if Park himself did scarcely any empirical research, Turner (1967, p. ix), for example, stated that hardly anybody "has so deeply influenced the direction taken by American empirical sociology as Robert Ezra Park." Park had a spectacular talent of enthusing his students to do empirical research (Bulmer, 1984, pp. 83–108). Reviewers of Park seldom forget to tell the advice he gave the students in the beginning of their field work: "Write down only what you see, hear, and know, like a newspaper reporter" (Rogers, 1994, p. 181)

Park did not develop any systematic sociological theory, but made conceptual interventions into many questions ranging from urban ecology and race relations to the role of news and the press in society. According to Coser (1977, p. 382), "Park rarely set out deliberately to write a theoretical essay"; rather his custom was "to think about a conceptual issue in terms of concrete research problems raised by his students." This made his thought multidimensional and somewhat incoherent. On the other hand, one can find in it certain recurring patterns that render it amenable to a more coherent description.

Competition and Communication as Basic Social Forces

In an abstract sense, a society consists of people who are in touch or who interact with one another. There are, naturally, many different forms of concrete interactions. Abstracting from them, Park singled out two forms, competition and communication, which he regarded as the basic social forces. They "seem to be the two fundamental processes, or forms of interaction, by which a social order is initiated and maintained" (Park, 1940b/1955, p. 314). They are opposite forces: "Competition seems to be the principle of individuation in the life of the person and of society," whereas communication "operates primarily as an integrating and socializing principle" (Park, 1939/1953, p. 168). Where competition tends to scatter, communication tends to integrate.

From these forces, Park (e.g., 1936a/1967, pp. 81–84; 1936b/1967, pp. 90–94) derived two basic social orders: the ecological (or symbiotic) order marked by competition, and the moral (or cultural) order marked by communication. In mature societies, he singled out two more orders, an economic order closer to the ecological one, and a political order closer to the moral one (1936a/1967, p. 84; see also Park, 1940b/1955, pp. 309–314).

Distinct to the ecological order is a "Darwinian" struggle for existence. Individuals "act independently of one another," they "struggle with one another for mere existence, and treat one another, as far as possible, as utilities" (Park, 1929, cited in Turner, p. xxvii). In this order, people "coexist without much sympathy, empathy, or even communication" (Matthews, 1977, p. 141). In the economic order, communication is already more significant. Economic competition is "regulated to some extent by convention, understanding, and law"—in short, "by custom" which "is a product of communication" (Park, 1939/1953, p. 166, 167).

Communication becomes even more important in the political order where the "struggle for existence" terminates in a competition "for status, for recognition, for position and prestige" (Park, 1926/1950, p. 150). Finally, the moral order consists purely of communication and social phenomena solidified by it, such as "custom, convention, tradition, ceremonial, language, social ritual, public opinion" (Park, 1921/1955, p. 222). Such things bind people together and enable them, "through their collective action, recreate the world in the image of their collective aspirations and their common will" (Park, 1929, cited in Turner, p. xxvii).

As abstractions, these orders do not exist as such in society, where their elements are intermixed. Through abstracting them,

Park intended to catch the dynamics of the movement of society. For him, the orders marked by competition make up "the origin of social change" (Park, 1936b/1967, p. 93) whereas the orders marked by communication, and the social control exercised through them, stabilize society and keep it together through its changes. According to Turner (p. xxix), Park especially saw the moral order "as restricting the intensity and softening the impact of the struggle for existence, by the operation of custom and sentiment," whereas he looked at the ecological order as offering an

> explanation for many failures in control at the social level, and for innovations and deviations from the patterns of human collaboration. . . . If the system of values and norms that men erect is conservatizing, the ecological order is like the unconscious realm in the individual, constantly unsettling the stable order and precipitating change.

Although competition is above all an individualizing and unstabilizing force, is also has integrating effects. Economic competition leads to specialization and, through it, to a division of labor which, again, makes people dependent on each other. For Park (1936b/1967, p. 91), the "effect of competition has been to bring about everywhere a division of labor that has diminished competition." Respectively, even if communication is mainly a unifying and stabilizing factor, it also has dissolving effects. This can be illustrated with the interaction cycle, Park's other important frame of reference in addition to that concerning the orders.

The cycle describes, by utilizing a four-stage division, the development of the interaction between people. The first stage is competition, "interaction without contact" (Turner, p. xxxiii). At this stage, people are unaware of their competitors or have a purely impersonal relation with them. As communication between the competitors increases,

> competition tends to assume a new character. It becomes conflict. In that case the struggle for existence is likely to be intensified by fears, animosities, and jealousies, which the presence of the competitor and the knowledge of his purposes arouse. Under such circumstances a competitor becomes as enemy. (Park, 1939/1953, p. 168)

This is the second stage of conflict, and it is just at this stage where the dissolving effects of communication appear most clearly. On the other hand, Park (p. 168) continued,

> it is always possible to come to terms with an enemy whom one knows and with whom one can communicate, and, in the long run, greater intimacy inevitably brings with it a more profound understanding, the result of which is to humanize social relations and to substitute a moral order for one that is fundamentally symbiotic.

This moves the interaction at the third stage, called accommodation by Park. At this stage, the unifying force of communication overcomes its dissolving force. Accommodation "is a cessation of overt conflict, an agreement to disagree" (Turner, p. xxxiii). Once it is reached, "a slower process of assimilation sets in" in which the "absorption of cultural heritage and a thoroughgoing transformation of personality take place under the influence of intimate and concrete contacts" (p. xxxiii).

Although the main direction is from competition to assimilation, contacts can also develop in the opposite direction. Conflict and accommodation, especially, are critical stages because they are "characterized by greater instability than those at either end of the cycle" (Matthews, p. 161). Thus, an attained stage of accommodation is always in danger of dissolving back into that of conflict. For Park, society is basically an unstable formation, also in regard to the development of people's contacts and interaction.

Economy and the News

Park considered economy a particularly unstable domain of society. Being an organization composed of "competing groups of individuals," it is "in a state of unstable equilibrium, and this equilibrium can be maintained only by a process of continuous readjustment" (Park, 1925, p. 17). Consequently, there have in society "grown up a number of special organizations which exist for the special purpose of facilitating these readjustments" (p. 19). One of the devices serving this purpose is the news.

For Park (1939/1953, p. 171), there has always been an "indissoluble relation between commerce and the news": the centers of trade have invariably been "the centers of news." But first in the

modern society, the news has become a sine qua non for the functioning of its ever complicating economy. For instance, in order to be able
to react adequately, such modern organizations like the stock
exchange are in sore need of reports conveying data of changes "in
economic conditions all over the world" (Park, 1925, p. 19).

> These reports, in so far as they are calculated to cause readjust-
> ments, have the character of what we call news. It is the exis-
> tence of a critical situation which converts what were otherwise
> mere information into news. Where there is an issue at stake,
> where, in short, there is crisis, the information which might
> affect the outcome one way or another becomes "live matter," as
> the newspaper men say. (p. 19)

In the modern economic order, the function of news is to
assist the economic actors to readjust their action in the capriciously
changing market—actually one in permanent crisis, because "crisis
may be said to be the normal condition on the exchanges" (p. 21).
Moreover, the instability has spread out to other modern domains of
life as well: "Concentration of populations in cities, the wider markets, the division of labor, the concentration of individuals and groups
on special tasks, have continually changed the material conditions of
life, and in doing this have made readjustments to novel conditions
increasingly necessary" (p. 19). Thus, in so far as the news assists the
readjustments in all the changing conditions, society survives.

The News, the Public, and Public Opinion

Park viewed the public basically from an angle similar to Dewey:
Both considered the public as an acting body of people rather than a
structural "public sphere" of society in the sense of Habermas
(1962/1989). On the other hand, where Dewey reflected on the preconditions for a concrete, modern Great Public, Park attempted to
define the public abstractly in terms of interaction and collective
behavior. In the public, the interaction "takes the form of discussion,
individuals act upon one another critically, opinions clash, parties
are formed, the opposing opinions modify one another" (Matthews,
1977, p. 55). Because "within the public, opinions are divided," the
objective of the discussion and debate is to reconcile the disagreements and to attain a common public opinion for the guideline of further action (Park, 1904/1972, p. 80).

Approaching the news from the point of view of the discussing public, Park regarded it as a resource for fueling discussion. He remarked that the news "does not so much inform as orient the public" (Park, 1940a/1955, p. 79). However, what the function of news "to orient man and society" (p. 86) requires to be fulfilled is discussion. Indeed, when talking about news, Park (e.g., 1923/1955, p. 100) used to refer to the conceptions from the yellow press days, according to which news is anything that will make people talk or at least to cry out: Gee Whiz! And modern newspapers print "anything that would make people talk" (p. 100).

Besides fueling discussion in already formed publics, news can give rise to the formation of new discussing publics, as the following description of Park (1940a/1955, p. 79) indicates:

> The first typical reaction of an individual to the news is likely to be a desire to repeat it to someone. This makes conversation, arouses further comment, and perhaps starts a discussion. But the singular thing about it is that, once discussion has been started, the event under discussion soon ceases to be news, and, as interpretations of an event differ, discussions turn from the news to the issues it raises. The clash of opinions and sentiments which discussion invariably evokes usually terminates in some sort of consensus or collective opinion—what we call public opinion.

News has an important role in the formation of public opinion. But, for Park, news is no hypodermic needle injecting opinions of this or that kind into defenseless people. Although "public opinion" rests "on the basis of the information" supplied by news, it becomes actually formed in the discussion prompted by that information (Park, 1925, p. 39). A widely accepted public opinion is incorporated into society's moral order and imposes itself on individuals as relatively external force "stabilizing, standardizing, conventionalizing as well as stimulating, extending, and generalizing individual representations" (Park, 1921/1955, p. 225).

But nothing guarantees that a discussing public will finally reach some common opinion. Sometimes the disagreements are so profound "that further discussion appears unprofitable, if not impossible" (Park, 1941/1955, p. 131). The breaking down of communication relations has easily the consequence that a stage of accommodation dissolves into an open conflict. As can be seen, Park's conception of modern society as basically unstable formation informed also his view of the processes of public opinion, characteristic of this society.

Concluding Remarks on Park

Park has been evaluated very differently by the historians of sociology, some elevating him to the rank of the masters of social thought, others placing him among the minor figures in early U.S. sociology (see e.g., Bottomore & Nisbet, 1979; Coser, 1977; Martindale, 1981; Swingewood, 1984). Fischer and Strauss (1979) counted him, with good reasons, among the founders of the interactionist sociology. Park was, together with Dewey and some others, a forerunner of what was later called symbolic interactionism.

Park quite heavily drew on preceding social thought, especially on Simmel's sociology (Coser, 1977, pp. 373–376). For his thought on communication he was greatly indebted to Dewey. Like Dewey, but also like many classical sociologist, he saw mass communication—above all, the press—as one of the most focal channels connecting the parts of modern society together. The responding of one part "to the news from another" is "the mechanism which holds together and coordinates the activities of The Great Society" (Park, 1942/1955, p. 328).

On the other hand, Park took a more cautious stand than Dewey in the capacity of mass communication to rehabilitate the previous local democracy in the scale of modern society. Although he admitted that, for instance, the press functioned in the same way as the personal intercourse, which had kept up the local democracy, he still argued—referring to Lippmann's critical views—"that a newspaper cannot do for a community of 1,000,000 inhabitants what the village did spontaneously for itself through the medium of gossip and personal contact" (Park, 1923/1955, p. 94).

Also Park was on a bit different track than Dewey in his view of communication. Whereas Dewey painted a rosy picture of communication as a unifying force in people's community life, Park considered communication not only as an integrating power but as a force that, depending on situations, can have also dissolving effects. It seems that this important insight has still not attracted the attention that it clearly merits.

Park's views of the public, as well as of the forms of collective action more generally, inspired particularly Blumer (1946/1961, 1947/1965) to take the job of specifying them. With the term public, Blumer (1946/1961, p. 373) referred "to a group of people (a) who are confronted by an issue, (b) who are divided in their ideas as to how to meet the issue, and (c) who engage in discussion over the issue" (see also Mills, 1956/1995, pp. 79–80). This way of looking at the public fell into oblivion for some decades, but the recent interest, for instance, in public journalism or in the civic-oriented uses of network technology seems to be bringing corresponding ideas of the public back on the agenda.

Some of Park's ideas concerning news anticipated the constructivist view of modern news research. He "clearly saw that 'news' was a constructed account, not a mirror image of what was happening" (Gouldner, 1976, p. 120). This view notwithstanding, Park regarded the relations between reality and its representation in communication as highly important, privileging in this way the referential function of communication to its expressive function. As Czitrom (1982, p. 119) remarked, there is "a real irony in Park's inability to see how his theoretical principle of cultural integration through communication operated in American life, precisely through the expressive function"—that is, through the popular culture he despised.

5

THE "REALIST" CRITIQUE OF DEMOCRACY

Walter Lippman and Harold D. Lasswell

The belief, cherished still by Cooley, that the expanding net of mass communication could weave traditional democracy and the modern Great Society together, began to seem doubtful in the first decades of the 20th century. Dewey's diagnosis of the public's problems was one sign of this doubt, although he still believed that a participatory democracy might be restored, provided that journalism would improve its performance and keep a living public discussion going. There were others, however, who did not share Dewey's optimism. In particular, the so-called "realist critics of democracy," among them Lippmann and Lasswell, looked at the matters quite pessimistically.

"THE WORLD OUTSIDE AND THE PICTURES IN OUR HEAD": LIPPMANN

As a young man Walter Lippmann (1889–1974), the only child of a wealthy New York family, was quite radical in his thought: He was attracted by the critical "muckraking journalism" and even by social-ist ideas that he, however, soon discarded (about his vicissitudes, see

Luskin, 1972; Steel, 1980). After graduation from Harvard, he began his career as journalist, which lasted, with a few interruptions, until the age of retirement. He is especially known for his columns, which were published daily from 1931 to 1967 in many leading newspapers all over the world. Thanks to these columns, he was the most influential journalist of his time. Besides this work, he wrote several books touching on journalism and mass communication. His Public Opinion, published in 1922, is regarded by Carey (1989, p. 75), for example, as "the founding book of American media studies."

Starting Points of Lippmann's Thought

The seminal significance of Public Opinion appears in the mere fact that Dewey's The Public and Its Problems was largely a response to it (Carey, p. 78). Although Dewey came to a contrary conclusion than Lippmann concerning democracy and its possibilities in the modern Great Society, they were on similar tracks in certain issues. Most importantly, they both saw that the modern society is a huge organization, of which the experience of an individual cannot cover but a tiny fraction, and that, for this reason, the face-to-face forms of local democracy were inappropriate for the changed conditions. Despite sharing this view of democracy, they had very divergent conceptions of what the situation required. J. Peters (1986, p. 128) has described their basic difference as follows:

> Dewey thought that education, art, and science—the creation of intelligence—could make it [democracy] possible; Lippmann thought that democracy at best could be improved by providing the public with objective facts about the outside world. Dewey wanted to improve people's lives and discourse; Lippmann wanted to improve their data-base.

Thus, Dewey was for participation; Lippmann for knowledge. This difference indicates that they had a differing conception of communication: Where Dewey looked at it as communion, sharing, Lippmann viewed it—without, though, explicating this—as transmission of knowledge.

Lippmann (1922/1965, pp. 3–20) started Public Opinion by considering the relationship between the social "world outside" and the pictures of it "in our heads." In his view, the correspondence between them depends on whether or not our contacts with the world outside are direct and intimate. In a small community, one could have such contacts with its various parts, but as we move into a modern society, our contacts with its parts become more and more indirect and mediated. "In a society that is not completely self-contained and so small that everyone can know all about everything that happens, ideas deal with events that are out of sight and hard to grasp," Lippmann (p. 8) wrote and continued that in such a society

> the real environment is altogether too big, too complex, and too fleeting for direct acquaintance. . . . Although we have to act in that environment, we have to reconstruct it on a simpler model before we can manage with it. (p. 11)

This model inserts between people and the real world "a pseudo-environment" (p. 10). Instead of the real world, people base their actions on this pseudo-world, that is, "what each man does is based not on direct and certain knowledge, but on pictures made by himself or given to him" (p. 16). The wider the gap between the real world and "the pictures in our heads" becomes, the flimsier is the ground for social action. Acts based on the pseudo-world lead often to errors, for which reason it is important to inquire into "the reasons why the picture inside so often misleads men in their dealings with the world outside" (p. 18).

Lippmann (p. 17) particularly praised "the new psychology" for its "study of dreams, fantasy and rationalization" which had "thrown light on how the pseudo-environment is put together." In fact, the "realist" critique of democracy was heavily indebted to the view, cultivated in psychology around the turn of the 20th century, that human beings are irrational, led by instincts and drives (Westbrook, 1991, pp. 282–286). This fed the thesis that democracy in an ideal sense is impossible: People are, simply, incapable of that rationality presupposed by the ideal. The conclusions drawn by Lippmann were not so extreme; yet his thesis also was that the interpretation of reality, which constructs the pictures in out heads, "is essentially emotional and irrational" (J. Peters, 1986, p. 119).

Why Are the Pictures in Our Heads Defective and Distorted?

For Lippmann, the basic reason for the widening gap between social reality and people's pictures of it is the huge scope of modern society that simply oversteps people's capacity to experience it directly and, consequently, to act rationally. Moreover, their obtaining of knowledge is hampered by additional factors: by the hiding or censoring of information, by people's narrow social circles that prevent them from having multiple contacts with reality, by their lack of time for entering into public affairs, by the deficient ways in which the affairs are presented in the media, and so on (Lippmann, pp. 23–49). Yet, for Lippmann, a more grave obstacle was people's tendency to think stereotypically. He wrote about this as follows:

> For the most part we do not first see, and then define, we define first and then see. In the great blooming, buzzing confusion of the outer world we pick out what our culture has already defined for us, and we tend to perceive that we have picked out in the form stereotyped for us by our culture. (pp. 54–55)

People are prone to stereotypical thinking, for instance, because "the attempt to see all things freshly and in detail, rather than as types and generalities, is exhausting" and, thus, uneconomical (p. 59). Moreover, stereotypes function as a guarantee of a world where "people and things have their well-known places, and do certain expected things" (p. 63). On the other hand, stereotypes are harmful in that they "intercept information on its way to consciousness" (p. 57) or turn fresh information to support old, ingrained beliefs.

Also people's character and interests may distort pictures in their heads. For instance, when "people of highly varied character" hear a story, "lacking precise character of its own," they "give it their own character" (p. 111). And, since "'self-interest' determines opinion" (p. 112), interests deviating from one another tend to give rise to dissimilar opinions, that is, to pictures distorted in different directions. To cap it all, these pictures vary continuously because people's character and interests are not stable but variable.

But if individual opinions are so different and variable, how is it possible to speak of a public opinion? Lippmann thought that it is produced by political leaders in a top–down fashion; they create symbols that in themselves matter little but that can be saturated with different feelings, images and conceptions. "In the symbol emotion is discharged at a common target, and the idiosyncrasy of real ideas blotted out," he remarked (p. 150) and continued that a symbol

> enables people to work for a common end, but just because the few who are strategically placed must choose the concrete objec-

tives, the symbol is also an instrument by which a few can fatten on many, deflect criticism, and seduce men into facing agony for objects they do not understand. (p. 151)

Journalism and Its Problems

Lippmann blamed the preceding thought of democracy for the belief that people are inherently capable of democratic action and that mass communication is able to keep them in touch with a society sliding increasingly out of sight. He criticized the press largely on the same grounds as Dewey. In its aim to "present us with a true picture of all the outer world in which we are interested" (p. 203), the press is restricted by economic conditions, in particular by its dependence on advertising and people buying the advertised goods. But an ever more restricting factor is the nature of news.

Lippmann (p. 215) noted that before matters become news they must "make themselves noticeable in some more or less overt act." Therefore, "the news is not a mirror of social conditions, but the report of an aspect that has obtruded itself" (p. 216). The narrowing influence of this is amplified by the journalistic habit of casting the news into a stereotypical form. For Lippmann (p. 224), the reader wants "to feel a sense of personal identification with the stories he is reading"; for this "he must find a familiar foothold in the story, and this is supplied to him by the use of stereotypes."

Due to such narrowing factors, "news and truth are not the same thing" (p. 226). "The function of news is to signalize an event, the function of truth is to bring to light the hidden facts, to set them into relation with each other, and make a picture of reality on which men can act" (p. 226). News contains a lot of uncertain and questionable information. Actually, one only can be sure of knowledge stemming from the "social bookkeeping," that is, from statistical and other official records.

> Wherever there is a good machinery of record, the modern news service works with great precision. There is one on the stock exchange, and the news of price movements is flashed over tickers with dependable accuracy. There is a machinery for election returns, and when the counting and tabulating are well done, the result of a national election is usually known on the night of election. In civilized communities deaths, births, marriages and divorces are recorded, and are known accurately except where there is concealment or neglect. . . . It will be found, I think, that

there is a very direct relation between the certainty of news and the system of record. (pp. 216–217)

There are, of course, many things that cannot be recorded similarly for which reason news on such "subjects is bound to be debatable, when it is not wholly neglected" (p. 217).

The situation might be improved by expanding the "social bookkeeping" and by developing means for reporting "of an unseen environment" (p. 166). For the latter task, there is a need for expertise, capable of mediating "between the private citizen and the vast environment in which he is entangled" (p. 238). Even if there is a lot of technical and organizational problems to be solved, Lippmann (p. 248) believed "that unseen environments can be reported effectively, that they can be reported to divergent groups of people in a way which is neutral to their prejudice, and capable of overcoming their subjectivism."

Expertise as the Solution to the Problems of Democracy

Like Dewey, Lippmann saw that democracy sorely needs the expert knowledge produced, for instance, by social research, but he had a totally different view of the relationship between this knowledge and acting people than Dewey. Where Dewey conceived knowledge as a resource for the lay public to discuss and act, Lippmann identified "acting people," in the last instance, with society's political élite. To keep democracy going, it was more important to impart the knowledge uncovered by the experts to the élite than to disseminate it to the citizens. There is no reason "to burden every citizen with expert opinions on all questions, but to push that burden away from him towards the responsible administrator" (pp. 250–251).

For Lippmann, the public at large is unable to take directly part in society's government because, consisting of private citizens with their private concerns, it "has neither time, nor attention, nor interest, nor the equipment" for managing all the facts needed for administrative decisions (p. 251). Nevertheless, it is able to judge the soundness of the procedures through which the decisions are arrived at. A private member of the public can watch the procedure especially "when the news indicates that there is something to watch" (p. 251). Thus, for Lippmann, the news fulfills its social responsibility by exposing the deciding élite "to the hot light of publicity" and by keeping the public alert to its doings (Carey, 1987, p. 7).

The ideal democracy in Public Opinion comes close in many respects to a view of it as a kind of "aristocracy of experts." Lippmann's mistrust in people's capacity for self-government and in the role of public opinion as a guiding line for public action became even more pronounced in The Phantom Public, published in 1925 (Westbrook, 1991, pp. 299–300; B. Wright, 1973, pp. 58–64). He conceived democracy as a "rule for people" on the basis of science and expertise, not as a "rule by people" themselves (Steel, 1980). No surprise, then, that in his review Dewey regarded Public Opinion "as 'perhaps the most effective indictment of democracy as currently conceived ever penned'" (Westbrook, p. 294).

TECHNIQUES OF PROPAGANDA: LASSWELL

Where Lippmann was a metropolitan by birth, Harold D. Lasswell (1902–1978) came from small Midwestern town milieu (about his vicissitudes, see Almond, 1990, pp. 290–308; Rogers, 1994, pp. 203–233). And, unlike Lippmann, Lasswell took an academic path right after his graduation from the University of Chicago. In 1927, he defended there his doctoral thesis Propaganda Technique in the World War. For the rest of his life he served as professor in political science in a couple of universities. Regardless of the differences between their background and career, Lasswell's and Lippmann's thought had quite many points in common.

Some Basic Features of Lasswell's Thought

Although Lasswell specialized in political science, it has been said that "his mind was so eclectic and wide-ranging that he did not fit into any disciplinary box" (Rogers, 1994, p. 203). He attempted "to develop a theory about man in society that is comprehensive and that draws on all the social sciences" (Lerner, 1968, p. 405). Perhaps incited by this aim, he enriched political theory with ingredients from psychology and psychoanalysis. In this, he was close to Lippmann. Furthermore, where Lippmann flirted with socialism, Lasswell was one of the few Americans, who, in the 1920s, became versed in Marxism. He was also influenced by the Chicago School's pragmatism and by logical positivism, then in the ascendancy in the U.S. social sciences (see McDougall, 1984, pp. 1–17).

Lasswell influenced communication studies especially with his analysis of propaganda and work on content analysis. In fact, Berelson (1959/1964, pp. 503–504) named him as one of the field's founding fathers. For Lerner and Nelson (1977, p. 1), again, the "story of communication research begins with the publication in 1927 of Lasswell's Propaganda Technique in the World War." Yet, to be frank, Lasswell contributed mostly to the establishment of the behavioral tendency within communication studies. When considering this tendency later, we meet him occasionally. Here, I focus on young Lasswell and his dissertation thesis.

Starting Points in the "Propaganda Technique"

Like Lippmann, Lasswell has been counted among the "realist" critics of democracy (Westbrook, 1991, pp. 283–284). And indeed, in the beginning of his dissertation, Lasswell (1927/1938) already shows mistrust in people's ability to self-govern. The sheer existence of propaganda as a means of controlling public opinion "testifies to the collapse of the traditional species of democratic romanticism" (p. 4). Instead of ruling, the public is ruled with the aid of propaganda. This was also his critical conclusion (p. 222): "To illuminate the mechanisms of propaganda is to reveal the secret springs of social action, and to expose to the most searching criticism our prevailing dogmas of sovereignty, of democracy, of honesty, and of the sanctity of individual opinion."

Lasswell sided here with Lippmann without, however, referring to him. On the other hand, he did not, in distinction from Lippmann, specify his critique and seek for some remedy to the troubles of democracy. This reserved attitude to normative judgments implies already the stand of a value-free scholar—a stand that was alien to Dewey and Lippmann but that became more and more valued along with the rise of positivism and the behavioral discourse.

Lasswell (p. 5) stressed that social science must start with an "analytical motive": it has to explain "how the social wheels go round, wholly apart from any pressing anxiety to steer them in any particular direction." The researcher's "business is to discover and report, not to philosophize and reform" (p. 5). This notwithstanding, it is wholly legitimate for social research to give advice in particular problems. Compatible with this view, Propaganda Technique was written in an advisory spirit, as if its readers would be future propagandists. Lasswell was also a central name in the subsequent development of policy research, geared to obtain data for social planning and guidance (see Lasswell, 1971).

Lasswell showed his bent also by criticizing the theorists of public opinion for approaching the subject too speculatively, without sufficient empirical grounds. He found that "much of the literature of public opinion is of such abstruse and indefinite character that it defies empirical verification"—admitting, however, that this sad situation resulted partly from the lack of means for "exact measurement" (pp. 5, 6). The same lack manifests itself clearly in his own dissertation. In any case, in it he made a strong plea for the replacement of theoretical speculation by empirical research—a plea taken subsequently by the behavioralism as its guiding principle.

Lasswell's Views of Propaganda

Lasswell (p. 12) undertook "to evolve an explicit theory of how international war propaganda may be conducted with success." With propaganda he meant "the control of opinion by significant symbols" or by "forms of social communication" (p. 9). The aim of war propaganda is "(1) To mobilize hatred against the enemy; (2) To preserve the friendship of allies; (3) To preserve the friendship and, if possible, to procure the co-operation of neutrals; (4) To demoralize the enemy" (p. 195). In his book, Lasswell described, with the aid of examples picked up from multifarious propaganda materials, what kind of propaganda was used to serve these purposes in the United States, Great Britain, France, and Germany. There is, unfortunately, no room for entering into his results in more detail here.

As to Lasswell's methodology, it seems that he first developed theoretical views of what propaganda is and what forms it has, and then illustrated these views with suitable examples. Afterward, when arguing for the use of quantitative content analysis in propaganda studies, Lasswell (1949/1968, pp. 40–52) assessed self-critically the way of study and presentation in the Propaganda Technique. He apologized, for instance, for not telling what criteria had guided the selection of examples. More generally, he rebuked his study, as well as many later studies conducted in its spirit, for being too impressionistic and unsystematic. This deficit could only be remedied by the use of quantitative content analysis (pp. 48–52).

Concluding Remarks on the "Propaganda Technique"

As was pointed out in the first chapter, the received view of the field's past claimed that the theory preceding behavioralism articulated a hypodermic needle model of omnipotent media and defenseless people as their victims. As observed, Dewey and Park did not have this kind of view. With certain grounds, one might argue that they are present, at least dimly, in Lippmann's thought. But in Lasswell's dissertation they are present quite clearly. In other words, of the notable predecessors of the behavioral tradition it is Lasswell—himself one of the founders of that tradition—who can most legitimately be counted as a representative of the notorious hypodermic needle model!

At the end of his dissertation, Lasswell (p. 220) took up the question of why "propaganda is one of the most powerful instrumentalities in the modern world." To explain this, he said that, along with the coming of modern Great Society, "the bonds of personal loyalty and affection which bound a man to his chief have long since dissolved" (p. 222). Modern society "is an atomized world, in which individual whims have wider play than ever before, and it requires more strenuous exertions to co-ordinate and unify than formerly" (p. 222). For Lasswell, it is precisely propaganda that wields "thousands and even millions of human beings into one amalgamated mass of hate and will and hope" (p. 221).

In another context, Lasswell (1927, pp. 631, 630) attributed the force of propaganda "to the social disorganization" and said that "the language of stimulus-response" describes adequately its functioning. Referring to such phrases, some historians of communication studies have concluded that Lasswell, if anyone, believed in the omnipotence of the media in their encounter with atomized individuals (e.g., Bineham, 1988, p. 235; Delia, 1987, p. 26; Sproule, 1989, pp. 232–233). Here they agree with Nye (1975, p. 186) that Lasswell's "debt to turn-of-the-century collective psychology is readily apparent." It needs to be remarked, however, that Lasswell did not elaborate the issue but quitted it with a few scattered and general statements.

ASSESSING LIPPMANN AND LASSWELL

Lippmann approached both the prevailing democratic polity and the press without illusions, even cynically, and many of his insights into them are pertinent still today (cf. T. Patterson, 1994). On the other hand, his way of looking at matters wiped out effectively all perspectives for a radical overcoming of the prevailing conditions. The ideas Lippmann had for the improvement of democracy remained wholly within the system into which democracy had evolved in the conditions of the Great Society. One can even argue that those ideas represented an early form of social technology—a form of "administrative" thought that became subsequently a distinct characteristic of the behavioral discourse.

Lippmann has been criticized further for his inclination to approach knowledge from a Cartesian perspective as a relationship between what is inside and what outside of our heads. From this perspective, "we can know the world if we can represent accurately what is outside our mind" (Carey, 1989, p. 76). This led him to place much confidence in institutions collecting seemingly accurate data, and to look at the knowledge from the angle of an administrator, not from that of an acting citizen. For Carey (p. 78), Lippmann came thereby to endorse "the notion that it was possible to have a science of society such that scientists might constitute a new priesthood: the possessors of truth as a result of having an agreed-upon method for its determination." Also this view paved way for the behavioral tradition.

Lasswell's inclination to the hypodermic needle model was previously commented on. All in all, his dissertation expresses clearly a transition period from the old-fashion theoretical work to the "brave new world" of empirical research. It opened doors into the future by demanding that the old way of legitimating theoretical insights with examples, often chosen to lend them plausibility, ought to be replaced with a new way of systematic empirical inquiry. "The demand today is for verifiable facts as a basis for generalizations rather than even the most brilliant individual insights," as Woodward (1930, p. 9) wrote some years later. However, unlike Woodward who already worked in the spirit of this demand, Lasswell's dissertation remained trapped still largely in the same manner of proceeding that it criticized.

6

THE IMPACT OF THE MOVIES

The Payne Fund Project

In 1916, psychologist Hugo Münsterberg, a pioneer in film theory, considered the possible influence of movies or "photoplays" as follows (cited in Jowett, 1992, p. 213):

> The intensity with which the plays take hold of the audience cannot remain without social effects. . . . The associations become as vivid as realities, because the mind is so completely given up to the moving pictures. . . . But it is evident that such a penetrating influence must be fraught with dangers. The more vividly the impressions force themselves on the mind, the more easily must they become starting points for imitation and other motor responses.

Münsterberg's concern reflects a common phenomenon in the history of communication: The introduction of a new medium has always called forth discussion about its possible dangerous effects. For example, the birth of the press in the 17th century soon prompted writings that doomed it outright as harmful for plain people or that at least advised how to use it profitably (Groth, 1948, pp. 14–61). The emergence of the movies and radio—and later television—gave rise to similar reactions. Such reactions have often motivated inquiries into whether or not the worries are justified. The "moral panic" stirred up by the movies was the prime reason behind the Payne Fund Studies (PFS) on the possible impact of movies on children and youth.

THE MOVIES UNDER FIRE

Already before World War I, the movies had become "a major entertainment activity, particularly for adolescents" (Delia, 1987, pp. 39–40). Their enormous popularity "did not go unnoticed" by individuals sometimes called "the 'custodians of culture'" (Jowett, 1992, p. 214). "Everyone from clergymen to private detectives offered advice on how to 'improve the movies,' while the more zealous appealed to their political representatives for action to prevent what they considered to be a gross and dangerous misuse of the medium's innate potential" (p. 214). Especially worrisome was "that the ubiquity and popularity of the movies would cause children to forgo other recreational activities of a more wholesome character" (Jowett, Jarvie, & Fuller, 1996, p. 26). According to Lowery and DeFleur (1983, pp. 34–35):

> by the mid 1920s, pressure began to mount on motion picture industry. Numerous editorials, sermons, magazine articles, and other forms of public criticism raised questions and made charges that the movies were a negative influence on children.

For Jowett et al. (p. 12), all this fuss and concern resulted from the fact that, as a mass medium, the movies "were new sources of social control that did not run along the grooves of established power and class relations," but "served the masses without special regard for the élites." Therefore, they "represented a threat to the established hegemony of the Protestant groups" that had imposed their "values on American life" (Jowett, p. 214). Sklar (1976, pp. 123–124) spoke of a "struggle between the classes" in which the élites defended "their social and economic status" under the guise that "the general welfare" required the prohibition of "the circulation of any product that might cause people harm."

Despite the fact that not all voices were against the movies, the movie industry was, in the beginning of the 1920s, mostly under hostile fire. To stave off these attacks, as well as the government intervention continually threatening it, the industry, in 1923, established a board for self-regulation, the Motion Picture Producers and Distributors of America. According to Jarvis (1991, p. 128), the board was, however, "much ado about nothing" because, being short of "enforcement procedures," it "frequently ignored violations of the production code." Thus, its operations did not prevent people from becoming "increasingly dismayed at the quality of the pictures" (p. 128). It was this situation that prompted the PFS.

ON THE STARTING POINTS AND RESEARCH POLICY OF THE PFS

The undertaking was initiated by William M. Seabury, a film industry lawyer who had become worried about "movie morality" (Jowett, p. 216). Seabury proposed the establishment of a public organization to "consider and grapple with the problems presented by the motion picture as controlled by the monopolized industry" (Seabury, 1926, cited in Jowett, p. 216). Prompted by Seabury, Reverend William H. Short, a veteran of organized activity, set up an organization known as The Motion Picture Research Council. However, Seabury and Short soon realized that they had divergent views as to how to criticize film industry most effectively.

In fact, what was at stake was a controversy between a traditional rhetorical criticism, based on moral arguments, and a new, social scientific criticism, based on facts obtained by seemingly objective research methods. The cultural transitions brought about by World War I had given the social scientific activity a decisive push (Sklar, p. 134; Rowland, 1983, pp. 90–91). Unlike Seabury, Short realized the changing conditions, and he set the organization up on condition that "an adequate program of fact-finding be undertaken prior to determining a program of propaganda and action" (Short, 1927, cited in Jowett, p. 217). It was thought that "only 'scientific' proof of the potentially harmful influence of the movies" will persuade the government to take measures against the film industry (Jowett et al., p. 29). Seabury, favoring attempts at "immediate legislative action" (p. 48), had to leave the undertaking.

With his connections in organized action, Short was able to procure the funding for the fact-finding from the philanthropic Payne Fund, which had already before funded juvenile research and that was, in the late 1920s, involved also in attempts to promote a nonprofit and noncommercial radio (McChesney, 1996, in Jowett et al., pp. 303–335).

Notwithstanding the emphasis put by Short on fact-finding, the project was imprinted with a conviction that movies were harmful. Jowett (p. 218) observed "that while a great effort was made to cloak the research in the cloth of scientific objectivity," basically the discourse "was one of hostility toward the existing motion picture industry." And for Jarvis (1991, p. 129), Short's organization "had predetermined that movies were bad and wanted evidence to prove it." Jowett et al. (p. 60) argued that this predetermination regulated the choice of researchers: "Short preselected his research group, choosing social scientists who already shared his belief that movies had a suspect influence on children." However, this bias (if there was any) did not manifest itself in the research reports in any clear fashion.

The individual studies carried out within the project fell into two broad categories: Some studies described "the content of the films" and determined "the size and composition of their audience," whereas others tried to find out their "major effects," the investigated effects being, in brief, "acquisition of information, change in attitudes, stimulation of emotions, harm to health, erosion of moral standards, and influence on conduct" (Lowery & DeFleur, 1983, p. 36).

Besides Seabury's and Short's controversy, the undertaking was troubled by an opposition between what was regarded as scientific objectivity and the project's value-laden policy. Results indicating that the influence of movies might be slighter than believed "did not please Short at all" (Jowett et al., p. 77). Consequently, there was a continuous hunt for methods that would bring forth the desired effects. At the project's final conference in 1931, some researchers believed they had found "conclusive evidence that movies were harmful and that the movie industry must be confronted and charged" whereas others had not found any "measurable evidence whatsoever and cautioned against placing any blame at the movies' doorstep" (pp. 81–82). The opposition also manifested itself in the fact that the results were presented and discussed on two levels (Jarvis, pp. 129–130):

> One was a serious, academic study presented in the carefully limited language of trained scholarship. Articles about the research appeared in scholarly journals and academic monographs. The other was emotional and inflammatory, written not as a discussion of research but to influence readers. It appeared in religious literature, popular magazines and a summary volume about the research, Our Movie-Made Children by [journalist] Henry James Forman.

This popular book "sensationalized the research results" (p. 132). Forman's unqualified message was that films had a "dramatic effect on youth" (p. 131). In his scientific summary, the project's head of research, W.W. Charters, stressed, in contrast, that the PFS had not found out what the influence of movies is "in relation to the influences of the ideals taught in the home, in the school, and in the church, by street life and companions or by community customs" (Charters, 1933, cited in Rowland, 1983, p. 94). Nevertheless, it was Forman's summary that represented "the PFS in the public mind" giving "the false impression that the researchers had lent themselves to a moralizing crusade" (Jowett et al., p. 7).

Of the investigations started in the project, 10 were completed and reported in book form. The conclusions of one study appeared only in a journal article (Cressey, 1938, in Jowett et al., pp. 336–345). Jarvis (p. 130) has implied that the conclusions were, from the viewpoint of the project's policy, too favorable for the movies, but, according to Jowett (p. 224), the study did not remain unpublished for this reason but simply for that that it was never finished. For Jowett et al. (p. 126), this study was the most promising of all because it did not approach movies as a separate phenomenon but "as one part of the 'total situation' or 'configuration' in which they were experienced."

The project's researchers "were pioneers both in research methods and in research design" (Jowett et al., p. 5). Even if, in this respect, much of the "lineage and inspiration" of the PFS traces back to the Chicago School—Robert Park was among the project's planners—many researchers applied experimental designs and statistical methods untypical of the Chicagoans (p. 4). In fact, there was some controversy between the users of qualitative and quantitative methods which "probably contributed to dissension and animosity among the research group during the studies' publication" (p. 65).

The qualitative methodology was represented especially by Herbert Blumer (1900–1987), a disciple of Park. According to Astala (1989, p. 277), for one, Blumer's Movies and Conduct (1933/1970) is "perhaps the most influential and, at the same time, most interesting" of the PFS's reports. Also many others have placed it in a class of its own, in good (Lowery & DeFleur, 1983, pp. 46–54; Mayer, 1946, pp. 145–168) as well as in evil (Rowland, 1983, pp. 93–94; Sklar, 1976, pp. 136–140). Therefore, it merits a closer presentation.

MOVIES AND CONDUCT

Blumer studied the possible influence of movies on the conduct of children and adolescents. Like the other reports, Movies and Conduct was opened by Charters' preface in which he argued that the talk on movies and their possible effects had hitherto been based on mere opinions and convictions. Therefore, "it is obvious that a comprehensive study of the influence of motion pictures upon children and youth is appropriate" (Blumer, p. vii). In this way, Charters created an impression that the PFS represented an objective research devoted merely to finding the truth. However, by taking a closer look at the preface Sklar (p. 135) concluded that "all its assumptions about motion pictures were negative."

Blumer's Research Design

Blumer (p. 2) set his study as an opposite to those that resorted to "experimental and control situations" by introducing "a number of subjects to a given kind of picture" and testing their reactions through questionnaires or other devices. He based his analysis "chiefly on personal accounts given by people of their experiences with motion pictures" (pp. 2–3). He got such accounts from more than 1,800 respondents, most of whom were high school, college, or university students. They were asked to tell of their actual experiences with the movies, not to judge how they believed "they were affected by them" (p. 3). The accounts were written under strict confidentiality so that the informants would not feel embarrassed at also telling about awkward situations. This material was supplemented by other materials collected with other methods.

Blumer (pp. 6–8) checked the reliability of his data in several ways. These checks showed "convincingly that there was little tendency to exaggerate or falsify; if anything, there was a tendency to withhold information" (p. 8). Despite the confidentiality, the respondents were somewhat reluctant to uncover particularly their movie-related sexual experiences in their "movie-autobiographical" accounts.

In Movies and Conduct, Blumer analyzed these autobiographical accounts qualitatively, but there is no detailed description of his way of proceeding. In the presentation he let the accounts "speak for themselves" and limited his own remarks "mostly to interpretation" (p. 12). Occasionally, he summarized some results in a statistical form. In regard to the large material Blumer himself claimed to have collected, it is quite surprising to learn from Jowett et al. (pp. 237–238) that the excerpts that he used to illuminate the movie-related experiences stemmed from a handful of the autobiographies and that he, for unknown reasons, varied the identification of these excerpts so that the pool of them looks in the book larger than it seems to have been in reality.

An Overview of Blumer's Results

The autobiographies enabled Blumer to analyze the role of the movies with respect to aspects in the life of children and youth, such as childhood play, imitation by adolescents, day-dreaming and fantasy, emotional possession (through stimulation of feelings like fear, sorrow, love, thrill, etc.), emotional detachment, and schemes of life. In assessing the possible impact of the movies in these respects, he was quite cautious. Thus, if he was "one of the most antimovie of the PFS researchers," as Jowett et al. (p. 79) claimed, this did not show in his exposition. More visible is the attitude that Blumer (1931, cited in Jowett et al., p. 82) expressed in the project's final conference by saying: "As I look back on my own results, I don't know whether types of experiences that children have are something to be commended or to be regarded as harmful."

For instance, the experiences told in the autobiographies implied that the movies offered "content for children's plays" providing them in this way with "certain stereotyped conceptions" of life (Blumer, p. 28). On the other hand, this kind of experience seems to have been "of little consequence on their subsequent attitudes and conduct" (p. 29). There emerged thus a dilemma: The movies incontestably "have a profound influence on children's plays," but the significance of this influence "is uncertain" (p. 29).

The autobiographies revealed further that the movies had provided a rich array of patterns for adolescents to imitate, especially in the area of love behavior. Many also had tried to employ these patterns in real life, often with meagre results but sometimes even successfully. In the following excerpt a high school girl tells about her experiences (p. 55):

> I have learned how to flirt, and how to "handle 'em." I have also learned different ways of kissing, and what to say when made love to. I have had all kinds of chances to use what I've learned from moving pictures, and I've taken advantage of them. If it hadn't been for what I've learned from the movies and seen what the actresses did in such cases, it would go hard with me at times.

Even if it appeared to be quite common to probe the effectiveness of film mannerisms and techniques in real life, Blumer (p. 58) judged the impact of the movies in this respect again in quite a balanced way:

> Much, perhaps most, of what is selected for imitation is rejected in the process; much is confined to limited use in separate situations and on special occasions. Yet much is taken over and is incorporated into conduct.

It also appeared to be quite common to extract from the movies stuff for day-dreaming and fantasy. Understandably, "the chief theme" in adolescent day-dreaming was "that of love" (p. 65). For Blumer (p. 72), it was again difficult "to interpret the meaning of this day-dreaming in the life of the individual." Due to "the absence of an acceptable interpretation of the effect of day-dreams on conduct" (p. 73), it was impossible to say whether the movies are beneficial or harmful in this respect.

For Blumer (p. 74), the "most interesting motion-picture data" consisted of descriptions of episodes in which the movies aroused the viewers' emotions—their fright, sorrow, love, and/or thrill—to such an extent that they lost their "self-control." Inferred "from the accounts given," this "emotional possession" appeared, in particular, through

> physical expressions such as the shouting, jumping, and excited movement occasioned by the witnessing of "thrillers"; such as the shrinking and avoidance in the case of fright; such as the weeping in the case of sadness; such as the sighing and breathing and fondling in the case of romance or passionate love. (pp. 126–127)

In this area of the stimulation of emotions, the movies seemed to have powerful but mostly short-lived effects: Usually the "state of emotional possession" disappears soon and "the old state usually reappears," even if this "return is probably never complete" (pp. 127–128). Yet, because being "usually transient," the emotional possession is "perhaps not ordinarily significant in the life of the individual," albeit in some cases it "may leave some enduring effect" (p. 128). A familiar example is children's tendency to avoid dark places for a long time after seeing a frightening film (pp. 83–87).

Along with individual maturation, the disposition of losing oneself emotionally in the films seemed to give gradually room for a more detached, rationally analyzing attitude. Important for this was the recognition that films were technically manipulated artifacts, not reflections of reality (pp. 135-136). But, for Blumer (pp. 134-135), the "chief source of emotional detachment" lies in the peer group pressures:

> If one's companions or associates look askance at a certain kind of picture, make depreciating remarks about it, ridicule its character and term one's interest in it as childish, one's attitude is likely to change by adopting the attitude of the group towards the picture. One tends to withdraw oneself from its hold. . . . Group conversation tends to define and set the individual attitude.

Leaning on viewpoints he presented of emotional detachment, Blumer (p. 140) saw that, compared to censorship or other restrictive forms of film control, a "more effective and so desirable form" would be "the development of attitudes of emotional detachment." Such attitudes could be created for "children and adolescents through instruction and through frank discussion of motion pictures instead of categoric condemnation of them" (p. 140). With such views, Blumer clearly anticipated critical media education (cf. Masterman, 1985).

On the Conditions of the Influence of the Movies

Astala (1989, p. 264), for example, claimed that all the reports of the PFS—including, thus, Movies and Conduct—approached the influence of motion pictures "in very simple and linear terms: the influence was conceived as a direct reaction to the film or its scenes." Rowland (1983, pp. 93–94) suggested that Blumer assumed, in this book, "a direct media-stimulus to audience-response process" and took only later a critical stand toward this kind of conception of mass media effects. In my mind, however, Blumer's view is more complicated.

In the first place, even if the movies might have even drastic direct effects, these effects were mostly short-lived or at least their significance for subsequent conduct remained unclear. Often real-life experiences—such as backlashes experienced in testing the suitability of film mannerisms to everyday practice—were sufficient to prevent the adoption of patterns from the dream world of films into one's conduct. In the second place, the emotional detachment, brought forth by maturation and peer-group pressures, narrowed the scope of direct effects. So it is somewhat problematic to maintain without qualifications that Blumer would have underwritten the doctrine of direct effects.

Moreover, Blumer (p. 179) was clearly aware that the possible effects of films were dependent on "the different interpretations which people may place upon what is seen."

> There is a wide variety in what people may select out of a picture. Its influence, consequently, is dependent not solely upon its content but also upon the sensitivity and disposition of the observer. A picture which to one may be quite devoid of stimulation may be highly exciting to another. A picture which some may regard as highly moral may be construed in an opposite light by others. . . . Sometimes the meanings which movie-goers may get from the same picture are diametrically opposite. (pp. 179–180)

Thus, for instance, The Birth of a Nation was interpreted differently by two girls:

> The Birth of a Nation made me see the Negro of the South as he was and not as the Northerners have always portrayed him. . . . The picture did not make me an advocate of slavery as it existed but made me see things from a Southerner's point of view.

> I remember coming home and crying because the poor colored people were so mistreated. . . . For weeks I looked with sympathy at every colored person and got eleven cents together . . . and gave it to a little Negro boy. (pp. 180-181)

In brief, the way in which a person "responds to a motion picture depends considerably on his own attitude" (p. 182). Blumer derived these attitudes largely from the peer-group pressures. "An individual's sensitivity and perception are built up very frequently in response to what his associates think and say," he (p. 186) said, and continued that "the different interpretations that are made of pictures are explicable to some degree in terms of the interests of one's group." The following experience of a boy gives an example (p. 186):

> There was a time, however, at about the age of sixteen, when I took more of an interest in this sex part of movies. The interest was developed largely through the comments of other boys who suggested that a certain actress was beautiful, or had a nice fig-

ure, or that it would be fun to kiss her, or that they envied the actor playing opposite her, etc.

Thus, Blumer recognized the peer group's mediating role in the experience and influence of the movies long before the behavioral tradition claimed to have discovered it. Blumer was ahead of this tradition also when he stressed that the movies influence the viewers most in regard to those areas of life where they "do not already have definitely shaped images" (p. 190). In his influential summary of mass media effects research, Klapper (1960, pp. 53–61) stressed the same idea—without, however, referring to Blumer with a single word. For Blumer, the fact that children's knowledge and experience is on the average more limited than that of the adults explains their greater susceptibility to movies (pp. 188–190).

AN EXAMPLE OF THE QUANTITATIVE RESEARCH OF THE PFS

Where Blumer's study was qualitative, that of Peterson and Thurstone, reported under the title Motion Pictures and the Social Attitudes of Children, exemplifies the quantitative-experimental work of the PFS. They studied "the degree to which commercial motion pictures could change the attitudes of youthful subjects toward different topics" as, for instance, "toward different nationalities and races" (Lowery & DeFleur, 1983, p. 41). The study comprised of more than 20 experiments, some of which concerned the effects of single pictures, others the cumulative effect of two or three pictures dealing with the same topic, whereas the rest assessed the persistence of attitude change over time (p. 42).

The example here is an experiment geared to find out to what extent Griffith's The Birth of a Nation had power to affect the attitudes toward Black people—"the film portrays Negroes in negative terms and is considered an anti-Negro statement" (pp. 42–43). The group studied consisted of 434 White high school students of whom only a few "had known or ever seen a Negro" (p. 43). First their attitudes toward Black people were measured with a scale ranging from extremely unfavorable to extremely favorable. After some 2 weeks, the film was shown to them, and their attitudes were measured again the following day. The group's attitudes had clearly become more unfavorable: the mean value, which in the first measurement was 7.41 (the maximal favorable score was 10), was in the second measurement 5.93 (p. 44).

In his summary of the PFS, Charters (1933/1953, pp. 400–401) said that the experiments of Peterson and Thurstone indicated "that single pictures may produce a change in attitude, that the influence of pictures is cumulative, and that their effects are substantially permanent." However, besides noting that, Peterson and Thurstone also emphasized that "young people's social attitudes generally conformed to group values and resisted easy redirection by mass media" (Jowett et al., 1996, p. 76). Thus, both Blumer, from the qualitative camp, and Peterson and Thurstone, from the quantitative camp, demonstrated that "movies had a definite impact" on children but that "everywhere that influence was modified" by group pressures and other intervening variables such as "age, gender, [and] social background" (p. 91).

ON THE INFLUENCE OF THE PFS

The PFS failed to influence the government in the intended way. According to Rowland (1983, p. 94), in 1934 only a committee considering the establishment of "a Federal Motion Picture Commission to inspect, classify and license films," heard witnesses who referred to the results of the PFS. However, "none of the researchers themselves testified" (p. 95). Most of the witnesses were "religious or educational leaders" whose claims that the PFS had demonstrated "the deleterious social and moral impact of film" did not convince the congressmen of the necessity of any control commission (p. 95).

On the other hand, the PFS had, at least for Sklar (1976, pp. 173–174) and Jarvis (1991), a more powerful effect on the film industry. In Jarvis' (p. 134) view, writings popularizing and dramatizing the project's results prompted Catholic bishops to appoint in 1933 The Episcopal Committee on Motion Pictures "to plan and conduct a campaign against immoral movies." The campaign resulted in a wide boycott of films, and it "did not take long for Hollywood to get the message" (p. 135). The industry tightened the production code, controlled its observance more closely, and gave more prominence to films geared to children and the youth. For Jowett et al. (1996, pp. 9, 57), however, the "industry was engaged in self-reform" already when the Payne studies were under preparation; therefore it "would be wrong to say that the PFS played a major role" in that reformation.

Although the Payne Fund project was ground-breaking "in a new field" and, for its time, "sophisticated social science" (p. 2), it had no discernible effect on the development of research. It seems that the scientific community largely ignored it—definitely so after a furious attack against it by philosopher Mortimer Adler in 1937 for the intermingling of facts and values (pp. 8, 95). This repudiating attitude is represented pertinently by Klapper (1960) who listed the Payne studies in the bibliography of his book but scarcely bothered to mention them in the text. The PFS were, in effect, practically forgotten for a long time.

In seeking reasons for this, Jowett et al. (pp. 7–10) pointed out, for instance, that scientific conjectures had turned unfavorable for an approach utilized in the PFS, that the researchers had "no clearly articulated framework in which to present their results as advances in science" or that they, almost immediately after having finished their work, "turned their backs on this line of research and made their careers elsewhere." Yet it seems that the most decisive reason was Forman's book, which effectively helped "to discolor" the researchers' "academic reputation" (p. 111). Maybe it was just this which prevented the scholars for a long time for according the PFS "the recognition that are their due" (p. 1).

ASSESSING THE PFS

There are quite dissimilar interpretations as to how the PFS conceived the phenomenon of influence and how the researchers assessed the power of the movies in this respect. As stated, for Astala (1989), the PFS considered influence as a direct linear process. In Rowland's (1983, p. 93) view, such a conception was especially pronounced in the quantitative studies approaching the effects "in conventional S $\rightarrow$ R, experimental terms." The assumption that the PFS started with a direct effects model seems to nourish an interpretation that the studies were overall "confident in their discovery of effects" (p. 94) or, what amounts to the same, that the researchers overstated the power of film to influence confirming so "the worst fears of the critics of the medium and the movie industry" (Lowery & DeFleur, 1983, p. 55).

Others have stressed that most of the studies had a more sophisticated view of effects than that implied by a direct effects model. As Jowett et al. (p. 58) stated, to a

> casual observer the PFS might seem to be illustrations of long-discredited "hypodermic needle" or "direct influence" theories of media effects. . . . But when we look more closely at the actual undertaking of the studies, we see that they reached cautious

conclusions that emphasized limited, indirect models of media influence and the extent to which individual, social and environmental differences moderated film's impact on the youth.

Similarly, for Wartella and Reeves (1987, pp. 163–164), the logic of the PFS did not depend "on stimulus–response models," but emphasized to such an extent the role of the variables intervening "between exposure and effect" that to blame the project for representing "the 'hypodermic needle' model of media effects" is untenable. In fact, the project's results anticipated in many respects those obtained subsequently by the behavioral approach to mass communication (Delia, 1987, p. 40). Thus, it seems to be quite to the point to say that the PFS "revealed nothing alarming" (Jarvie, 1970, p. 121) or that their "overall conclusions hardly attributed a pervasive influence to the film in shaping youth culture" (Janowitz, 1968, p. 42).

Sklar (1976, p. 136) criticized the project of having ignored an essential comparison: "How does the influence of movies compare with that of other stimuli in the environment?" This, however, was a defect of which the project's researchers were well aware: for instance, as previously shown, Charters deplored it in his summary of the project's results. Anyway, this and other defects seen by Sklar (p. 139) in the project prompted him to doom it by saying that, "despite their vast array of scientific procedures," the PFS "hardly advanced an understanding of the impact of movies on American society beyond the Chicago physician who claimed they caused St. Vitus dance."

For some scholars, the PFS failed to advance this understanding mostly because "no study of the ownership and control of the industry were undertaken" and because, moreover, the studies were based on "only a commonsense view of society and its workings" (Jowett et al., pp. 12, 114). Similarly, Rowland (pp. 95–96) charged the project for ignoring the analysis of "the nature and impact of motion pictures as an industry" and for taking no cognizance of the "temporal and political context" of its studies. Jowett et al. (pp. 48–53) implied that, had the project taken the course proposed by Seabury instead of that advanced by Short, it would have concentrated on the economic and legal aspects of the industry. But then it would most certainly have been met with charges for neglecting the question of whether or not the movies influence their audiences.

Because of concentrating solely on the possible individual effects of movies, the PFS indeed "took place in a vacuum" (p. 114). Yet, to offset this blame one should keep in mind that, for being a pioneer in the field of mass communication research, the project was unusually extensive. There are few studies with a corresponding scope among the later research. The project's pioneering nature also explains why the PFS often made mistakes, for instance, by saddling "themselves with topics that were too broad, experiments that failed and assumptions that were initially naive, misguided or biased" (p. 59). Even if Lowery and DeFleur (1983) overstated the impact of the PFS on subsequent research, their overall judgment of the project hits the mark in my view:

> The Payne Fund studies were clearly the pioneer studies that established the field of media research within the perspectives of science. They anticipated contemporary interest in meaning theory and the influence of models, and focused the new field on such topics as attitude change, the sleeper effect, uses and gratifications, content analysis, modeling influences, and the social construction of reality. They placed an emphasis on quantitative, experimental, and survey methodologies, but they still made use of more qualitative approaches. Above all, the studies shifted the the long-standing pattern of concern on the part of communication scholars with propaganda criticism that represented an earlier rhetorical form of analysis. (p. 55)

II

CONSOLIDATION FROM THE 1930S TO THE 1960S

During the 1930s, the field underwent such drastic changes in the United States that it is wholly legitimate to speak of a transition from one phase to another. The most visible sign of this transition was the birth and rise of what I call classical behavioral mass communication research. In its mature form, it was a somewhat heterogenous collection of empirical approaches to different facets of people's mass communication behavior. However, what particularly captivated the researchers' attention was the question of whether or not the mass media have an effect on people. Effects were repeatedly researched in different contexts with varying empirical methods. What these studies had in common was a sort of "natural scientific attitude"—the phenomena under study were approached causally, measured quantitatively, and analyzed statistically.

Another sign of the transition is the rise of the functionalist approaches to mass communication on both individual and societal levels. Its causal bent notwithstanding, the behavioral tradition was ecumenical enough to promote such a development. In fact, the individual level uses-and-gratifications (U&G) approach got started under its auspices. Instead of examining effects, the U&G was interested in what gratifications receivers obtained from their media fare. This was tackled initially from a functionalist-qualitative perspective, but afterward the research moved more toward a causal-quantitative framework. The behavioral tradition also extended the field's scope by promoting societal level functionalism in mass communication theory. The objective of functionalism was to find out what kind of functions the mass media are fulfilling in society.

The transition in question was part of a larger transformation process that took place in the U.S. social sciences from the end of World War I onward. Scholars turned more and more from theoretical speculation to empirical research, focusing especially on human behavior and the factors affecting it. This turn gave rise to the term behavioral sciences. Although the term was coined first in the 1940s (Berelson, 1968), one can find use of the terms behavioral psychology, behavioral sociology, and so on already in the 1920s. Behavioral mass communication research was born in the wake of these developments. This is one indicator of the fact that the fortunes of the field have often depended on changes in other disciplinary fields.

For Rowland (1983, p. 46), this transformation was fueled especially by "the rise of a large governmental regulatory apparatus" in the United States after World War I. For the purposes of planning, the apparatus needed information that could be supplied by the means of empirical social research. This precipitated the rise of applied "administrative" research geared toward social technology (cf. Lazarsfeld, 1941). Such research does not criticize the prevailing system but seeks means to improve its functioning (see Popper, 1952, pp. 22–25). Behavioral mass communication research also developed in this affirmative direction. It served the government, in particular, during World War II and the subsequent Cold War (Simpson, 1993). In addition, it also served the interests of the communication industry (Gitlin, 1981, pp. 93–101).

Although the affirmative behavioral tradition dominated the field from the 1930s to the 1960s, there were also some other notable discourses that took a more critical stand to the media and media industries. One of them is the critical (media) theory of the Frankfurt School, which was formulated in the beginning of the 1940s. It approached the media as institutional practices that are subordinated to serve the pursuit of profit and that keep up the status quo in society by preventing people from realizing the system's inequities. Also, the somewhat later Canadian theory of media technology was partly critical of the media even if its representatives had clearly divergent accents in this respect. What was unique to this theory was its attempt to tell the world history in terms of changes in media technology.

Both of these theories also deviated from the behavioral tradition and its protégés in the respect that they continued certain themes that had surfaced already during the field's prehistory. The critical theory of the Frankfurt School took up specifically the critique of mass culture, although establishing it on a more comprehensive theoretical basis than the earlier critics had done. The theory of media technology, again, has predecessors in earlier views of the press as a technological vehicle that extends contacts over space and time. Moreover, the emphasis put on theory shows that both theories have an affinity with the way in which mass communication was approached in earlier times.

This glance backward must be balanced with a look forward. Both of these theories have been important sources of inspiration for some of the main reorientations that have taken place in the field during the third phase, that is, in the 1970s and afterward. The critical theory of the Frankfurt School fueled Marxism particularly during the period of its formation. The Frankfurtians' view of the media industry as subordinated to the economic imperatives of capitalism had an especially strong impact on the Marxist way of approaching mass communication. The Canadian theory of media technology, for its part, has inspired much of the discussion around the so-called information society and the new information and communication technologies. Thus, both theories link the field's past with its future.

7

THE CLASSICAL BEHAVIORAL
MASS COMMUNICATION
RESEARCH

Besides general causes, specified in the prologue, there were other factors also contributing to the rise of the behavioral mass communication research. One of them was a public concern of the possible omnipotence of the media. As noted earlier, many feared that the movies in particular would have harmful effects on the public. Additionally, the effectiveness of propaganda in World War I nurtured "popular images of the pervasive effects of the mass media" (Janowitz, 1968, p. 41). "A postwar wave of autobiographies, exposés, and popular articles helped further a belief in the deceitful power of propaganda and the ease with which modern media could be insidiously controlled in its service" (Czitrom, 1982, p. 123). The use of mass agitation "in the rise of European totalitarian movements" increased these fears (Janowitz, p. 41).

Due to such public fears, there was a "social order" for research concerning media effects. But pressure toward it came from another direction, too—from commercial radio broadcasting on one hand, and from the advertising business on the other. To be able to price their advertising time adequately, the "broadcasters needed evidence concerning their audiences," whereas advertisers "needed information concerning the effectiveness of the media and of their advertisements" (Delia, 1987, p. 47; cf. also Czitrom, 1982, pp. 125–127; Hurwitz, 1988). These needs could only be fulfilled with empirical inquiries into the behavior of radio audiences and the possible effects of radio on them.

As noted in chapter 6, the Payne Fund project was the first to approach the possible effects of the media in empirical and behavioral terms. However, it did not establish the behavioral mass communication research and fell into oblivion. In fact, the classical behavioral tradition began to grow in the 1930s out of the empirical-behavioral research on radio audiences. Throughout its golden age through the late 1960s, it maintained good relations with the broadcasting industry and with the media industry in general (Gitlin, 1981; Rowland, 1983).

During World War II, the tradition entered into close relations with the government, too. For Simpson (1993), these relations gained specific significance during the subsequent Cold War when the behavioral communication research was articulated as a part of psychological warfare against Soviet Union. In Simpson's view, it is unlikely that the behavioral current "could have emerged in anything like its present form without constant transfusions of money for the leading lights in the field from U.S. military, intelligence, and propaganda agencies" (p. 316). Surely such a support must have had its impact (see pp. 330–341), but despite this it seems far-fetched to derive the whole progress of the behavioral tradition from its collaboration with military circles.

THE NATURE OF THE CLASSICAL BEHAVIORAL TRADITION

What distinguished the behavioral tradition most clearly from the previous currents in the field was the emphasis it put on empirical research. This emphasis prompted Katz and Lazarsfeld (1955, pp. 15–17), to quit the earlier thinking on mass communication as pure speculation. Wilbur Schramm (1907–1987), the great synthesizer of the classical tradition, stated that "communication research in the United States is quantitative rather than speculative" (Schramm, 1963, p. 5). He continued that scholars are, of course, "interested in theory, but in theory they can test"—thus, "they are behavioral researchers" (p. 5). This kind of premise gave the classical behavioral tradition in communication studies its specific flavor.

A Quest for a Discipline

In the heyday of the classical tradition, the empirical measurement of behavioral phenomena was generally regarded as a precondition for the scientific status of any field of social research. No surprise, then, that the tradition's representatives were occupied by the question of whether or not mass communication research was a scientific discipline of its own. For example, Lazarsfeld and Stanton (1949, p. xiii) did not hesitate to proclaim it "a specific discipline." Most, however, considered it a multidisciplinary field of research—so did, for instance, Berelson (1959/1964) in his "funeral speech for communication research." In his comment on Berelson, Schramm (1959/1964, p. 511) emphasized in particular that "communication research is a field, not a discipline." Some 20 years later he contended that it is "a new discipline," but was quite unsure whether it will "be recognized" as such (Schramm, 1983, pp. 6, 17).

An obstacle in the way to a full scientific status was that the classical tradition lacked a theory of mass communication process. In an early assessment, the field's too "practical orientation" was criticized for this lack (Freidson, 1953/1971, p. 197). The development of communication models, especially in the 1950s, aroused a spark of hope for a theory, but this spark soon died out. In his retrospective view of the already marginalized classical tradition, Schramm (1983, p. 14) asked whether it had produced "an interrelated body of theory on which the practitioners of a discipline can build and unify their thinking," and answered: "I am afraid that it has not." This lack was not substituted for by specific theories—such as Festinger's (1957) theory of cognitive dissonance—developed to explain particular aspects of mass communication process.

On the other hand, the lack of a general theory did not prevent the entry of mass communication research into the universities in the form of the behavioral tradition. This took place through the foundation of specific academic institutions of communication research. The first was founded by Schramm at the University of Illinois at the end of the 1940s (Chaffee & Rogers, 1997, pp. 139–141; Rowland, 1983, pp. 82–85; Rogers, 1994, pp. 451–457). Despite the resistance coming from established journalism schools and speech departments, such institutes spread step by step to several universities, although this entry "did not follow a singular pattern" (Chaffee & Rogers, 1997, p. 159). Yet, in all their dissimilarity, the institutes had the common feature that they were imbued by an empiricist-positivist spirit and turned a deaf ear to "more critical and interpretive traditions of communication research" (Rowland, 1983, p. 84).

Communication Process as an Object of Research

Mass communication behavior may seem simple as a term but as a phenomenon it is quite complex, consisting of multiple forms of behavior having multifarious causes and consequences. One problem was how to render this complexity an orderly object of research. It was this problem that called forth the manner of considering mass communication as a unified process, the core of which is the transmission of messages from the senders through the media to the receivers. Lasswell (1948/1960, p. 117; see also Gary, 1996) crystallized this process model by saying that communication research studies "who says what in which channel to whom with what effect."

Lasswell's model was based on a view of communication as a technical transmission process—a view opposite to the conception of communication as a sharing of common sociocultural world. The same view underpinned also the influential communication model of Shannon and Weaver (1949), which, according to Rogers (1994, p. 440), constituted "the root paradigm" for the behavioral tradition. It stimulated subsequent modeling work, especially in the 1950s, in the (vain) hope of in this way providing the field with a general theory. Influenced by cybernetics (see pp. 405-407), some models took also feedback into account, shaping communication as a two-way transmission process (for models, see Fiske, 1982, pp. 6–39; McQuail & Windahl, 1981).

The idea that all communication amounts to message transmissions led to the view that, instead of being focused on single media, communication research "is concerned with all the ways in which information and ideas are exchanged and shared" (Schramm, 1963, p. 6). In view of this, it is not surprising that the behavioral tradition was characterized by a "trend toward a unified field of communications research" (Czitrom, 1982, p. 131)—a trend that ignored the differences between the media and saw them as similar instances of mass communication in general. Such a field of research was outlined already in 1940 in the memorandum Research in Mass Communication, compiled by request of the Rockefeller Foundation (Czitrom, p. 131; Gary, 1996). In this way, the tradition, which had emerged as radio research, abstracted mass communication or, still more broadly, communication in general as its area of research.

Besides articulating an object of research, Lasswell's (1948/1960, pp. 117–118) catch phrase also divided the study as follows: "who" referred to control analysis, "what" to content analysis, "channel" to media analysis, "whom" to audience analysis, and "effect" to effect analysis. Gatekeeper study focusing on how the messages were selected in the media exemplifies control analysis (for a summary, see G. Robinson, 1973). Content analysis was deployed to describe many kinds of communication content (see Berelson, 1952). Media analysis was rare. In addition to the composition of audiences, audience analysis also studied "why people choose to be in a particular audience and what they think of what they receive" (Schramm, 1960, p. 424). Effect analysis, the absolutely most significant subtype, is taken up later.

The classical behavioral tradition operated mostly on the level of individuals or small groups leaving the broader social and cultural aspects aside. Its sight did not extend to social processes maintaining the unequal distribution of power and wealth, for example (cf. Hall, 1982, pp. 56–62). Explanations for phenomena were derived, as a rule, from psychological or social psychological theories. If society happened to catch attention, it was usually seen as a functional system where the subsystems—the media among them—produce functional or dysfunctional consequences, the former supporting and the latter disturbing its equilibrium.

Causal-Quantitative Methodology

The scholars who had the greatest impact on the classical behavioral tradition represented different orientations—Hovland was an experimental psychologist, Lasswell a political scientist, Lewin a social psychologist, and Lazarsfeld a methodologist with a predilection for survey analytical social research (Berelson, 1959/1964). Due to these differences, there were dissimilar emphases within the classical tradition. The most distinct cleavage separated the Hovlandian type experimental laboratory study from the Lazarsfeldian style survey analytical field research.

On the other hand, the tradition was integrated by its manner of measuring quantitatively the aspects or variables of behavior under study and analyzing statistically the data obtained in this way. Moreover, the relations between behavioral aspects were approached in causal terms. For instance, in effect analysis the characteristics of media content were seen as causal factors that may produce specific behavioral consequences—for example, the amount of violence in TV programs may stimulate aggressive behavior among viewers. This led to the application of such research designs that allow the presumed cause and the presumed consequence to be measured independently of one another and their (possible) causal relationship to be tested reliably.

The design regarded as most appropriate for this purpose is the experimental one (Hsia, 1988, pp. 261–278; Tannenbaum, 1963). Its rationale in bare outlines is the following. The subjects are first divided into experimental and a control groups. The variable indicating the consequence to be studied is measured in both groups. After that, the experimental group, but not the control group, is subjected to the influence of the causal variable. Then the variable indicating the consequence is measured again in both groups. If it has changed in the hypothesized direction in the experimental but not in the control group, the conclusion is that this confirms the existence of the presumed cause–consequence relationship. In survey research, such a design can be neared with certain research arrangements and statistical techniques (Hyman, 1955, pp. 178-329; Lazarsfeld, 1955).

Despite the emphasis that the classical behavioral tradition put on quantitative methods, it did not look awry at qualitative methods either. It was usual to supplement larger quantitative survey materials with a small number of qualitative "intensive interviews" (Schramm, 1997, p. 55). The studies of Cantril, Gaudet, and Herzog (1940) and Merton (1946) give evidence of this. For Berelson (1949, p. 113), qualitative data do not suffice "as scientific proof," but they can offer "a set of useful hypotheses." In summary, the classical tradition preferred quantitative methods but resorted to qualitative ones when reasonable.

PAUL F. LAZARSFELD: THE PERSONIFICATION OF THE CLASSICAL TRADITION

For Rogers (1994, p. 246), as for many others, "the most important intellectual influence shaping modern [behavioral] communication research" was Paul F. Lazarsfeld (1901–1976), an Austrian-born scholar, who studied mathematics at the University of Vienna and defended his dissertation there in 1925 (about his vicissitudes, see Rogers, pp. 246–311; Morrison, 1988; Neurath, 1983). He felt particularly attracted by empirical social study that challenged him to employ his mathematical talents for creating appropriate research methods. He also realized that, in order to be efficient, such a study must be conducted by a research institute team. To test his ideas in practice he founded a small-scale research institute in Vienna. Its most remarkable achievement was the famous Marienthal unemployment study (Jahoda, Lazarsfeld, & Zeisel, 1933).

In 1933, Lazarsfeld got a Rockefeller scholarship for familiarizing himself with the U.S. social research. The political development in Austria soon made it clear that it would be wisest for him to remain in the United States, as he was of Jewish descent and a known socialist in Austria. He got his first workplace at the University of Newark where he created a research center. In 1937 he began to co-direct the Radio Research Project, established at Princeton University and funded by the Rockefeller Foundation. Soon the project was extended to the Office of Radio Research, with Lazarsfeld as its head. As Rogers (1994, p. 265) put it, Lazarsfeld became a communication scholar in an accidental way: "he was the right man, in the right place, at the right time."

In view of Lazarsfeld's focal position in communication research, it is interesting to hear him confess that he had "no interest whatsoever in mass communication" (cited in Morrison, 1988, p. 204). He entered communication studies because there the research activity was still in its incipiency allowing him to devote himself to creating empirical methods and organizing the carrying out of research—both things that he had loved already in Austria. He achieved his position largely "through the establishment of a new form of academic enterprise—the research bureau—and mass communication research was the hard core for his institutional brickwork" (p. 185). "Intellectually his commitment was to methodology and educationally to the idea of research centers as training schools for the social sciences" (p. 186).

The Office of Radio Research was formed around a large radio research project motivated by the Rockefeller Foundation's conviction that radio programs left much to be desired (pp. 196–198). Although the radio industry did not find the project very useful for this reason and did not greatly contribute to its finance, Frank Stanton, a researcher from the CBS—subsequently the head of research and finally the president of the corporation—took part in it. So the project had both scientific and commercial links. This setting recurred in many Lazarsfeld's projects. He was also more directly involved in commercial undertakings. For example, together with Stanton he developed a device to measure the emotional effects of program or advertising content on audience members. By pushing the buttons of this "program-analyzer" audience members indicated what they liked and disliked when listening to the content (Rogers, 1994, pp. 274–277). The device had immediate commercial value.

Lazarsfeld has told that the objective of the Princeton project was "to determine eventually the role of radio in lives of different types of listeners, the value of radio to people psychologically, and the various reasons why they like it" (cited in Rowland, 1983, p. 61). Adorno, the best known critical theorist of the Frankfurt School, who was active in the project for a short time, characterized it quite differently (cited in Rowland, p. 61):

> There appeared to be little room for . . . critical social research in the framework of the Princeton Project. Its charter, which came from the Rockefeller Foundation, expressly stipulated that the investigations must be performed within the limits of the commercial radio system prevailing in the United States. It was

thereby implied that the system itself, its cultural and sociological consequences and its social and economic presuppositions were not to be analyzed.

The plan of the project was loose, which "gave free rein to Lazarsfeld to take it in directions that he would choose" (Rogers, 1994, p. 270). The first years were spent mainly in developing adequate research methods. The initial purpose had been to concentrate on experimental studies with radio programs, but Lazarsfeld extended the scope to cover, inter alia, survey research and content analyses of radio programs. The project did not limit itself to radio but comparisons were made, for example, between the audiences of radio and the printed page (Czitrom, 1982, pp. 128–131). Many results were published in Radio Research collections edited by Lazarsfeld and Stanton.

Besides radio research, the Office also carried out pure commercial research "for Life and Time magazines, Green River Whiskey, wine, Sloan's Liniment, refrigerators, greeting cards, toothpaste (Kolynos Tooth Powder), vitamins, and Bisodol (a stomach powder)" (Rogers, 1994, p. 290). Market research yielded about half of its revenues already "in its early years," the other half coming from the Rockefeller Foundation (p. 291). When the Office was moved in 1939 to New York and annexed to Columbia University, other than radio research increased its share so much that the Office's name was changed in 1944 into the Bureau of Applied Social Research (pp. 289–296; Rowland, 1983, p. 63). Thanks to its research activity, Columbia sociology achieved a leading position in the U.S. sociology similar to that of the Chicago School.

Lazarsfeld combined in his activity different things, even such that seemed deeply discordant. Some have wondered, for example, how a socialist could advance market research contributing to the valorization of capital (Rogers, 1994, p. 256). The reason is that Lazarsfeld was a practically-minded person, who conducted commercial research in order to get means for scientifically more ambitious studies. His ecumenic leaning came into sight also in his attempt to combine so-called "administrative" fact-finding research with the ideas of the Frankfurt School's critical theory (Lazarsfeld, 1941). With this intention, he hired Adorno in the Princeton project, but there soon emerged so deep disagreements that Adorno had to leave (Morrison, 1978). Lazarsfeld was also a methodological ecumenist in that although he was fond of statistical-quantitative methods, he did not despise qualitative research either. In fact, the first U&G studies that were conducted within the Princeton project, had a clear qualitative slant.

As previously mentioned, Lazarsfeld's favorite—survey analysis—represented one branch within the classical behavioral communication research. Under his influence, the so-called "Columbia School" researched the possible effects of the media with the aid of large-scale surveys. An opposite branch consisted of psychologically oriented experimental laboratory studies. This experimental work on media effects split actually into two tendencies, with their roots in different psychological doctrines, the "Yale School" representing neo-behaviorist psychology and the "cognitive tendency" Gestalt psychology. In what follows, I elucidate the classical effects research from the Yale School through the cognitive tendency to the Columbia School.

MEDIA EFFECTS AS LEARNING: THE YALE SCHOOL

The basic tenet of psychological behaviorism was, grossly stated, that human behavior consists of reactions to various stimuli: a certain stimulus (S) gives rise to a certain reaction (R), or S ➤ R. It was soon realized, however, that the relationship between S and R depends on the reacting organism (O) that led to a neo-behaviorist model of three members: S ➤ O ➤ R. This model underpinned also the neo-behaviorist learning theory that equated learning with conditioning (see Bower & Hilgard, 1981). If a reaction is experienced as rewarding, it tends to be "learned," that is, it is reinforced and tends to become a recurring manner of reacting. On the other hand, a reaction leading to punishment is not "learned." In the neo-behaviorist view, the organism is constituted of this kind of conditioned ways of reaction or behavior.

The top name at the Yale School was Carl I. Hovland (1912–1961). Although he and his colleagues were more fact-finders than theorists (McGuire, 1996), they approached media effects loosely from the perspective of learning theory. Starting with Hull's neo-behaviorist version of this theory, they equated media effects with learning (Hovland, Janis, & Kelley, 1953, p. 10): "Exposure to a persuasive communication which successfully induces the individual to accept a new opinion constitutes a learning experience in which a new verbal habit is acquired."

The researchers thought that, when exposed to a certain opinion, the individual compares it with the opinion he or she already has. In order to be able to change the individual's opinion in such a situation, the communicator must "create a greater incentive" for making the new response "than for making the old one" (p. 11). The incentives involve "anticipated rewards and punishments" (p. 11). The individual must, then, be brought to see that the adoption of the new opinion is more rewarding than the clinging to the old one. Of course, what individuals experience as rewarding and what punishing depends on how their previous experiences have conditioned them.

It was hypothesized, for example, that individuals learn through rewards and punishments which communicators or sources of information are credible and which are not and that, consequently, the adoption of opinions coming from credible sources is more rewarding than the adoption of opinions coming from noncredible sources. Thus, messages coming from credible sources should be more effective than messages coming from noncredible sources.

To study this experimentally, Hovland and Weiss (1954) let two groups of subjects read same articles. The difference was that the articles of one group were ascribed to sources held generally trustworthy, whereas those of another group were ascribed to sources held generally untrustworthy. As the hypothesis predicted, "subjects changed their opinion in the direction advocated by the communicator in a significantly greater number of cases when the material was attributed to a 'high credibility' source than when attributed to a 'low credibility' source" (p. 341). What was most interesting, however, was that in a posttest a month after the experiment the differences between the groups had vanished. It seems that the subjects had forgotten from which kind of source the information they had received had originated.

The Yale School began to take form during World War II when Hovland worked in the Research Branch of the Information and Education Division, U.S. Department of War (Lowery & DeFleur, 1988, pp. 105–161; Rogers, 1994, pp. 358–383). The work started there was continued after the war in the Department of Psychology, Yale University. The war focused attention on the ways of rendering war propaganda more effective. One question intriguing the researchers was whether it is "more effective to present only the materials supporting the point being made" or to present arguments opposing to this point as well (Hovland, Lumsdaine, & Sheffield, 1949, p. 201).

The experiment concerning this question was carried out in early 1945 when the end of the war was yet not in sight. The researchers prepared two radio programs—an "one-side" program which contained only arguments indicating that the war will be prolonged and a "both sides" program that included also some arguments emphasizing that the war may end up even quite soon (pp. 202–206). The subjects were divided into two experimental groups and one control group. Before the experiment, all subjects filled out a questionnaire where they had to evaluate, among other things, how long the war will still last. After that, one experimental group heard the one-side program and another the both sides program, whereas the control group did not hear any program. Then all subjects filled out again a questionnaire, serving seemingly a totally different purpose than the former one but containing the same evaluation task of the continuance of war.

The researchers condensed the results shown in Table 7.1:

Table 7.1. The experimental effectiveness of one-side versus both-sides propaganda (adopted from Hovland et al., 1949, p. 210).

	One-Side Program	Both Sides Program	Control Group
Before	37 %	38 %	36 %
After	59 %	59 %	34 %
Difference	22 %	21 %	-2 %

The programs increased the belief in the prolongation of the war in the same proportion—"no advantage for one program over the other for the audience as a whole is revealed" (p. 210). But the scrutiny of the effects in different subgroups revealed interesting things. For example, the one-side program was found to affect more the lower educational group and the both sides program more the higher educational group (pp. 213–214). The researchers did not take pains to interpret this result closely, but in view of their theoretical bent, the most probable interpretation would be that education fosters ability to complex thinking and that, therefore, the more complex both sides program would have been more rewarding for the high than the low educated men, for whom the plain one-side would have been more rewarding (cf. pp. 147–160).

MEDIA EFFECTS AS A FUNCTION OF COGNITIVE CONSISTENCY: THE COGNITIVE TENDENCY

The neo-behaviorist learning theory is challenged most powerfully by cognitive-organizational theories. The contrast between them stems from the antagonism between philosophical empiricism and rationalism (Bower & Hilgard, pp. 2–8, 14–17). Like empiricism, neo-behaviorism views individuals as "empty containers" that are filled with $S \to O \to R$ links constituted through learning-as-conditioning. Cognitive-organizational theories, again, take the road of rationalism in that, for them, individuals possess an inherent mental structure which mediates between them and the world out there.

This starting point was specified by the theories of cognitive consistency with the argument that individuals' behavior in relation to their environment is governed by an innate tendency to avoid inconsistencies among their "beliefs, feelings, and actions" (McGuire, 1966, p. 1). Leon Festinger's (1919–1991) theory of cognitive dissonance is one of these theories (Festinger, 1957). It "grew out of the group-dynamics movement founded by Kurt Lewin" (McGuire, 1996, p. 50)—a movement that, for its part, was partly rooted in Gestalt psychology (Rogers, 1994, pp. 317–320). Also Heider's (1944/1958, 1946) Gestalt psychological balance theory may have influenced Festinger's theory. This background explains why Festinger had a somewhat critical attitude to behaviorism (see Lawrence & Festinger, 1962, pp. 1–59).

Festinger's theory can be condensed into following propositions (Markus & Zajonc, 1985, p. 202):

1. Cognitive dissonance is a noxious state.
2. In the case of cognitive dissonance the individual attempts to reduce or eliminate it, and the individual acts so as to avoid events that will increase it.
3. In the case of consonance, the individual acts so as to avoid dissonance-producing events.
4. The severity or the intensity of cognitive dissonance varies with the importance of cognitions involved and the relative number of cognitions standing in dissonant relation to one another.
5. The strength of the tendencies enumerated in Propositions 2 and 3 is a direct function of the severity of dissonance.
6. Cognitive dissonance can be reduced or eliminated only by adding new cognitions or changing existing ones.
7. Adding new cognitions reduces dissonance if the new cognitions add weight to the one side and thus decrease the proportion of cognitive elements that are dissonant, or the new cognitions change the importance of the cognitive elements that are in dissonant relation with one another.
8. Changing existing cognitions reduces dissonance if their new content makes them less contradictory with others or their importance is reduced.
9. If new cognitions cannot be added or the existing ones changed by means of a passive process, behaviors that have cognitive consequences favoring consonance will be recruited. Seeking new information is an example of such behavior.

Festinger (1957, p. 3) stated that because dissonance is "psychologically uncomfortable," it leads to attempts at "dissonance reduction just as hunger leads to activity oriented toward hunger reduction." For McGuire (1966, p. 13), "inconsistency reduction is reinforcing in much the same sense as pain reduction is reinforcing." As these remarks reveal, the theory of cognitive dissonance is quite mechanical in its implication that a state of dissonance always leads to attempts at its reduction and that there is "no individual exceptions" (Pepitone, 1966, p. 270). So, in the end, this theory is not very far away from behaviorist tenets.

The theory of cognitive dissonance was developed with the intention to create a theoretical view capable of integrating results obtained in an area ranging "from studies on the effects of the mass media to studies on interpersonal communication" (Festinger, 1957, p. v). And indeed, the theory seems to be able to explain a wide array of observations. Take, for example, the observation that people tend to select from the media messages corresponding to the conceptions they already have for which reason there is not much room for media effects. The explanation is that in this way they are avoiding dissonance. On the other hand, if people continually face messages challenging their opinions, the probability increases that they will change these opinions in order to escape the state of dissonance. So there is an explanation ready for cases, in which the media have no effects, as well as for cases in which they have tremendous effects.

Although the theory was developed to explain available observations, it was also tested with specifically arranged studies. Often their design was similar as in the experiments of the Yale School. The design in the following example is, however, a bit different. The theory predicts that a choice between important alternatives that are equivalent creates dissonance since the selection of one of them means the rejection of other, equally attracting ones (Festinger, 1957, pp. 32–47). The hypothesis is, then, that individuals strive to reduce the postselection dissonance, for instance, by seeking information that presents the chosen alternative in most favorable light.

Because advertisements present products in this way, the hypothesis was spelled out as follows: the "recent purchasers of some product should, provided the purchase is an important one, read advertisements of the company whose product they bought and avoid of reading advertisements of competing companies" (p. 50). The hypothesis was tested by scrutinizing whether ads about the purchased car were read more by new than by old car owners—it was namely presumed that the new owners suffered from an acute dissonance while that of the old owners would already have been reduced. The hypothesis was supported: 65% of new car owners and 41% of old car owners read ads dealing with their car. On the other hand—and this was against the hypothesis—new car owners did not avoid ads of other cars but "read more car ads of all types than did the old car owners" (p. 53).

MEDIA EFFECTS IN THE WEB OF OTHER INFLUENCES: THE COLUMBIA SCHOOL

In contrast to the cognitive tendency, in particular, the survey analytical work of the Columbia School was at its outset quite atheoretical. Its predecessor, the Princeton Radio Research project, was focused on describing people's mass communication behavior, not on developing theories of it. Also its first milestone, the People's Choice study on voting behavior (Lazarsfeld, Berelson, & Gaudet, 1944/1968), was started in an atheoretical spirit, although its results aroused theoretical consideration. In particular, the observation that people use the media selectively, paying notice to contents corresponding to their conceptions, put the selectivity on theoretical agenda.

The People's Choice study was conducted in the context of the U.S. presidential election in 1940. Rogers (1994, pp. 285) reported that Lazarsfeld's initial plan was to study "the impact of U.S. Department of Agriculture radio broadcast promoting federal farm policies." The quick change of the research theme describes aptly Lazarsfeld's research policy. It has been said that he simply wanted to do a panel study, whatever the theme (p. 286). Another incident describing his policy is that in order to secure the funds for the study—the grant from the Rockefeller Foundation was not enough—he sold the rights to report the study to Life Magazine and included in the interview schedule questions, sponsored by the manufacturers, about which make of radio and refrigerator his panel respondents preferred (pp. 286–287).

The study was not limited to mass communication and its possible effects; its scope was broader as the following posing of objectives reveals (Lazarsfeld et al., p. 1):

> We are interested here in all those conditions which determine the political behavior of people. Briefly, our problem is this: to discover how and why people decided to vote as they did. What were the major influences upon them during the campaign of 1940?

This formulation notwithstanding, it is said that Lazarsfeld expected the study "to find that the mass media had direct, powerful effects in making up people's minds about how to vote" (Rogers, 1994, p. 287). The study proved this expectation wrong. Interestingly—and paradoxically—this seems to be the reason why the study has become, despite its extensive objectives, a classic expressly in the domain of media effects research.

The study was carried out in small Erie County, Ohio, because there the earlier presidential election results "had deviated very little from the national voting trends" (Lazarsfeld et al., p. 3). The study made use of a panel design. A group of 600 persons were interviewed six times before election day and once after it. In some rounds, additional respondents were also interviewed. The questions dealt with the respondents' interest in politics, their political preferences, their exposure to the media and other channels of influence, and so on. To trace the possible effects of mass communication, respondents were asked to what extent they followed the campaigns of the main candidates—Franklin D. Roosevelt, the Democrat, and Wendell Willkie, the Republican—and to whom they decided to give the vote and when. If somebody changed his or her vote intention, "detailed information was gathered" on the reasons for this (p. 5).

A problem hampering the causal approach in survey research is that a correlation between two variables does not tell which of them possibly is the cause and which the consequence. A positive correlation, say, between the exposure to a candidate's campaign and the willingness to vote for him or her may be due to the influence of the campaign or due to the predisposition of the voters to vote for that candidate and their willingness, caused by the disposition, to expose themselves to his or her campaign. A panel design escapes this problem, because the time order between the variables can be taken into account. If the vote intention comes after the exposure to the campaign, the hypothesis of a campaign effect is more plausible, but if the intention is formed before to the exposure to the campaign, the hypothesis of a predisposition effect is supported.

Lazarsfeld and his colleagues observed that a correlation between the exposure to the campaign and vote intention emerged mainly through the predisposition effect. "Half the people knew in May, before the campaign got underway, how they would vote in November, and actually voted that way" (p. 87). The campaign exposure of those who had made up their mind "was consistently partisan"—Republicans tended to expose themselves to Willkie's and Democrats to Roosevelt's campaign (p. 89). Moreover, "the more partisan the person," the more likely he or she was to insulate him- or herself "from contrary points of view" (p. 89).

The researchers concluded that the campaign had hardly any effects, if by an effect is meant "a change in vote" (p. 87). There were specific factors warding off such conversion effects. The most important was that those who had made up their mind did not expose themselves to a campaign speaking against their decision. Moreover, people resorted to their relatives and friends much more than the media in making their minds. Persons, "who made up their minds later in the campaign were more likely to mention personal influences in explaining how they formed their final vote decision" and also those making "some change during the campaign" mentioned most often "friends and members of their family" as sources of the change (p. 151). Sure, the campaign converted some people "but they were few indeed" (p. 94).

On the other hand, the campaign had other kind of effects. It activated indifferent people to vote (pp. 73-86), and the exposure to the campaign backing one's decision reinforced the conviction that the decision was the right one (pp. 87-93). Perhaps the most important observation was the one that led subsequently to the so-called hypothesis of the two-step flow of communication. The researchers found that some respondents, who were opinion leaders in politics, "reported that the formal media were much more effective as sources of influence than personal relationships" that suggested to the researchers that "ideas often flow from radio and print to the opinion leaders and from them to the less active sections of the population" (p. 151). The media effects were seen, then, as being involved in a web of other influences.

In People's Choice, selectivity was approached only in regard to its consequences, of which the most important was the reinforcement of the dispositions having led to the selections made. In their second voting study, conducted in the context of the U.S. presidential election in 1948 (Berelson, Lazarsfeld, & McPhee, 1954), Lazarsfeld and his colleagues considered also what leads people to select content according to their dispositions. With an explicit reference to Gestalt psychology, they suggested that people have a tendency to form "strong Gestalts," an example of which is the congruence between dispositions and the corresponding selective behavior (pp. 277–285). This anticipates clearly the theory of cognitive dissonance. However, the researchers themselves did not develop a clear-cut theory, neither in the study at hand nor at the subsequent work of Personal Influence (Katz & Lazarsfeld, 1955).

In any case, the finding of selectivity had an important impact on behavioral communication research. It provided an explanation for the observation that the effects of the mass media on people's political opinions and behavior were, at the most, indirect by-effects, and not direct and powerful as Lazarsfeld had expected. With reference to selectivity one could argue for the view that the mass media were not particularly effective. It is mostly due to this that People's Choice has been regarded as the study that "launched the era of limited effects in mass communication research" (Rogers, 1994, p. 287; see also Gitlin, 1981; Lowery & DeFleur, 1988, pp. 79–103).

THEORY OF MODERNIZATION

The doctrine of minimal effects was derived on the basis of studies conducted in the United States. On the other hand, behavioral mass communication researchers were also involved in research activities concerning other countries, especially the developing ones. In the Cold War era the United States and the Soviet Union "tried to expand their own interests to the developing countries" (Servaes, 1999, p. 18). Development and modernization were the catchwords of the day. Development was defined in the United States, according to Servaes (p. 18), "as the replica of its own political-economic system and opening the way for transnational corporations." Modernization was viewed as a process through which traditional societies will gradually turn into Western model societies (Hellman, 1981, pp. 76–85). The research was charged with a task of finding out the parameters of that process.

The results indicated that, lo and behold, the mass media did have effects on people. In fact, the media were seen as key agents in the modernization process. Lerner's (1958) version of the modernization theory, for example, run as follows. The most important precondition for the modernization process is empathy, a psychological "capacity to see oneself in the other fellow's situation" (p. 50). In Lerner's (1967, p. 120) view, the advanced Western model society "presents to the less developed country 'a picture of what it may become'." But if people in the less developed country lack empathy, they are not able to put themselves into that picture and see themselves in the situation portrayed by it. That's why empathy is indispensable.

The mass media have a key role in cultivating empathy. Lerner (1958, p. 54) argued that the media have "disciplined Western man in these emphatic skills which spell modernity" and that the continuing spread of the media "is performing a similar function on a world scale." Resting on empirical material collected in Middle Eastern developing countries he concluded that, "in accelerating the spread of empathy," rising media participation "also diffuses those other modern demands to which participant [modern] institutions have responded: in the consumer's economy via cash (and credit), in the public forum via opinion, in the representative polity via voting" (p. 60). Of course, this influence takes place in the context of other relevant factors.

Lerner's view of the effectiveness of mass media in the modernization process was endorsed by many behavioral researchers. Schramm (1967, p. 11), for one, had no doubts that the development of the mass media is "one of the requisites for and signs of a modernizing society." Therefore, "the mass media have a particular importance at this point of history" (Schramm, 1964/1974, p. 179). In Pye's (1963) view, it is communication coming from outside that has pushed traditional societies in the state of transition. Moreover,

> throughout the transitional world the hopes and the fears about a new kind of life are ceaselessly stimulated by communication from abroad. . . . The pattern of development is inevitably governed in each particular setting by whether the modern world has been communicated as being friendly and sympathetic or hostile and forcing, as being benign and comforting or harsh and intractable. (pp. 3–4)

CLASSICAL MEDIA EFFECTS RESEARCH: A SUMMARY AND A CRITIQUE

In his summary of the classical behavioral effects studies, Klapper (1960) crystallized the limited effects model by generalizing the findings of the research as follows. First, "mass communication ordinarily does not serve as a necessary and sufficient cause of audience effects, but rather functions among and through a nexus of mediating factors and influences" (p. 8). Second, on these conditions the media influence mostly by strengthening opinions people already have; "reinforcement, or at least constancy of opinion, is typically found to be the dominant effect" (p. 15). A minor change in intensity of opinion is "the next most common" whereas conversion—the shift from an opinion to the opposite one—"is found to be most rare" (p. 15).

For Klapper, most significant in the effects research was the discovery of the factors that mediate the media influence: selectivity caused by predispositions, group norms, interpersonal dissemination of mass communication, opinion leadership, and the nature of the media in a free enterprise society (pp. 19–43). Only in cases in which these factors do not function, or function differently from their normal way, mass communication may have direct conversion effects (pp. 62–97). For instance, in experiments the factors protecting against effects are normally eliminated, which explains why the media have been observed as more powerful in experimental studies than in survey analyses where the mediating factors mingle with the game.

These generalizations were supplemented by some others. For example, Klapper emphasized that if people do not yet have an opinion of an issue, the media may influence even decisively on its formation (pp. 53–61). Here, "mediating forces which normally hinder conversion seem likely to be inoperative" (p. 61). Furthermore, relevant characteristics of the sender, the medium, the message content and the prevailing opinion climate may foster or restrain the effects (pp. 98–132). An example is the credibility attributed to the sender (pp. 99–103)—a factor studied by the Yale School. It is worth noting that Klapper presented his generalizations with a caveat warning that they may easily lead one "to go overboard in blindly minimizing the effects and potentialities of mass communications" (p. 252).

It has been pointed out that Klapper's book was very useful for the broadcast industry—in fact, Klapper's "work was directly underwritten by CBS" and it earned him "a position with CBS, where Stanton made him director of a new Office of Social Research" (Rowland, 1983, p. 72). Another question is whether or not Klapper formulated his generalizations with the industry's interests in his mind. What is beyond dispute, however, is that the generalizations corresponded to those interests: On their basis the industry could argue that public fears of the omnipotence of the media were gross exaggerations.

From the end of the 1950s onward, critique on the limited effects model began to mount. One point of criticism was the research design applied in experimental and field studies. For Blumer (1959/1986, p. 184), the researchers had a too simple view of "the operation of mass media in the real world." They disregarded three important things. First, the media supply varies enormously and continually. Second, how receivers are sensitized to the supply and how they interpret it, varies similarly. Third, the media operate interdependently. These things "challenge seriously the methodology" that requires, in order to be meaningfully applicable, homogeneity and constancy, not heterogeneity and fluctuation, in all these three respects (pp. 185–186).

Another point of criticism was the limited effect model's view of effect as a measurable change in individual opinions or behaviors (Gitlin, 1981). Such a view is incapable of catching hold of the long-term effects mass media may have. The view of an effect as a change ignores, further, that mass communication may influence by preventing possible changes and, thus, support the status quo. An influence acting against change is not the same thing as reinforcement, which was taken into account by the classical effects research (see pp. 83–85). Finally, clinging to effects on individual level kept the possible societal effects of mass communication out of sight. In summary, the classical effect studies

> could not possibly explore the institutional power of mass media: the degree of their power to shape public agendas, to mobilize networks to support the policies of state and party, to condition public support for these institutional arrangements themselves. Nor could they even crack open to the questions of the sources of these powers. (pp. 83–84)

The third point of criticism was that the researchers' conclusions glaringly contradicted at places the results that served as their basis. Gitlin (pp. 87–88) picked up from the Personal Influence results speaking against its conclusion that personal influence overshadows that of the media. Chaffee and Hochheimer (1985, pp. 272–273) noted that in the postelection interview of the People's Choice study "more than two-thirds mentioned newspapers or radio as a 'helpful' source while less than one-half mentioned any type of personal source" and that "more than one-half said either radio or newspapers had been the single most important source, but less than one-fourth cited a personal source as important." An intriguing question is why the researchers did not even relativize their conclusions in the light of such discordant results.

A fourth point of criticism was that the researchers made a habit to present results, gained under specific conditions, as universal truths (Gitlin, 1981, pp. 88–92). For example, the Personal Influence is fraught with broad generalizations regardless of the fact that the study "was completed before the general introduction of television," as Katz and Lazarsfeld (1955, p. 312) remind us in a footnote. On the other hand, the rapid dissemination of television in the 1950s was one of the focal reasons for why the limited effects model began to seem suspect. With the new research stimulated by the rise of television there began to accumulate evidence "which suggested that the limited effects image was at best oversimplified and under many circumstances quite misleading" (Chaffee & Hochheimer, 1985, p. 288).

In the name of fairness it should be noted, however, that the classical effect researchers were generally aware of the shortcomings troubling their studies even if they did not highlight them sufficiently. For example, many footnotes of the Personal Influence contain remarks relativizing the study by reminding that mass communication may have many such effects—indirect, long-term, societal—that cannot be traced with the methods employed in the study (Katz & Lazarsfeld, pp. 18–19, 24, 133; see also Gitlin, 1981, pp. 79–80). It should also be kept in mind that Klapper presented his generalizations with a grain of salt.

Not only was the minimal effects position harshly criticized but so also was the behavioral theory of modernization. A summary of this critique by Servaes (1999, pp. 27–31) shows that it was criticized partly on the same grounds as the minimal effects view. Some claimed, for instance, that the role of the media in modernization was derived questionably from studies concerning "primarily specific, quantitatively measurable, short-term, and individual effects" (p. 27). The theory was charged, further, for regarding communication as a linear transmission process, for abstracting from the sociohistorical contexts in which communication takes place, for its belief that research produces objective facts, and so on. In the late 1960s, this theory was challenged by the dependency theories to which I return in the context of the theory of culture imperialism.

MARGINALIZATION OF THE CLASSICAL BEHAVIORAL TRADITION

During the 1960s, the classical tradition of behavioral communication research was driven into an ever deepening crisis. The first signs of the crisis came into sight at the end of the 1950s. One of its prophets was Berelson (1959/1964), who argued, in his "funeral speech for communication research," that the field was withering away. Of the "founding fathers" of the behavioral tradition Lewin was dead and Lasswell and Lazarsfeld had moved on to other interests. Also Hovland's contribution had begun to fade out. For Berelson (p. 508), this situation signaled

> that "the great ideas" that gave the field of communication research so much vitality ten and twenty years ago have to substantial extent worn out. No new ideas of comparable magnitude have appeared to take their place. We are on a plateau of research development, and have been for some time.

According to Nordenstreng's (1968) documentation, Berelson saw that the field had taken on a too academic-theoretical-methodological character and forgot problem-centered research. Also Lasswell, another veteran of the field, charged it for concentrating on the finesses of method at the cost of the development of a policy-relevant theory (Nordenstreng, 1968).

A particular thing precipitating the crisis was the critique leveled against the minimal effects position both from inside and outside the classical tradition. Some researchers who had worked within the tradition began to feel that the research had run into a blind alley, because it had approached people as passive targets of messages without noticing that people use the media actively. Therefore, more important than to ask what the media do to people is to ask what people do with the media. With this question in its banner, the U&G research, lingering long in the shadow of the effects research, began to prosper in the 1960s. But also the effects research began to renew at the end of the 1960s with the consequence that the classical form of that research lost conclusively its prior leading position.

Besides the limited effects doctrine, certain other premises of the tradition were also questioned during the 1960s, at least by some of its representatives. For example, Schramm began, at the beginning of that decade, to distance himself from the view that communication amounts to a linear transmission of messages from the sender to the receiver. He stressed that messages consist of signs having "only such meanings as, by agreement and experience, we give them" (Schramm, 1963, p. 7). So he replaced linear transmission with an active interpretation. Later he took an even more critical stand to the transmission model by saying that communication has "to be thought of as a relationship, an act of sharing, rather than something someone does to someone else" (Schramm, 1971, p. 8).

The crisis described here also had its external reasons. Perhaps the most important of them was the 1960s social turbulence that undermined ingrained ways of thinking and opened up roads to approach mass communication—and, of course, other social institutions and processes as well—in fresh ways. In these turbulent conditions, a real ferment was started in the social sciences as new critical tendencies, both Marxist and cultural ones, began to compete for a legitimate status. Communication studies made no exception. Challenged by the new tendencies and torn by inner controversies, behavioral research underwent such profound changes that, as the 1970s progressed, one could hardly speak any longer of a classical style of thinking and the research within it.

8

USES-AND-GRATIFICATIONS APPROACH AND FUNCTIONALISM

In many respects, the individual level uses-and-gratifications (U&G) approach and the societal level functionalism are quite close to the classical behavioral mass communication research. In fact, both tendencies were adapted to communication study by the Lazarsfeldian circle in the 1940s. There is, however, one fundamental difference: Where classical behavioral research considered the role of the media in causal terms of effects, both the U&G approach and functionalism consider it in functional terms of purposes and consequences. In brief, where the classical behavioral current looked at the media as (possible) masters dominating over individuals, both the U&G and functionalism regard them as servants, the former for individuals, the latter for society.

U&G APPROACH

The difference between the classical effects research and the U&G approach has often been summarized by stating that where the former studies what the media do to people, the latter explores what people do with the media. The U&G approach looks at individuals as

127

beings who use the media as a means for particular purposes. Such a use implies that the media fulfill certain functions for them. Consequently, McQuail (1987, p. 72) has called the approach individual functionalism. In fact, it came to communication studies "on the shoulders of functionalist paradigms in sociology and psychology" (Blumler & Katz, 1974, p. 15).

But as the approach has grown older, there has emerged attempts to detach it "from its former functionalist moorings" and to reinterpret it in causal terms—that is, to replace the functionalist language of serving-a-purpose with a causal language of need satisfaction (Blumler & Katz, p. 15; see also Palmgreen, Wenner, & Rosengren, 1985, pp. 16–18). The causal language states, shortly, that needs are causes motivating one to seek to satisfy them, for example, through media consumption that is the cause for the gratifications, if the satisfaction takes place. The emergence of this causal view has produced tensions within the U&G approach and blurred its initial difference from classical behavioral research.

Qualitative Start

The U&G approach sprang up in the context of the Princeton Radio Project at the beginning of the 1940s. The early studies resorted largely to qualitative methodologies (Katz, Blumler, & Gurevitch, 1974, p. 20). Data were collected mostly through open-ended interviews with the aim of detecting what kind of gratifications people derived from their media fare. There was almost no attempt at ascertaining the quantitative distribution of gratifications in the population or at finding out how gratifications were related to preceding variables possibly qualifying as their causes. With the introduction of quantitative methods in the 1960s, the early research began to seem as nonscientific fumbling that had, at the most, created some tentative ideas about media uses and gratifications to be tested with more rigorous research.

An example of the early research is Herzog's (1944/1961) study of the gratifications experienced by listeners of radio day-time soap operas. Qualitative interviews suggested that the gratifications were divided into three types: the soaps offered "a means of emotional release," provided "opportunities to wishful thinking," and gave advice (pp. 50–51). The third gratification was so unsuspected that it was investigated closer. A quantitative study showed that it was quite common—only 28% of the respondents claimed "not to have been helped" by the soaps (p. 51). The sense of being helped was most pronounced among less educated women who felt that they worried "more than other people" (p. 51). A qualitative study specified that the

> over-all formula for the help obtained from listening seems to be in terms of "how to take it." This is accomplished in various ways. The first of these is outright wishful thinking. The stories "teach" the Panglossian doctrine that "things come out all right". . . . A second way in which the listeners are helped to accept their fate is by learning to project blame upon others. . . . Thirdly, the listeners learn to take things by obtaining ready-made formula of behavior which simply requires application. (p. 55)

Another example comes from Berelson (1949, p. 112), who explored "the function of the modern newspaper for its readers" during the New York newspaper strike in 1945. A strike offers good chances to find out what the missing medium means for its users. Berelson observed that although people said they used the newspaper for this or that rational purpose—as for obtaining information about important events—many seemed to miss it simply for the reason "that the act of reading provides certain basic satisfaction, without primary regard for the content of reading matter" (p. 124). Furthermore, the respondents implied that the newspaper gave them "a safeguard" and "an assurance with which to counter the feelings of insecurity and anomie pervasive in modern society" (p. 125). It thus seems that one needs to be in touch with the surrounding world in order to avoid feelings of alienation.

Quantitative Continuation

The U&G approach was quite dormant during the 1950s but was reawakened just at the end of that decade—roughly at the same time that Klapper (1960) formulated the doctrine of minimal effects. It seems, indeed, that the belief that the media do not have marked effects pushed the researchers to ask, among other things, what kind of "use" people have for media contents in the social and psychological contexts where they live (Katz, 1959). Around the turn of the 1960s there appeared a surge of writings outlining in different ways conceptual and theoretical starting points for the study of that subject (Blumler, 1964; Katz, 1959; Katz & Foulkes, 1962; Klapper, 1963; White, 1964; C. Wright, 1959/1975, 1960/1964).

The form in which the approach resurrected differed in two important respects from its earlier form. In the first place, it was located firmly within the functionalist theory. This is probably due to the hegemonic position of functionalism in 1950s social thinking (Friedrichs, 1970). For example, C. Wright (1959/1975) worked in those days on a functionalist theory of mass communication. Starting with Merton's (1949/1968, pp. 73–136) distinction between manifest and latent functions and dysfunctions (to which I return later), he summarized the object of study for a functionalist mass communication research with the following question:

> What are the (1) manifest and (2) latent (3) functions and (4) dysfunctions of mass-communicated (5) surveillance (news), (6) correlation (editorial activity), (7) cultural transmission and (8) entertainment for the (9) society, (10) individual, (11) subgroups and (12) cultural systems? (C. Wright, 1959/1975, p. 11)

The part of the question dealing with the individual implies the U&G approach. Wright did not himself study empirically what manifest and latent functions and dysfunctions diverse mass media contents have for the individual, but was satisfied with presenting an array of hypotheses about possible functions and dysfunctions.

In the second place, many of those reviving the approach advocated a methodological turn. When Klapper (1963, p. 524) reproached the earlier researchers for relying too much on their "insight" and "the qualitative analysis" of their data, his message was unmistakable: The researchers should resort to quantitative methods. However, already before this request Schramm, Lyle, and Parker (1961) had paved the way for the methodological turn with their quantitative study of the functions of television for children. They analyzed two kinds of rewards: pleasure and enlightenment (p. 64). These types of gratification resemble those that Schramm (1949) had distinguished, on the basis of Freud's pleasure principle and reality principle, in his earlier theoretical treatise on the news. There he had coined them, respectively, "immediate reward and delayed reward" (p. 260; cf. Schramm et al., 1961, pp. 109–111).

In later quantitative research, the gratifications, or the reasons for media use, were approached in a more differentiated manner (Blumler & McQuail, 1968; Lundberg & Hultén, 1968; McLeod, Ward, & Tancill, 1965). A standard procedure was to compile a list of possible reasons for use in advance and to ask the respondents to what extent each of the reasons applies to their use of a given medium or content. In McLeod et al.'s (1965) study, for example, the list contained such reasons for the use of newspapers as "to keep me up with things," "to bring some excitement into my life," and so on. Interested in how the reasons for use depended on the degree of alienation, the researchers observed that alienation correlated positively with "vicarious" reasons (or escape reasons such as "to bring some excitement into my life") and negatively with informational reasons (such as "to keep me up with things").

The quantitative measurement of the reasons for use enabled, by using factor analysis, the study of whether or not they are structured along some more basic dimensions. I found in my studies that the reasons resolved into three basic dimensions: The media were used for purposes of information, for purposes of diversion, and for purposes of practical utility (V. Pietilä, 1974). A quite surprising result was that reasons associated with the library use and with the participation in adult education displayed the same factor structure. It should be noted, however, that the basic factor structure heavily depends on how many reasons for use are included in the study and how they are verbalized (see, e.g., Greenberg, 1974).

The later refinement of the U&G approach took place mainly within the quantitative and causal way of thinking. One example is the application of the expectancy value theory to media gratifications (Palmgreen & Rayburn, 1985). This theory postulates that the seeking of a given gratification from a given medium is a function of (a) expectancy or the perceived probability that the medium will provide it, and (b) evaluation or the positive affection attached to that gratification (p. 62). This proposition, which can be formalized into an equation, predicts that the use of a certain medium for certain gratification is more probable the more one believes that the medium at issue is capable of providing it and the more one appreciates this outcome.

Conceptual Models Behind the U&G Approach

The U&G approach developed principally as a specific form of empirical research. Yet, there has been debated quite a lot whether or not it has a theory of its own (Swanson, 1979; see also Palmgreen et al., 1985, pp. 15–18). To settle the issue, Blumler (1979, p. 11) suggested that there "is no such thing as a or the uses and gratifications theory, although there are plenty of theories about uses and gratifications phenomena." Indeed, instead of a theory, one can speak, at the most, of conceptual models which underlie the approach and give it a specific shape. These models have been formulated with the causal need-satisfaction language with the concept of need as the most fundamental starting point.

For example, Katz et al. (1974, p. 20) formulated such a model by stating that the U&G is "concerned with (1) the social and psychological origins of (2) needs, which generate (3) expectations of (4) the mass media or other sources, which lead to (5) differential patterns of media exposure (or engagement with other activities), resulting in (6) need gratifications and (7) other consequences, perhaps mostly unintended ones." Rosengren (1974, p. 270) specified a more detailed model that also starts with basic human needs. Under interaction with individual characteristics and social structures, these needs lead an individual to perceive problems and solutions to them. The perceived problems and solutions constitute motives for attempts at gratification-seeking or problem-solving behavior, involving media use or other activities, which lead or do not lead to gratifications. This outcome may finally affect individual characteristics and/or social structures.

The different parts of these models can be seen as those phenomena of which Blumler spoke and for which—as for needs—there are various theories. For U&G researchers, the view that needs really guide people's gratification-seeking can be argued for with reference to particular individual and social situations—for example, one "might expect 'substitute companionship' to be sought [in the media] especially by individuals with limited opportunities for social contacts" (Katz et al., 1974, p. 27). This expectation is fulfilled if people with a minimum of social contacts answer in a survey that they use the media especially "to get companionship." However, it has been more usual to think that a reason for use reveals directly the motivating need behind it—that, for example, the use of the media for the reason "to keep me up with times" reveals that the use is motivated by a need for security (p. 24).

Within the just discussed models, one important question is whether or not the reasons for use lead one to select content matching these reasons. For example, do people who use a certain medium especially to get excitement into their life choose predominantly thrilling content from it? The answer seems to be "no"—there are no close dependencies between types of reasons for use and types of content chosen (V. Pietilä, 1974). The lack of such dependencies has been explained by arguing that "almost any content may serve practically any type of function" (Rosengren & Windahl, 1972, p. 166). This insight has led to investigations, for example, to what extent different media are each others' substitutes in need-satisfaction (Katz et al., 1974, pp. 25–26) and to what extent the media are capable of fulfilling the wants people bring to bear on them (Katz, Gurevitch, & Haas, 1973).

Critical Discussion

The U&G approach has been assailed from many directions. For some critics, it is, behind its functionalist facade, nothing but atheoretical variable analysis (Swanson, 1979). It fails to meet the functionalist requirements: An individual-level functional analysis should concern "consequences" that contribute to maintaining "the individual personality" (Carey & Kreiling, 1974, p. 235), but typical variables in a U&G survey measure reasons for media use, not consequences of that use for "the maintenance" of the individual (Swanson, 1977, p. 216). Moreover, the approach has ignored "dysfunctions, the necessary complement to functions" (p. 217; Carey & Kreiling, 1974, p. 237). This criticism has not shaken Katz (1979, p. 78), who sees that few functional analyses have in practice tackled "system maintenance" and that, therefore, the U&G research qualifies "as functional analysis, in the rather loose sense in which the paradigm has generally applied."

In the 1970s there was a "movement away from functionalism" (Swanson, 1977, p. 217). Need became the new buzzword. This did not, however, improve the situation because, if one believes Elliott (1974, p. 251), "the concept of need is the source of most of the difficulties" of the U&G research. It leads easily to "circularity of the argument" because mostly the existence of needs "can only be assessed indirectly" (p. 252). Argument is circular if one infers from a reason for use (say, "to keep me up with the times") the underlying need (say, the need for security) and then argues that the inferred need explains the use of the media for that reason. The U&G scholars admitted that this is a problem, and tried to resolve it by seeking such psychological or social conditions that could indicate the influence of the need in question (Blumler, 1979, pp. 21–29). But if a given condition correlates with a given reason for use, is there any need for a concept of need—in other words, is not the condition itself a sufficient explanation for that reason?

Thus, it is unclear how the typical U&G variables, the reasons for media use, are related to needs—or to consequences, for that matter. Moreover, it is unclear what these variables actually measure. Are people really capable of recognizing the true reasons of their media use and to report how far they apply at each specific case? Katz et al. (1973, p. 179) endorsed this argument but, as Elliott (1974, p. 255) observed, they brought "no evidence" for it. It might well be that the reasons people give for their media use do not result from their "genuine" needs but from the cultural images of the media (V. Pietilä, 1974, p. 6). In that case, reasons-for-use variables would measure cultural significations rather than reasons for use, let alone gratifications. They measure certainly also the social acceptability of the different reasons for use (pp. 7, 78–79).

The U&G approach detached itself from the classical effects research with its notion of an active audience (Katz et al., 1974, p. 30). But also this notion has been questioned by the critics. For Swanson (1979, p. 42; see also 1977, pp. 219–220), the approach has ignored the most important characteristic of an active audience, namely receivers' "activity of interpreting or creating meaning for messages." The approach has failed to link the question of use with "the symbolic content of mass communicated materials or with the actual experience of consuming them" (Carey & Kreiling, 1974, p. 232). Katz (1979) replied to the critics with the argument that to define "'activity' as the act of interpretation" is far too narrow—people are active also when they "consult the TV Guide" or discuss "a program with their friends." Yet, such aspects have not been included in normal U&G studies.

A related charge is that U&G research supports the status quo because, for example, it ignores "all the problems associated with the differential distribution of power and opportunity in society" (Elliott, 1974, p. 254). A more general accusation of conservatism and blindness to change has been laid at the door of the whole functionalist thinking (see Anderson & Meyer, 1975, p. 12; Carey & Kreiling, 1974, p. 230). Palmgreen (1984, p. 48) rebutted this charge by claiming that the U&G research does not ignore change but sees in the "discrepancies between gratifications sought and obtained" a motor that stimulates "changes in media consumption" and, through this, "changes in media structure and content." He implies, thus, that the media structure and the supply of content depend on people's changing content choices—a popular thesis in conservative circles.

This multifarious criticism notwithstanding, the U&G researchers have not given up its specific problematics. For them, research since the mid-1970s bears "witness to systematic progression" (Rubin, 1994, p. 425). A specific feature has been the extension of the problematics to cover media effects in relation to uses (Rubin & Windahl, 1986; Windahl, 1981; see also Rubin, 1994, pp. 426–430). The approach has also returned to qualitative concerns, for example, by counting Lull's (1980b, 1985) qualitative ethnographic study of the social use of the media to its body. Furthermore, it has sought contact with cultural studies (see Blumler, Gurevitch, & Katz, 1985; McQuail, 1985; Rosengren, 1985). Cultural researchers, however, have rejected the view that there would be affinities between their approach and the U&G (cf. Ang, 1989, pp. 99–102; Morley, 1992, pp. 22–26).

FUNCTIONALISM

Although individual-level U&G research has been regarded as a functionalist approach, initially functionalism was born as a societal-level approach. It has been characterized as follows: "Functional analysis studies the functions which a structural item of the social system has for the state of the system as a whole, and how these functions bear on the structural item itself" (Isajiw, 1968, p. 25). There are two conceptions of functions. From the system perspective, functions are "contributions which structural elements make towards the satisfaction of given needs," needs being "those of the social system as such," while from the structural elements perspective functions "are consequences of structures or structural items" (pp. 72, 76-77). As can be seen, the latter perspective tries to do without the notion of system needs.

Merton (1949/1968, p. 105) has specified functionalism by making a distinction between functions, which "make for the adaptation" of the system, and dysfunctions, which "lessen the adaptation." Furthermore, he distinguished manifest functions, which "are those objective consequences contributing to the adjustment or adaptation of the system which are intended and recognized by the participants in the system," from latent functions "which are neither intended nor recognized" (p. 105). With the latter distinction, he in a way divided society into a conscious and unconscious level: Consciously intended beneficial consequences may carry with them unintended and unrecognized harmful consequences.

Mass communication theory has involved functionalist views from the 19th century's press theories onward, but as a specific approach functionalism was brought into the field particularly by Robert K. Merton (1910–2003), Lazarsfeld's close co-worker in the 1940s (Rogers, 1994, pp. 244–246; Sills, 1996), who contributed to the empirical mass communication research largely in the spirit of the Columbia School (Merton, 1946, 1949). Although functionalism made some important openings from the 1940s to the 1960s, it never succeeded in becoming a major orientation within communication studies. As functionalism lost its prominent position in sociology at the end of the 1960s, it also disappeared as an approach from communication studies, albeit one can continually discern glimpses of functionalist thinking within other approaches.

The Beginning of Functionalism in Communication Studies

Functionalism was introduced to communication studies through two articles that appeared in 1948. One of them was written by Lazarsfeld and Merton, another by Lasswell. Lazarsfeld and Merton (1948/1960, pp. 497, 499) singled out two media functions: "status conferral" and "the enforcement of social norms." The media confer status on "public issues, persons, organizations and social movements" simply by telling about them (p. 497). Similarly, the media "reaffirm social norms" by reporting about cases "at variance with public moralities" (pp. 499, 501). The writers implied that these functions are manifest because they are "evidently well recognized by the operators of mass media" (p. 501).

Additionally, Lazarsfeld and Merton (p. 501) noted one negative social consequence of the mass media, namely, "the narcotizing dysfunction" that they obviously considered latent because it had gone largely unnoticed. Their view was that individuals are subjected to growing outpourings of media content. Even though this enables them to "keep abreast of the world," the drawback is that "this vast supply of communications may elicit only superficial concern with the problems of society, and this superficiality often cloaks mass apathy" (p. 502). This is dysfunctional, for "it is not the interest of modern complex society to have large masses of population apathetic and inert" (p. 501).

Lasswell (1948/1960, p. 118), for his part, singled out three media functions but no dysfunctions; the functions being the surveillance of the environment, the correlation of the parts of society in responding to the environment and the transmission of the social heritage from one generation to the next. The media serve the first function by keeping an eye on what is happening, the second function by disseminating information from one part of society to other parts so that activities in different parts can be adjusted to each other, and the third function by reproducing a picture of society that is adopted by the growing-up generations. It is not clear whether Lasswell considered these functions manifest or latent.

Charles R. Wright's Theoretical Viewpoints

The outlines just given did not go far toward building a functionalist theory of mass communication but were satisfied with bringing forth tentative ideas of consequences that the media may have in relation to society. C. Wright (1959/1975) outlined theoretical viewpoints in a more systematic fashion. Guided by Merton's functionalist views he asked, as already stated, what manifest and latent functions and dysfunctions mass communication might have for the society, individual, subgroups, and cultural systems. His list of the general functions includes, besides the three Lasswellian functions of surveillance, correlation, and social heritage transmission, a fourth one of entertainment (pp. 11–17).

Wright split these general functions into more specific ones. For example, the surveillance function, fulfilled especially by the news, was resolved into three subfunctions for society—a warning function (news warns of oncoming dangers), an instrumental function (news is essential to the economy and other institutions), and an ethicizing function (news enforces social norms) (pp. 12, 15–16). On the other hand, news can also be dysfunctional for society because reports on "better" societies can threaten social stability and warnings may foster panic (p. 12). It remained unclear whether these and other (sub)functions were manifest or latent.

Typical of the outlines considered hitherto is that they have all looked at the functions from the structural elements perspective. That is, they have reflected on the probable consequences of a specific structural item—the mass media—for society without any particular theory of those needs or prerequisites of the system that the consequences might satisfy. The gravest problem in this way of proceeding is that without any theory it is hard to justify the lists of functions and dysfunctions one has compiled. Consequently, such lists are often quite arbitrary. Wright's extensive list is a point in case— namely, excluding what is self-evident, he does not succeed in giving convincing reasons why mass communication should have those and only those functions and dysfunctions that he enumerates.

Parsonsian Functions and Mass Communication

Another way of proceeding is to start with a theory concerning the needs or functional problems of society, and to consider the structural items—as the mass media—as elements called forth by these needs or problems. According to Talcott Parsons' (1902–1979) theory, in order to survive, societies must be able to resolve four functional problems: adaptation, goal attainment, integration and latent pattern maintenance (see Parsons, Bales, & Shils, 1953, pp. 179–190; Parsons & Smelser, 1956, pp. 13–23). In other words, societies must be able, respectively, to produce means for attaining goals, to set common goals and to attain them, to guarantee inner solidarity and integration, and to create and maintain a common value system.

According to this theory, the necessity of resolving these problems calls forth different structural means from the economy to the communication system. Such means are not created intentionally to solve the problems but they operate functionally, although not manifestly but latently, in so far as they take actively part in the resolution of the problems. One should further note that structural means and functional problems do not have a one-to-one correspondence but that one and the same means may take part in the solution of different problems and that different means may be active in solving one and the same problem (Merton, 1949/1968, pp. 86–91).

What problems do the mass media resolve? In his only text about mass communication, Parsons did not go into this question (Parsons & White, 1960). Of those, who have applied his theory, Hemánus (1966, pp. 9–10) argued that hardly anyone denies the significance of the media in keeping society together and maintaining its integration. Moreover, the media take part, for Hemánus (p. 10), in latent pattern maintenance or in the resolution of the problem of creating and maintaining a common value system. These functions of integration and latency resemble those of correlation and social heritage transmission in Lasswell's list. So the detour via theory has led to quite the same result as the more untheoretical considerations.

Critical Discussion

Functionalism has been criticized partly for the same faults as the U&G. One charge has been that both tend "to be blind to change" (Anderson & Meyer, 1975, p. 12) or that "their methodology is conservative and defensive of the status quo" (Carey & Kreiling, 1974, p. 230). Functionalism—according to Gouldner (1970, p. 332)—takes the existing "institutions as given and unchangeable," counseling for "acceptance of or resignation to what exists rather than struggling against it." Opposing such charges, Merton (1949/1968, p. 107) argued that the concept of dysfunction "provides an analytical approach to the study of dynamics and change" (p. 107). Moreover, it is not alien for a functionalist to think that the intensification of a functional problem may bring on an extensive social restructuration lasting until "the problem gets resolved in a manner that guarantees the survival of society" (V. Pietilä, 1980, p. 148).

The accounts of the mass media functions, described here, have not been commented on very extensively. There are mainly scattered remarks, such as claims that "Merton's paradigm of functional analysis" has been followed by media scholars "somewhat mechanically," with "a considerable over-emphasis on functional integration" (Brown, 1970, p. 55). Furthermore, the division of media functions into surveillance, correlation, transmission of culture, and entertainment has been judged as a scientific failure because each function "operates with an easy face validity without providing an adequate operational definition" (Anderson & Meyer, 1975, pp. 12–13). Without such a definition, they cannot be put to an empirical test. This has been countered by claiming that such charges reflect a skimpy understanding of functional analysis (Pryluck, 1975, p. 415).

The gravest problems of functionalism, as well in communication studies as in general, concern methodology (see Merton, p. 73). The question, simply, is how to empirically test a hypothesis that a structural element fulfills a given function for society—that, for example, the mass media fulfill the integrative function. In principle, one should find two societies that are in every other respects similar save that one has a mass media system whereas the other does not. If the society with the media system would be better integrated than the other society, one would be tempted to conclude that it is the media that serve the integrative function. In practice, however, the problem cannot be meaningfully posed in this way as it is impossible to find such societies.

To circumvent this problem, C. Wright (1960/1964, p. 106) suggested that one should take advantage of mass communication disturbances such as media strikes. But would a fall in social integration during a media strike prove that the media attend to the function of integration? No, it would not, because the decline of integration may result from many other causes. On the other hand, if the problems of integration would not worsen during a strike, would this prove that the media have nothing to do with the integration? No, it would not, because the case might be that other structural elements have begun to act as substitutes for the missing media.

In fact, C. Wright (p. 105) took the individual as "the unit or system" he was concerned with. Following his advice one might study, for example, whether those with rich opportunities for media use are better integrated in society than those with poor opportunities (pp. 106-107). But there is again a problem—if those with rich opportunities are found to be better integrated than those with poor opportunities, the result can be due to many other factors than the availability of the media. Thus, even on individual level it is difficult to get conclusive proof for functional hypotheses. Moreover, it is questionable whether societal phenomena, with which functionalism is concerned, can be studied on individual level without compromising their societal character.

Perhaps historical research offers best chances to seek support for functional hypotheses. If one could show that the birth of a structural element is related to a certain structural change of society, there would be at least some empirical ground to reflect upon its possible functions. An example is the birth of news transmission, in the 15th and 16th centuries, in the context of the form of social organization produced by the expanding trade. This coincidence gives some empirical support to the conclusion that the function of news transmission was to enable people's activity in this new (modern) form of social organization (K. Pietilä, 1980, pp. 167–189). One should realize, however, that to explain the birth of a structural element is not the same as to explain its persistence (Bredemeier, 1955), and that functionalists have been more interested in the persistence of the elements than in their birth (Mullins & Mullins, 1973, p. 53).

Theoretical insights of social functionalism have often been seen as hypotheses that, like those of biological functionalism, require empirical verification or falsification. Another possibility, however, would be to regard those insights—as, for example, Parsons' views of the functional imperatives—as formulations that do not make "an empirical statement" but propose instead "that it would be fruitful to categorize and interpret social structures in terms of their contribution" to the resolution of the functional problems (Cancian, 1968, p. 34). The acceptance of this kind of a view as a guideline would release functionalism from empirical criticism, but at the same time it would be rendered purely conceptual activity.

9

THE FRANKFURT SCHOOL
AND ITS THEORY
OF CULTURE INDUSTRY

The birthplace of the Frankfurt School is the Institut für Sozialforschung (the Institute of Social Research), established in 1923 in Frankfurt am Main, Germany, and connected loosely to the University of Frankfurt. The nuclear group of the school consisted of scholars who rose in the foreground after Max Horkheimer (1895–1973) had become the leader of the institute in 1931. Despite the fact that the group represented a wide array of disciplines, its work displayed so many common features that its achievements have been synthesizingly called the critical theory. However, one should not exaggerate the unity of this work (Held, 1980, pp. 13–16; Kausch, 1988, pp. 71–78; on the school's history see also Jay, 1974; Wiggershaus, 1994).

The school's theory represented Marxism, but it rejected the orthodox Marxist conception of society as determined by naturelike laws and took instead the road opened by Georg Lukács and Karl Korsch. The emphasis was laid on human practice (praxis) as the key of the revolutionary transformation of society (Held, 1980, pp. 19–23; Jay, 1974, pp. 3–5). The future of a Marxist organization of this kind, staffed, in addition, "almost exclusively by men of Jewish descent," was obviously bleak in Germany after Nazi assumption of power in 1933 (Jay, p. 29). This compelled the institute to emigrate abroad. It landed eventually in New York where it made a loose connection with Columbia University (pp. 29–40). After World War II, the institute returned to Frankfurt, although most of its members, who had emigrated to the United States in the 1930s, remained in their new homeland (pp. 281–287).

An early incentive to the critical theory was the question why the attempts at socialist revolutions had failed in western Europe after World War I (Dubiel, 1988, pp. 40-41; Kausch, 1988, pp. 20–22). More generally, the objective was "to understand the disappearance of 'negative,' critical forces in the world" (Jay, p. 84). This focused the school's attention on what the traditional Marxism had despised, the subjective factor, human consciousness, and the "cultural superstructure of modern society" (p. 84) conditioning it. The superstructure refers to more or less institutionalized forms of "mental" activity, in distinction from "material" economy. For critical theory, the core of the superstructure of modern society was mass culture, represented among others by the mass media. To provide a background for the school's view of mass communication, I elucidate first its theoretical and methodological approach.

STARTING POINTS OF THE SCHOOL'S THINKING AND RESEARCH

After his appointment as the leader of the institute, Horkheimer initiated an interdisciplinary research project with the objective of finding out

> the interconnection between the economic life of society, the psychic development of the individual and transformations in the realm of culture . . . including not only the so-called spiritual contents of science, art and religion, but also law, ethics, fashion, public opinion, sport, amusement, life style etc. (Horkheimer, 1931, cited by Held, 1980, p. 33)

The project's starting points were fetched from the tradition of German idealist philosophy, on the one hand, and from "Marx—his theory of history, his theory of capitalism, his view of emancipation," on the other (Kotkavirta, 1991, pp. 170–171). After the school had settled in the United States this project of multidisciplinary materialism was displaced by "a more philosophical approach" (pp. 171–177). Kausch (1988, pp. 5–7) called it "the negative philosophy of history." During this phase, the school also began to strip its most conspicuous Marxist accents.

Nevertheless, the Frankfurtians did not compromise with the principles of their thinking and research. These can be illuminated by taking positivism, which underpinned the behavioral tradition, as a point of comparison (see Hardt, 1992, pp. 133–142). To positivism, empirical facts are all the world. They make up the source for generalizations and theoretical ideas, and compose the criterion against which the soundness of such ideas is tested (see V. Pietilä, 1979, pp. 11–17). The Frankfurtians, again, argued that the consecration of empirical facts restricts the research to the immediate appearances of things. They considered this problematic in two respects.

In the first place, as Theodor W. Adorno (1903–1969) stressed, a theory based on immediate observation "will be reduced to the phenomenon against which it is tested" and cannot therefore penetrate "the context of delusion which it desires to penetrate" (Adorno, 1957/1976, p. 69). For Horkheimer (1937/1972, pp. 197), the acceptance of the existing conditions as given prevents one from realizing, for instance, that seemingly free people do nothing "but exemplify the working of incalculable social mechanism." This implies the Marxist view that (capitalist) society has been divided into observable appearances and the social mechanism of essential relations regulating them—relations that do not show themselves in the appearances as they really are. Therefore, if the research pledges itself positivistically to mere appearances, "then the essential connections—what actually matters in society—are protected a priori from knowledge" (Adorno, p. 79).

In the second place, the clinging on appearances serves "the conservation and continuous renewal of the existing state of affairs" (Horkheimer, p. 196). In doing so, positivism privileges "the existing reality," as Herbert Marcuse (1898–1979) put it (Marcuse, 1937/1979, p. 235). The Frankfurtians themselves approached society as "a historically changing object" (Horkheimer, p. 239). This cannot be done by sticking to appearances that always describe society in its current form. Therefore, what was pursued was an articulated critical theory capable of both explaining the existing society and criticizing it in order to advance the coming of a new, better society—one for which previous development had already paved the way.

The intention of the theory to "go beyond prevailing social ways of acting" (Horkheimer, p. 209) prompted the Frankfurtians to criticize the conception that sees social phenomena as unshakable facts. Although these phenomena are conditioned in modern society by "an incalculable social mechanism," they originate in human action. As such, they "lose the character of pure factuality" (p. 209). Hence, it is entirely possible to eliminate "the dismemberment and irrationality of society" whereby society becomes the "object of planful decision and rational determination of goals" (pp. 207, 217). Then there is no longer any room for an "incalculable social mechanism."

The starting point of the school's work was Marx's theory of capitalism which concerns "an economy based on exchange" (Horkheimer, p. 225). It is the capitalist mode of economy where the essential relations are operative that regulate modern societies. On the other hand, the Frankfurtians regarded Marx's theory as limited to the competitive capitalism. Hence, it could not explain such new social facts as the monopolization of production, or the involvement of the state with the economy, and so forth (Held, 1980, pp. 40–76). There was, however, no unanimity as to how this new situation might be grasped (see also Jay, 1974, pp. 143–172).

Despite their critique of appearances, and the empirical research based on them, the Frankfurtians also saw the merits of both. Although the empirical phenomena and the essential relations conditioning them are not reducible to one another, "appearance is always also an appearance of essence and not mere illusion" (Adorno, 1957/1976, p. 84). So "if the task of a theory of society is to relativize critically the cognitive value of appearance, then conversely it is the task of empirical research to protect the concept of essential laws from mythologization" (p. 84). Although the empirical phenomena do not directly qualify to test a theory, theoretical work should nevertheless sustain connections with the empirical world.

Because critical theory drove at social change, it was not only a theory but at the same time a critique of modern society. The aim was the so-called immanent critique that tries to find the measures of critique within the object to be criticized, not to bring them from outside. The measures for the critique of the bourgeois-capitalist society were offered by those concepts depicting the ideals and promises that its development had produced but that had not become true. On the other hand, the critique should not only weigh reality against concepts but also concepts against reality. Jay (1984, p. 61) has described this dialectics of Adorno's immanent critique as follows:

> To move from error to truth requires a critique of concepts that pits their ambiguous implications against the social world to which they imperfectly refer; the result will not merely be that the concept is inadequate to the world, but also that the world as it presently is constituted is inadequate to certain meanings of the concept. It is the interaction of these complementary inadequacies that gives thought, so Adorno contended, its critical power to transcend the status quo.

Critical theory was never brought to a united whole. It remained a body of theoretical-critical interventions directed to a spectrum of social issues—a body that grew out of a somewhat incoherent foundation. In what follows, I discuss the intervention that dealt with mass culture or culture industry as it was called by Horkheimer and Adorno who were particularly fond of this topic (Adorno, 1963/1991, p. 85).

THEORY OF THE CULTURE INDUSTRY

Although Adorno (e.g., 1932/1984, pp. 729–777; 1938/1991, pp. 26–52) had touched on mass culture in some earlier writings, the theory of culture industry was shaped at the outset of the 1940s. The basic question addressed was seemingly a simple one: What is mass culture? For Adorno and Horkheimer, one cannot get an adequate answer by approaching mass culture as an isolated empirical phenomenon. It must be considered in its social relations. Because the starting point was this broad, the theory evolved into a quite complex one. I illuminate its three main aspects, which concern economy, (class) structure of society, and ideology.

Economy

Adorno's and Horkheimer's ironical talk of culture industry—common wisdom sees culture and industry as opposites (Kellner, 1989a, pp. 130–131)—hints already at the weight they put on economy. Not being economic determinists who reduce all in the end to economy, they still saw that the essential relations concealing themselves in the capitalist economy also condition culture in specific ways. This economy is based on commodity production whose determining motive is the pursuit of profit and the valorization of the capital invested in production. The owners of capital have always been "in search of new opportunities for the realization of capital" (Adorno, 1963/1991, p. 86). Mass culture was born when they recognized that capital can be valorized by investing it in the production of cultural commodities.

As the mental production of culture became expandingly captured by capital valorization, it became increasingly a specific domain of commodity production. The pursuit of profit requires, under the market laws typical of capitalism, that industry and business must be continuously rationalized and the costs minimized. One means is the standardization of products. For Adorno (p. 87) the term culture industry referred "to the standardization of the thing itself . . . and to the rationalization of distribution techniques."

In the realm of culture, standardization dresses the products in rigid formats impressing "the same stamp on everything" (Adorno & Horkheimer, 1944/1986, p. 120). Within the saleable formats into which the contents are packaged "the details are interchangeable" (p. 125). All of them are "ready-made clichés to be slotted in anywhere; they never do anything more than fulfill the purpose allotted them in the overall plan" (p. 125). The likeness of products is the foundation on which are then built the strategies that differentiate them and envelope them with individual air. Individuality is important because it creates an impression that what is "completely reified and mediated is a sanctuary from immediacy and life" (Adorno, p. 87). These strategies have, for their part, contributed to the development of culture industry into a system that finally takes hold of everybody:

> Something is provided for all so that none may escape; the distinctions are emphasized and extended. The public is catered for with a hierarchical range of mass-produced products of varying quality, thus advancing the rule of complete quantification. Everybody must behave (as if spontaneously) in accordance with his previously determined and indexed level, and choose the category of mass product turned out for his type. (Adorno & Horkheimer, p. 123)

The dialectics of making the products at the same time alike and different is not only an instrument in the rationalization of production but attempts also at guaranteeing their continuous salability. However, not all products of culture industry are similarly on sale for the customers—some of them are seemingly free. Horkheimer and Adorno (pp. 158–159) illuminated this with the American commercial radio which, because "it collects no fees from the public," has "acquired the illusory form of disinterest, unbiased authority" (p. 159). This illusion, however, "is made possible by the profits of the united automobile and soap manufacturers, whose payments keep the radio stations going—and, of course, by the increased sales of the electrical industry, which manufactures the radio sets" (p. 158).

(Class) Structure of Society

Because critical theory drove at social change, a burning question was, of course, how and by whom it could be brought about. According to classical Marxism, the change takes place through a revolution effected by the working class. Because its interests are opposite to those of the capital-owning bourgeoisie, the overthrow of the capitalist system would occasion no loss for it—it would only lose its irons. It was realized, of course, that the overthrow had its objective and subjective preconditions: the sharpening of the inner contradictions of capitalism and the development of the workers to recognize their revolutionary interests. When these preconditions come into force, the capitalist system "is burst asunder. The knell of the capitalist private property sounds. The expropriators are expropriated" (Marx, 1867/1990, p. 929).

When reflecting on why the attempts at socialist revolutions had failed in western Europe, the Frankfurtians paid particular attention to the subjective factor. Initially they were confident that despite the backlashes, the workers composed the motor of the change. What was needed was an advancement of their revolutionary consciousness. The Frankfurtians regarded their own work as contributing to this. For instance, Horkheimer felt at that time, according to Held (1980, p. 50), "that the thought of critical intellectuals could be a stimulating, active factor in the development of political struggles . . . by fostering a debate between theoreticians, the advanced elements of the class, and those in need of greater awareness about social conditions."

However, the weakness of the workers' movement in front of the Nazi appropriation of power had already sown seeds of doubt, and the pessimism deepened as the 1930s drew to the end. For Jay (1974, p. 43), "signs of the proletariat's integration into society were becoming increasingly apparent; this was especially apparent for the members of the institute after their emigration to America." They began to incline toward the view that such developments as the involvement of the state with economy were producing a one-dimensional society into which all, including the working class, were gradually absorbed.

For the Frankfurtians, this development dissolved the working class and the old class structure in general, a process in which the mass culture did its share. "The culture industry intentionally integrates its consumers from above," Adorno (1963/1991, p. 85) said. And, according to Jay (1974, p. 50), as Horkheimer's pessimism deepened he appreciated Nietzsche for having "been perceptive in refusing to romanticize the working classes, who were even in his time beginning to be diverted from their revolutionary role by the developing mass culture." Due to the culture industry, "the redeeming power of negation was almost totally absent . . . in what Marcuse was later to make famous as 'one-dimensional' society. . . . The only course open to those who could still escape the numbing power of culture industry was to preserve and cultivate the vestiges of negation that still remained" (p. 276). The numbing power of culture industry refers to ideology.

Ideology

Ideology has been conceptualized in different ways (see Larrain, 1979). Within classical Marxism, there were two basic views: For some, ideology denoted the world-views of different classes, representing their interests; for others, "false consciousness" (Koivisto & V. Pietilä, 1993; Larrain, 1983). False consciousness refers to a way of conceiving society as it appears in everyday experience. This kind of consciousness enables one to act even with success but, on the basis of it, the individual is unable to conceive what kind of forces, which conceal themselves in appearances, make society function as it does. Therefore, the individual cannot recognize the seeds of change that mature within it, not to speak of promoting the change with his or her actions.

The Frankfurtians regarded ideology as false consciousness. Mental activity that is content to reflect reality as it appears always supports "the status quo" (Adorno, 1963/1991, p. 90), legitimizing it and wiping off the perspectives for its changing. This ideology is represented, for instance, by positivist science but above all by products of the culture industry. They are "advertisements produced for the world"; they disseminate "a general uncritical consciousness" (p. 86). This is not so much intentional misleading as a process that takes place behind mens' backs, so to say. According to Adorno (1940/1953, p. 312), for instance, "radio music's ideological tendencies realize themselves regardless of the intent of radio functionaries. There need be nothing intentionally malicious in the maintenance of vested interests."

A more detailed description by Adorno (1966, cited by Kausch, 1988, p. 96) runs as follows:

> Culture industry has grown out of the capital's tendency to valorization. It has developed under the market law, under the force

to adjust itself to its customers, but has later on been swung round into an instance which fixes and strengthens consciousness in its particular forms corresponding to the mental status quo prevailing at each time.

The adjustment means that, in order to be saleable in mass quantities, the products of culture industry must find their way onto the golden route of conventionalism so that they would offend the taste of the smallest possible number of solvent people. The inversion means, for its part, that by adjusting themselves in this way, the products begin to sustain the conventionalism prevailing at each time. It is the force of market law that makes the culture industry ideological because that law conditions it to generate "a pattern of one-dimensional thought and behavior in which ideas, aspirations and objectives that, by their content, transcend the established universe of discourse and action are either repelled or reduced to terms of this universe" (Marcuse, 1964, p. 12).

The products are adjusted into the limits of the established universe of discourse by fabricating them of ready-made pieces according to standard schemes that create between the pieces an illusory, "prearranged harmony" (Adorno & Horkheimer, p. 129). As such, the products are devoid of tensions that would reflect contradictions operating beneath the surface of reality. They leave "no room for imagination or reflection on the part of the audience" (p. 129), no starting points for the critique of the existing conditions. The production of ideology is amplified by the development of the culture industry's techniques—as in sound movies or television—to serve the representation of the existing conditions in increasingly perspicuous and sensuous ways. So "a disagreeable existence" is elevated "into the world of facts in representing it meticulously" (p. 148). This strengthens the ideology of "the world as such" (p. 148).

For Adorno and Horkheimer, the culture industry produced amusement that arouse in people needs that its products promise to fulfill, but the promise is always broken. The dialectics of promise and its deceiving yokes people to continuous consumption in which they are seeking need-satisfaction that is postponed endlessly:

> The culture industry perpetually cheats its consumers of what it perpetually promises. The promissory note which, with its plots and staging, it draws on pleasure is endlessly prolonged; the promise, which is actually all the spectacle consists of, is illusory: all it actually confirms is that the real point will never be reached, that the diner must be satisfied with the menu. (p. 139)

Adorno and Horkheimer (p. 135) stressed that "'light' art as such, distraction, is not a decadent form." In principle, it could poke sarcastic fun at the existing conditions by, for instance, falling "mischievously back on pure nonsense, which was a legitimate part of popular art, farce and clowning, right up to Chaplin and the Marx Brothers" (p. 137). But to the extent that culture industry abandons subversive elements of this kind, it degenerates into the apology of society. Then the pleasure it produces is devoid of any resistance: It

> means not to think anything. . . . Basically it is helplessness. It is flight; not, as is asserted, flight from a wretched reality, but from the last remaining thought of resistance. The liberation which amusement promises is freedom from thought and negation. (p. 144)

A Different View

Not all Frankfurtians shared Adorno's and Horkheimer's harsh view of the culture industry and its amusements. Walter Benjamin (1892–1940) did not hesitate to proclaim cinema, mistreated by Adorno, as the most powerful tool for socialist movements (Benjamin, 1936/1977, p. 14). Although "as long as the film capital" holds the sway, "movies cannot be ascribed any other revolutionary merit as the promotion of a revolutionary critique of obsolete conceptions of art," still cinema and other technically reproducible art forms are progressive by transforming "the relation of the masses to art"—the reactionary character of looking at a detached, unique work of art "is turned round into the most progressive when one watches, say, a Chaplin film" (pp. 28, 32-33).

Benjamin's view of mass culture was closely related to that of Bertolt Brecht (who, by the way, kept a critical distance to the Frankfurt School). Brecht appraised, for instance, the possibilities of radio as a mass medium very differently from Adorno when making the following proposal:

> Radio should be converted from a distribution system to a communication system. Radio could be the most wonderful public communication system imaginable, a gigantic system of channels—could be, that is, if it were capable not only of transmitting but of receiving, of making the listener not only hear but also speak, not of isolating him but connecting him. This means that

radio would have to give up being a purveyor and organize the listener as purveyor. (Brecht, 1930/1983, p. 169)

As to newspapers, Benjamin (p. 29; see also 1937/1978) remarked that the initial difference between editorial staff and the audience had already begun to disappear:

> An ever bigger part of the readers has become writers, albeit in the beginning only occasionally. . . . Thus, the difference between the writer and the audience will lose its fundamental character. It will be reduced to a functional one appearing from case to case in this or that way. The reader is continually ready to become a writer.

According to Kausch (1988, pp. 175–179), Benjamin did speak not only of the changing role between writers and receivers but more generally of activating the audience to "take mentally part" in the production of what it receives. The products ought to be composed— as Brecht's theory of the epic theater implied—in a way that would alienate people from their conventional habits: They should be brought to think, interpret and analyze instead of being fed with ready-chewed food. Consequently, Benjamin did not appreciate mass culture as such but the opportunities it had generated for creating with aberrant methods products deviating from conventional ones, and for obtaining broad masses as their audiences.

HIGH ART AS A COUNTERWEIGHT TO CULTURE INDUSTRY

In conditions in which the ideological culture industry is transforming society increasingly into one dimension only, art may have a "a liberating function" (Dubiel, 1988, p. 34) But not any art would do. Adorno, in particular, demanded it be "avantgardist, difficult to decipher," and stressed that in modern times "only modern art can be critical" (Kausch, 1988, p. 139). Only it refuses to copy things as they appear and so preserves "the gap between art and reality, so important for the transcendent qualities of art" (Held, 1980, p. 89). "An art that self-consciously debunked its illusory claim to wholeness and self-sufficiency was more capable of negating reality than one that kept up the pretence" (Jay, 1984, p. 54).

For the Frankfurtians, art can be subversive only "by remain-ing autonomous" (Held, 1980, p. 86). According to Held (p. 83), Adorno thought that "art is most critical" when it, as an autonomous force, "negates the empirical reality from which it originates." Autonomy requires that artworks "reject and react against market requirements" (p. 89). Adorno (1955/1977, p. 16) wrote that authentic artworks' "insistence on independence and autonomy, on separation from the prevailing realm of purposes, implies, at least as an uncon-scious element, the promise of a condition in which freedom would be realized."

Adorno and other Frankfurtians recognized, of course, that art always has had its bonds, first to art patrons and later to the market. But confinement has different degrees. For Adorno (1963/1991, p. 86), works of art and products of culture industry dif-fer from each other in this respect: Whereas the former are "also com-modities," the latter are "commodities through and through." The tighter art becomes bound to the market the more its products lose their autonomous and authentic character. This is completed when "art renounces its own autonomy and proudly takes its place among consumption goods" (Adorno & Horkheimer, p. 157). At this point, it is swung round into culture industry pure and simple.

Autonomy does not mean that art steps outside of society. According to Kausch (1988, p. 95), Adorno saw that both art and cul-ture industry have a mediating relationship to society: Social circum-stances, attitudes, and the like are mediated into the products and, through their reception, back into society. So "society mediates itself through art or culture industry" (p. 95). The content of mediation, however, is different in these two cases. Authentic "art that wants to express society's general tendency, does this against the resistance of society. It represents 'the social antithesis of society' [Adorno] since its brings forth society's general tendency in its whole contradiction" (p. 147).

For Adorno, art can avoid the traps of ideology only by expressing openly the social contradictions contained in its material (pp. 145–146). He found in Beethoven an artist who did not "succumb to the ideology" like "those who cover up the contradiction instead of taking it into the consciousness of their own production" (Adorno & Horkheimer, pp. 157–158). Adorno looked on him, however, as a rep-resentative of his own time to which there is no return. As an aes-thetic modernist "Adorno ruthlessly rejected any calls for the restora-tion of an allegedly 'healthy' realism or classicism, either in bourgeois or proletarian guise" (Jay, 1984, p. 106). Beethoven does not offer a model for the present day but supports as an example Adorno's (1955/1977, p. 27) stand that authentic art "is not one which resolves objective contradictions in spurious harmony," but one which brings forth "those social problems that it contains down to the innermost cells of its technique" (Adorno, 1932/1984, p. 731).

Among the Frankfurtians, Adorno's view was the most extreme. Although Horkheimer and Marcuse shared it at certain points, they had a different conception of the critical nature of art. Instead of putting weight on its capacity to reflect the contradictions of society and to criticize it in this way, they emphasized more the utopian potentialities inherent in art. For instance, in Horkheimer's mind, the images of beauty and harmony offered by art promise "a utopia—a vision of an ideal life—that could motivate thought and a critique of reality" (Held, 1980, p. 84). In so doing, art "preserves an ideal in danger of being forgotten" (p. 84). Marcuse saw as well that art, even in its bourgeois form, expresses ideals of bourgeois society that have not been realized. Thus, "bourgeois artistic culture is not simply ideology, for it contains remembrance of what might have been and what could be" (p. 85). In this way, it unwittingly gives weapons for the immanent critique of the existent.

ON THE EMPIRICAL RESEARCH OF THE SCHOOL

Although the Frankfurtians took a brusque stand toward positivism, they did not reject empirical research. In fact, the school carried out several empirical studies with critical theory as their starting point. The most remarkable of these studies was a project called Studies in Prejudice concerning people's anti-semitic attitudes, and their prejudices in general (Jay, 1974, pp. 219–252; Wiggershaus, 1994, pp. 408–430). Adorno took part in the empirical charting of the attitude dimensions of the so-called authoritarian personality (Adorno, Frenkel-Brunswik, Levinson, & Sanford, 1950/1969).

On the other hand, the school's empirical research into mass culture and communication remained scant. Adorno, for one, was involved in it shortly in the beginning of the 1950s when he was the head of research at the Hacker fund (Wiggershaus, pp. 456–466). At that time, he studied interpretatively meanings contained in television serials and analyzed the content of the horoscope columns of The Los Angeles Times (Adorno, 1953/1957, 1953/1994). He had already earlier analysed the fascist-colored content of an American radio station (Adorno, 1943/1975). Nevertheless, the empirical research into mass culture remained a sideline in his work, at least as compared with the mass of his more theoretical writings.

The most prominent figure of the school's empirical research on mass culture and communication was Leo Lowenthal (1900–1993), an Austrian-born literary sociologist. His most known study, carried out at the beginning of the 1940s, focused on popular biographies in U.S. magazines. With an array of such stories, collected from the outset of the century through the 1940s, Lowenthal investigated from which spheres of society—politics, business and professions, or entertainment—the stories picked out their subjects during each period. Additionally, he analyzed the sociology and psychology of the stories, that is, whether the focus was on the person's private or public life and what characteristics and traits the stories ascribed them.

Table 9.1 presents the distribution of the stories according to hero's or heroine's profession in four different periods:

Table 9.1. Distribution of the stories according to hero's or heroine's profession in four different periods (adopted from Lowenthal, 1944/1968, pp. 111–112)

	1901-1914	1922-1930	1930-1934	1940-1941
Politics	46	28	31	25
Business and Professions	28	18	14	20
Arts and Entertainment	26	54	55	55
	100%	100%	100%	100%
N =	177	395	306	125
The percentual share of artists within arts and entertainment	77	38	29	9
N =	47	211	169	69

The proportion of persons coming from arts and entertainment has gone up clearly from the first to the second period at the expense of those coming from politics or business and professions. After that, the distribution has remained quite constant. An even more notable change has taken place within arts and entertainment: The proportion of artists has gone down dramatically whereas that of entertainers has risen respectively. Lowenthal (p. 115) concluded that the focus of the biographies has shifted from idols of production to idols of consumption. Since the 1920s, persons offered for the idols of masses were no more, "as they were in the past, the leading names of the battle of production, but the headliners of the movies, the ball parks, and the night clubs" (p. 116).

For Lowenthal, the stories of the first period mirrored "an open-minded liberal society which really wants to know something about its own leading figures on the decisive social, commercial, and cultural fronts" (p. 113). At that time an

> unbroken confidence in the opportunities open to every individual serves as the leitmotiv of the biographies. To a very great extent they are to be looked upon as examples of success which can be imitated. They are written—at least ideologically—for someone who the next day may try to emulate the man whom he has just envied. (p. 113)

The biographies of the latter periods were characterized by Lowenthal in a clear mass culture critical spirit. The idol selection in them

> corresponds to needs quite different from those of genuine information. They seem to lead to a dream world of the masses who no longer are capable or willing to conceive of biographies primarily as a means of orientation and education. They receive information not about the agents and methods of social production but about the agents and methods of social and individual consumption. (p. 116)

In the stories of the last period, Lowenthal "looked almost in vain for such vital subjects as the man's relations to politics or to social problems in general" (p. 118). Sociologically, the stories were reduced "to the private lives of the heroes" (p. 118). With respect to psychology the stories contained "mainly a static image of a human being to whom a number of things happen, culminating in a success which seems to be none of his doing" (p. 118). This figure is totally of another kind as the former one who gained success with his or her own efforts and energies (see p. 123).

Although not explicated by Lowenthal, his interpretation of the idol evolution is clearly in line with the view of critical theory as to the destiny of individuality. For Adorno and Horkheimer (1944/1986, p. 155), bourgeois society made individuality possible, and it was at least in germ in the phase of liberalism, but the subsequent monopol or state capitalist development toward a totally administrated society stifled it in its infancy. In Lowenthal's study, this development is indicated by the fact that whereas the stories of the first period reflected the rugged individualism of liberalism, "the pride of being an individual with his own very personal ways and interests becomes the stigma of abnormality" in the subsequent stories (Lowenthal, pp. 114, 129).

A parallel to Lowenthal's results can be found in Riesman's (1950) view of the change of U.S. social character from inner- to other-directed. The former is exemplified by an undertaker who in a strong-minded way and unconcerned with others cuts a road to economic success; the latter, again, by a person who sensitively takes into account the expectations of the others and who in this way gains social approval and success (pp. 14–17, 19–25, 115–120, 131–144). The change in the focus of the biographies seems to reflect such a turn. This is indicated by Lowenthal's (p. 128) observation that the yardstick with which the stories of the last period valued their principals was social adjustment. An other-directed person is typically a socially adjusting conformist. It was the growth of conformism that Adorno and Horkheimer regarded as a sign of the end of individual.

EVALUATING THE WORK OF THE FRANKFURT SCHOOL

The Frankfurtians' work has been evaluated in quite contradictory ways. Undoubtedly, this depends partly on their—especially Adorno's and Horkheimer's—style of writing. They abstained from streamlining the complexity of their thinking, on the one hand, and cultivated paradoxes, irony, mockery, and intentional exaggeration, on the other. All this has led to even opposite interpretations of what they wrote, which makes it difficult to conclude how just their evaluation in this or that direction is. This should be kept in mind when considering the criticism leveled at the theory of culture industry.

Some have claimed that this theory amounts to a theory of mass society that is invalid in regard to modern societies. This criticism was formulated most aggressively by Shils (1957/1978, pp. 26–27) who asserted that if the theory of culture industry is taken seriously,

> one would believe that the ordinary citizen who listens to radio, goes to films and looks at television is not just l'homme moyen sensuel known to past ages. He is something new in the world. He is a "private atomic subject," utterly without religious beliefs, without any private life, without a family which means anything

to him; he is standardized, ridden with anxiety, perpetually in a state of "exacerbated" unrest, his life "emptied of meaning," and "trivialized," "alienated from his past, from his community, and possibly from himself," cretinized and brutalized.

Shils looked at the school's views from a perspective of a pluralist theory of society seeing society not as one-dimensional but as a multidimensional one where groups with divergent values compete for power. This perspective predetermines one to label the Frankfurtians as mass society theoreticians. But they were labeled this way also by certain other scholars not representing the pluralist theory of society (see, e.g., Bennett, 1982, pp. 41–47; Curran, Gurevitch, & Woollacott, 1982, pp. 22–23; Swingewood, 1977, pp. 10–23). The school was seen to reproduce an elitism á la Le Bon or Ortega y Gasset, although in an inverse form—while the elitism of the latter abominated "the uproar of the masses," the elitism of the Frankfurtians allegedly regarded the masses as being stunned apathetic by manipulation.

Interestingly enough, this criticism ignored the question, central to the school, whether or not the "negative" critical forces are disappearing in the world. The school answered this question affirmatively, and its diagnosis of modern society—with views of the end of individual and family or of mass culture as an agency of a one-dimensional society—can be regarded as an attempt to justify this position. Because this justification can be interpreted to imply a view of mass society, it is not easy to defend the Frankfurtians against charges of mass society theory, as Jay's (1984, pp. 94–95, 108–109) effort to defend Adorno shows. If one would like to stand up for the school, the discussion should be removed from the critics' agenda and directed expressly at the question what has happened to the "negative," critical forces (as the Frankfurtians understood them).

Claims that the theory of culture industry viewed media texts "as monolithic, containing a well-marked preferred meaning," and the audience as "passive, prisoner of the text" (Abercrombie & Longhurst, 1998, p. 18), make up the standard critique of that theory. The critics speak of "Frankfurt School notions of passive audiences and mislead masses" (Schröder, 1999, p. 45), or of the fear, felt supposedly by the Frankfurtians, that the media would homogenize the audiences into an "unthinking mass" (Fiske, 1986/1998, p. 194). Adorno especially is charged for such misconceptions—it was he who portrayed the consumer of cultural commodities "as a helpless victim of all-pervasive media reality" (Honneth, 1985, p. 93).

According to some critics, the theory of culture industry over-stated the capacity of mass culture to integrate society. For Kellner (1982, pp. 507–508), it ignored social contradictions and individual crises "which all undermine the alleged unity and harmonious inte-gration." Against the theory was stressed, furthermore, that culture industry is not uniform, but that its products are, on the contrary, quite diverse. Neither do people receive them in a uniform way but "respond to them with different interpretations and reactions" (Kellner, p. 508). And last, the theory neglected the "utopian moments of transcendence, moments of opposition and rebellion" con-tained in mass culture (Kellner, 1989a, p. 141). As such, the theory "left no room for any interplay between the authentic desires and utopian impulses of the masses and their expression in the content and use of the mass media" (Czitrom, 1982, p. 145).

As a countercritique, Crook (1994, p. 24) remarked that the Frankfurtians did not regard the consumers of culture industry as "passive dopes" swallowing all without interpretation. Adorno, for one, was of the mind that people "'actively' make sense" of the prod-ucts relating them to their own conditions (p. 24). Moreover, people feel "deep unconscious mistrust" of those products and have thus not totally "accepted the world as it is constructed for them by the cul-ture industry" (Adorno, 1963/1991, p. 91). Also, the claim that the Frankfurtians saw each single product of having only a single mean-ing is problematic in the light of Adorno's (1953/1957, p. 179) view that the meaning structure of television serials is multilayered even if there is a built-in "tendency to channelize audience reaction." Cook (1996, p. 70) has summarized that "one needs not read Adorno against the grain in order to avoid attributing his work a simple-minded thesis about the total manipulation of consciousness by the culture industry."

Some of the critics, most notably Kellner (1982, 1989a, pp. 140–145), have balanced their criticism with viewpoints going in the same direction. Kellner (1989a, p. 141) has also been ready to admit the Frankfurtians' unquestionable merits by stressing that the theo-ry of culture industry "is more than a piece of history, because it con-tains a unified, critical approach to the study of culture and commu-nications within the context of critical social theory." Although shar-ing willingly his point, I emphasize, for my part, that the theory of the culture industry is not so much a theory as a challenging theoret-ical and critical intervention into the world of mass culture. As such, it has prompted, from the late 1960s on, a lively and multifaceted discussion on this subject. It has also been a lasting source of inspira-tion for critical inquiries into popular culture as, to take only one example, the study by Gripsrud (1995) on the show Dynasty.

10

TECHNOLOGIES OF COMMUNICATION

Harold A. Innis and Marshall McLuhan

The theory of culture industry was not the only critical counterpoise to the affirmative behavioral mainstream in mass communication studies from the 1930s to the 1960s. In addition, the chief figures of the Canadian mass communication theory at that time, Innis and McLuhan, "were critics of modernity" (Stamps, 1995, p. xv). Their views, in fact, had certain points in common with the Frankfurt School's critical theory, even if the divergences are much more marked. The main difference is that the Canadians focused above all on media technology, which for the Frankfurtians remained a minor issue.

It is a specific feature in the Canadian mass communication theory in general that it has been preoccupied with communication technology. For Kroker (1984, p. 7), the attractiveness of technology to the Canadian mind results from the country's history and geography: "situated midway between the future of the New World and the past of European culture" the Canadian discourse "is neither the American way nor the European way" but "that in-between: a restless oscillation between the pragmatic will to live at all costs of the Americans and a searing lament for that which has been suppressed by the modern, technological order."

Innis and McLuhan started with the view that the nature of different historical epochs is attributable to the possibilities of development opened up by the forms and means of communication employed at each epoch. However, within this broad problematics they focused, according to Carey (1968, p. 281), on different things: Whereas

> Innis sees communication technology principally affecting social organization and culture, McLuhan sees its principal effect on [human] sensory organization and thought. McLuhan has much to say about perception and thought but little to say about institutions; Innis says much about institutions but little about perception and thought.

Even if this distinction has later been problematized (G. Patterson, 1990), it nevertheless provides useful guiding lines for a closer elucidation of Innis and McLuhan.

COMMUNICATION TECHNOLOGY AND SOCIAL ORGANIZATION: INNIS

Harold A. Innis (1894–1952) actually won fame as an economic historian. He is well-known for the so-called staples theory with which he explained the economic development and the territorial structuration in Canada. Being based on staples—fur, fish, timber, and so on—the economy required transportation routes connecting the staple sources in peripheral areas to the trade centers located within the St. Lawrence River region. In this territorial center/periphery structure, the centers exploit the periphery's "staple, or natural resources" (Melody, 1981, p. 4).

In the 1940s, Innis moved from this kind of theme to analyze communication technologies and their role in the historical development of civilizations. At the beginning of the 1950s, he published some books on this subject. The best known are Empire and Communications (1950/1980) and The Bias of Communication (1951/1982). According to Buxton (1998, pp. 322–323), the accounts of Innis' thought have usually been based on these books instead of his massive but unpublished manuscript A History of Communication. My account here is no exception to this usual way of proceeding.

Some commentators have discussed what prompted Innis to go into communication. Creighton (1981, pp. 22–25) argued that he started from one of the staples—wood and pulp—and moved through pulp industry to print communication and finally to communication in general. G. Patterson (1990, pp. 6–10), again, has paid notice to Innis' bent for thinking with analogies. The shift would, then, have grown out of the structural similarity between transportation system—one of the main ingredients in Innis' economic theory—and communication system. Innis (1950/1980, pp. 5–6) himself admitted an analogical bent in his thought without, however, referring to the structural similarity spoken of by Patterson.

For Buxton (1998, pp. 322–325), such accounts are limited to a "received view" of Innis as a general media theorist not interested in any particular medium. Buxton (pp. 323, 337) rejected that view and argued instead that Innis' vision of the role of communication in the fates of civilizations should be viewed "as largely a prelude" to his main analysis of print and newspaper industry "from the Gutenberg era through to the modern period." Moreover, this analysis did not ensue along the route suggested by Creighton, but it was related to Innis' "moral concerns about the decline of public life in Western civilization" (p. 324).

In what follows, I first make an overview of Innis' synoptic vision of the role of communication technologies in the history of civilizations and go then into his views of how the developing monopolies of knowledge—especially the newspaper—have served "to stifle debate and discussion about public affairs" (p. 325).

Speech and Writing

The first great divide within communication technologies goes between speech and writing. The properties of oral speech enabled "the co-operation of individuals" and maintained "group life" (Innis, 1951/1982, p. 105). In archaic oral cultures, tradition could only be maintained through memory. As such it could not be schematized, but it remained elastic favoring "a flexible civilization but not a civilization which could be disciplined to the point of effective political unity" (p. 10). In other words, oral speech enabled only narrow kinship or tribal communities.

More extensive civilizations became viable only after the invention of writing. It "provided man with a transpersonal memory," and the swiftly transmitted written record was essential to "the extension of government"—through this invention "small communities were written into larger states and states were consolidated into empire" (Innis, 1950/1980, p. 10). Moreover, the "language, characteristic of the oral tradition and a collective society, gave way to private writing" (p. 10). Thus, where oral speech made for collectivity, writing advanced individuality. For Innis (1951/1982, p. 9), the "writing age was essentially an egoistic age."

Egoism was one of the drawbacks of writing compared to oral speech. Innis saw in it also other harmful aspects. For instance, it "introduces monopolistic elements in culture which are followed by rigidities and involve a lack of contact with the oral tradition" (p. 4). It implies "a decline in the power of expression and the creation of grooves which determine the channels of thought of readers and later writers" (p. 11). In general, writing fosters the establishment of fixed, dogmatic systems of thought. In this sense, it is the antithesis of the openness and elasticity of oral speech.

For Innis, however, this kind of generalization tends "to obscure the differences between civilizations insofar as they are dependent on various media of communication" (Innis, 1950/1980, p. 11). Consequently, he took as his objective to analyze "the roles of different media with reference to civilizations and to contrast the civilizations" (p. 11).

Time and Space as the Main Axes of Communication Technologies

Before going on, Innis' basic concepts need to be clarified. One of them is empire denoting established power systems such as "specific states" or "historical 'empires' like Byzantium" or "the church in the middle ages" (Salter, 1981, p. 195). Monopoly refers to "the nature and means of control" exerted by the empires or by their inner power centers (p. 196). By rigidities Innis meant, for example, "inherent tendencies in any institutionalization of power to resist change and adaptation" (p. 196). For him, all empires seek to extend their control through time and/or over space. The possibilities for this depend on the nature of the available media of communication, of which some are biased toward time and others toward space.

For instance, face-to-face speech is biased toward time. It does not enable the transmission of knowledge over vast spaces but allows it to endure through time—naturally only as memorized. Writing supports time or space depending on the material or medium on which the writing is recorded. Time-biased media are durable "such as parchment, clay, and stone" whereas space-biased media are less durable and light "such as papyrus and paper" (Innis, 1950/1980, p. 7). Writing on a clay tablet endures over time, but the heavy tablets are not easily moved over distances. A message on papyrus, again, can be transmitted swiftly over distances, but it does not withstand the ravages of time equally well as a clay tablet.

It depends on the media's bias what kind of institutions and forms of social organization they tend to support: Time-biased media "favour decentralization and hierarchical types of institutions," whereas space-biased media "favour centralization and systems of government less hierarchical in character" (p. 7). This is illuminated by the divergence between a religious organization persisting in time and a political organization expanding over space (p. 170): the "temporal culture" characteristic of the former "is one of faith, afterlife, ceremony, and the moral order" whereas the "spatial culture" typical of the latter "is secular, scientific, materialistic and unbound" (Czitrom, 1982, p. 156).

For Innis (1951/1982, p. 64), a stable society requires a proper balance between time- and space-biased media. Such a balance has been attained "only at rare intervals" (p. 64), and it has been regularly upset. Most often, a space-biased medium has risen into the position of monopoly. One example is classical Greece. At its golden age, time-biased oral speech checked the bias of a papyrus-based writing culture. This civilization began to get ruined when, in the second half of the fifth century,

> writing began to make its encroachments on the oral tradition. . . .
> An increase of writing in Athens created divergences in the Greek community and accentuated differences particularly with Sparta. The Athenian Empire proved unable to meet the strains imposed by diverging cultures. . . . Interstate co-operation imposed demands which could not be met. The end came with the outbreak of war and the defeat of Athens. (pp. 43–44, see also Innis, 1950/1980, pp. 75, 83)

The power struggle between time- and space-biased media and between the organizations supported by them can be exemplified with Europe from the middle ages on. The rule of the Catholic church in the middle ages was based on the "dominance of parchment" with its "bias towards ecclesiastical organization" (Innis, 1950/1980, p. 170). This began to be balanced by "the introduction of paper with its bias towards political organization" (p. 170).

> By the end of sixteenth century the monopoly of knowledge built up in relation to parchment had been overwhelmed and a fusion achieved with a new monopoly of knowledge built up in relation to paper in the establishment of separate kingdoms in which the Church was dominated by the state. (p. 148)

The Monopolization of Knowledge and the Question of Public Life

The rise of a medium into dominance monopolizes knowledge into the hands of those controlling that medium. This results in rigidities because those benefitting from the situation oppose changes. "The conservative power of monopolies compels the development of technological revolutions in the media of communication in marginal areas" (Innis, 1949/1978, p. 5) An example is the invention of the alphabet in Phoenicia, which was peripheral in relation to established centers of knowledge monopoly and which itself had no such monopolies (Innis, 1950/1980, p. 43).

Innis seems to have loathed all kinds of monopolies and concentrations of power. Looking for a counterweight to the mechanical media disseminating messages over distances or preserving them over time, he put weight on the tradition of the face-to-face spoken word because it "inhibits the emergence of monopolies of knowledge" (Heyer, 1988, p. 117). Innis (1950/1980, p. 170) urged that "limitations of mechanization of the printed and spoken word must be emphasized and determinate efforts to recapture the vitality of the oral tradition must be made." His bias was, thus, "with the oral tradition" (Innis, 1951/1982, p. 190).

From this viewpoint, he took a critical stand toward the First Amendment, which usually has been celebrated as the cornerstone of democracy. He claimed that it "did not so much grant freedom of speech and press as give constitutional protection to technology and in this sense restricted rather than expanded freedom" (Carey, 1989, p. 163). In his view—so Carey (p. 166) interpreted—it hindered democracy and public life:

> Modern media of communication, largely for commercial purposes, created a system of communication that was essentially private. Private reading and the reading audience replaced the reading public and the public of argument and discussion. The system of communication that actually evolved was grounded, therefore, not merely in a spatial bias but in a privatized one as well. . . . With that the public sphere goes into eclipse.

For Innis, only with the revitalization of the oral tradition "the public could take an autonomous existence and not be subject to the easy control of the state and commerce" (p. 166). For freedom and knowledge to extend, the growth of mechanical communication should be balanced by "a parallel and dialectical growth of the public sphere, grounded in an oral tradition" (p. 167). Here Innis agreed with John Dewey.

Reflections on the Mass Media

Because of their capacity to transmit messages increasingly faster over distances, the modern mechanical media—the press and radio—had, for Innis, a bias differing from that of the earlier media, the bias "to undermine both space and time" (Carey, p. 134). As such, they were supportive of the centralizing tendencies of society; however, the impact of the press on this varied from time to time depending on other factors from technological developments to commercial arrangements (Buxton, 1998, p. 336). Because the "press and the radio address the world instead of the individual" (Innis, 1951/1982, p. 191), they contributed progressively to a "shift from local and regional units to national and international ones" (Carey, p. 156).

In his analysis of the press, Innis noticed particularly its increasing commercialization for which the First Amendment had opened the doors by providing "a rigid bulwark for the shelter of vested interests" (Innis, p. 138). With increasing advertising the significance and quality of the news went into decline (Buxton, pp. 327–328).

> The low prices of newspapers incidental to the need for circulation demanded by advertisers assumed an emphasis on changes in the content of the newspaper which would attract the largest number of purchasers. The newspaper was made responsive to the market. . . . News became a commodity and was sold in competition like any other commodity. (Innis, 1949/1978, p. 12)

Under the market pressure "the journalist has been compelled to seek the striking rather than the fitting phrase, to emphasize crisis rather than developmental trends" and "to rely on topics with a universal appeal, notably on sex" (pp. 15, 18). Another change was "the decline of the editorial as an influence on public opinion" (p. 21). All this "accentuated the importance of the ephemeral and of the superficial" (Innis, 1951/1982, p. 82). As a result, the ability of the press to contribute to a stable public opinion diminished radically.

This trend was strengthened by the acceleration of the message transmission, also caused by the market requirements. In principle, news could, by reflecting the past, give guidance of action in the future, but with the accelerating speed the press became obsessed with the immediate (Buxton, pp. 328, 333). Due to this, it "became increasingly difficult to achieve continuity and to ask for a consideration of the future" (Innis, p. 83). Through this present-mindedness, public opinion lost its anchor to the past and became even more unstable.

The "instability of public opinion" was increased further by the centralized distribution systems of the mechanized media, because those on the receiving end of these systems "are unable to make any direct response" being thus "precluded from participation in healthy, vigorous and vital discussion" (Innis, 1949/1978, p. 37). Only the invigoration of the oral tradition could remedy this unhappy situation. Innis (p. 39) saw that the unbalanced bias of the mechanical media was guilty of grave consequences in the first decades of the century:

> The . . . maladjustments were evident in the boom of the twenties and the depression and were to an important extent a result of expansion of the press and . . . the radio. Public opinion became less stable and instability became a prime weakness serving as a forced draft in the expansion of the twenties and exposed to collapse in the depression.

Regarding the relationships between nations, centralized media systems were contributing, for Innis, to a cultural center/periphery structure reminiscent of the territorial structure resulting from the transportation routes in a stable economy. He noted, in particular, that in its relation to Canada the United States was becoming an imperialistic center whose newspaper industry expropriated cheap paper from Canada subjugating it, with products printed on this paper, to the U.S. cultural hegemony. He saw this as extremely perilous for the Canadian cultural identity (Innis, 1952, cited in Buxton, pp. 331–332):

> We are indeed fighting for our lives. The pernicious influence of American advertising reflected especially in the periodical press and the . . . impact of commercialism have been evident in all the ramifications of Canadian life. . . . We can survive by taking persistent action . . . against American imperialism in all its attractive guises.

Evaluating Innis

Innis' work on communication has provoked quite conflicting evaluations. It has been regarded by many, who admire his work on economic history, "as an idiosyncratic preoccupation" having not much worth (Heyer, 1988, p. 112). This judgement may be partly due to his style of writing, which has been characterized as "difficult, highly condensed, extremely elliptical, and not infrequently obscure" (Creighton, 1957, cited in Patterson, 1990, p. 26). On the other hand, this cryptic style was praised by McLuhan (1982, p. viii) as aiming at a "form of conversation or dialogue," that is, at an oral way of expression in writing. Stamps (1995, p. 85), too, is of the mind that Innis' "style made for a new, oral kind of writing."

Some remarked critically that Innis put too much emphasis on media technology as a source of social change—that he, in brief, was a technological determinist (Carey, 1968, p. 272; Czitrom, 1982, p. 148). Therefore, he explained the world history in terms that were too mechanistic and simple (Creighton, 1981, p. 25). Others have rejected such views. Heyer (1981, p. 257) said that, "for Innis, communication technology never determines the character of a historical epoch; in his words it 'hastens,' 'facilitates,' or 'helps to define' that character." And according to Parker (1981, p. 133), Innis did not represent a naive form of technological determinism, but emphasized "the dialectical interdependence" of technology and other factors.

Professional historians criticized Innis for dilettantism. One appraisal was, for example, that he was not "an expert in ancient or medieval history" (G. Patterson, 1990, p. 26). Some rejected his way of approaching media in terms of temporal and spatial bias by insisting that his application of the terms is too "vagary and inclusive" (Heyer, 1988, p. 121). Also his view of the oral tradition has been judged very limited because it was based only on the Greek experience, taking no notice of that tradition among different native cultures (p. 118). More generally, in outlining his view of the evolution of civilizations he did not look outside of "the Western lineage" (p. 119).

Much of the criticism has been based on the assumption that Innis was, as the "received view" has portrayed him, a general media theorist whose aim was to account for the world history in terms of media technology. Some have stressed, however, that his aim was not to provide such a historical panorama but to look "to ancient forms of communication as an aid to understand the implication of modern media" (Czitrom, 1982, p. 155) or "to scrutinize the past in order to more effectively engage with the present" (Buxton, 1998, p. 325). If this is the case, the criticism loses much of its pertinence. What then would be worth to discuss is whether or not Innis' diagnosis of the ills caused by the mechanized media is to the point.

COMMUNICATION TECHNOLOGY AND SENSORY ORGANIZATION: MCLUHAN

Marshall McLuhan (1911–1980) began his scholarly career as a traditional literary critic (Gordon, 1997). In 1946 he was appointed as professor of English literature at the University of Toronto where he met Innis. Heyer (1988, p. 111) believes that it is thanks to McLuhan that Innis did not sink into oblivion: In various contexts McLuhan (see, e.g., 1962, p. 50; 1980, 1982) emphasized his significance and claimed a discipleship with him. There are, however, differing opinions as to their scholarly relationship. For some, McLuhan brought Innis' ideas forward (Olson, 1981, pp. 139–140; Rantanen, 1997, p. 104) whereas, for others, he at the most shaped a few ideas taken from Innis to support his own outline (Carey, 1968, p. 281; Czitrom, 1982, pp. 172–173; Heyer, 1988, pp. 118, 121; see also Cooper, 1981; Winter & Goldman, 1989).

Czitrom (p. 166) divided McLuhan's career into three phases. During the early phase he moved from literary criticism to study popular culture and the mass media; this phase ended with the publication of The Mechanical Bride (1951/1967). During the interim phase McLuhan laid the foundation for his ideas of media technology as the molder of human sensory organization. With the publication of The Gutenberg Galaxy (1962) and Understanding Media (1965) at the beginning of the 1960s he entered the mature phase. Especially the latter book elevated him to an almost worldwide fame. In the following, I first glance at the Bride and go after that into his main ideas contained in the Galaxy and the Media.

The Critique of Mass Culture

As a critique of mass culture, Bride has been compared with Barthes' Mythologies (Heyer, 1988, p. 128). McLuhan analyzed there the products of mass culture as the "folklore of industrial man." As instances that "manipulate, exploit, control" they are bringing about "public helplessness" (McLuhan, 1951/1967, p. v). It is not easy for us to resist these products because we live immersed in them and are, therefore, short of abilities to take critical distance from them and to analyze them consciously. McLuhan (p. v) saw it as his duty to "assist the public to observe consciously the drama which is intended to operate upon them unconsciously."

To accomplish this task, McLuhan relied on the method of the sailor who rescued himself from the whirlpool in Edgar Allan Poe's story "A Descent into the Maelstrom": Being locked in by the whirling walls of the products of the press, radio, movies, and advertising, one must take on an attitude characterized by rational detachment and the amusement it gives rise to. That is to say, to grasp the maelstrom of mass culture it must be arrested for this kind of contemplation. "And this very arrest is also a release from the usual participation" (p. v). However, the method was after all not particularly successful—at least Compton (1968, p. 112) argued that the Bride does not contain "very convincing hints" about how to escape from the unhappy situation.

The Bride's structure, in some respects, is reminiscent of a whirlpool. It consists of a host of mass culture fragments—ads, newspaper pages, comic strips, and so forth—each of which is accompanied by a short critical commentary. What connects the commentaries is their attempt to diagnose through the fragments "the 'collective trance' or 'dream state' into which industrial society had fallen" (Czitrom, 1982, p. 170). The diagnosis revealed "an unrelenting diet of sex, death, and technological advance, ingeniously interwoven in cluster patterns designed to sell merchandise" (p. 170). The kaleidoscopic or mosaic nature of the book's structure—"there is no need for it to be read in any special order" (McLuhan, p. vi)—repeated itself also in McLuhan's later works.

Media Technology and Human Sensory Organization: An Overview

Though McLuhan's thought had its turns, there were also certain continuities. One of them was his way of considering the history of Western culture in terms of a dualism "in which 'grammarians' are ranged against 'dialecticians'" (Compton, 1968, p. 108). The grammarians believed in the primacy of action over knowledge and emphasized form at the cost of content, whereas the dialecticians regarded knowledge superior to action and stressed content at the cost of form. In his media theory, McLuhan followed the grammarians when considering the technological form of a medium more decisive than its content.

The basic design of this theory is aptly summarized in the introduction to McLuhan's Playboy interview in 1969 (Playboy, 1969/1989, p. 102): He contends that all media—in and of themselves and regardless of the messages they communicate—exert a compelling influence on man and society. Prehistoric, or tribal, man existed in a harmonious balance of the senses, perceiving the world equally through hearing, smell, touch, sight and taste. But technological innovations are extensions of human abilities and senses that alter this sensory balance—an alteration that, in turn, inexorably reshapes the society that created the technology. According to McLuhan, there have been three basic technological innovations: the invention of the phonetic alphabet, which jolted tribal man out of his sensory balance and gave dominance to eye; the introduction of movable type in the 16th Century, which accelerated this process; and the invention of telegraph in 1844, which heralded an electronics revolution that will ultimately retribalize man by restoring his sensory balance.

Because McLuhan was a devout Roman Catholic, some have seen in this synoptic vision "a secularized version of the basic Christian story of Eden, the Fall, and Redemption" (Carey, 1998, p. 294; see also Czitrom, 1982, pp. 174–175; Ferguson, 1991, p. 74; Macdonald, 1968, pp. 30–31).

McLuhan's starting point was the view that technologies are extensions of human organs and abilities. Prior to McLuhan, this idea had been put forth, for example, by Mumford (Carey, 1981, pp. 173–174). McLuhan's contribution to it was a conception of technologies as "closed systems . . . incapable of interplay" (McLuhan, 1962, p. 5). In this respect, they are the reverse of our innate senses that "are endlessly translated into each other" and, therefore, capable or "interplay or synesthesia" (pp. 5, 265). This being so, technologies extending our senses undermine their ability of synesthesia by isolating them from each other and preferring some of them to others: Man "has long been engaged in extending one or another of his sense organs in such a manner as to disturb all of his other senses and faculties" (p. 4).

From Speech to Printed Letter

As an innate faculty, speech is not yet an isolating technology. In fact, "the spoken word involves all of the senses" (McLuhan, 1965, pp. 77–78). "The sensuous involvement" is "natural to cultures in which literacy is not the ruling form of experience" (p. 78). The interplay of the senses in communication began to dissolve first when writing, being an extension of sight, started its triumphal march. In this process, "the visual component" became abstracted "from the sensory complex" (McLuhan, 1962, p. 39).

This evolution was realized step by step. Hieroglyphs or ideograms did not yet change much because they are complex Gestalts "involving all the senses at once" and affording thus "none of the separation and specialization of the sense" (p. 34). What actually undermined the balance of the senses was phonetic writing. In it, "semantically meaningless letters are used to correspond semantically meaningless sounds" (McLuhan, 1965, p. 83). The sensuous richness preserved in hieroglyph or ideogram is shorn of in letters: they address only the eye. Thereby, "the phonetically written word sacrifices worlds of meaning" (p. 83).

The isolation of sight from other senses still took a long time after the invention of the alphabet. For hundreds of years, the writing was done manually. The manuscript phase was not intense enough to split the visual entirely from its relation to other senses (McLuhan, 1962, p. 54). This was mostly due to the fact that "in antiquity and the middle ages reading was necessarily reading aloud" which still favored "synesthesia" (pp. 82, 83). As an event of communication, reading aloud for an audience reminds one of an ancient tale-telling situation—with the difference, of course, that the reader is related visually to the text.

This situation changed when, thanks to the invention of typography, all became potential readers. Typography created "the first uniformly repeatable commodity, the first assembly-line, and the first mass-production" (p. 124). Before printing, texts existed as rare exemplars; now they could be copied in mass quantities. "It was not until the experience of mass production of exactly uniform and repeatable type, that the fission of the senses occurred, and the visual dimension broke away from the other senses" (p. 54). The change was not instantaneous, however, but "print gradually made reading aloud pointless" (p. 125). Print communication became a private act where the text addresses the eyes leaving the other senses out.

By reducing the "experience to a single sense, the visual" (p. 125), print decisively molded people's way of perceiving the world. The acoustic tribal man lived in a "world of simultaneous relations" (p. 22) and so within a space of noncontinuous, kaleidoscopic events. Typography provided man with "a fixed position or 'point of view'" from which the world appears as a one-way linear, uniform, continuous, and homogenous one where "things move and happen on single planes and successive order" (pp. 19, 58-60, 125).

Despite its uniformity, this world was not united, as was that of the tribal man, but characterized by "the separation of senses, of functions, of operations, of states emotional and political, as well as of tasks" (p. 43). One aspect of this separation was individualization. Tribal man regarded "himself as a rather insignificant part of a much larger organism—the family and the clan—and not as independent, self-reliant unit" (Carothers, 1959, cited in McLuhan, p. 18). This tribal unity began to dissolve along with phonetic writing. The detribalization was completed by print, "the technology of individualism" (p. 158).

Print also had other social consequences. For example, it substituted vernacular for Latin, and the vernacular, rendered visible in national literature and the press, helped to generate a "collective national awareness" (p. 199). "Within vernacular boundaries" (p. 217) these media contributed to an "one-way extension" or even an "explosion outward from center to margins" (McLuhan, 1965, pp. 36, 92). In general, print had, for McLuhan, explosive effects—from the explosion of the unity of the senses through that of the unity of the tribal society to the explosion of connections from centers to margins within nations.

The Electronic Global Village

Although all other technologies function in an isolating way, electronic technology functions, for McLuhan, in an integrative way. Where other technologies "only extended a single sense or function," the electronic one externalizes "our entire nervous system" (Playboy, 1969/1989, p. 113). As an extension of the central nervous system electric technology "is total and inclusive," in contrast to the "partial and fragmentary" nature of the "previous technologies" (McLuhan, 1965, p. 57).

The explosive process of fragmentation, advanced by print, is inversed by electricity. Consequently, McLuhan spoke of the impact of electricity as implosion which refers to fusion, in contradistinction to explosion, which refers to fission (pp. 92–93):

> Our speed-up today is . . . an instant implosion and interfusion of space and functions. Our specialist and fragmented civilization of center-margin structure is suddenly experiencing an instantaneous reassembling of all its mechanized bits into an organic whole. This is the new world of global village.

Especially the electronic media are contributing to this process. They are replacing the center-margin structure with another corresponding to the tribal man's acoustic space that "permits any place to be a center" (p. 36). There is no longer a fixed point of view available; so the world is no longer perceived as a uniform and continuous succession of events but, like in the tribal conditions, as a mosaic of simultaneous and noncontinuous things. Most importantly, the "electric technology dethrones the visual sense and restores us to the dominion of synesthesia" (p. 111). In brief, through the electronic media man "becomes tribal once more. The human family becomes one tribe again" (p. 172).

Of course, "post-literacy is a quite different mode of interdependence from pre-literacy" (McLuhan, 1962, p. 46). McLuhan (1965, p. 4) characterized it as follows:

> In the electric age, when our central nervous system is technologically extended to involve us in the whole of mankind and to incorporate the whole of mankind in us, we necessarily participate, in depth, in the consequences of our every action.

McLuhan found a deficiency here, however. Although we live in a global village, we have not yet reached a corresponding global consciousness. Hence, there is a need for a technology "that would raise our communal lives to the level of world-wide consensus" (p. 108). However, McLuhan saw this technology coming in the form of computers: As we already have translated our nervous system into the world of electronic technology, we ought to translate "our consciousness to the computer world as well" (p. 60). Through computers, human consciousness can be amplified "on a world scale, without any verbalization at all," McLuhan, a devout Catholic, uttered in his Playboy interview, and continued:

> the real use of the computer [is] not to expedite marketing or solve technical problems but to . . . orchestrate terrestrial—and eventually galactic—environments and energies. Psychic communal integration . . . could create the universality of consciousness foreseen by Dante when he predicted that men would continue as no more than broken fragments until they were unified into an inclusive consciousness. In a Christian sense, this is merely a new interpretation of the mystical body of Christ; and Christ, after all, is the ultimate extension of man. (Playboy, 1969/1989, pp. 130–131)

"The Medium is the Message"

With his slogan of the medium as the message McLuhan (1965, p. 7–21) stressed that, regarding the impact of the media, it is less important what they contain than what they are as technologies. So, for example, print communication isolates and privileges sight and individualizes men regardless of its particular content. Of course, content plays its own role, but it is "distinctly subordinate" to that of technology (Playboy, p. 115). The obsession of media researchers with content had precluded them from noticing this or even from realizing that the content of one medium is another medium: the content of writing is speech, the content of print is writing, and so on (McLuhan, 1965, p. 8).

For McLuhan, the ignorance of the media as media has other reasons, too. Leaning on some physiologists' views, he argued that the technological extension of some bodily area exposes that area to much stronger stimuli than before (pp. 41–47), for what reason the central nervous system self-protectively numbs that area, "insulating and anesthetizing it from conscious awareness of what's happening to it" (Playboy, p. 105). Therefore, men remained unaware of what, for instance, their typographic extension really meant, which accounts for the puzzling "lack of understanding" of its psychic and social effects (McLuhan, 1965, p. 172).

Moreover, because the media are the air we breathe, it is difficult to take a conscious, let alone analytic, stand to them. As from a rearview mirror, we can see past things but not the present ones (Playboy, pp. 106–107). Thus, people living in the present electronic global village do not quite understand how the electronic media are impinging on them. Here, we meet McLuhan, the critical educator from the Bride. If the media are not paid proper attention to, "we will become their servant," he warned (p. 137), and continued that "the world-pool of electronic information movement will toss us about like corks on the stormy sea, but if we keep our cool during the descent into the maelstrom, studying the process as it happens to us and what we can do about it, we can come through."

Hot and Cool Media

McLuhan (1965, pp. 22–32) elaborated his view of the relationship between the media and the senses by dividing media into hot and cool. A "hot medium excludes and a cool medium includes;" hot media are low and cool media high in participation by the audience (Playboy, p. 114). A hot medium, such as a photograph, expresses its data with high definition leaving little to be filled in by the viewer while a cool medium, such as a cartoon, is low definition, "because the rough outline drawing provides very little visual data" requiring the viewer to "complete the image himself" (p. 114).

Among the electronic media, movies and radio are hot, telephone and television cool—so it is the latter media, especially television, which are the actual creators of the retribalized global village. For McLuhan (1965, p. 313), television is a cool medium because it is "visually low in data." Its screen is "a mosaic mesh" of horizontal lines and millions of tiny dots, of which the viewer must shape the image; thereby he or she becomes involved deeply in the screen and brought into a "creative dialog with the iconoscope" (Playboy, p. 114). If one would claim (cf. Czitrom, 1982, p. 180) that the TV image has improved since the 1960s and no longer requires an in-depth involvement, McLuhan's (1965, p. 313) answer is that an improved TV would no more "be television!"

Moreover, in McLuhan's view TV addresses touch more than sight and hearing—and, for him, "'touch' is not so much a separate sense as the very interplay of the senses" or "a kind of synesthesia" (McLuhan, 1962, pp. 65, 41). The spaces in the mesh of the TV image must be closed "by a convulsive sensuous participation that is profoundly kinetic and tactile, because tactility is the interplay of the senses, rather than the isolated contact of skin and object" (McLuhan, 1965, p. 314). Through this, TV tattoos "its message directly on our skins" (Playboy, p. 114). By operating like this, television partakes in the construction of a new tribal world for which it creates, for example, new national leaders that are, like Fidel Castro, more tribal chieftains than politicians (p. 115).

Evaluating McLuhan

Few ideas within communication studies have prompted so much critical debate than those of McLuhan. In addition to the ideas, the debate was extended also to their way of presentation.

McLuhan himself said that he used his data as a means of "pattern recognition" (Playboy, p. 104). As he told in the beginning of the Galaxy, the pattern—"causal operations in history"—can only be revealed by "a mosaic image of numerous data and quotations." This seems to be the reason that, in the books considered here, he adopted a nonlinear, incoherent, and fragmentary mosaic style of presentation instead of the linear, orderly, and coherent one. Perhaps also, his interest in modern poetry has something to do with this choice of style.

This style was not met with acclaim. DeMott (1968), for example, saw it as an indication of the weakness of McLuhan's thinking in general. For Carey (1968, p. 291), McLuhan's "terminology is ill-defined and inconsistently used and maddeningly obtuse." Macdonald (1968, p. 33) abused the Media's style as follows:

> A writer who believes that truth can be expressed only by a mosaic, a montage, a Gestalt in which the parts are apprehended simultaneously rather than successively, is forced by the logic of the typographical medium into "a fixed point of view" and into much too definite conclusions. And if he rejects that logic, as McLuhan tries to, the alternative is even worse: a book that lacks the virtues of its medium, being vague, repetitious, formless and, after a while, boring.

Commenting on this kind of critique Zingrone and E. McLuhan (1995, p. 6) remarked that those clinging to the literate tradition were inherently unable to comprehend a presentation style suited to a totally different, electronic culture: "One should not have expected the dinosaurs blissfully to embrace their own ends."

McLuhan, the theorist, has been charged above all with being "a technological determinist" (Carey, 1968, p. 272). Slack (1984, p. 56), for one, viewed him as an "explicit example of a simple causal position, the assumption of direct and unmediated effects of autonomous, isolated technologies." For Czitrom (1982, p. 180), he was a technological naturalist who "substituted mythology for history by ignoring or distorting the real historical or sociological factors that shaped media institutions." Fekete (1977, p. 187) regarded McLuhan as a technological fetishist and as "perhaps the major bourgeois ideologue of the one-dimensional society."

For Kroker (1984, pp. 78, 81), McLuhan's blindness to the economic forces behind technology resulted from that fact that his theory, being "a direct outgrowth of his Catholicism," moved on utopian and transcendent tracks, for which reason he was unable

> to embrace the problematics of capitalism and technology. In McLuhan's lexicon, the privileging of the "economic" relationship belonged to an obsolete era. . . . McLuhan viewed himself as living on . . . the coming age of "cosmic man" typified by "mythic or iconic awareness" and by the substitution of the "multi-faceted for the point-of-view".

Some, as Jeffrey (1989, pp. 19–23) and Zingrone and E. McLuhan (1995, p. 7), rejected the claims of McLuhan's technological determinism without, however, proving convincingly that these claims are wrong.

McLuhan did not arrive at his ideas through a painstaking scrutiny of archaeological and historical material. Instead, he relied mostly on other scholars' writings and used also art "as primary evidence" in his analysis (Curtis, 1981, p. 149). For critics, this kind of a method does not give sufficient proof of the validity of his ideas. Compton (1968, p. 115) scorned that "McLuhan wisely relies upon literary intimations of a pre-alphabetic cultural Eden, rather than attempting to prove that such condition ever actually existed." Heyer (1988, p. 133) was on the same track in his remark that McLuhan made "minimal use of archaeological sources."

To go into details: Bross (1992) found McLuhan's view of human sensory experience incompatible with the modern psychophysical findings even if it contains some valuable insights. The slogan the medium is the message provoked many to blame McLuhan, a bit unjustly, for a total ignorance of the media content (e.g., Burke, 1968, pp. 169–177; Kostelanetz, 1968, pp. 219–220; Roszak, 1968, pp. 260–265). Furthermore, the division of the media into hot and cold has irritated many (e.g., Carey, 1968, pp. 289–290; Roszak, 1968, pp. 265–269; G. Wagner, 1968). Czitrom (1982, p. 180), for one, found the idea of TV's tactility totally pseudoscientific. Many booed also to McLuhan's electronic visions. Macdonald (1968, p. 37) compared McLuhan in this regard with Madame Blavatsky, the mother of all clairvoyants.

Offsetting this kind of critique, S. Becker (1975, p. 236) remarked that it is unfruitful to respond "to McLuhan's work as though it is scientific research, historical or anthropological observation, or even serious criticism":

> We ought not to read it for what it or McLuhan means, but rather for its help in loosening our imaginations, for stimulating us to think about communication in fresh and imaginative ways, for causing us to dredge up out of the very deep recesses of our own minds the ideas of communication which are lurking there.

III

MULTIPLICATION FROM THE 1960S ONWARDS

The situation that persisted in the field of mass communication studies for about three decades was revolutionized from the late 1960s on. As in the 1930s, this upheaval was part of a larger transformation taking place in all social sciences. This time, one of the main issues was "rebellion against positivist-behaviorist tradition" (Nordenstreng, 1977, p. 280). A conviction began to spread especially among the younger academic generation that the dominant behavioral currents were incapable of finding answers to the urgent questions of the time. A need for fresh ways to look at those problems was felt. The turn of the 1970s witnessed an unprecedented surge of Marxist thinking, followed by a "linguistic turn" raising various cultural approaches on the agenda. The behavioral currents were forced to rethink their premises, at least in some respects, but this did not prevent them from losing their hegemony.

The context undermining the accustomed patterns of thought and fueling the whole transformation was the socially and politically tumultuous atmosphere of the 1960s. Students in the Western countries, in particular, began to realize that the world where they lived was deeply unequal and unjust. They affixed their gaze to the capitalist economic-political system, which was seen to uphold inequality and to oppress people worldwide. Such a viewpoint enticed the observer to envision capitalist society, along Marxist lines, as totality where its various structures, the mass media as one of them, tend to contribute to the rule of the capitalist class over other social classes.

179

Even if there has not been a single, unified Marxism, a common denominator for its strains has been an inclination to approach society quite theoretically, and in holistic and structural terms.

Some currents of Marxism, however, did not consider society so much as a structural reality than as a reality lived by people. In broad lines, this same orientation was shared by cultural approaches that have counted such figures as John Dewey and Robert Park among their ancestors. Although Marxist culturalism and other cultural perspectives differ in many respects from one another, they have joined in placing an emphasis on meanings as a means through which people make sense of the world. This emphasis indicates that an important context for the rise of cultural studies has been the spread of the view that the contact of human beings with the world is not direct but mediated through meanings they attach to the world.

In contrast to the structural variants of Marxism, cultural discourses have focused their attention on the same level where the more or less changed behavioral approaches have also been working. In mass communication studies, this level consists mainly of phenomena concerning the media, the audience, and the relationship between these two. On the other hand, although the behavioralists, like their classical predecessors, have been preoccupied with the possible effects of the media on the audience, the culturalists have concentrated on the meanings through which the production and reception of mass-mediated messages takes place. Furthermore, although the behavioral approaches have usually utilized quantitative methods, the cultural discourses have resorted to qualitative-interpretive procedures.

This description of the revolutionized situation is still far too simple. Besides various Marxist, cultural, and behavioral currents there are also discourses that combine elements from these currents in different ways. Some of these discourses have started from premises of their own. One example is feminist theory and research that, like Marxism, gained an impetus from the recognition that societies were deeply unequal and unjust. However, unlike Marxism, which derived the inequality from the economic imperatives of capitalism, feminist theory derived it from the patriarchal nature of societies where women have been relegated in a subordinate position. At least in mass communication studies, this starting point has been enriched, above all, with ingredients from cultural studies.

Another example is postmodern discourse. In a way, its starting point is opposite to that of Marxism. Where many of the Marxist currents have been inclined to consider societies as centralized, at least to a certain point, by the operative logic of capital, the postmodern discourse has looked at them as decentralized and dispersed. It has supported itself with a reference to social processes that are centrifugal rather than centripetal. Advanced information and communication technologies seem to fuel such processes—at the same time as they, paradoxically, seem to serve the solidification of the capitalist rule on a global scale. This has raised these technologies and the so-called information society as objects of scholarly debates that have implications also for mass communication studies.

The information society has not yet given rise to a specific discourse comparable, for example, to the postmodern discourse. Actually, the information society has been more like terrain that different theories try to capture and to accommodate from their special points of view. In contrast, in this respect, there is information-processing theory. Where the information society is an object for different discourses, information-processing theory, with its ideas of mental schemata or scripts as instruments for social cognition, is a source from which different, even conflicting, discourses have appropriated concepts and viewpoints. For instance, the concept of framing has attained so much popularity in different discourses—also in the field of mass communication studies—that it now seems to be a coverall term for just about anything.

As this account shows, the discursive field in social sciences in general and in mass communication studies in particular has multiplied drastically since the late 1960s. But this multiplication has not been the only outcome of the social scientific upheaval. Another impact has been the internationalization of mass communication studies, its break out from its former parochialisms. There have been certain facilitating elements in this process. The role of the scientific journals, for example, has been indispensable. Their growing number has made room also for voices coming from outside the established circles of traditional orthodoxies. The Journal of Communication, in particular, had a notable role, during George Gerbner's editorship in the 1970s and 1980s, in advancing the "ferment in the field" (see Journal of Communication, 1983). The activity of the field's international scientific associations has been significant as well. For example, the International Association for Mass Communication Research (IAMCR) gave the processes of internationalization and diversification a definite push in the turn of the 1970s when James Halloran was appointed to its presidency (cf. Nordenstreng, 1994; see also Halloran's interview in Lent, 1995). The International Communication Association (ICA), particularly under Brenda Dervin's leadership in the 1980s, made notable work enriching U.S. communication study with influences from abroad and in initiating discussions between different paradigms (see Dervin, Grossberg, O'Keefe, & Wartella, 1989). But one should not forget that UNESCO also had, in the 1970s, a seminal role in promoting international communication studies and international discussion on world communication problems (Nordenstreng, 1994).

11

"RETURN TO THE POWERFUL MEDIA"

The Renewal of Effects Research in the 1970s

The marginalization of classical effects research made room for new trends that brought "the social power of the mass media" once more "at the centre" (McQuail, 1977, p. 74). The main question no longer concerned the influence of the media on attitudes and opinions—the earlier research had concluded the media to be quite ineffective in this respect—but their effects on beliefs and knowledge. Agenda-setting approach and knowledge-gap research, in particular, put this cognitive side in the forefront. Another important aspect of this renewal of the effects research was the location of the problematics of mass media influence into broader social contexts; this was done especially by the spiral of silence approach.

Despite their apparent differences, these three approaches share certain basic points that they actually inherited from the earlier effects research. Most importantly, they all rest on an underlying view of communication as a linear transmission process where the media operate as agents imparting messages to the receiving individuals. This view specifies effects, quite similarly to earlier research, as changes caused by the messages in the individuals. The question is whether or not the messages have such effects and whether or not there are external and internal conditions that may influence effectiveness.

AGENDA-SETTING APPROACH

In his book The Press and Foreign Policy, Cohen (1963, p. 13) remarked that the press "may not be successful much of the time in telling people what to think, but it is stunningly successful in telling its readers what to think about." This remark was one incentive to the basic hypothesis of agenda setting research, namely that the attention given by the mass media to various issues teaches people which issues are important and worth thinking about. This way, "the media may set the 'agenda'" for the people (McCombs & Shaw, 1972, p. 176).

The rationale for this hypothesis was given, as early as in the 1920s, by Lippmann (1922/1965) through his view that "the mass media are the principal connection between events in the world and the images of these events in our minds" (Rogers, Dearing, & Bregman, 1993, pp. 70-71). The media enable people to have contact with "issues that lie far outside their own experience" (Iyengar & Kinder, 1987, p. 2). Thus, as some of Lippmann's contemporaries had already stressed, the media are "important in turning attention toward certain topics"—even if they do "not actually form public opinion," they act "as a pointing finger" (Willey, 1926, p. 20). Agenda setting researchers have approached the media precisely as pointing fingers.

The idea of the media as agenda setters was in the air long before the first empirical agenda study was conducted at the end of the 1960s, when disenchantment with the old effect research made room for new initiatives (McCombs, 1981, p. 121). In this study, Maxwell McCombs (1938–) and Donald Shaw (1936–) compared the attention given by the media to the main campaign issues in the 1968 U.S. presidential election in Chapel Hill, North Carolina, with the assessed importance of these issues among 100 undecided voters (McCombs & Shaw, 1972). The fit between the order of importance of the issues in the voters' sample and the amount of attention given to them in the media was almost perfect.

McCombs and Shaw concluded that, although agenda setting "is not proved by the correlations," the results still indicated that "mass media influence seems more plausible than alternative explanations" (pp. 184–185). However, the cross-sectional research design they adopted does not allow one to draw conclusions concerning causal relationships (Brosius & Kepplinger, 1990; Iyengar & Kinder, 1987, pp. 6–8; MacKuen, 1981, pp. 22–27). The problem of causality is one of the puzzles that have kept agenda-setting researchers busy.

What Is an Agenda?

According to Dearing and Rogers (1996, p. 2), an agenda "is a set of issues that are communicated in a hierarchy of importance at a point in time." In the McCombs and Shaw (1972) study, the issue set consisted of such broad and abstract topic domains as foreign policy, law and order, fiscal policy, and so on. The media agenda is the order of importance of such topic domains in the media; the public agenda, again, their order of importance among samples representing the public in the studies.

The media agenda is ascertained by measuring how much attention they give to the topics. A problem has been which of the possible attention variables—such as quantity of space or time devoted to the topics, conspicuousness of presentation, and so on—"provide the cues from which audience notions of salience are constituted" (McCombs, 1981, p. 138). Information about the public agenda has either been gleaned from already existing data, especially in longitudinal studies (e.g. Funkhouser, 1973; MacKuen, 1981; Winter & Eyal, 1981), or gathered with purpose-designed surveys. The importance of the topics can be asked in various ways—for instance, by open-ended questions like "In your mind, what is the most urgent problem facing us today?" or by letting the respondents choose from ready-made topics. Different procedures have produced dissimilar agendas (see Dearing & Rogers, 1996, pp. 45–49; Ehlers, 1983, pp. 168–169, 173).

There are certain problems involved in working with broad topic domains. For instance, it is often difficult to say which domain is represented by a particular event reported in the media. Did the Chernobyl accident reflect the domain of energy supply (as in Brosius & Kepplinger, 1990)? Furthermore, abstract topic labels do not reveal anything of the reality of the domains as of the "controversy and contending forces" in them (Kosicki, 1993, p. 104). Both the media and people may consider a certain domain highly salient, but, nevertheless, pay notice to totally different aspects of it. Admittedly, there have been attempts to take into account the "attributes of these topics" (McCombs, 1981, p. 134), as well as the topics, but some scholars see that this has only led to new problems (Swanson, 1988, pp. 612–614).

Research Design and the Problem of Causality

Researchers have employed both cross-sectional and longitudinal designs (McCombs, 1981, pp. 122–123). Cross-sectional studies have been used to compare the media agenda with an aggregate-level public agenda. L. Becker (1982, pp. 527–528) criticized this and stressed that to test the agenda-setting hypothesis adequately, one must move on the individual level and compare the agenda of the individuals with that of the media they follow. This has been uncommon, however. Moreover, even if the agenda variables would correlate positively, a difficult problem would still persist: There is no way to tell whether the correlation is due to the influence of the media on the individuals or of the individuals on the media.

To solve the problem of causality, the time factor must be taken into account. One option has been to make the measurements at two points of time and to look, with the aid of cross-lagged correlations, at whether the earlier media agenda correlates more strongly with the later public agenda than the earlier public agenda with the later media agenda (Tipton, Haney, & Baseheart, 1975). If this is the case, the view of the media agenda as a causal agent gets support.

Truly longitudinal studies with measurements at several points of time have often focused on a single issue. The purpose has been to ascertain whether or not the media coverage of that issue and its salience among the public rise and fall in tandem. The agenda setting for the civil rights issue, for example, has been analyzed in this way (Winter & Eyal, 1981). With appropriate statistical methods one can ascertain whether turns in media coverage are followed by corresponding turns in public attention or vice versa. An analysis of time-series data of several topics in this way showed that for some topics, media coverage preceded the public attention, whereas for other topics the reverse held true (Brosius & Kepplinger, 1990).

The result that the turns in public attention follow those in the media coverage does not settle the causality problem because this may only reflect the real development of the issue in question. Taking this possibility into account, Funkhouser (1973) found that the coincidence between the relative importance of certain issues in the media and in public opinion during the 1960s did not depend on their development in reality. Results in some other studies have been supportive (Beniger, 1978; Kepplinger & Roth, 1978), but it has also been observed that if an issue is close to people—unemployment, energy supply, and inflation, for example—then its salience follows its fluctuations in reality rather than its coverage in the media (MacKuen, 1981, pp. 81–101).

Experimental design is generally regarded as most appropriate for causal analysis. It has been applied to agenda-setting research particularly by Iyengar and his colleagues (e.g. Iyengar & Kinder, 1987). For instance, these researchers showed their experimental groups in six consecutive days specially edited TV news bulletins, each of them with one story on the same topic, while the control groups saw no stories of that topic (pp. 16–21). Before and after the experiments the participants in both groups assessed the importance of several topics, including the topic covered in the news bulletins viewed by the experimental groups. The result was that the salience of this particular topic rose for the experimental groups, but not for the control groups. Also, other experiments supported the agenda-setting hypothesis so strongly that the researchers concluded that TV news "shapes American public's political conceptions in pervasive ways" (p. 116).

However, it is risky to declare these experimental results outright as definitive because there are, in real situations, different factors at work. For instance, the reality necessarily contributes to the agenda setting because it is just the real development of the issues that gives the stuff for the media. The case is even more complicated because there exists also a policy agenda consisting of issue preferences among policymakers (Rogers & Dearing, 1988, pp. 556–565; Rogers et al., 1993). Thus, besides the relationship of the media agenda to the public agenda, there are many other possible relations that do not yield themselves easily to experimental testing but that can affect decisively the agenda-setting process.

Contingent Conditions

In any case, agenda-setting research has mostly started with the view of the mass media as the setter of the public agenda. One important question has been which conditions "constrain or enhance" the role of the media in this respect (McCombs, 1981, p. 132). Such contingent conditions have been looked for in the nature of the issues, on one hand, and in the characteristics of the media audiences, on the other.

The issues have often been divided into obtrusive, which one is likely to encounter personally, and unobtrusive, which only can be experienced vicariously through the media. Conventionally, the hypothesis has been that the media have greater power to set the public agenda with regard to unobtrusive than obtrusive issues— simply because the less people have direct contact with an issue, the more they must "rely on the news media" (Zucker, 1978, p. 227). This hypothesis has often been supported (Palmgreen & Clarke, 1977; Zhu, Watt, Snyder, Yan, & Jiang, 1993; Zucker, 1978). On the other hand, some have presumed that persons being "personally affected by a particular problem" may be quite "sensitive to news about it"

(Iyengar & Kinder, 1987, p. 48), in which case the media would have power to set also the public agenda of obtrusive issues. The support given by research to this hypothesis has been partial, at best (pp. 48–51; Demers, Craff, Choi, & Bessin, 1989).

Of the audience characteristics found to play a role in agenda setting, the most interesting is a motivational factor called the need for orientation. An example of an individual considered to have a high need for orientation is a voter who is highly committed to vote in an election but unsure about the important issues on which to base his or her choice of the candidate for whom to vote (McCombs, 1994, p. 8). Such individuals have generally been found to be "open to considerable agenda setting influence" (p. 8). Agenda-setting effect has also been perceived, not surprisingly, to increase with increasing media exposure (Winter, 1981, pp. 237–238). On the other hand, results concerning, for instance, the role of interpersonal discussion in agenda setting have generally been inconclusive (pp. 238–239; McCombs, 1981, p. 134; but see Wanta & Wu, 1992).

Critical Discussion

Agenda-setting research critics have fixed their eyes especially on the inconstancy of its results. Arguments claiming that the "findings concerning the agenda-setting hypothesis are both conflicting and inconclusive" (Carragee, Rosenblatt, & Michaud, 1987, p. 39) or that "the one consistent attribute" of agenda studies is "inconsistency of conceptualization, method, and result" (Swanson, 1988, p. 604) are indicative of this critique.

This inconsistency appears to stem from an attempt to push a complex subject—the relation of the media to people—into a far too simple formula. L. Becker (1982, p. 533) referred obviously to this attempt when he advised: "Be suspicious of the simple explanation of social phenomenon, no matter how promising it sounds; things are probably always more complex than they seem on first notice." It seems that the processes, which agenda-setting approach intends to grasp, cannot be accounted for adequately with a mechanistic model of statistical relationships between highly abstracted variables as, for instance, the topic sets with which the researchers are working,

A correlation—usually a low one—between the media agenda and the public agenda tells, in the end, very little about how people have assessed the importance of the issues under study. Different people may make their assessments under different influences, some coming from the media, some from own experience, some from other people, and so on, and, to cap it all, these influences may be complicatedly interwoven. Thus, for G. Lang and K. Lang (1983, p. 27), the agenda-setting hypothesis attributes to the media both too much and too little influence:

> "Too much" because it ignores the contextual and political factors that limit the power of the media to set the public agenda; "too little" because it sheds little light on the process through which public agendas are built or through which a problem, having caught public attention by being big news, gives rise to a political issue.

It seems futile to try to prove once and for all that the media determine causally the public agenda or, more generally, that there is a permanent pattern of causal relationships between the real-world indicators, the media agenda, the public agenda, and the policy agenda because the dependencies between the variables seem to vary from case to case (see Dearing & Rogers, 1996). On the other hand, the agenda-setting perspective offers a useful frame of reference for concrete studies of public opinion processes. One can map the development of issues in reality and analyze the interrelations among the media agenda, the public agenda, and the policy agenda against this background. G. Lang and K. Lang's (1983) inquiry into the relationships among the press, the public, and the polity during the Watergate affair is a case in point. There are some signs that agenda-setting research is indeed moving in this direction (Dearing & Rogers, 1996).

KNOWLEDGE-GAP RESEARCH

In 1970, George A. Donohue (1924–), Clarice N. Olien (1933–) and Phillip J. Tichenor (1931–) put forth the following hypothesis establishing the knowledge gap approach:

> As the infusion of mass media information into a social system increases, segments of population with higher socioeconomic status tend to acquire this information at a faster rate than the lower status segments, so that the gap in knowledge between these segments tends to increase rather than to decrease. (Tichenor, Donohue, & Olien, 1970, pp. 159–160)

The hypothesis grew out of information campaign studies that had shown that the campaigns usually failed to reach those that were judged to be most in the need of the information—that is, less educated people lower in social status (Hyman & Sheatsley, 1947; Star & Hughes, 1950). Tichenor et al.'s (p. 161) hypothesis suggested itself "as the fundamental explanation" of such failures. The researchers supported the hypothesis further with the observation of R. Budd, McLean, and Barnes (1966) that information of a news event spread more rapidly among the more educated than the less educated people (Tichenor et al., p. 163). This rule is not without exceptions, however (cf. R. Hill & Bonjean, 1964; Spitzer & Denzin, 1965). A bit surprising is the fact that the researchers did not support their hypothesis with the finding, obtained in the diffusion of innovations research, that socioeconomic status has proven to be an important factor in the adoption of innovations—"as you move from early to late adopters you also move from the highest to the lowest in social status, income [and] education" (Larsen, 1962, p. 19; also see Rogers, 1962).

The Context of the Hypothesis

The knowledge-gap hypothesis was spelled out against the common belief that information growth will "equalize knowledge among the different groups in the social system" (Olien, Donohue, & Tichenor, 1983, p. 455). In studying the information flows in communities, the researchers had observed that the mass media tend to control information "in the interest of system maintenance," including "the maintenance of power" (Donohue, Tichenor, & Olien, 1973, pp. 652–653). This control "limits the ability of general population members to acquire information which may be used as inputs for public decisions" (p. 658). Moreover, the mass media tend to define issues to fit "the interest of established power groups" increasing in this way "the gaps in social power between established groups and other groups" (Olien et al., 1983, p. 459).

Another side of the coin is that the differentials in knowledge also depend on the competencies of the receivers of information. The knowledge-gap hypothesis was grounded on the view that "education is a powerful determinant of information reception" (Donohue et al., 1973, p. 658). The socioeconomic status, spoken of in the hypothesis, has mostly been measured by using "formal education" as its indicator (Olien et al., 1983, p. 456). For the research team, education is paramount simply because it cultivates the ability to acquire and process information. For example, better educated people tend to have "stored information" about a broad range of topics, which is why they are "likely to be aware of a topic when it appears in the mass media and are better prepared to understand it" (Tichenor et al., 1970, p. 162).

Researching Knowledge Gaps

The knowledge-gap hypothesis can be tested either by scrutinizing longitudinally, on the basis of time-series data, whether or not the "acquisition of knowledge of a heavily publicized topics" proceeds faster "among better educated persons than among those with less education," or by investigating cross-sectionally, at one point in time, whether or not there is "a higher correlation between acquisition of knowledge and education for topics highly publicized in the media than for topics less highly publicized" (Tichenor et al., 1970, p. 163).

When presenting the hypothesis, the researchers backed it with longitudinal data extracted from polls, conducted in 1949, 1954, 1959, and 1965, "asking respondents whether they believed man would reach the moon in a foreseeable future" (p. 164). The acceptance of the belief increased quite rapidly among college-educated persons but quite slowly among grade-school educated persons so that the initially slight difference in 1949 had grown into a glaring gap in 1965 (p. 166). Because the data had not been collected to test the hypothesis, this result has several weaknesses as a proof. For instance, there is no way to show that the increase in beliefs would "reflect increased knowledge," as the research team was forced to assume (p. 164). In any case, this is one example of what a time-series analysis would look like.

Even though not longitudinal in a time-series sense, a panel design nevertheless takes the time axis into account. In his two-wave panel survey, conducted in the beginning and at the end of a gubernatorial campaign, Moore (1987) investigated whether or not his respondents knew the candidates' stands on two issues, one relatively simple and the other more complex. At the beginning of the campaign, the stands were already known better among the higher educated than the lower educated respondents. The campaign increased the knowledge in both groups: In regard to the simpler issue the increase was the same, but in regard to the more complex issue it was far greater among the higher educated respondents. The campaign seemed to widen the knowledge gap for the more complex issue.

When presenting the hypothesis, Tichenor et al. (1970, pp. 167–169) also supported it with a cross-sectional analysis. They let the respondents read articles on two scientific topics, one that received a lot of publicity versus one that did not. Because the hypothesis claims that knowledge gaps will widen with the increasing flow of information, the difference between the more and less educated respondents in the intake of knowledge from the articles should be greater in regard to the more publicized than the less publicized topic. This indeed proved to be the case.

Over the course of years, many studies have been carried out representing, in one way or another, the knowledge-gap research (for overviews, see Gaziano, 1997; Viswanath & Finnegan, 1996; Wirth, 1997, pp. 62–87). In regard to the gap processes, results have varied greatly. One problem has been that only a few studies have met correctly the requirements of the knowledge gap hypothesis (Gaziano, 1983, 1997, pp. 242–245). On the other hand—as Donohue, Tichenor, and Olien (1975) had to admit already in the early 1970s—there are also conditions that may prevent the gaps from widening or may even lead to their narrowing.

One such condition was found in a study concerned with how information of controversial issues was diffused in communities (Tichenor, Rodenkirchen, Olien, & Donohue, 1973; Tichenor, Donohue, & Olien, 1980). In contrast to what the hypothesis predicts, the increase in the press coverage of such issues did not cause the knowledge gaps to widen. The researchers thought this was due to the local and controversial nature of the issues that may lead to "frequent interpersonal communication" and so "create the conditions under which the knowledge tends to become more equally distributed among persons higher and lower in social status" (Tichenor, Rodenkirchen, Olien, & Donohue, 1973, p. 72). This would restrict the validity of the hypothesis only to "non-local public affairs" (p. 67; also see Tichenor et al., 1980, pp. 175–203).

In the aforementioned study, knowledge was measured simply by asking the respondents to recall what they had seen or heard about the issues, and by coding the responses "according to the number of accurate and inaccurate statements" (Tichenor et al., 1980, p. 46). As Bentele (1985, p. 91) remarked, this captures only "a fraction of what is commonly meant by 'knowledge.'" Indeed, one problem in the studies has been that the focal concept of knowledge has been applied in quite unreflecting and unsophisticated ways. According to Wirth (1997, p. 94), for instance, about 80% of studies have given no theoretical justification for the way in which knowledge has been conceived and applied in them.

Other Looks at the Gaps

The result that controversial local issues did not lead to gaps implies that persons higher and lower in social status were equally interested in them. This suggests that it may be the motivation to acquire information of a given issue, and not the socioeconomic status, that explains the knowledge gaps in regard to that issue. Ettema and Kline (1977, p. 188) reformulated the initial gap hypothesis from this perspective as follows:

> As the infusion of mass media information into a social system increases, segments of the population motivated to acquire that information and/or for which that information is functional tend to acquire the information in a faster rate than those not motivated or for which it is not functional, so that the gap in knowledge between these segments tends to increase rather than to decrease.

Ettema and Kline (pp. 181–197) called the initial hypothesis a deficit interpretation because the knowledge gaps were connected to presumed transsituational deficits in basic cognitive ability. They saw their own hypothesis, again, to represent a difference interpretation that pays notice to situational factors motivating or not motivating individuals to use their abilities. On the basis of this hypothesis, the observation that the knowledge gap between persons higher and lower in social status is widening could be explained with a reference to situational factors not motivating the persons in lower position "to acquire information from the particular knowledge domain (e.g., public affairs) under study" (p. 190).

Ettema and Kline did not themselves test their hypothesis. Some studies carried out afterward have given it some support (Genova & Greenberg, 1979; Lovrich & Pierce, 1984), whereas others have found the influence of the socioeconomic status on the existence or increase of knowledge gaps more persistent (Viswanath, Kahn, Finnegan, Hertog, & Potter, 1993; McLeod & Perse, 1994; for summary, see Viswanath & Finnegan, 1996, pp. 203–205). Perhaps the interests and motives should be regarded "as mediating between social location and information acquired concerning a specific topic" (Fredin, Monnet, & Kosicki, 1994, p. 177) in which case social status would affect the knowledge acquisition not directly but through different interests and motivations it gives rise to.

Dervin (1980, 1989a, 1989b) approached the gaps from a different angle than Ettema and Kline. In her view, the usual way of approaching them is based on a conception of communication as an one-way transmission process. This has led to "inappropriate assumptions about the nature of human information seeking and use" (Dervin, 1980, p. 81). Within such a model, people are looked at from the sender's perspective as empty containers to be filled with information. What people themselves think of the situation, is mostly disregarded. If the filling fails—if there emerges gaps, for example—it is more common to blame the audience than the sender for this. The initial knowledge-gap hypothesis exemplifies this kind of a model of thought.

Dervin reversed this model by implying that the problem does not lie in people's capacities of information intake but in the reified communication systems, in their unresponsiveness for the users' needs. Being designed on the basis of the transmission view of communication, the systems make the gaps between the "haves and have-nots inevitable" (1989b, p. 218). More important, then, would be how a given system of communication "could change itself than how it could change the audience" (1989a, p. 84).

One aspect of the reversal concerned the research strategy: The analysis should be started, not with the sender's, but with the audience's point of view—or, more precisely, with a view of everyday situations in which people stumble on diverse discontinuities or gaps. This led to "the sense-making approach" the core of which "is the idea of gap—how people define and bridge gaps in their everyday lives" (1989a, pp. 76, 77). The object of this approach is outlined as follows:

> The human moves cognitively through time-space using whatever sense he or she has already constructed based on personal as well as vicarious experiences. Given that life is inherently discontinuous, sense frequently runs out. A gap is identified. The human must build a bridge across the gap. In doing so, the human will answer questions, create ideas and/or obtain resources. (p. 77)

As can be seen, gaps are here not differences in knowledge between people in different social positions but concrete cognitive problems that people try to solve by seeking and using information. From this perspective, people's information-seeking and information-using behavior, "is best predicted based on how they see their situations, the constraints they face, the gaps they need to bridge, and the kind of bridges they would like to build across these gaps" (p. 80). Here, Dervin has a point in common with Ettema and Kline who also stressed, in regard to people's orientation to knowledge, the importance of situational factors at the cost of such transsituational variables as education or socioeconomic status. On the other hand, she stands clearly closer to cultural views than Ettema and Kline or other gap researchers.

Critical Discussion

In addition to Ettema and Kline's and, in particular, Dervin's critical views, the main criticism of the knowledge-gap approach has argued that it suffers from similar problems as the agenda research. Its results, like those of agenda research, have been inconsistent, which indicates that the model on which the studies rest does not meet adequately the complexity of the processes that the studies want to account for. Moreover, the statistical way of approaching these processes is mechanical and external which is why the results tell almost nothing of what the information at stake at each time means to people, how they process it, and what exactly is the reason for the gaps to widen (or to remain the same or to narrow, for that matter).

It is also surprising that, despite the central role cognitions necessarily play in gap research, the cognitive aspect has been taken into account only indirectly through the level of schooling. The view of knowledge has remained very simple (Wirth, 1997, pp. 94–122), and the ways people receive and process information and make sense of it have remained a black box. This holds true also with agenda research (Kosicki, 1993, pp. 110–116). Both currents seem to imply—like the cultivation research considered in chapter 13—that a closer analysis of reception is not necessary if one studies the influence of broad information flows. Recently, however, some gap scholars have emphasized the importance of a more detailed study of reception, for instance, from the perspective of schema theory (see, e.g., Wirth, pp. 122–153).

THE SPIRAL OF SILENCE APPROACH

The spiral of silence approach was initiated by Elisabeth Noelle-Neumann (1916–) in (West) Germany in the early 1970s. Unlike the quite nontheoretical approaches of agenda setting and knowledge gap, this approach was built on specific theoretical premises. In effect, its aim has been to give a theoretically articulated and empirically sustainable explanation to transformations taking place, under certain conditions, in public opinion. The mass media are not in the main focus, but have nevertheless an important place in this construction.

Basic Theoretical Points

Presume there is an issue that is supported by one part of the population and opposed by another part. If one of the stands receives more positive publicity than the other, a peculiar dynamic may get started. Those adhering to the opinion that has got the wind of publicity behind it will become ready to speak openly for it, whereas those adhering to the opposite one tend to fall silent. In the end, the stand that was backed by the positive publicity dominates the public scene, whereas the other stand has disappeared from the sight. "This process can be called a 'spiral of silence'" (Noelle-Neumann, 1980/1993, p. 5).

One should note that the spiral-of-silence theory does not aim at universality—it claims validity only on conditions that the opinions under consideration are not stable but labile, that they are moral ones that cannot be shown as factually right or wrong and that they are discussed in the mass media (Donsbach, 1987, pp. 329–330).

But why should there be, on these conditions, such spiral-of-silence processes? To account for this, two additional factors must be noticed. In the first place, "the force that sets the spiral of silence in motion" is "the fear of isolation" (Noelle-Neumann, p. 6). If individuals feel that their opinion is not supported, they are inclined to remain silent on their stand in order to avoid being isolated. In the second place, people are continually monitoring, through a quasi-statistical sense, the climate of opinion in order to know which opinions are widely supported and which are not (pp. 9–16). For this monitoring, the mass media are paramount because without them one's reach would be limited to the closest surroundings.

This theory rests on a certain conception of public opinion. For Noelle-Neumann (pp. 58–69; 1992), there are two basic conceptions of public opinion, one viewing it as an outcome of a rational public discussion and the other considering it as social control that ensures a sufficient level of consensus for society to function. Noelle-Neumann represented the latter conception seeing public opinion like a court that, by dealing out popularity and unpopularity, promotes conformism. Consequently, public opinion consists, for her, of opinions "that one can express in public without isolating oneself" and/or "that one must express or adopt if one is not going to isolate oneself"

(Noelle-Neumann, 1980/1993, p. 63).

In seeking support for her theory, Noelle-Neumann (p. 7) thought that if silence-of-spiral processes really exist, "then many authors from earlier centuries" must have noticed them. And, as it was, she perceived this to be true, even if the topic never was "a major theme" (p. 7). For example, she found "a precise description of the dynamics of the spiral of silence" in Tocqueville's comment on the decline of the French church in the middle of the 18th century (p. 7). Tocqueville stated that, because the church chose to be silent vis-à-vis the criticism leveled against it,

> those who retained their belief in the doctrines of the Church became afraid of being alone in their allegiance and, dreading isolation more than error, professed to share the sentiments of the majority. So what was in reality the opinion of only a part . . . of the nation came to be regarded as the will of all and for this reason seemed irresistible, even to those who had given it this false appearance. (Tocqueville, 1856, cited in Noelle-Neumann, p. 7)

Noelle-Neumann (pp. 37–41) supported the theory also with Asch's experiments on conformity. Asch (1963, p. 178) let the participants match, in a group situation, "the length of a given line with one of three unequal lines." The situation was, however, faked as all but one of the participants, the critical subject, were Asch's helpers, giving in turn the same manifestly incorrect estimate before the critical subject, unaware of the arrangement, had his or her turn. The question was what he or she will do. With each critical subject, the experiment was repeated 10 times. Three of four critical subjects was found to agree at least once with the incorrect estimate. For Noelle-Neumann (p. 38), this confirms empirically Tocqueville's expression: "Dreading isolation more than error, they professed to share the sentiments of majority."

On the other hand, of all judgments made by the critical subjects, 68% "was correct despite the pressure of the majority" (Asch, p. 181). Noelle-Neumann ignored this as, equally, the fact that if there was one helper giving a correct estimate, the critical subjects were much less prone to incorrect judgments. When charged for neglecting the latter fact (Salmon & Kline, 1985, pp. 6–8), Noelle-Neumann (1985, p. 71) replied that it only "shows the limited applicability of the Asch situation to public opinion processes." Obviously it applies only when it fits her hypothesis!

The media have a specific role in the theory. Noelle-Neumann (1991, p. 276; also see 1985, pp. 80–82) asserted to have "never found a spiral of silence that goes against the tenor of the media." For her, the media may even produce so-called pluralistic ignorance by backing an opinion that actually is in the minority, and creating this way the illusion that it is in the majority, with the consequence that the actual minority gets noisy and the actual majority silent (Noelle-Neumann 1989, pp. 420–423). Thus, in her view, the media are much more powerful than they were seen to be in the minimal effects model of the classical behavioral tradition.

As a matter of fact, Noelle-Neumann (1973, 1982) has been very critical of the minimal effects model and of the thesis of selective exposure on which it was built. In her view, there is not much room for selection because the content of the media is highly consonant. This is due to the conformism of the journalists—they are politically close to one another (Noelle-Neumann, 1973, pp. 34–35; 1980, pp. 227–239), and the spiral-of-silence processes among them tend to keep them on the same track (Noelle-Neumann 1990). The assertion of the consonance of the media is one point on which many critics have fixed their eyes as will be seen later on.

Testing the Theory Empirically

One consequence of the comprehensiveness of the theory is that empirical testing has only been possible in a piecemeal fashion (Donsbach, 1987, pp. 324–327; Donsbach & Stevenson, 1986, pp. 8–9). As an opinion researcher, Noelle-Neumann tested the theory with survey methodology, not experimentally. This forced her to develop intricate indirect procedures to measure, for example, the dependent variable of the theory, the willingness to speak out or to keep silent. Most often, each respondent in the survey has been put into a situation where he or she has to imagine whether or not to talk, in a public occasion, with people having the opposite (or, in some cases, the same) opinion as he or she in the question under study (Noelle-Neumann, 1980/1993, pp. 16–22).

For instance, to find out whether or not fear of isolation causes reticence, Noelle-Neumann (pp. 42–50) proceeded as follows in a survey conducted in 1976. First, half of the respondents were put in an imaginary situation condemning the smoking in the presence of nonsmokers (the experimental group), half were not (the control group). Second, all the respondents had to imagine whether or not they would converse publicly with others about the right to smoke in the presence of nonsmokers. It was presumed that the collision with the condemning situation would provoke fear of isolation among the actual smokers in the experimental group so that they would more likely keep quiet than the actual smokers in the control group. "The results confirmed the expectation" (p. 44). The validity of the variables is not beyond doubt, however.

In this study, variables measuring how and with what result the respondents have monitored the opinion climate were lacking from the analysis, even if such variables are "most crucial in a proper analysis of the spiral of silence," because the theory holds that it is precisely people's views "of what constitutes majority opinion" that makes them talkative or reticent (Salmon & Kline, 1985, p. 22). This notwithstanding, Noelle-Neumann often ignored respondents' perceptions of the distribution of opinions, being content to explore merely whether those whose stand accords with the major opinion as indicated by an opinion poll, are more prone to talk than those whose stand accords with the minority opinion.

Table 11.1 presents a case where respondents' views of the opinion climate have also been taken into account.

Table 11.1. Willingness to speak out among supporters of major opinion who think they represent the majority vs. the minority, and among supporters of minority opinion who think they represent the majority vs. the minority (adopted, through Salmon & Kline, 1985, p. 22, from Noelle-Neumann, 1973, p. 49).

If, during a 5-hour train ride, someone in the compartment had a different opinion on the subject under discussion, I would:	supporters of majority opinion who think they represent the majority (N= 748)	supporters of majority opinion who think they represent the minority (N= 271)	supporters of minority opinion who think they represent the minority (N= 47)	supporters of minority opinion who think they represent the majority (N= 198)
Contradict him	79 %	75 %	53 %	78 %
Not contradict him	14	20	45	19
No statement	7	5	2	3
	100%	100%	100%	100%

As the theory predicts, respondents believing that their opinion is in the majority, regardless of whether or not it actually is, are prone to talk. Of those respondents who feel that their opinion is in the minority, one group supports the theory by being relatively reticent, but another contradicts it also by being prone to talk. Donsbach and Stevenson (1986; see also Donsbach, 1987) thought, paying attention to the fact that the deviant group represents actually the majority opinion, that perhaps these respondents had somehow sensed that theirs was the major view although they had not yet become aware of it. It is not unusual to resort to this kind of auxiliary hypotheses if the results have contradicted the theoretical predictions.

Despite the focal place of the mass media in the theory, analysis of media content has often been ignored. Sometimes, the media have been evoked merely rhetorically to explain some intriguing result. For instance, in a study conducted in 1976, the opinion climate was found to be strongly against having Communist Party members appointed as judges (Noelle-Neumann, 1980/1993, pp. 170–173). Yet, those holding this majority opinion were more willing to keep quiet than those holding the minority opinion. This disconcerting result led Noelle-Neumann (p. 173) to ask rhetorically (referring to those holding the majority opinion): "Could it be that words failed them because the opposition of communists as judges has scarcely ever been articulated in the mass media . . . ?" No data on the mass media coverage were supplied, however.

Of course, there are studies that have analyzed the media. One interesting study was carried out in the context of the federal election in 1976 (Noelle-Neumann, 1980/1993, pp. 157–166). It was observed that long before the election, most people expected Christlich-Demokratische Union (CDU) would win, but, as the election day came closer, the majority began to expect the Sozialdemokratische Partei Deutschlands (SPD) would win, which was what happened. A closer analysis revealed that those watching more political programs on television began to expect the SPD to win earlier than others. Furthermore, data on journalists disclosed that they also began to expect this result quite early. Additionally, among them the support to the SPD was much higher than among the population in average. Because, for Noelle-Neumann (1985, p. 80), the political stand of journalists is indicative of what they will present, she implied that the CDU "might have won if the media climate had not been against it" (Noelle-Neumann, 1980/1993, pp. 167–168).

Such an implication aroused much public indignation (Atteslander, 1980; Kiefer, 1977). Maybe that's why Noelle-Neumann's colleague Kepplinger (1979, 1982) took it on himself to analyze the political content of the media at the time preceding the election. The result was that the verbal content was impartial but that, on the TV, the CDU's leader Helmut Kohl was presented visually slightly more often in an unfavorable way than the SPD's leader Helmut Schmidt. Merten (1985, p. 41), for example, wondered how such a minuscule difference would have been decisive in "the whole election campaign of six months."

Another example of how research has tried to take media content into account is a study comparing time-series data on the media coverage of nuclear energy with those on people's own nuclear energy attitudes and their assessments of the opinion climate of that issue (Noelle-Neumann, 1991, pp. 272–278). On the basis of this comparison, Noelle-Neumann asserted that, "in the long run, much of the population adjusts its attitudes to the tenor of the media" (p. 272). Yet, even if the opposing stand to nuclear energy increased both in the media and among people during the period under study, the data are too inconclusive to warrant any causal statements.

Critical Discussion

The spiral-of-silence approach has been criticized both theoretically and empirically. First, for many critics, the anchorage of the theory merely on the fear of isolation is restrictive since reticence in public may result from many other motives (Glynn & McLeod, 1985, pp. 60–61; Price & Allen, 1990, pp. 372–373; Salmon & Kline, 1985, pp. 9–13). Katz (1981, pp. 30–32) suggested that people act according to a sort of cost–benefit principle and that this would offer a better starting point than the fear of isolation alone. It has been remarked further that the theory overstates people's inclination to conformity (Katz, 1981; Price & Allen, 1990, pp. 376-377) and paints a far too gloomy picture of their capacity to self-sustaining democratic action (Simpson, 1996, pp. 163–164).

Second, the theory has been charged for its conception that the opinion formation of individuals depends directly on an anonymous public opinion presumed to become visible in the mass media. What is thereby completely overseen is the role of primary groups to which people belong and which can prevent the influence of a more remote and alien public opinion (Glynn & McLeod, 1985; Katz, 1981; Kennamer, 1990, pp. 397–397; Salmon & Kline, 1985, pp. 7–8). Spurred by this critique, Donsbach (1987, pp. 340–341) urged the spiral-of-silence research to take primary groups as well as reference groups into account as contingent conditions that can constrain—or perhaps in certain cases also enhance—the influence of public opinion on individuals.

Third, as already stated, the role attributed to the media by the theory has annoyed many. For some scholars, the assertion of a consonance of media content is not applicable "to Western democratic societies other than West Germany" (Price & Allen, 1990, p. 375). Katz (1981, p. 30) said that with her consonance assertion Noelle-Neumann, ironically, joins forces with the critical theory of the Frankfurt School, albeit "from the other side of the political spectrum." Here one might intervene by stating simply that the consonance or nonconsonance of media content is not a theoretical but empirical question. Unfortunately, the empirical evidence put forth by the spiral-of-silence research in support for the consonance assertion is next to nothing.

Noelle-Neumann and her colleagues presented only such empirical results that support the theory or are at least adjustable to it through interpretation. On the other hand, the results of some outside researchers have clashed with the theory (e.g., Fuchs, Gerhards, & Neidhardt, 1992). For example, the proportion of those who would speak out only among like-minded people was observed in one study to be as insignificant as 3.5% (Gerhards, 1996). Most would speak out or keep silent regardless of the opinion of others. Some other "outsiders," again, have obtained results that are at least partly in keeping with the theory (Glynn & McLeod, 1985; Gonzenbach, 1992; Taylor, 1983). An overview of several studies showed that most of them supported the spiral of silence, albeit quite weakly (Glynn, Hayes, & Shanahan, 1997).

Because the empirical support to the theory has remained, at best, only weak and, at worst, contradictory, it seems that the theory does not adequately meet the complexities of the processes it intends to explain. Therefore, one must indeed doubt whether the theory as such can ever be confirmed. In this respect, the state of affairs of spiral of silence research is comparable with that of agenda-setting and knowledge-gap approaches. On the other hand, there surely are such aspects in public opinion processes that are rooted in people's inclination to conformity and that can be fruitfully interpreted from the perspective of the spiral of silence.

12

INFORMATION-PROCESSING THEORY

Although the three preceding approaches focused on media effects, none of them has paid much attention to how the intake of information from the media takes place and what happens to it in the individual mind. This lacuna was filled by the information-processing theory, which began to gain ground in mass communication studies from the early 1970s on. It is not, like the preceding approaches, a narrow string, based on clear-cut premises, but a more broad and diffuse current running through many disciplines from psychology to text linguistics and literary science. Its broad nature comes into sight also in the fact that that it has attracted scholars who otherwise differ very much from each other.

In mass communication studies, the closest predecessor of information-processing theory is the cognitive tendency considered in chapter 7. They both see, for example, that the information intake depends on what there already is in the individual's mind. On the other hand, where the cognitive tendency emphasizes the importance of the pursuit of cognitive consistency as the regulative mechanism, information-processing theory sees the intake being determined also by factors that may disturb cognitive consistency, such as curiosity or the expected utility of information, for example (Donohew & Tipton, 1974; see also Schenk, 1987, pp. 132–141).

The information-processing theorist approaches the human mind as consisting of certain structures called models, frames, schemata, scripts, and so on. The structures not only determine "what information will be noted, processed and stored," but also help people to fit new information "into their established perceptions" and enable them to "fill in missing information, which permits them to make sense of incomplete communications" (Graber, 1988, p. 29). Such framing processes have caught much attention in recent mass communication studies. That's why the so-called schema theory, explicating these structures and processes, is the main object of the following considerations.

SCHEMATA, REMEMBERING AND UNDERSTANDING

One of the founding fathers of schema theory is Frederic Bartlett (1932/1954), an English psychologist who studied experimentally perception and memory in the 1910s and 1920s. He thought that what a person perceives or remembers is not simply given through sense organs or memory, but is, to a great extent, a result of his or her (re)constructive work. For instance, situational perceptions are constructed largely on the basis of what the perceiver has experienced in similar situations before or "what he takes to be 'fit,' or suitable, to such a situation" (p. 14). "He may do this without being in the least aware that he is either supplementing of falsifying the data of perception" (p. 14).

Bartlett studied this by flashing at his subjects diverse figures and asking them to reproduce the figures. He found that the subjects typically named what they had seen or attacked it by analogy. This occurred "immediately and unreflectingly: for the presented visual pattern seemed at once to 'fit into' or to 'match' some preferred scheme or setting" (p. 20). The process of connecting a given pattern with some scheme was called by Bartlett "effort after meaning" (p. 20; cf. also 43-46). Thus, there was one single process of perceiving and signifying, organized by the schema that the presented figure had provoked in the perceiver's mind.

On the basis of similar experiments on memory, Bartlett concluded that also "remembering appears to be far more decisively an affair of construction rather than one of mere reproduction" (p. 205). This construction also was found to be based on some schema that the object to be remembered had called forth in the subject's mind. The schema transformed that object in the recall even drastically— details not fitting it were dropped out and new ones fitting it were added. The kind of a schema that was set as the basis for this constructing work seemed to depend on the individual's interests and attitudes at each time: The recall is motivated by some attitude, "and its general effect is that of a justification of the attitude" (p. 207).

Bartlett did not specify more precisely what schemata are and how they work but was content to state that a schema "refers to an active organization of past reactions, or of past experiences" (p. 201). In this sense, schemata would be condensations of individual experiences. On the other hand, schemata seem also to have a social origin since, for Bartlett (p. 296), "social organization gives a persistent framework" that "helps to provide those 'schemata' which are a basis for the imaginative reconstruction called memory." Moreover, in his view, the fixation and effect of schemata within an individual has a parallel in "social conventionalism": so individual schemata and social conventions seem to be analogical (p. 309).

Schema theory was further developed by Schank and Abelson (1977), who looked at interpretation and understanding from the schema perspective. They paid attention to specific schemata they called scripts. Their starting point was "an episodic view of memory," a view that "memory is organized around personal experiences or episodes" (p. 17). Episodes reminiscent of each other are preserved in memory as a prototype consisting of their similar features, as "a standardized generalized episode," which is just what is called "a script" (p. 19).

An example is the restaurant script consisting of typical events and acts of visiting a restaurant: entering, choosing the table, sitting, glancing the menu, and so on. It also has associated with it typical roles for persons acting in this kind of situation. It is on the basis of such a script that people behave in restaurants and understand what is going on there. More generally, people understand "what they see and hear" by matching it "to pre-stored groupings of actions they have already experienced" (p. 67). Of course, they can also understand situations, with which they have no previous experience, by applying general knowledge instead of the specific knowledge condensed in scripts. But, for Schank and Abelson (p. 67), "most understanding is script-based."

In addition to situations and actions, scripts also guide the interpretation and understanding of texts. In effect, they already guide the production of texts. Resting on scripts, people, for instance, "consistently leave out information that they feel can easily be inferred by the listener or reader" (p. 22). However, if the receiver does not master the scripts on which the text is based and with the aid of which the information left out can be filled in, there surely will emerge problems of understanding. What scripts "do is let you leave out the boring details when you are talking or writing, and fill them in when you are listening or reading" (p. 41).

Schank and Abelson (pp. 23, 31) exemplified understanding by considering, among others, the following sentence: "John cried because Mary said that she loves Bill." Generally, "in order to understand we must be able to fill in the gaps left implicit by a speaker" (p. 23), and we fill them in mostly with the aid of scripts. What is left implicit in the just presented sentence is the reason why John is crying. To fill in this gap most people would probably rely on the script of love and think that John is crying because he is in love with Mary. This is the most plausible explanation on the basis of the information provided by the sentence. Perhaps additional facts would lead one to conclude that John was crying for an entirely different reason.

SCHEMATA AND STORIES

Schema theory has been applied especially in the study of stories. A story is, of course, a text, but at the same time the term says something about the structures of human mind where stories are produced and received. It has been suggested that one of our basic modes of thinking—the narrative mode—is grounded on stories (see Höijer, 1995, pp. 12–15). This mode deals with events and actors, and as such it comes close to what Schank and Abelson meant by episodic memory. This story-formed mode of thinking is learned "early in childhood," and we "use it in our everyday interaction with the world" (Höijer, 1998, p. 75).

Because the story form indicates characteristics of both texts and mind, Mandler (1984) suggested the following conceptual distinction: story grammar refers to texts and story schema to the mind. The former describes the regularities found in the story structures, whereas the latter is "a mental structure consisting of sets of expectations about the way in which stories proceed" (p. 18). The expectations stem "from the experience with hearing and reading stories" (p. x). The study of grammar is pure textual analysis, but at the same time it provides the starting points to investigate the extent to which people have incorporated the regularities of the grammar into their story schema and how they make use of this schema when processing stories.

Story grammars are mostly explications of the parts of which stories are composed. According to the classical view, a story is made up of three parts: it starts with an equilibrium that is first disturbed and then restored on a new level. More generally, to qualify as a story or narrative a text must minimally include a stasis, its change through an occurrence or act, and a new stasis, all related to each other (see, e.g., Prince, 1973). Rumelhart (1975), for his part, distinguished between a setting and one or more episodes. The setting "is a statement of the time and place of a story as well as an introduction of its main characters" while an episode consists "of events which involve the reactions of animate . . . objects to events in the world" (pp. 213–214).

Usually there are many episodes in a story. The episodes can be linked with one another in different ways as, for instance, through a then-coupling (first happened A, then B) or causally (A caused B to happen). A single episode is often a minimal story in the above sense. According to Mandler (p. 22), an episode begins with one or more events. Then the protagonist reacts in some way to these events. This response can be an emotional reaction that often leads the protagonist to set up a goal to do something about the events. Attempts to reach the goal follow, with success or failure. The episode ends with some kind of commentary on the preceding events.

The question of whether or not people process stories through story schemata cannot be tackled straightforwardly because the schemata are not applied consciously (pp. 31–36). Their use must, then, be studied indirectly. For instance, Mandler (pp. 37–41) composed stories in which he utilized episode structure, and let his subjects divide them into meaningful parts. Because these divisions roughly corresponded to the partition in Mandler's story grammar, the conclusion was that the subjects had processed the stories through a story schema reminiscent of that grammar. Furthermore, experiments on memory have shown that stories with a canonical story grammar are easier to recall than stories deviating from it. Moreover, there was a tendency to recall the deviant stories in the canonical story form (Mandler, 1978; Mandler & DeForest, 1979).

Thus, there is some evidence supporting the view that people process and understand stories through a story schema reminiscent of story grammar. On the other hand, being heavily biased toward structuralism, this view has ignored the role of the content in story reception. There are experiments indicating that a story is not comprehensible unless it succeeds in calling into the receiver's mind appropriate scripts or schemata of content (see, e.g., Bransford & Johnson, 1972). For some, the structure of stories is even a minor factor in their understanding (e.g., Wilensky, 1982). Be that as it may, it is in any case necessary to take both the grammar-based story schema and the content-based schemata into account in the inquiry into story processing and comprehension (Höijer & Findahl, 1984, pp. 19–23).

SCHEMA THEORY AND THE STUDY OF JOURNALISM

I illustrate the application of schema theory in mass communication studies by using the study of journalism as an example. Within it, this theory has nourished particularly the study of how journalistic texts are structured and what thematic frames they contain. Also the schemata, through which the texts are processed in reception, have been investigated in some degree. On the other hand, the question of how schemata guide the text production—that is, what kind of schemata journalists apply and in which ways in different cases—has received less attention.

Within textual studies, a notable name is Teun A. van Dijk, a Dutchman who was involved in the 1980s in shaping a news grammar, comparable to a story grammar (van Dijk, 1983, 1985, 1986, 1988, pp. 49–59; 1991, pp. 118–124). This grammar divides the structure of the news first into the summary and the text proper. Summary, consisting of a headline and a lead, gives the main topic of the subsequent text. It functions like the setting in a story. The text itself divides into episode(s) and verbal reactions aroused by them, quite as a story according to the Rumelhartian grammar. Both of these structural parts split further into smaller units; the episode, for example, into main event(s), background, consequences, and so on.

This model condenses a conventional or canonical order for the structural parts in the news text. So canonically the journalist, for example, takes up first the main event before going on to the verbal reactions aroused by it. However, in actual cases, the journalist may deviate from this order. For instance, if verbal reactions are judged most newsworthy, they are taken up before going on to the event that has given rise to them. Because such things as newsworthiness, relevance, and recency may overstep an orderly presentation form, news narration seldom proceeds linearly from one structural part to another but often jumps to and fro between the parts.

The formal structure of news is one thing; the way in which the matters told in it are framed, is another. This brings us to the frame analysis of news. The term frame comes from Goffman's (1974) Frame Analysis, in which he equated it with the schemata of interpretation that people utilize to make sense of the world around them. This term has been taken into use even by scholars who actually are not "cognitivists." Gitlin (1980), for example, adapted the term to news analysis. For him, frames help journalists select what to portray and to emphasize some points at the cost of others. In this way frames enable the journalists "to process large amounts of information quickly and routinely" and to "package the information for efficient relay to their audiences" (p. 7; see also Gamson & Modigliani, 1989).

Through framing—that is, through selection, emphasis, and exclusion—news texts construct specific versions of the matters they deal with. A striking example is provided by a study of Halloran, Elliot, and Murdock (1970) that was conducted before there was any explicit schema theory. These researchers followed news reporting of a demonstration against the Vietnam War before and after it took place in London in 1968. They found that the journalists had developed, before the event, an "underlying frame of mind" (p. 26) foretelling that the event would go violently. This frame determined how the pre-event period and the event itself were reported. Most remarkable is that, although the event was overwhelmingly peaceful, journalists focused on some violent incidents as if they had been forced to certify the frame that had guided their whole work.

Studies focusing on the news coverage of strikes have found that there is often an "us–them" frame in use. It relegates the strikers as "troublemakers" to the negative pole of "them," while the positive pole of "us" is mostly filled with people seen as innocent victims of the strike (Fiske, 1987, pp. 296–301; Hartley, 1982, pp. 115–129). Also, civic activists and social protesters slip easily to the negative pole of "them." Gitlin (1980) observed that the leftist student movement, SDS, was handled through a frame that depicted it both as a threat and as a marginal phenomenon. The coverage often disregards the aims of those in the negative pole, and focuses instead on what they do. There seems in general to be a shift from an issue frame toward a performance frame (Adatto, 1990; Hallin, 1992; T. Patterson, 1980, 1994). For example, in election coverage the candidates' success in the "horse-race" has begun to weigh more than their political aims and goals.

The reception process of news has been tackled with the view that people bring "an array of collected experiences and world-knowledge" to this process and that it is within these "frames of reference" or "cognitive structures" that every piece of news "will be understood and interpreted" (Höijer, 1990, p. 30). These schemata concern the formal structure of news, on one hand, and matters dealt within the news items, on the other. Regarding the former aspect, van Dijk (1988, p. 151) maintained that people have "an elementary news schema" corresponding to his news grammar. In some studies, he found that what was best recalled from newspaper news was the information favored by the formal news structure, that is, reported in the summary part of headlines and leads (pp. 165–174).

The processing of information about the matters told in the news has attracted more attention. In an extensive study, Graber

(1988, p. 188) observed, for example, that the schemata through which people processed information provided by policy issue news consisted of six dimensions:

> (1) a very brief, basic description of the objectives of the policy; (2) who or what caused particular problems or could resolve them; (3) the nature of institutions involved in the policy; (4) the roles played by human actors in the political drama; (5) the relation of the policy to American interests and cultural values; and (6) the policy's relation to humanistic concerns, including . . . self-interest.

Because ordinary people generally lack "direct experience with the complexities of politics," the schemata composed of these dimensions—not necessarily always even of all of them—were quite simple and "the individual schemata" revealed "a good deal of shared stereotypical thinking" (pp. 189, 214). This, however, "should not be surprising since the news in general, and political events in particular, are comparatively remote from the individual's life" (p. 214).

The inquiry into the ways in which people interpret single news items has shown that the interpretation tends to keep to some script or schema called by the item in the receiver's mind. Lewis (1985, p. 208) named the schemata narrative contexts and found, for instance, that a simple item about the quantity of jobs lost and created was interpreted differently depending on the context or schema into which it was put. Some read it as a story about the ratio of new jobs to jobs lost, whereas for others, it was a story telling where jobs were going and coming or what kind of jobs were lost and created (pp. 208–209). K. Jensen (1988) observed that people were inclined to interpret news items in relation to what he called super-themes. For instance, news about the unrest in the world was often related to the super-theme (or schema) of war (pp. 294–295).

As these examples deal with interpretation, they actually are close to cultural studies. They have not specifically tackled the question of media effects. Within the schema theoretical approach, this question has been paid more notice to since the early 1990s. McLeod and Detenber (1999), for example, produced different frames for a TV news item relaying a clash between anarchist protesters and the police, and studied experimentally how these frames influenced the way the viewers saw the event. The framings gave the police weak, mediate, or strong support. The result was that the framing giving the police strong support led the viewers "to be more critical of, and less likely to be identified with, the protesters; less critical of the police; and less likely to support the protesters' expressive rights" (p. 3; see also McLeod, 1995; Rhee, 1997; Scheufele, 1999).

CRITICAL DISCUSSION

Schema theory, or information-processing theory in general, has focused principally on cognition. It sees people as "active, goal seeking and purposeful" who "use schemata to comprehend news and information, leading to sensible interpretations of day-to-day events" (Wicks, 1992, p. 126). But are people so rational in their news reception? Dahlgren (1985, p. 84), for one, doubted this and argued that the excessively rationalistic angle of information processing theory may leave the most focal points of news reception "lingering in shadows." Also van Dijk (1988, p. 173), a promoter of the theory, considered it obvious that news reception "does not primarily serve the permanent updating of our world knowledge, but rather more direct functions such as the satisfaction of curiosity about actual developments, daily conversation about events, and so on."

Critics have picked out terminological and methodological problems. For instance, besides the term schema there are in use many other terms such as frame, model, representation, and the like, whose boundaries of meaning have remained blurred. Even the concept of schema itself has not obtained a "standard or consensual definition" (Woodall, 1986, p. 151). Its "fuzziness" has been charged for that it has not become "a more widely used theoretical construct" (Wicks, 1992, p. 151). As a matter of fact, the term became, "due to its loose and ambiguous use," an anathema in psychology in the beginning of the 1990s (Brosius, 1991, p. 290). Anyway, in communication studies it is still in use (see Clausen, 1997; Kepplinger & Daschmann, 1997).

Critics have remarked further that it is unclear under what conditions schemata are activated and how they "are acquired and modified" (Woodall, 1986, p. 151). The term itself implies that schemata exist in mind as ready-made structures waiting to be used. But do people indeed carry such structures in their heads? Höijer and Findahl (1984, p. 203) tell that Roger Schank, the father of the script idea, began to think already at the beginning of the 1980s that, instead of being ready-made, schemata are "constructed as occasion requires" and that the outcome of this process is quite fragmentary, not so well-rounded as he initially thought.

A further problem is that terms such as interpretation, comprehension, remembering, and recall are used as if they had same meanings. Yet comprehension and remembering, for example, refer to "separate and different cognitive processes" (Woodall, Davis, & Sahin, 1983, p. 176; see also Woodall, 1986, pp. 145–147; Son, Reese, & Davie, 1987). The nonseparation between the terms has led to methodological confusions. Because the data for studies claiming to focus on comprehension are usually collected by the method of recall, one must ask whether such studies concern really comprehension or simply recall—one can namely recall things that one has not understood. Admittedly, there are methods for distinguishing between comprehension and remembering (see J. Robinson & Davis, 1986; Son et al., 1987), but the role of recall has continually been obscure here.

Despite its shortcomings, schema-theoretical thinking has fruitfully advanced the idea that all comprehension is rooted in preunderstanding. Preunderstanding is a phenomenon difficult to pin down. Perhaps the terminological obscurities reflect this fact. Some have proposed a new opening with the concept of heuristics (Brosius, 1991, pp. 293–294; Woodall, 1986, pp. 153–157). This proposal seems to start with the view that information is processed not through ready-made cognitive structures but rather by utilizing elastically heuristic devices available at each time. Of course, also in this case the adapting of the devices would be semi-autonomous or something not done with clear awareness (Bargh, 1988).

13

CULTURAL INDICATORS

George Gerbner

Like the approaches described in chapter 11, the cultural indicators (CI) project, initiated by George Gerbner (1919–), also represents the study of effects. But where the previously mentioned discourses drew almost exclusively from the positivist behavioral legacy, the CI project also utilized elements from the critical theory of the Frankfurt School. To a certain extent, it has taken the course Lazarsfeld (1941) had in mind when suggesting the collaboration between critical-theoretical and administrative-empiricist research. This suggestion fell for a long time on deaf ears—the contrasts between these two types of research were simply far more drastic than Lazarsfeld could envisage (see Slack & Allor, 1983).

Gerbner (1983, p. 59), too, admits these contrasts: critical and administrative research cannot be united because "there is between them an inner contradiction; you cannot represent both at the same time." Yet, the CI project was built on theoretical premises resembling those of the critical theory although it has utilized the empirical methods of administrative research (see Smythe & Dinh, 1983). Gerbner was influenced theoretically by Adorno during their collaboration in the beginning of the 1950s (Gerbner, 1994, pp. 106-107; Kellner, 1982, p. 502), although he himself has downplayed this fact (Potter, 1993, p. 566). The methodological course taken by the CI project, on the other hand, is perhaps explained by the fact that Gerbner was, already in the 1950s, well versed in quantitative content analysis.

THE BACKGROUND OF THE CI PROJECT

One of the starting points of the CI project is Gerbner's (1958/1964) long-standing conviction that, in order to have real significance, content analysis should be focused in a critical way on broad flows of cultural commodities instead of on limited message sets. It was this view that prompted him to search for a synthesis of critical theory and empirical methods: The objective was "to combine empirical methods with the critical aims of social science, to join rigorous practice with value-conscious theory" (p. 499). Gerbner introduced this with an explicit reference to Lazarsfeld's suggestion. Quoting Lazarsfeld, Gerbner said that the consequences of mass communication should be approached by asking "what endangers and what preserves the dignity, freedom and cultural values of human beings" (p. 493).

The point that mass communication should be looked at as broad streams of cultural commodities conforms to the Frankfurtians' view of media "as a system, which is uniform as a whole and in every part" (Adorno & Horkheimer, 1944/1986, p. 120). It also conforms with Adorno's (1963/1991, p. 91) view of the effectivity of a culture industry that "steady drops hollow the stone, especially since the system of culture industry that surrounds masses tolerates hardly any deviation and incessantly drills the same formulas on behavior." Because the "drops" of the mass media act on the "stone" of mass audience slowly, their effect is not easy to discern: that's why the task is

> to scientifically gather and test inferences about content that may involve generally unrecognized and unanticipated consequences [and] to isolate and investigate consequential properties of content which escape ordinary awareness or casual scrutiny. (Gerbner, pp. 482–483)

On the other hand, although the Frankfurtians utilized empirical observations, at the most, to illustrate theoretical insights, Gerbner (1967, p. 433) stressed that social science is obligated "to deal systematically, rather than selectively or only qualitatively, with problems of social life." Therefore, the message flows and their consequences should be submitted to empirical-quantitative research. For instance, the messages should be classified systematically "into categories for the purpose of description and measurement" (Gerbner, 1958/1964, p. 488). Here, critical and administrative research "join in common concern over the development of research design and methodology" (p. 489). Still, critical research ought to transcend the limits of administrative content analysis and "to harness its methodological insights to more critical social uses" (p. 483).

THE GENERAL OUTLINES OF THE CI PROJECT

Cultural indicators refer to such aspects of media production and message flows on which continuous statistics can be compiled in order to describe the states of and trends in mass communication in the same way as economic states and trends are described with the aid of economic indicators (Gerbner, 1973, pp. 555–558). The CI project focused its work on television—perhaps because the project was initially funded by the National Commission on the Causes and Prevention of Violence to research the influence of television on violence (Gerbner & Gross, 1976, p. 174). The project, launched in the late 1960s, was continued subsequently with the support of state agencies and private funds. Since the late 1970s, its discourse has also attracted scholars outside the original project group (see Signorielli & Morgan, 1990).

Unlike the talk of cultural indicators implies, the CI project has not limited itself to compiling statistics of message production but has gone on to study how the media's institutional frames shape their output and how this output shapes people's conceptions of various issues: (a) Institutional process analysis tackles the institutional operations, pressures and constraints on which message production hinges. (b) Message system analysis asks what are the predominating assumptions, viewpoints, images, and values included in the message flow. (c) Cultivation analysis attempts to discover the extent to which the predominant elements in the message flow cultivate corresponding elements among the audiences (Gerbner, 1973, pp. 558–572). Of these three, cultivation analysis generated the most focus, whereas the institutional processes have attracted only minor attention (see Morgan & Signorielli, 1990).

Gerbner and his colleagues approached the output of television as a program flow. This view, which comes close to the Frankfurtians' standpoint, was justified with the argument that the whole output of television composes a specific symbolic world of its own:

The symbolic composition and structure of the message system of
a mass medium defines its own synthetic "world". Only what is
represented exists. All that exists in that "world" is represented
in it. . . . The "world" has its own time, space, geography, demog-
raphy, and ethnography, bent to institutional purposes and rules
of social morality. (Gerbner, 1973, p. 563)

The viewing of television means "living" in its "symbolic
world" (Gerbner & Gross, p. 178). Of course, heavy viewers spend
more time there than light viewers. This brings us to the question of
cultivation. For Gerbner (1967, p. 433), it is futile to ask, like the
behavioral tradition did, whether or not messages change attitudes
or behavior immediately; instead one should ask "what public perspectives, conceptions and actions different types of mass communication systems tend to cultivate." Cultivation denotes a process in
which a person, living in a symbolic world, absorbs conceptions typical of it. The question is "of broad enculturation rather than of narrow changes in opinion or behavior" (Gerbner & Gross, p. 180):

The environment that sustains the most distinctive aspects of
human existence is the environment of symbols. We learn, share,
and act upon meanings derived from that environment. . . .
Common rituals and mythologies are agencies of symbolic socialization and control. They demonstrate how society works by dramatizing its norms and values. They are essential parts of the
general system of messages that cultivates prevailing outlooks.
(p. 173)

For Gerbner and his colleagues, today's symbolic environment is dominated by TV's message system. As a cultivating agent,
TV does not change culturally prevailing conceptions but reinforces
them—its "chief cultural function is to spread and stabilize social
patterns, to cultivate not change but resistance to change" (p. 175).
Thus, "stability may be the significant outcome" of the system (p.
180)—a standpoint that again reflects the Frankfurtians' view of
mass culture.

TELEVISION AND PEOPLE'S CONCEPTIONS OF VIOLENCE

The CI project has studied, in particular, how television influences
people's views of violence. The question was not whether or not tele-

vision causes violent behavior in reality, but whether or not it induces people to imagine that their environment is violent and they themselves unprotected. Thus, Gerbner's view was not that TV violence disrupts the social order by fostering violent behavior, but, on the contrary, that it

> maintains the status quo by demonstrating and protecting the power of the powerful. By cultivating fear, apprehension, and mistrust, television might contribute to a climate in which demands for security outweigh any remnants of concern about repression and violation of civil liberties. (Morgan, 1995, p. 110)

To obtain a basis for their research on cultivation, Gerbner and his colleagues registered the violent content in TV fiction yearly since the 1967 (Gerbner & Gross, p. 181). For them, violence consists of "the overt expression of physical force against self or other, compelling action against one's will on pain of being hurt or killed or actually hurting or killing" (p. 184). All such instances occurring in fiction programs during the sample week at each year were recorded. A time-series extending to the 1978 tells, for instance, that the proportion of the U.S. networks' fiction programs containing violence varied from 73% to 89% and the number of violent incidents per hour from 7 to almost 10 (Gerbner, Gross, Morgan, & Signorelli, 1980a, p. 408). Such figures have led to the conclusion that the "symbolic world" of television is "ruled largely by violence" (Gerbner & Gross, p. 178).

The cultivating power of TV violence was studied by asking respondents how often they watched television and how violent they considered their environment to be—for instance, how high they judged their chances of being involved in some type of violence. The rationale of asking the respondents only about the amount of their television viewing, not about the programs they used to watch, was that "television is used non-selectively" (p. 177). Thus, instead of particular programs, people watch the program flow. Even if some would watch selectively, this would change nothing since—as Gerbner (1967, p. 433) stated metaphorically—people can swim in a river in different directions, but in the end all directions "are relative to the direction and speed of the current itself."

The basic hypothesis of cultivation analysis is "that the more time one spends living in the world of television, the more likely one is to report conceptions of social reality that can be traced to television portrayals" (Gross & Morgan, 1985, p. 226). The way to test the hypothesis is to look into how the conceptions of social reality differ between heavy and light TV viewers. It is supported if the conceptions of heavy viewers tilt more toward the world of television than those of the light viewers—in other words, if the former experience their environment as more violent and are more worried about this than the latter.

The CI project's results have mostly supported the cultivation hypothesis. For example, when respondents were asked in one study about the chances of being involved in violence, 52% of heavy viewers and 39% of light viewers gave an answer tilting towards the world of television. Furthermore, when asked "Can most people be trusted?" 65% of heavy viewers and 48% of light viewers chose the answer "Can't be too careful" (Gerbner & Gross, pp. 192–193). It is, however, difficult to say whether these differences stem from the watching of TV or from other relevant factors in regard to which heavy and light viewers might differ. Being aware of this problem, the project group has investigated the differences between heavy and light viewers by holding demographic and other factors constant. The results obtained have generally supported the cultivation hypothesis.

On the other hand, the differences between the viewer groups often have been small. Morgan and Signorielli (1990, p. 20) explained this by saying that even light viewers

> may watch a substantial amount of television per week and in any case live in the same cultural environment as heavy viewers; what they do not get through television can be acquired indirectly from others who watch more. It is clear, then, that the cards are stacked against finding evidence of cultivation. Therefore, the discovery of a systematic pattern of even small but pervasive differences between light and heavy viewers may indicate far-reaching consequences.

DISCUSSION AROUND THE CI PROJECT

Debate around the CI project has dealt especially with (a) the project's way of approaching TV violence, (b) its way of drawing conclusions of the cultivating effects of television, and, more broadly, (c) the basic premises of its work.

Comparing the project's results with some other content analyses on TV violence, researchers from NBC concluded that the project's findings gave too gloomy a picture of the subject (Coffin & Tuchman, 1972–1973). In their view, if one wants to assess the amount of TV violence reliably, violence should be defined more strictly than the project has done. Most importantly, the research should "discriminate between 'harmful' and 'harmless' violence" (p. 19). A voice from CBS pronounced that the meaning of the project's "arbitrarily chosen" and "arbitrarily weighted" violence measures is "totally unclear," that the project's definition of violence is too inclusive and that measuring violence "during one week a year" does not yield reliable results (Blank, 1977, pp. 273, 276).

In their rejoinders, the project group stressed that their definition pays attention to the multidimensionality of violence. This has enabled the construction of specific Violence Profiles (Eleey, Gerbner, & Tedesco, 1972–1973; Gerbner et al., 1977). The suggestion that only such violence should be taken into account, which is considered harmful by the citizens, was countered with the remark that the citizens do not necessarily realize what is harmful for them (Gerbner et al., 1977, pp. 281–282). That's why "independent research is needed"—the issue "cannot be left to conventional wisdom, and even less to rationalizations of the corporate interests involved" (p. 282). Gerbner et al. (pp. 284–285) argued, furthermore, that a week is a long enough period for reliable measurements.

Some scholars were intrigued by the question of whether or not the correlations between the amount of TV watching and the view of a violent world are genuine or spurious, caused by other variables (Doob & Macdonald, 1980; Hirsch, 1980; Hughes, 1980). By reanalyzing a NORC data set utilized by the CI project itself, and by making their own replications, the researchers came to the conclusion that many of the correlations that at the first glance seemed to support the cultivation hypothesis were in fact spurious. Thus, for Hirsch (p. 408), the assertion of the cultivating effect of TV violence remained an unproven "armchair hypothesis."

The project group answered that, due to its problems, the NORC data had not been central in their analysis and that in other data the correlations had proven genuine (Gerbner, Gross, Morgan, & Signorelli, 1980b, 1981a). Moreover, even if the correlations would not hold good on the level of the whole data, they would do this in some subgroups. And finally, the cultivation effect can appear also otherwise than in the form of a linear dependency. In his reply, Hirsch (1981a) argued that the claim of the cultivation effect's nonlinearity watered down the project's starting points and effectively immunized it against all criticism. The debate continued for a while without bringing forth new viewpoints (Gerbner, Gross, Morgan, & Signorelli, 1981b; Hirsch 1981b). This discussion was continued by Potter (1993).

The project's basic premises were tackled by Newcomb (1980). Although he praised the project's way of foregrounding the symbolic environment—this brought it close to humanist cultural studies—Newcomb saw that its analysis remained very mechanistic. For instance, the project lumped together indiscriminately all violence portrayed in television without noting that different violent scenes might have very different meanings. Moreover, the project ignored the possibility that different people may interpret the same scenes differently. For Newcomb, these problems resulted from the project's view of communication as transportation regardless of certain hints towards a view of it as sharing or ritual.

In their rejoinder, Gerbner and Gross (1980) took up, once again, the Frankfurtians' position that the production of TV fiction is assembly-line work. Therefore, with regard to its violent content, the recurrence weighs much more than nuances of meaning. Even people's different interpretations are not relevant in a research that focuses on the uniform program flow instead of detached programs. Gerbner and Gross rejected also the claim that the CI project represents a transportation model of communication—what is at stake in cultivation is not transportation but enculturation. As the most forceful argument against Newcomb, they resorted to the project's findings according to which

> heavy viewers do tend to answer questions in line with the television presentations, even when we control for demographic and other characteristics. Therefore, it seems that they do learn at least some of the lessons brought out in our analysis. . . . Newcomb does not offer an alternative explanation for these findings, nor another way to assess TV's contribution to what people think and do. (p. 474)

14

MASS MEDIA AS THE PROP
OF THE SYSTEM

Marxism

The launching of Gerbner's critical project was only a prelude to the rebellion against the positivist-behavioral orthodoxy that began to penetrate the field of mass communication studies in the late 1960s. This revolt was headed by Marxism—or, in plural, Marxisms, because what was at issue was no unified camp but a real mixture of conflicting ingredients ranging from the traditional Party orthodoxies to the anti-authoritarian and undisciplinary views entertained among student and other New Left movements. The composition of this amalgam varied also by countries—for instance, it differed in Britain from what it was in the United States (see, e.g., Dworkin, 1997; Lent, 1995; G. Turner, 1992; Unger, 1974).

What connected the trends of this multiple Marxism was their opposition to the dominant capitalist economic-political system. They criticized things they regarded supportive to this system— among them the positivist-behavioral research, and the mainstream communication study as a part of it. The critique was fueled partly by the bitter experiences of the student movements that taught the academic Marxists, among other things, that most media were not impartial disseminators of information, as the research had made people believe. In conflict situations, the media supported the prevailing system and exposed in this way their close ties to the economic-political power (Gitlin, 1980; Jansen & Klönne, 1968; Zoll, 1971). This offered the basic perspective from which the Marxists approached mass communication.

BASIC FEATURES OF THE MARXIST THINKING OF MASS COMMUNICATION

One important source from which the rebellion drew inspiration was the critical theory of the Frankfurt School. Gerbner already had made use of it, but it gained more widespread attention in academic circles first with the turn to Marxism. The appropriation of critical theory was particularly marked in West Germany (Hoffmann, 1983). There, the student movement's thinking was fueled by stuff extracted from the Frankfurtians' writings, many of which circulated as pirate publications among the radicals (Wiggershaus, 1994, pp. 676–705). In Anglo-American circles, the school's thinking was noticed later, but none the less the critical leftist thinking there resembled it "in intent and practice" (Kellner, 1989a, pp. 140).

In the following section, I first make an overview into the shared points and divergences within Marxism. In order to be able to compare it to the Frankfurt School, I employ the same division— economy, the class structure of society, and ideology—that organized the description of the theory of culture industry earlier. After that, I take a closer look at three Marxist tendencies singled out by Curran et al. (1982, pp. 23–28): the structuralist Screen theory, the political economy of mass communication, and the Birmingham critical cultural studies. This consideration is limited to the period from the 1970s to the beginning of the 1980s, during which these trends blossomed especially in Great Britain.

Economy

Like the Frankfurtians, the Marxists thought that the structure and functioning of Western mass communication is determined by the capitalist mode of economy. The commercial media, in particular, but also the public service media are subjected to the economic laws of market sphere. Differing from the Frankfurtians, many Marxists saw that even if the capitalist economy leashes most of the media as props for the bourgeois hegemony, there are also alternative media, critical of the system, although their circulation remains small. For example, Negt and Kluge (1972) brought this forth in their theory of the proletarian public space, based on the authentic experience of the working class, as an opposite to the dominating bourgeois public sphere oppressing that experience.

Although the Frankfurtians approached the culture industry in economic terms, they did not analyze its economy concretely. Like them, many Marxists used the economy, at the most, only as their starting point. However, the political economists of communication were not satisfied with this but set out to analyze how the capitalist economy determines the production and distribution of media products nationally and globally (e.g., Mattelart, 1979; H. Schiller, 1969; Smythe, 1981). It was found, for example, that the world information flows were firmly in the hands of Western transnational corporations and that the flows were extremely skewed running mainly from the world's developed centrum to the less developed periphery.

Within the economic discourse, the functioning of the media was considered in terms of commodity production and distribution. But what actually were the commodities that were sold by the (commercial) media? For instance, Hofmann (1968/1983) shared the Frankfurt School's view of media products—news, entertainment, and so on—as commodities. For Smythe (1981, p. 4; see also 1977), on the other hand, the commodity is the audience collected by the media to consume their products: "the mass media produce audiences and sell them to advertisers." Smythe's thesis that media were increasingly organized around the production and sale of audiences, and that what had been studied as their ideological working was a secondary issue raised a lively debate (see Meehan, 1993; Murdock, 2000). Mosco (1996, pp. 140–172) later proposed a balanced view according to which the media industry is involved in capitalist commodity production in many ways other than only by manufacturing media products and/or audiences.

Some strove to develop a theory about the functions fulfilled by the media in capitalism. From the economic point of view, the attention was naturally turned to their economic functions. For Holzer (1973, pp. 129–137), the media have two such functions: (a) they enable the direct and indirect valorization of capital, and (b) they support the circulation of commodities and the realization of the (surplus) value incorporated in them. The first function means simply, as the Frankfurtians already recognized, that mass communication offers options for capital to make profitable investments. The second function means that the media support the commerce of commodities by selling space or time for their advertising. Corresponding distinctions were also made by others (Cheesman & Kyhn, 1975, pp. 135–151; Hund, 1976, pp. 175–193; V. Pietilä, 1978, pp. 76–82).

Beside the economic functions, the media were also seen to fulfill ideological functions which I will refer to later.

Class Structure

With regard to economy, the Marxists were on the same track as the Frankfurt School, but not so with respect to the class structure of society: They rejected the view that the classes had disappeared and society was becoming totally one-dimensional. Here, the school found an enemy even within itself: Hans-Jürgen Krahl, "Adorno's most brilliant, and most critical, student" (Slater, 1977, p. 82), stressed that even if the school's critical theory approached society as a totality, it

> was none the less unable to grasp this totality in its concrete expression as class-antagonism. . . . The practical class standpoint, to put it crudely, did not enter into that theory as an active constituent of that theory. (Krahl, 1971, cited by Slater, p. 82)

It was claimed that the theory was doomed to elitism because it lacked "any concept of a continuing confrontation of wage-labour and capital" (p. 135). With the ignorance of the working class its starting point, praxis was ruined as the genuinely "revolutionary opposition was confined to a privileged élite and a subversive art" (Swingewood, 1977, p. 18).

For Marxism, the focal structural feature of capitalist society is the class division into the dominant bourgeoisie and the subordinated proletariat. Being grounded on the exploitation of wage-labor by capital, class-antagonism endures as long as the capitalism itself. "The life process of the bourgeois society as class-struggle derives its origin from the material-economic process of production" (Hoffmann, 1973, p. 194). Therefore, Marxist communication studies should be focused on "the class-struggle in its concrete forms and on the role and function that communication has in it" (Cheesman & Kyhn, 1975, p. 24) or on "the question about the constitution of class consciousness" (Dröge, 1973, p. 183).

There was, however, no unanimity of what kind of entities classes are. The orthodox Marxists saw them as formations which, because of emanating from the antagonism between capital and wage-labor and having thus opposite interests, were predestined to (political) class struggle. It was typical to speak of the dominating class (= bourgeoisie) as if it were a pregiven uniform monolith. The problem was, then, how the working class might grow from a class as such (an sich) to a class for itself (für sich) in conditions where the dominating class is able, thanks to its intellectual hegemony, to present its interests as the interests of all—in other words, where its views "receive insistent publicity and come to dominate the thinking of subordinate groups" (Murdock & Golding, 1977, p. 15).

Others, for their part, saw that although the antagonism between capital and wage-labor remains as the foundation of classes, it does not produce them as ready-made political camps (Laclau, 1977; Poulantzas, 1977). They stressed that classes are not pregiven, uniform monoliths, but that, for instance, "the ruling class" is "a shifting and often precarious alliance of different social strata" (Curran, 1990, p. 142). So they replaced "the view of society as dominated by the ruling class" with "an alternative model which stresses the fissures and tensions within the dominant power bloc" (pp. 143–144). This, however, did not entail the abandonment of the basic starting point that the structures of capitalist societies are determined by the class division and class struggle.

Ideology

The Marxists used to distinguish between ruling ideology and ideologies opposing it. The ruling ideology was seen as supporting the capitalist social order and its power relations. There was, however, no unanimity as to its nature and way of acting. The orthodox Marxists spoke of it as the class ideology of bourgeoisie, as a worldview that reflects the interests of the capitalists and that is disseminated among people primarily through the mass media controlled by the bourgeoisie. This keeps the development of the proletarian class consciousness back. Those entertaining this view often called the mainstream media not mass media but class media (e.g. Cheesman & Kyhn, 1975; Dahlmüller, Hund, & Kommer, 1974; Dröge, 1972).

This view was often clothed into the so-called double function theory of the mass media. Lenin (1921/1983, p. 248) expressed it as follows: "Under capitalism, a newspaper is a capitalist enterprise, a means of enrichment, a medium of information and entertainment for the rich, and an instrument for duping and cheating the mass of working people." In this theory, the economic functions just described were supplemented with ideological ones like "duping and cheating the mass of working people." This was often seen as manipulation pure and simple (Arens, 1971; Jansen & Klönne, 1968; Zoll, 1971). In a more detailed analysis of the ideological functions, a distinction was made between the function of securing the exploitation and that of reproduction of individual working capability by offering possibilities for relaxation (Holzer, 1973, pp. 129–137).

Others subjected the double function theory to strict criticism. One of its main problems resides in its assumption that a privately owned mass medium (e.g., a newspaper) represents the interests of the bourgeois class against the working class. But how could this be so when every individual capital, "be it even in the form of newspaper production, has to take care of only itself as against all other competing capitals" (K. Pietilä, 1980, p. 34)? In fact, the newspaper capitals cannot defend "the common interest of the capitalist class, but only their own interest" of capital valorization (p. 34). Because the interests of single capitalists are often contradictory, there simply cannot be a unified bourgeois class having a uniform worldview ready to be disseminated among people.

Many of the critics were inclined to see ideology, like the Frankfurtians, as "false consciousness" that sticks in the phenomena as they appear and does not penetrate into the essential relations behind them (Geras, 1972; Larrain, 1979; Mepham, 1979; Sayer, 1979). From this perspective, ideology is not produced purposely to advance particular (class) interests but it grows up unintentionally due to the fact that the real relations of capitalist society are hidden behind the appearances. Thus, the origin of ideology "is not the subject who deceives himself, but reality which deceives him" (Godelier, 1972, p. 337). Despite its unintentionality false consciousness supports the permanence of capitalism because without a grasp of the real relations one cannot realize capitalism as an exploitative system requiring overthrowing.

This false consciousness was seen as being kept up by a mental activity that is content to reflect the existent as it appears. There is no need for a conscious ideological activity. For instance, journalism nurses false consciousness by acting exactly as it does—this is how

> it prevents, in most masterly way, the recognition of the real laws
> . . . that produce their effects beneath the surface of bourgeois
> society, prevents people's revolutionary activity and guarantees
> the prevailing social order. . . . By presenting as much as possible
> true information about itself—information that rests on percep-
> tions and is combined of them—bourgeois society conceals, in
> most masterly way, its true nature. (K. Pietilä, 1978, p. 238)

There were also attempts to outline ideology in more functional or structural terms. The most influential outline is the one by

Louis Althusser (1918–1990). He spoke of "Ideological State Apparatuses" (Althusser, 1971, pp. 141–148) stressing thereby that ideology is not, in the first place, a form of consciousness—a world-view or false consciousness—but a form of practice. He condensed his view into three theses (pp. 162, 165, 170): (a) "Ideology represents the imaginary relationship of individuals to their real conditions of existence." (b) "Ideology has a material existence." (c) "Ideology interpellates individuals as subjects." To get a hold of his thoughts, the theses should be deciphered from the last to the first one.

Althusser (p. 171) specified the third thesis by saying that "the subject is constitutive of all ideology" because "all ideology has the function (which defines it) of 'constituting' concrete individuals as subjects." Here he utilized the ambiguity of the term subject, which means

> (1) a free subjectivity, a centre of initiatives, author of and responsible for its actions; (2) a subjected being, who submits to a higher authority, and is therefore stripped of all freedom except that of freely accepting his submission. This last note gives us the meaning of this ambiguity. . . : the individual is interpellated as a (free) subject in order that he shall submit freely to the commandments of the Subject [the authority], i.e. in order that he shall make the gestures and actions of his subjection "all by himself." (p. 182)

We live from the cradle to the grave within ideology. Therefore, it is for us the air we breathe. This is the bridge to the second thesis. With it, Althusser transposed ideology from consciousness to practice: Ideology embraces specific actions, practices, rituals, and so on and the ideological state apparatuses they make up. Our participation in them feeds a self-conception "that we are indeed concrete, individual, distinguishable and (naturally) irreplaceable subjects" (pp. 172-173). Ideology interpellates us when we participate in those practices seeing us as free actors, that is, as subjects in the first but not in the second meaning of this concept.

The first thesis of ideology as people's imaginary relation to their conditions of existence refers just to this matter. The recognition of subjectivity as free is illusion because we do not become aware of the structural constraints of society that set the frameworks of our living and steer our seemingly free action. Through this very action we reproduce the structural constraints. Also, there are always, of course, "bad subjects" who recognize the structural pressures and struggle against them, but most people are "good subjects" whose relation to the (structural) conditions of their existence remains illusory and who "work all right 'all by themselves,' i.e. by ideology" (p. 181).

Althusser's theory was an important source of inspiration for even divergent Marxist accounts of mass communication. On the other hand, it was also severely attacked. Its conception of ideology was regarded as quite mechanistic, and it was seen to ascribe to ideology an irresistible force (see especially E. Thompson, 1978). Hence, it became accustomary to supplement or even replace it by Antonio Gramsci's (1891–1937) theory of hegemony. Where Althusser seemed to conceive the rule of ideology as static and total, Gramsci's concept of hegemony was interpreted to refer to a more shifting power settings, to "a process of cultural domination that was never static or total but was continually defended, challenged, reformulated, and reproduced" (Dworkin, 1997, p. 152). This view has also left it traces to divergent Marxist accounts of the media.

THE SCREEN THEORY

The Screen theory, concerning the relations between text, subject, and ideology, was developed in the 1970s by scholars gathered around the film journal Screen (see Paech, Borchers, Donnerberg, Hartweg, & Hohenberger, 1985). Instead of the mass media proper, this theory focused on film and literature, but later its ideas were applied, for instance, in the study of news (see, e.g., Kunelius, 1996; Selucky, 1984). The theory concentrated on film and literature as texts leaving the production of texts in the capitalist economic system without notice and ignoring also largely the social classes (but see Coward, 1977).

Forms of Textual Structures

The basic idea of this quite complex theory can be summarized by saying that the way a text is structured determines the way its receiver becomes structured as receiving subject. This idea is clearly indebted to Althusser (see Coward & Ellis, 1977, pp. 62-92). Regarding the forms of textual structures, Screen theorists singled out two ideal types: realist and avantgardist texts. The former type was represented especially by the 19th-century realist novel, "the classic realist text" (MacCabe, 1974, p. 7). It was analyzed in regard to its linguistic-presentational and discursive structures.

For Screen theory, the realist use of language is based on the idea of the naturalist language philosophy that the meanings of words and other signs are fixed and correspond to the reality reflecting its beings, objects, states of affairs, and so forth. In realism, "language is treated as though it stands for, is identical with, the real world. The business of realist writing is, according to its philosophy, to be the equivalent of reality, to imitate it. This imitation is the basis of realist literature" (Coward & Ellis, p. 47).

In a realist text, signs are combined according to their "reality-copying" meanings so that the world represented by the text appears to reflect the real world. Screen theorists themselves argued, in accordance to the poststructuralist conception of language, that in using language or other sign systems one produces meanings instead of simply reflecting reality (pp. 1-11). Sign systems are capable of producing meanings limitlessly, but in realism this productivity is limited, "through the establishment of certain positions of signification" (p. 44), to meanings that seemingly reflect reality.

A further thing noted by the Screen theorists was that there is, in the classic realist text, a double-leveled discourse hierarchy. The lower level consists of characters' discourses. At the higher level is the narrator's discourse. It "achieves its position of dominance" (MacCabe, p. 10) by virtue of explaining issues left open by the lower level discourses and, in so doing, making sense of them. It "wields" the various occurrences and dialogues of the text "into a coherent whole" (MacCabe, 1979, p. 23) and leads in the end to closure "at which the events of the story become fully intelligible to the reader" (Belsey, 1980, p. 70).

An avantgardist text is the antithesis of a realist one. Instead of imitating reality avantgardist texts turn "their attention to their own material, to language" (Coward & Ellis, p. 6). Employing the capacity of language and other sign systems to produce meaning limitlessly they unsettle the accustomed connections between signs and meanings that realism treats as fixed. Additionally, avantgardist texts do not contain a hierarchy of discourses: none of their discourses "can master or make sense of the others" (MacCabe, 1979, p. 14). Their events, dialogues, and so on, do not get an explanation that would bring a closure, but the text remains open.

Forms of Subject

Both types of texts construct a specific receiving subject by positioning the receivers in certain relation to the texts. A reality-imitating realist text makes receivers spectators watching reasonable events in the outside world. In this way, the text positions them "in place as the point of intelligibility of its activity" where they are "in a position of observation, understanding, synthesising" (Coward & Ellis, p. 50). Thereby, the receiver is constituted as "a homogenous subject, fixed in a relation of watching"—this unified identity "is not questioned by the flux of the text" (p. 50). Every realist text positions the receivers similarly producing them, over and over again, as united spectator-subjects.

An avantgardist text, for its part, does not construct a reasonable world to be watched. Readers cannot find in it a position that would produce them as homogenous subjects. Because the text itself does not offer coordinates for an identifiable position it is left for the readers themselves to decide how to position themselves in relation to the text. The space needed for a unified subject "is dissolved. The dissolution is a function of the dissolution of the fixed system of meanings found in classic [realist] representations. In this way, textual practice makes it felt that meaning and the subject are only produced in the discursive work of the text" (p. 6).

In other words, because of the lack of fixed meanings the receiver of an avantgardist text cannot gain an identity of a unified and homogenous subject watching reality, but this subject form is dissolved and supplanted by a form of a subject "in process" (p. 6).

Subjectivity and Ideology

Screen theorists viewed a united subject form as ideological, basing this view on Jacques Lacan's (1901–1983) psychoanalytic thoughts about language (pp. 93–121). Lacan argued that when entering into language, a child becomes split into conscious and unconscious halves. But because language covers the unconscious, the child does not recognize this splitting but misrecognizes him or herself as a united whole. Screen theorists specified this idea: What constructs this misrecognizing subjectivity is "realist" language that limits "the endless productivity of the signifying chain" by fixing certain meanings to certain signs (p. 67). This ideological subject form is produced initially through its entering into language but is reproduced over again in the reception of realist texts.

This ideological misrecognition accounts for the situation that the subject does not experience his or her unity as produced but as his or her natural property. Therefore, the influence of "realist" language remains outside awareness: What, in effect, the language defines for the subject appears to him or her to be unquestionably "the way things are." Ideology has succeeded "when it has produced this 'natural attitude,'" when "the existing relations of power are not only accepted but perceived precisely as the way things are, ought to be and will be" (p. 68). Screen theory's Marxism came in sight particularly in the view that "the social relations of capitalism" are only possible with this "'free' and consistent" subjectivity (p. 68). MacCabe (1974, p. 23) saw that this subject form was historically "tied very closely to the rise of the bourgeoisie."

An avantgardist text dissolves this bourgeois-united subject form, thereby freeing people from limits imposed on them by the realist texts. Another question is whether or not this can be considered an anti-ideological process. Kristeva (1974/1984, p. 186), who inspired Screen theory, wrote that avantgardism opens up "toward a revolutionary ideology capable of transforming the social machine." Thus, also a subject-in-process would be an ideological form. Screen theorists left this question open. They saw, however, that a crucial precondition for the overthrow of the capitalist system is the destruction of the bourgeois-united subjectivity. An avantgardist text that displaces the fixed relations of the sign and meaning therefore contains revolutionary potential.

Some Critical Points

Screen theory's conception of the relation between text and subject, in particular, was received critically by other Marxist trends. It was interpreted to represent a view "of the near total effectivity of a text . . . in the 'positioning of the subject'" (Morley, 1980a, p. 148). For critics, this view ignored the argument that readers are "already constituted in other discursive formations and social relations" (Morley, 1980b, p. 163) that have provided them with "resources against particular 'subject positions' in particular 'texts'" (Corrigan & Willis, 1980, p. 300). Critics emphasized that when entering into language the subject steps into a space criss-crossed by diverse discourses which, due to this diversity, cannot simply reproduce or dissolve a certain—that is, the bourgeois-united—subject form.

This criticism hit a point to which Screen theory had paid scant attention. However, they seem not to have thought as straightforwardly as the critics claimed. For Coward and Ellis (p. 68), for example, one can occupy "sometimes conflicting subject positions, given in a plurality of representations," even if, in the case of realist representations, this takes place within the unified subject form reproduced by realism. Personally, I see as the theory's greatest deficiency that it left the working of avantgardist texts undertheorized. To view avantgardist art without firm theoretical and empirical grounds as a counterforce to the mechanisms adjusting people to the existing conditions remains unconvincing, as it also did in the Frankfurtians' case.

THE POLITICAL ECONOMY OF COMMUNICATION

The political economy of communication is quite a wide territory containing an array of other discourses besides the Marxist discourse (see, e.g., Dyson & Humphreys, 1990; see also Picard, 1989). Here I take up only the Marxist discourse which is based on "the recognition that the mass media are first and foremost industrial and commercial organizations which produce and distribute commodities" (Murdock & Golding, 1974, pp. 205-206). Thus, the political economists urged the study of mass communication to start with a view of the media "as economic entities" (Garnham, 1979, p. 132) which take part both directly and indirectly in surplus value production and capitalist profit-making. Beginning with the "economic structure" of mass communication, the analysis should explore how "its organization and underlying dynamics shape the range and forms of media production" (Golding & Murdock 1979, p. 199). Only in this way could the media be studied adequately "as ideological agencies" (p. 198).

Mass Media as Ideological Agencies

Many Marxist analyses of the media as ideological agencies use the following statement of Marx and Engels (1846/1970, p. 64) as their starting point:

> The ideas of the ruling class are in every epoch the ruling ideas, i.e. the class which is the ruling material force of society, is at the same time its ruling intellectual force. The class which has the means of material production at its disposal, has control at the same time over the means of mental production, so that thereby, generally speaking, the ideas of those who lack the means of mental production are subject to it.

Within the Marxist political economy, this was interpreted to mean (a) that control over ideas is "in the hands of the capitalist owners of the means of production"; (b) that, due to this, views representing their interests gain wide publicity and come so to "dominate the thinking of the subordinate groups," and (c) that this "ideological domination" perpetuates "class inequalities" (Murdock & Golding, 1977, p. 15). On the basis of this, the media were regarded "as a kind of secretariat" of "ruling class interests" seeking to have them accepted as the interests of all (Hoch, 1974, p. 11).

The ideological control was seen to be exercised in multiple forms. In cases where the interests of the capitalists are directly at stake, the impact of the views of those owning or controlling the media "is likely to be immediate and direct" (Nedzynski, 1973, p. 418). Most often, however, the control is indirect. For example, the permanent threat "of losing one's job" accommodates the media workers' work to the prevailing power system (Garnham, pp. 135–136). Herman and Chomsky (1988, p. xii) condensed the view of the working of control within the media by saying that most ideological choices in them

> arise from the preselection of right-thinking people, internalized preconceptions, and the adaptation of personnel to the constraints of ownership, organization, market, and political power. Censorship is largely self-censorship, by reporters and commentators who adjust to . . . media organizational requirements, and by people at higher levels within media organizations who are chosen to implement, and have usually internalized, the constraints imposed by proprietary and other market and governmental centers of power. . . . In most cases . . . media leaders do similar things because they see the world through the same lenses, are subject to similar constraints and incentives, and thus feature stories or maintain silence together in tacit collective action.

For Murdock and Golding, many analyses of this kind derived their view of the control too directly from "the interests and motivations of the actors involved" omitting thereby the wider structural constraints (Murdock, 1982, p. 144). For Murdock and Golding, however, the way in which the ownership and control of the media influences the text production is regulated through market structures. The scrutiny of the development of the capitalist market structure in regard to media industry led the comrades to conclude (Murdock & Golding, 1977, p. 28):

The communication industries of the advanced capitalist countries are currently being shaped by two basic shifts in the corporate structure of capitalism. The first is the long-term trend
towards concentration which has led to an increasing number of
sectors being dominated by a handful of large companies. The
second is the more recent increase in diversification which has
produced conglomerates with significant stakes in several sectors
of the communications and leisure industry.

Due to this development, the major media markets "are only
effectively open to those with substantial capital" (Murdock, p. 144).
Therefore, "less and less voices survive in each media sector"
(Murdock & Golding, p. 37). The surviving voices belong largely "to
those least likely to criticize the prevailing distribution of wealth and
power," whereas those who would challenge it are unable to publicize
their "opposition because they cannot command the resources needed
for effective communication to a broad audience" (p. 37).

Furthermore, the need to secure advertising revenues in the
market competition compels the media to strive for maximizing audiences of solvent people. Also, public service media have increasingly
been forced to legitimize themselves with large audience quantities.
Under these pressures, the media tend "to avoid the unpopular and
tendentious" and to draw on what is "most familiar" (p. 37). Those
"oppositional views" not fitting easily into the prevailing frameworks
"tend to be excluded" (p. 38). Although critical of the Frankfurtians
(pp. 18–19), the comrades moved on their tracks when arguing that
the media tend to avoid risks by resorting to "formulae which are as
similar as possible to the tried and tested" (p. 39).

In Murdock's and Golding's outline, the dominating ideology
disseminated by the media consists of what remains after the views
critical of the the existing system become pushed into margins or
excluded totally. Material produced under market constraints "does
tend to support, or at least not to undermine, capitalism's central values of private property, 'free' enterprise, and profit" (Murdock, p.
143). In this way, mass communication becomes a key source of legitimation of "capitalism and of the structured inequalities in wealth
and power which it generates" (Golding & Murdock, p. 210).

Golding and Murdock (pp. 215-219) specified their view of
ideology closer when discussing how the market constraints have
shaped newswork. Under these constraints, broadcast news displays
three ideological features (p. 218). First, it concentrates on "institutions and events in which social conflict is managed" focusing the
attention thus on "consensus formation." Next, under demands of
impartiality, it draws "on the values and beliefs of the broadest con-

sensus" which do not "question existing social organization." Finally, it is incapable of portraying "social change and of displaying the operation of power in and between societies" for which reason its world is "unchanging and unchangeable."

For Murdock and Golding, then, the ideological working of the media is not a direct result of some deliberate conspiracy of the capitalist circles controlling them, but rather an indirect consequence of the capitalist market logic. Thus, they did not derive the media's ideological function directly from the interests of their owners or the bourgeoisie in general. This sets their outline positively apart from the crude reductionism that is not untypical of the Marxist political economy. On the other hand, their view of ideology remained quite narrow after all. Furthermore, they did not enter in more detail into the textual output of the media through which the ideological function was supposed to be realized (see J. Hill, 1979).

Theory of Culture Imperialism

Some of the Marxist political economists who approached the media industry more globally condensed their views into the theory of cultural imperialism (Mattelart & Mattelart, 1998, pp. 91–105). Its basic thesis was that the dissolution of colonialism had not broken up imperialism but only changed its form: The colonial rule of the world-system's periphery by the power centers had been replaced by an economic and cultural domination. For H. Schiller (1976, p. 9), the concept of cultural imperialism

> describes the sum of the processes by which a society is brought into the modern world system and how its dominating stratum is attracted, pressured, forced, and sometimes bribed into shaping social institutions to correspond to, or even promote, the values and structures of the dominating center of the system.

The cultural domination can be attained in various ways, but its "essential prerequisite" is the control of world communication system (p. 72). The world economy is dominated by transnational corporations, which in part operate in the media market (Mattelart, 1979). And because the bulk of them is in hands of U.S. capital, the world communication flow is ruled by beliefs and values incorporated into its products. This communication impregnates the periphery from outside, and also serves as a model for the periphery's own cultural production. What could be specific to it is therefore buried in a culture that becomes, as it follows "Uncle Sam," increasingly homogenous (H. Schiller, 1969, pp. 110–115). Thus, the information coming from outside to the developing countries is not the blessing for them that the theory of modernization assumed.

The theory of cultural imperialism saw the social class division being replicated in the world-system that was split into the ruling center and subordinated periphery. From this point of view, class struggle is worldwide struggle "between forces of domination and those that resist and challenge this domination" (H. Schiller, 1976, p. 70). For Schiller (pp. 68–97), one weapon in the struggle against the cultural imperialism of the U.S. and transnational corporations is the creation of national communication policies; not, however, through administrative decisions but through the vigor of the citizens.

This struggle is exemplified by the debate around the New World Information and Communication Order (NWICO) in UNESCO. Its purpose was to balance the one-sided information flow from the capitalist West to the developing countries and to help in this way the starting of a transformation in world power relations. The venture was driven into difficulties at the beginning of the 1980s as the United States, on the plea of the free flow of information, began to sabotage it. As the situation became aggravated, the United States withdrew from UNESCO and cut its payment to it (Journal of Communication, 1984; Preston, Herman, & H. Schiller, 1989; about the NWICO see Nordenstreng, 1993, 1999; Roach, 1990).

Some Critical Viewpoints

Marxist political economy has been criticized, above all, for the reduction of all things to the imperatives of the capitalist economy. On one occasion, Hall (1989, p. 50) stated sharply that it is marked by "crudity and reductionism"—its "view of the conspiratorial and class-originated source of ideology" is "woefully inadequate" and is "has no conception of the struggle for meaning." And for Grossberg (1991, p. 133), it makes "culture at best a reflection or mechanical reproduction of the social." Undeniably, there are expositions coming close to reductionism, but in its inclusiveness such a critique hits often off the mark. Consequently, Mosco (1996, p. 260) replied that the critics' "comprehension of economics and of political economy is painfully limited" and that it rejects "economic arguments on what amount to categorical grounds." Also for Garnham (1995, p. 62), the cultural scholars' criticism "is based on a profound misunderstanding of political economy."

The theory of cultural imperialism has raised much critical discussion as well. One charge is that "it overstates external determinants and undervalues the internal dynamics, not least those of resistance, within dependent countries" (Golding & Harris, 1997, p. 5). The critics have stressed that it has simply assumed—without making any empirical analyses—the manipulative effects of the Western media products in developing countries (Boyd-Barrett, 1982; Fejes, 1981). This seems to have been one motive prompting Katz and Liebes to conduct an empirical study of the reception of Dallas by people living in different cultures (see Katz & Liebes, 1985; Liebes & Katz, 1990). Their results indicated "that audiences are more active and critical, their responses more complex and reflective, and their cultural values more resistant to manipulation and 'invasion' than many critical media theorists have assumed" (J. Tomlinson, 1991, pp. 49–50).

In a way, Katz and Liebes revived the minimal effects view of the classical behavioral tradition. Therefore, their conclusions can be countered on the same grounds that were used by the critics of the minimal effects doctrine. Even if short-term empirical reception studies might problematize "the stronger versions of the cultural imperialism argument" (p. 56), they cannot say anything of the possible long-term effects of the Western mass mediated culture in non-Western parts of the globe. H. Schiller (2000, p. 119), one of the main targets of the critique, implied this when making the counterargument that the celebration of the active audience contributes "to a grotesque distortion of reality. It weakens, actually undermines, any effort to tangibly resist corporate cultural domination."

Within much of the political economy and cultural imperialism literature, the capitalist world economy has been mainly approached as it becomes empirically visible in commodity and money flows, that is, without penetrating into its essential but hidden relations—the "incalculable social mechanism"—on which the Frankfurtians put the prime weight and which also conditions the functioning of the world market. Maybe it was due to this that Schiller, for example, was not able to explain stringently the structure of domination described by him and "that his thesis of cultural imperialism remained loose" (Hellman, 1981, p. 100; see also Roach, 1997).

CRITICAL CULTURAL STUDIES

The birthplace of critical cultural studies is the Centre for Contemporary Cultural Studies established in 1964 at the University of Birmingham, England. In general terms, the Centre's research was focused on "the changing ways of life of societies and groups" and "the networks of meanings which individuals and groups use to make sense of and communicate with one another" (Hall, 1989/1992, p. 11; see also Nelson, Treichler, & Grossman, 1992). Media studies was one constituent of this transdisciplinary undertaking. It gained momentum after Stuart Hall (1932–) had become the leader of the Centre in 1969 (G. Turner, 1992, pp. 72, 77). Hall was the top name in the Centre's Media Group.

Meanings and Ideology

An apt starting point for deciphering Hall's and the Media Group's ideas is provided by the concept of meaning. Leaning on semiotics and (post)structuralism, they emphasized that the meanings of social issues are not given but produced. The issues do not have an intrinsic "meaning which is simply projected, through signs, into language" (Hall, 1977, p. 328). On the contrary, they have "to be made to mean" through "language and symbolization" (Hall, 1982, p. 67). Devoid of intrinsic meanings, the issues can be signified in different ways. Individuals and groups do indeed signify them differently striving to get their significations prevalent. This meaning struggle is significant because people act according to the meanings that define the issues: "how we act in certain situations depends on what our definitions of the situation are" (Hall, 1983, p. 77).

The Media Group focused especially on the relation between "the media and ideologies" (Hall, 1980c, p. 117) grounding its view of ideology on the idea of meanings as produced and contested. For Hall (1977, pp. 322–325; 1983), the conception of ideology as false consciousness provides a necessary starting point for a theory of ideology; yet it is problematic because it sees the social reality as being in itself divided into visible appearances and invisible real relations. Hall saw this division as resulting from an accustomed way to signify society—a way that is unable to bring the real relations into expression. But what is left in darkness by one discourse can be brought into daylight by another. In brief, society can be signified "by the use of different 'systems of representation'" (Hall, 1983, p. 77).

Instead of false consciousness Hall (1981, p. 31) referred with ideology "to those images, concepts and premises which provide the frameworks through which we represent, interpret, understand and 'make sense' of some aspects of social existence." Because these aspects can be signified from different viewpoints, the frameworks and the ideological discourses realized within them are divergent. Hall specified this characterization with three particular points:

1. Ideologies articulate "different elements into a distinctive set or chain of meanings" (p. 31). A certain term, say "freedom" or "democracy," can be articulated into different discourses. In their ideological struggle discourses often capture from one another terms that appeal to people, and articulate them in different contexts.
2. Ideological discourses are generated "unconsciously rather than by conscious intention" (p. 32). They "pre-date individuals," forming part of the social conditions "into which individuals are born" (pp. 31-32). Because one is born amidst them, he or she cannot readily see them as constructed but as grounded "in Nature itself" (p. 32).
3. Ideologies work

> by constructing for their subjects . . . positions of identification and knowledge which allow them to "utter" ideological truths as if they were their authentic authors. This is not because they emanate from our innermost, authentic and unified experience, but because we find ourselves mirrored in the positions at the centre of the discourses from which the statements we formulate "make sense". Thus the same "subjects" . . . can be differently constructed in different ideologies. (p. 32)

Hall stressed in particular that ideology is not a product of consciousness but consciousness is a product of ideological discourses. Here, as well as in some other of his points—as in the view that ideology works through constructing social identities—he followed Althusser. But he also deviated from Althusser in many respects. For instance, whereas Althusser fixed ideology firmly to the reproduction of capitalist production relations, Hall dissolved it to discourses signifying different things in different ways. And whereas Althusser did not enter particularly into the ideological struggle, Hall, leaning on Gramsci's theory of hegemony and Valentin Voloshinov's (1894–1936) theory of language, set it in central place. Referring to the latter he spoke of "the class struggle in language" (Hall, 1982, pp. 76–79) in which different groups advocate their interests by weapons of language and signification.

Ideology and Mass Media

Because the media produce frames making the world intelligible, they "are especially important sites for the production, reproduction and transformation of ideologies" (Hall 1981, p. 34). Unlike the political economists, Hall and his colleagues did not direct their main attention to the media's ownership and control relations, because, for them, the media are relatively "'free' of direct compulsion, and 'independent' of any direct attempt by the powerful to nobble them" (Hall, 1982, p. 86). Yet, despite their relative independency, the media tend to disseminate ideologies "which favour the hegemony of the powerful" (p. 86).

To explain this, the Media Group turned to the production practices of media texts. For instance, the production of news and current affairs programs—which was the group's main object of study in the 1970s (Brunsdon & Morley, 1978; Connell, 1980; Hall, 1975; Hall, Connelly, & Curti, 1981; Hall, Crichner, Jefferson, Clarke, & Roberts, 1978)—takes place under definite demands. The public service media have to operate impartially. Also, the commercial media must keep an eye on this because taking sides for one party would diminish their reliability and drive away customers belonging to other parties. Such demands open up certain possibilities, but restrict others. Hall et al. (1981, p. 115) concluded, for example, that the media are "not biased in favour of any one Party, but they are biased in favour of the Party-system as such," that is, in favor of a parliamentary-democratic system. Those who do not fit this consensus are discarded. This narrows down the spectrum of publicizable discourses.

Concerning the newswork, the group paid notice especially to the selection of topic and material, on one hand, and the encoding, the composing of the news text, on the other. For instance, in order to obtain material the reporters turn routinely to those "who know the things best," that is, to top persons of social institutions, authorities, experts, and so on. The pursuit of reliable information leads the media to offer the definitions of reality "which their 'accredited sources'—the institutional spokesmen—provide" (Hall et al., 1978, p. 58). In this way, the powerful are permitted to establish the "primary interpretation of the topic in question," and these interpretations are allowed the right of way to news (p. 58). This ensures for the media a key role in reproducing "the ruling ideologies" (p. 60).

Encoding/Decoding

The material available to the reporter is always already signified. In the encoding it is resignified, translated, for example, to a language regarded as understandable and appealing for the audience at large. As a result the encoding tends to correspond to the common sense, which refers to "prevailing schemes of interpretation" (Hall, 1972, p. 14). Consisting of "commonly-agreed, consensual wisdoms" it "helps us to classify out the world in simple but meaningful terms" (Hall, 1977, p. 325). As the news is encoded according to such common sense, it supports ideologies that consist of the "commonly agreed, consensual wisdoms" and are, by virtue of this, the most familiar and dominating ones. Ideologies deviating from the common sense become marginalized even if this is not intended.

By favoring certain ideologies, the practices of the newswork radically narrow down the scope of ideological contestation in the news. But these practices also cause other things. For example, news often signifies things by employing largely naturalized codes which, because of being widely distributed, do not appear as constructed but as "'naturally' given" (Hall, 1980b, p. 132). For instance, because visual codes "have been profoundly naturalized" (p. 132), the visuals in television news create a strong reality effect that is reinforced by the news' realist presentation mode. The reality effect, again, nourishes an image of news as a "window onto the world," thereby removing out of sight the fact that news is a product of multiple signifying activities. Hence, the ideological significations in the media begin to appear as the reality pure and simple and the ruling ideologies start to gain the status of self-evident truths.

The selection of the material and its (re)signification inscribe into the news text-specific preferred meanings that tend to harmonize with the views of those in hegemonic positions.

> The domains of "preferred meanings" have the whole social order embedded in them as a set of meanings, practices and beliefs: the everyday knowledge of social structures, of "how things work for all practical purposes in this culture," the rank order of power and interest and the structure of legitimations, limits and sanctions. (p. 134)

Preferred meanings are suggested by the text for its receiver. On the other hand, the Media Group had an "active conception of the 'audience'" (Hall, 1980c, p. 118). Audience members can decode the text in different ways that, however, relate themselves to the preferred meanings. The group distinguished three hypothetical positions from which decodings of a news text may be constructed.

The first is the dominant-hegemonic position (Hall, 1980b, p. 136), where the text is decoded according to its preferred meanings or in terms of the hegemonic code in which it has been encoded. The second position was called negotiated (p. 137). Here, the receiver decodes the text partly according to, partly deviating from, the preferred meanings. Often they are accepted as a general framework within which some deviant decodings are then made. The third position was called oppositional (p. 138). Here, the receiver identifies the preferred meanings, but decodes the text in a "contrary way" joining thereby "the struggle in discourse" (pp. 137–138). An initial horizon for specifying these positions was provided by Parkin's (1971) view of them as related to classes: the working class tends to the oppositional position, whereas the other classes are inclined to other positions (Morley, 1980a, pp. 16–21; 1983).

Some Critical Notes

The Media Group's work was not accepted without criticism. Political economists blamed it, of course, for ignoring the economic conditions imposed on the media. Golding and Murdock (1979, pp. 213-220) pointed out that even if it is right to allude to the news practices when explaining the ideological working of the news, the explanation remains half way if the market pressures shaping the practices are passed over. Among Screen theorists, Coward (1977) accused the Media Group of fixing the meanings and ideology too directly to classes, thereby omitting the specificity of signifying practices. The Media Group repaid this blame by emphasizing that Coward and other Screen theorists idealized the signifying practices as totally autonomous (Chambers et al., 1977–1978).

   The encoding/decoding model was a specific target of the critique. Among the Media Group, Morley (1980a, 1981) found in it several problems in his empirical study of decoding to which I return in chapter 16. He remarked that the preferred meaning came dangerously near to an intended one and that the model conceived, against its intentions, communication more as the transmission of meanings than as the interpretive work by an active audience. Moreover, the ideas concerning the decoding positions and their class ground turned out to be doubtful. Wren-Lewis (1983; see also Streeter, 1984, pp. 89–92) attacked similar problems. To Morley's (1981, p. 6) question of whether the preferred meaning was "a property of the text, the analyst or the audience," Wren-Lewis (p. 184) answered bluntly: "the audience." Afterwards, however, he has compromised with this view (see Lewis, 1991, pp. 61–66).

MARXISM UNDER THE FIRE OF POSITIVISM

The Marxist trends also received much critique from outside, especially from the quarters of positivist research against which they themselves raided most sharply. In certain respects, the positivist critique is closely related to that leveled against the Frankfurt School. Referring to the articles in the issue "Ferment in the Field" of the Journal of Communication (1983) Real (1984) distinguished in this critique three different lines. The following presentation follows them.

First, like the Frankfurtians, the Marxists and other critical scholars were accused of pessimism. For Blumler (1980, p. 38), they found the media to be so totally "comprised by, and locked into, the prevailing power structure that they cannot plausibly hold out any hope for the improvement from within." He described their problem as follows (pp. 35-36):

> On the one hand, there is an ideal world of social and communication relationships, in which man, if he inhabited it, could express and develop his humanity through cultural activity. But on the other hand, media institutions are so socially constrained as to be incapable of belonging in any way to that ideal domain.

According to Blumler, this starting point had a paralyzing effect on the socially relevant, policy-oriented research that the Marxists aimed at. This acid observation, however, hits the target only partly: It points to a real problem in a policy-oriented research directed against the prevailing system, but ignores, on the other hand, the fact that the Marxists did not aim at improving the media "from within" or within the system but at transforming the system itself.

Marxism was also accused of being severely biased by political commitments. For Rogers and Schement (1984, p. 161), the theory of cultural imperialism was mostly "of a polemic nature" that aimed "at political persuasion rather than a scientific testing of hypotheses." de Sola Pool (1983, p. 260) blamed the Marxists for condemning sound empirical research "as arid, naive, banal, and even reactionary and immoral." According to Wiio (1974, pp. 144–145), they consciously rejected scientific research and criticized "on political grounds" those scholars who founded their work on scientific principles.

These charges sprang forth from the positivist premise that research should be value-neutral. Those opposing the value-neutrality thesis have emphasized that even a politically uncommitted research cannot be value-neutral. Because research requires funds, it tends to serve one-sidedly those who dispose of them, on the one hand, and—as it avoids consciously taking a stand—it often takes an unconscious stand for the status quo, on the other. Consequently, the Marxists (e.g., Melody & Mansell, 1983; Mosco, 1983; Smythe & Dinh, 1983) attacked the positivist media research for serving the interests of the media industry. Therefore it is, regarding the political commitments, no better than Marxism.

Finally, the Marxists were labeled by the positivists as unscientific both logically and methodologically. de Sola Pool (1983, p. 260) ridiculed them by saying that they employed in their writings the following receipt:

> Avoid measurement, add moral commitment, and throw in some of the following words: social system, capitalism, dependency, positivism, idealism, ideology, autonomy, paradigm, commercialism, consciousness, emancipation, cooptation, critical, instrumental, technocratic, legitimation, praxiology, repressive, dialogue, hegemony, contradiction, problematic.

For him, the Marxists had simply replaced empirical research with a jingle of words. Stevenson (1983) charged that they made unwarranted generalizations and used pseudo data. Because they did not subject their theories "to rigorous and wide-ranging empirical tests," the theories were" merely polemic" (p. 269). Furthermore, they put forth such claims about reality that could not be tested (K. Lang & G. Lang, 1983) or that were illustrated with suitable examples without weighing to what extent all relevant cases spoke for or against the claims (Blumler, 1983, p. 170).

The critique has its point: The Marxists indeed largely neglected the duty of trying to prove their ideas with systematically collected empirical material. But the real message of the critique was, of course, that all sound study must fulfill the positivist criteria. Had Marxism done so, it would have avoided much of the criticism, but by doing so, it would have turned round into positivism. In all fairness it should be said that when criticizing positivism the Marxists measured it with their own criteria which positivism naturally could not fulfill. As a matter of fact, both parties created from each other a straw man all too easy to handle roughly.

15

AMERICAN INTERPRETIVE CULTURAL APPROACH

What I call the American interpretive cultural approach is a multiform set of meaning-based currents that began to gain ground in U.S. communication study in the 1970s. I speak of interpretive studies because what connects these currents is their objective to elucidate meaning—to understand "human behavior" and to "interpret its meaning" (Carey, 1977, pp. 416, 418) or "to explicate the meaning systems operating in a particular group or culture" (Lindlof & Meyer, 1987, p. 9). For Carey (p. 421), this kind of study

> views human behavior, or more accurately human action, as a text. Our task is to construct a "reading" of the text. The text itself is a sequence of symbols—speech, writing, gesture—that contain interpretations. Our task, like that of a literary critic, is to interpret the interpretations.

This way of looking at things was, however, nothing new in American social science in the 1970s. In fact, the interpretive cultural study of communication could establish itself on a long tradition to which Carey (1975, p. 10) referred when he said that in order "to get a fresh perspective on communication" one should go back to the writings of Goffman, Geertz, Duncan, Burke, Park, Dewey, and classical sociologists. This tradition, which approached society as meaning-based interaction, had also fed thinking about communication, although this thinking lingered in the margins during the behavioral tradition's period of domination.

Both interpretive cultural studies and the critical cultural studies considered above drew from this interpretive sociology, especially from symbolic interactionism (Carey, 1989, pp. 98–99; Hall, 1980a, pp. 23–24). Despite this, these two forms of cultural studies developed in divergent directions. Where the critical version approached meanings from the perspective of social power and inequality, as objects of ideological struggle, the interpretive variant regarded them as a means for creating a common, meaningful cultural world (cf. Grossberg, 1983; Hardt, 1992, pp. 173–216). Or where the former criticized the dominant form of mass communication in capitalist societies as ideological activity that fetters the tendencies for change, the latter celebrated communication as an activity through which societies, despite "all sorts of conflicts and contradictions, . . . manage to produce and reproduce themselves" (Carey, 1989, p. 110).

SYMBOLIC INTERACTIONISM AS THE BACKGROUND

Because symbolic interactionism is an important background for interpretive cultural study in communication, I begin with it, even if it did not yet represent the cultural approach, according to Denzin (1992, pp. 19, 47, 72). Nevertheless, the concept of meaning was paramount, as it considered social life as consisting of human interaction that takes place through meanings and their symbolic representations. The interacting people indicate "to others how to act" and interpret "the indications made by others"; that's why "human group life is a vast process of such defining to others what to do and of interpreting their definitions" (Blumer, 1974, p. 408). In other words, people guide their interactions or their actions in general "by defining the objects, events and situations which they encounter" (Blumer, 1956, p. 686).

To grasp what this defining means, one should realize that, for symbolic interactionism, not only words and other signs but all things from objects to actions to institutions are charged with meanings. For instance, "a 'chair' is not merely a collection of visual, aural, and tactile stimuli, but it 'means' an object on which people may sit; and if one sits on it, it will 'respond' by holding him up; and it has value for this purpose" (A. Rose, 1962, p. 5). These meanings exist culturally. Hence, to define a thing means to interpret it, a process in which people utilize their cultural capacities to unravel its meaning.

The interpretation is not always easy, however. For instance, meanings differ from one cultural community to another. Therefore, people from one community do not always understand what objects and actions within another mean. Even in the same cultural community, meanings are not necessarily common and clear to all. What objects are may be quite clear as, for example, that a chair is an object to sit on, but it is not equally easy to interpret what an action or people's behavior means. Thus, during their interactions, people often must test and rectify the conceptions they have formed of their actions and one another (see Wilson, 1970).

In any case, interpretation is, for symbolic interactionism as well as for the interpretive cultural approach, "a symbolic process whereby reality is produced, maintained, repaired and transformed." Admittedly, Carey (1975, p. 10) used this phrase to characterize communication, but, as shortly becomes clear, from the perspective of the interpretive cultural approach communication is essentially interpretation.

Remarks on the Transactionist Conception of Communication

Of the two perspectives on communication that have been entertained in communication studies—communication as transmission and as sharing—symbolic interactionism pledged itself to the latter one: As interacting people interpret situations and each other, they necessarily construct with their interpretations a shared reality. Transactionism followed this banner. For it, the partners of interaction "are not communicating meanings in the sense of simply exchanging information," but establish through their activity "a common repertoire of meanings which belong equally to both interactants" (Lincourt, 1978, p. 5).

Transactionists stressed that if the idea of interpretation as the basis of interaction is taken seriously, the view of communication as transmission does not hold good: communication does not transmit meanings but codified raw material that the receiver must interpret.

> If such codified data is to have any meaning . . . that meaning . . . will have to be attributed to it by some receiver; and that receiver, given his peculiar intellectual and culturally-derived competencies for doing so, must be de facto creator of whatever meaning . . . a message has for him. (Thayer, 1979, p. 57)

The idea is that "the 'message' the reader or listener 'gets' is not in the medium or in what is presented, but is in the receiver" (p. 56). "Meanings are found in people, not in words" (Berlo, 1960, p. 214; cf. R. Budd & Ruben, 1979, pp. 96–98). Thus, the basic transactionist tenet is that as people orient themselves to messages and to their environment in general, they look at them as meaningful signs—but what these things mean to them depends on their own, albeit culturally conditioned, reservoir of meanings.

Furthermore, if communication amounts to interpretation, then every act of interpretation is an act of communication. Thayer (1962, cited in Wiio, 1981, p. 39) said that "in its broadest perspective, communication occurs whenever an individual assigns significance or meaning to an internal or external stimulus." And as people do this all the time, all things in their environment are messages whether or not intended to be so. Consequently, "there is nothing in human or social life which does not involve communication" (Thayer, 1974, p. 1). For this conception, communication is a much wider phenomenon than it is for the usual view that confines it to the transmission of messages from the sender to the receiver.

Barnlund (1970) condensed these views into specific communication models. An intraindividual model, for example, depicts a person's communication with him or herself on the basis of cues coming from the environment. In Barnlund's example, Mr. A sits alone in the waiting room of a clinic waiting to see his doctor. There are several cues activating his communication with himself. For instance, the antiseptic odor in the room is a cue "which reinforces his confidence in the doctor's ability to diagnose his illness" (p. 98). Or the chair on which he sits cues him to think how nice it feels to sit "after a long day on his feet" (p. 98). As can be seen, communication with surrounding things includes not only their perception but involves also the moods and thoughts the perceptions give rise to.

Views of this kind have led the transactionists to emphasize that the concepts of mass communication and mass media, often used synonymously, should be kept apart because otherwise one supports the view that only the communication through mass media is mass communication (R. Budd & Ruben 1979, pp. 9-12). Supplementing these transactionist views we can state that there is conscious as well as unconscious communication and that one cannot avoid communicating even if he or she wishes to do so (Watzlawick, Beavin, & Jackson, 1967). The latter point means simply that "activity or inactivity, words or silence all have message value: they influence others and these others, in turn, cannot not respond to these communications and are thus themselves communicating" (p. 49).

The view of communication as interpretation was but one of the transactionists' theoretical ingredients. Among them, members of the so-called Palo Alto group, in particular, put together many kinds of theoretical ideas ranging from psychoanalysis to theories of signification and culture to general systems theory and cybernetics (see Mattelart & Mattelart, 1998, pp. 50–55; Rogers, 1994, pp. 87–101). However, because the thinking and research of the transactionists was focused predominantly on personal communication—the work of the Palo Alto group particularly on its pathologies and their therapy (Wilder, 1979)—I do not delve into this theoretical field any deeper.

MASS COMMUNICATION AS RITUAL: JAMES CAREY

Carey (1975, 1977), the leading figure of American cultural studies in communication, also started with the distinction between the views of communication as transmission and as sharing—or as ritual, as he called it. The former view arose "at the onset of the age of exploration and discovery" (Carey, 1975, p. 3). Since then, communication referred, for a long time, to the net of transportation consisting of roads, canals, post, and so on. Only the discovery of telegraph, at the latter part of the 19th century, put an end to this identity even if "it did not destroy the metaphor" (p. 3). For Carey, the transmission model is the dominant way of conceiving communication.

Whereas the transmission model sees communication as an "extension of messages across geography for the purpose of control," the ritual view—an older view that the transmission model has pushed aside—looks at it as a means for drawing "persons together in fellowship and commonality" (p. 6). This view, based on "the ancient identity and common roots of the terms commonness, communion, and communication" (p. 6), conceives of communication "as a process through which a shared culture is created, modified, and transformed" (Carey, 1977, p. 412). "It does not see the original or highest-manifestation of communication in the transmission of intelligent information but in the construction and maintenance of an ordered, meaningful cultural world which can serve as a control and container of human action" (Carey, 1975, p. 6).

As to mass communication, Carey paid particular attention to the newspaper and news journalism, stressing that the above models open quite divergent perspectives. The transmission model sees newspaper "as an instrument for disseminating news and knowledge . . . in larger and larger packages over great distances," whereas the ritual model views "reading a newspaper less as sending or gaining information and more like attending a mass: a situation in which nothing new is learned but in which a particular view of the world is portrayed and confirmed" (pp. 7-8). However, despite their differences

> neither of these counterposed views of communication necessarily denies what the other affirms. A ritual view does not exclude the processes of information transmission and attitude change. It merely contends that one cannot understand these processes aright except insofar as they are cast within an essentially ritualistic view of communication and social order. (p. 9)

It is, however, not enough only to consider how these views represent journalism or communication in general. They are not only representations of but also for communication (pp. 18-19). For example, an "obsessive commitment" to the transmission view has prompted the means of communication to develop into "a network of power, administration, decision, and control" (p. 20). The development of journalism along these lines has contributed to the eclipse of the public, to knit this with the Deweyan problematics so dear to Carey: "private reading and the reading audience [have] replaced the reading public and the public of discussion and argument" (Carey, 1989, p. 166). An audience consists of detached individuals silently receiving information mediated from above (see Carey, 1987).

Carey (1975, p. 21) urged, therefore, that the emphasis should be put on the ritual view that could help us "to rebuild a model of and for communication of some restorative value in reshaping our common culture." With regard to journalism, this would require it "to be conceived less on the model of information and more on the model of conversation" (Carey, 1987, p. 14). Journalism should not disperse people into an audience but bring them together and so doing "reconstitute the public" (p. 14) that once was alive. In his mind, the public will begin to reawaken when people "are addressed as a conversational partner and are encouraged to join the talk rather than sit passively as spectators before a discussion conducted by journalists and experts" (p. 14).

ON THE PHENOMENOLOGICAL STUDY OF NEWS

In the 1970s, modern newswork was often studied in terms of interpretive sociology or phenomenological thinking (Altheide, 1977; Epstein, 1974; Fishman, 1980; Gans, 1980; Golding & Elliott, 1979;

Roshco, 1975; Schlesinger, 1978; Tuchman, 1978). Within this study, news was approached not as information reflecting reality, like before; but rather, in Careyan terms, as an artifact that signifies reality and in so doing constructs it. Because news as an artifact is determined by journalistic practices, the focus of the study was on these practices. This emphasis was characteristic of critical cultural studies, too, but although it examined the practices on the basis of finished news, the phenomenologists studied them by participant observation—by observing, according to the canons of symbolic interactionism, "what goes on in social life under one's nose" (Blumer, 1969/1986, p. 50).

For Tuchman (1978, p. 183), "traditional view of news" implied that the newswork is guided by norms, defined by society, which point out for the journalists what is interesting or important. As they cover these issues, "news reflects society" by mirroring "its concerns and interests" (p. 183). Tuchman rejected this view to the benefit of an "interpretive approach to news" for which the norms guiding the newswork are not defined by society but arise in the work itself (p. 183). Therefore, news does not reflect society but constructs it. In other words, "in the process of describing an event, news defines and shapes that event" (p. 184).

Under the influence of Alfred Schutz's phenomenological sociology, Tuchman approached various aspects of news practice, conceiving them as means for getting along with external demands and the pressures inherent in the work. For example, the news events themselves cause stress, because they are "idiosyncratic" and cannot be dealt with in all their diversity (p. 45). To get out of this and other corresponding problems journalists need routine methods without which "news organizations, as rational enterprises, would flounder and fail" (Tuchman, 1973, p. 111).

Tuchman (1978, p. 50) referred here to Schutz, according to whom we "routinize the world in which we live" by typifying it, by combining idiosyncratic issues into particular issue types. Tuchman (1973, 1978, pp. 45–63) observed that journalists routinized their tasks by handling unique but nevertheless sufficiently similar events and issues as cases representing suitable news types—hard or soft news, for example. Such typifications, developed within the work, were so self-evident that journalists had great difficulties defining them formally. Their meanings come "from the settings in which they are used and the occasions that prompt their use" (Tuchman, 1973, p. 117). They construct and reconstruct social reality "by establishing a context in which social phenomena are perceived and defined" (p. 129).

News should be objective—all that it tells should be true. This not being the case, a news organization may not only lose its trustworthiness but may also suffer economically. In contrast, the busy rhythm of the work seldom enables journalists to check that all details included in their stories really are correct. This contradiction between the demand of objectivity and the pressure of work is resolved by utilizing specific routines to deflect potential criticism of nonobjectivity. In her studies, Tuchman (1972, p. 660) concluded "that 'objectivity' may be seen as a strategic ritual protecting newspapermen from the risks of their trade."

Let there be a source who has told the reporter that a certain issue is so and so. The reporter, however, has no time to check whether or not this claim holds true. But what is certainly true is that the source said so. "Newspapermen regard the statement 'X said A' as a 'fact,' even if 'A' is false." (p. 665) By using quotation marks, the reporter can ascribe the statement to the source and escape charges of nonobjectivity if it proves to be nonsense (pp. 668–669). Further, if the reporter finds another source who describes the issue differently, he or she can tell both views and claim objectivity because of having "presented 'both sides of the story' without favouring either man" (p. 665). With this kind of "objectivity rituals," journalists weave a web of facticity in their stories (Tuchman, 1978, pp. 82–103).

For Tuchman (1973, pp. 129–130), such procedures do not distort social reality because it is not given but constructed in different presentations: Hence, "the concept of 'distortion' is alien to the discussion of socially constructed realities." Altheide (1977)—a phenomenologist who observed television newswork—disagreed. For him, the news routines do distort events. The events are always imbued with "human intentions, interpretations, and meanings" (p. 17). It is these meanings that are distorted in the newswork, because, "for news purposes," the events are taken out of their "familiar circumstances and surroundings and meanings" and embedded "in a foreign situation—a news report" (pp. 24–25).

Altheide considered news reports as stories for which material from reality is selected and worked up to fit the chosen angle and storyline. Stuff that is unfit for this is not readily selected even if it were highly relevant (pp. 97–124). The U.S. television newswork followed in the 1960s a rule "that only the portions of film that fulfill the agreed-upon story should be used" (Epstein, 1974, p. 177). Furthermore, whatever the events meant before their selection to the news report, within it their meanings depend on how they are built in the storyline and may thus be "fundamentally altered in order to tell a story" (Altheide, 1977, p. 154). In order to avoid this bias, journalists should understand that social phenomena are constituted "by cultural and social meanings" and "cannot be divorced from the interpretive processes that create them" (p. 178).

EVALUATING THE INTERPRETIVE CULTURAL APPROACH

The common root of the currents reckoned among the interpretive cultural approach is the attempt to understand "social worlds from the perspectives of the social actors who inhabit them" (Carragee, 1990, p. 83). What is emphasized in particular is that even if human activity is conditioned by pregiven circumstances, it is not predetermined but depends on how the actors interpret the circumstances and define their situations. Taking the actors' point of view into account does not mean, however, that the study would merely reproduce their conceptions. The routines and rituals being examined are, paradoxically, too self-evident to be noticed. Thus, interpretive cultural studies undertook to clear up something

> what we already know about the ordinary, taken-for-granted experiences of daily life. But, because these experiences are daily rituals, we are not accustomed to "thinking" about what we do and why. We just seem "to do it." Such experiences are thus hidden from us and are only rarely illuminated, and then only when examined in some considerable detail. (Lindlof & Meyer, 1987, p. 25)

In contrast, the concentration on the interpretations of actions and situations has left the institutional and power structures shaping the actions and situations lingering in shadows (Carragee, pp. 87, 90; see Hardt, 1992, pp. 202–203). Surely, both Tuchman and Altheide noticed how external demands and work pressures guide the newswork, but the question of what forces shape these constraining circumstances and how was not paid particular attention to by them. Therefore, Altheide's news criticism remained incomplete because he ignored the larger organizational and power structures within which the practice, criticized by him, has been developed and which reproduce it the way it is.

A similar shortcoming troubles the transactionist theory of meaning, too. It is, of course, wholly legitimate to emphasize that it is, in the end, the individual itself who gives meaning to surrounding things. But the idea that meanings reside in individuals—implying, for instance, that the texts are devoid of meanings—is one-sided. Although the message one takes from a text depends on the individual's interpretation, this interpretation, for its part, depends on the possibilities opened by the text and on the socially developed, generic reading conventions that confine the scope of interpretations. The idea that meanings reside in individuals thus omits "the properties and structures of media messages, . . . the symbolic power of texts" (Carragee, p. 89).

16

CULTURAL STUDIES IN PRACTICE

Despite the theoretical divergences between the critical and the American interpretive variants of cultural studies, the logic of its empirical work has not been so different. Research has preferred interpretive-qualitative to statistical-quantitative methods drawing its inspiration more from the humanist disciplines than from the behavioral social sciences (cf. Lewis, 1997). As observed previously, the speciality of the 1970s was the interpretive study of media production practices. As the 1980s were drawing to a close, the interpretive study of media texts began to attract more attention and, later on, the focus has been on the question what the media texts mean in the life of the audience and how the receivers interpret them.

In the cultural studies of communication of the 1970s, there were differing views as to where the meanings were to be found. The critical cultural studies with its view of preferred meanings, found them in texts admitting, however, that they might be interpreted differently. Among the American interpretive cultural studies, the transactionists, again, argued that meanings reside on the receivers' side. This dilemma was resolved in the 1980s research with the view that meanings reside neither in texts nor in receivers but are generated in the encounter of texts and receivers. I begin the journey into the empirical work of cultural studies by elucidating this solution a bit closer.

MEANINGS AS PRODUCED IN THE ENCOUNTER
OF TEXTS AND RECEIVERS

Semiotics, especially in its Saussurean guise, was an important source of inspiration for cultural studies in communication (see Fiske, 1982). Especially important was his analysis of the sign into signifier, its physical form of existence, and signified, the mental concept to which it refers (Saussure, 1916/1974). According to Barthes (1964/1983, pp. 41–44), signifieds are connected to signifiers through meanings.

A writer composing a text has in his or her mind conceptual thoughts that he or she wishes to communicate. In order to do so, the writer articulates signifiers in a way that the result would correspond via the signifieds to the intended thoughts. Thereby, the writer charges the text with meanings in the sense of signifier/signified relations. Yet, the actual text may always deviate from the intended one. Even if the writer believes this is not the case, it may be that the articulations of signifiers do not express all the intended meanings and/or that they express meanings that were not intended.

In any case, from the writer's perspective the meanings are in the text, but not so from the point of view of the receiver. The text meets with the receiver always as an articulation of signifiers, and it is left to him or her to generate the meanings the text will have for him or her. These meanings depend on the meaning potential offered by the text, on the one hand, and on the receiver's cultural competencies of interpretation, on the other, but, on these conditions, they are produced in the encounter situation. For Fiske (1982, p. 49), the term negotiation describes this best by implying "the to-and-fro, the give-and-take between man and message." The resulting received text may differ even greatly from the actual, let alone the intended one.

The encounter has its specific contexts. The broadest of them is culture. It must be shared by the text and the receiver to such an extent that the receiver can, on the whole, generate any meanings. A narrower context is genre that mediates between the production and reception (Ridell, 1994). It tends to reduce the scope of possible interpretations by indicating what interpretation codes best suit this or that kind of texts. Another context is intertextuality, denoting the hints that a text makes at other texts, genres, and so on (Bennett & Woollacott, 1987, pp. 44–92; Fiske, 1987, pp. 108–127). Intertextuality tends to broaden the scope of possible interpretations by activating different interpretation codes. The encounter has also its everyday contexts, such as in whose company, in which mood, and so on, the text is met. All these contexts have their effect on the production of meaning.

INTERPRETING MEDIA TEXTS

The interpretive study of mass media texts is one step in the process that, from the 1970s on, dissolved the wall separating "high" and "low" culture more thoroughly. Many began to view products of popular culture as texts that are complex in their own ways, therefore deserving to be deciphered by interpretive analyses. Earlier, only products of high culture had been seen worthy of such analyses, but now the scope of study was enlargened to even jeans, shopping malls, and beach life as "texts" (Fiske, 1991a, pp. 13–76; 1991b, pp. 1–21). The prime attention, of course, was paid to mass media texts, especially to advertisements and to diverse television programs.

The intent of this research was to find out how the texts signified what they represented, what meanings the analyst could thereby produce of them, and what this would tell about the texts' cultural character and their possible significance in regard to wider social issues. It was thought that by employing sophisticated interpretive methods, based on linguistics, semiotics, or hermeneutics, and adequate theoretical insights the analyst could produce from the texts' meaning potential interpretations capable of answering socially relevant questions. Quite soon, however, this approach had to make room for another one, more interested in what the audience sees in the texts.

News Language and Ideology

As the first example of the interpretive text analysis, I describe the critical linguists' work as it is represented in the East Anglia group's linguistic-discursive analyses of the news in the late 1970s (Fowler, Kress, Trew, & Hodge, 1979; Kress & Trew, 1978; Kress, 1983; Kress & Hodge, 1979). The East Anglians did not represent the Birmingham critical cultural studies, but they shared the Media Group's interest in the relation between the media and ideology. For them, language was not to be studied as detached from society but explicitly as a social and ideological phenomenon. With ideology, they meant ideas "organized from a particular point of view" (Kress & Hodge, 1979, p. 6). Language is ideological if "it involves systematic distortion in the service of class interest" (p. 6).

The East Anglians focused their news analyses on the news language and its micro-structure. For a tool of analysis they developed a language model where the propositional sentences were divided into actionals representing actions and processes ("the batsman struck the ball") and relationals representing relations ("Bill has courage," pp. 7–10, 120). Well-formed actionals should be transactive that identify the actor ("the batsman"), the action ("struck") and the affected ("the ball"). In journalism, however, the transactive sentences are often replaced by, or transformed into, nontransactive ones where the actor ("the ball was struck"), the affected ("the batsman struck") or both ("strike") are deleted. For the East Anglia group, such transformations have a crucial place in linguistic-ideological activity.

Of the transformations the passive and the nominalization forms were seen as particularly important (pp. 15–28). There is first the passive inversion of actor and affected as, for instance, the transformation of the sentence "The opposition accused the government" into "The government was accused by the opposition." Even if the causality remains clear, the focus in shifted from the actor ("the opposition") on the affected ("the government"). A more drastic passive form is "The government was accused" where the information of the causal actor is deleted. The most drastic form of transformation is nominalization as, for instance, the transformation of the sentence "The workers picket a factory" into the noun "picketing," which contains no information of the actor and the affected. Consequently,

> although we know that there was an actor and an affected, the specific identities of both have been lost. . . . Second, in the resulting surface form the only thing that meets us is the verbal version of the action which was performed, and in this way our attention is directed to what is present and directed away from what is no longer there. (p. 21)

Nominalization has additional effects, too. Verbs tend to express actions and processes that, with the aid of verbs' tense, can be placed in time with some precision. Nouns, again, "tend to be about objects, abstract notions, and concepts" with no reference to time (p. 21). Therefore, the change of verbs into nouns tends to create a timeless world of "thinglike abstract beings or objects, which are capable of acting or being acted on" ("Picketing curtailed coal production") (pp. 23, 27). Nominalizations impose this abstract world on the real material world so that we no longer see "physical events" (p. 23).

With these kind of tools, the group analyzed, for instance, how two British newspapers changed their reporting of an incident that took place on June 1, 1975 in then Salisbury, Rhodesia (Fowler et al., 1979, pp. 94–116). There, police fired into a crowd of unarmed people killing five and, after people's angry reaction, six more. In the reporting, the incident was first transformed into passive form ("Africans were shot dead by police") and then into agentless passive form ("Africans were shot dead"). Next the cause of the deaths was deleted ("Africans were killed") and, finally, only the result was left over ("loss of life"). This was then connected with the angry reaction ("rioting and . . . sad loss of life") as if the "riot" was the cause of the deaths. This transformation process was interpreted to be in accordance with the ideology of the white minority ruling Zimbabwe at that time. A part of it was

> that "Africans" have to earn freedom by behaving like whites. To maintain this view it is necessary to ignore the real nature of the conflict. . . . This requires the suppression of the fact that the white regimes apply violence and intimidation, and suppression of the nature of exploitation this makes possible. It requires that the regimes and their agents be put constantly in the role of promoters of progress, law and order, concerned to eliminate social evil and conflict, but never responsible for it, and only killing unarmed people when forced to do so by those people themselves. (p. 106)

The East Anglians paid notice also to the use of nouns as classification devices—"rioters" instead of "demonstrators" or "terrorists" instead of "freedom fighters"—and to the role of modal auxiliaries in the ideological language use. This kind of a micro-analysis can indeed shed light on ideological processes even if it would be too far-fetched to interpret, for instance, all transformations to serve ideologically class interests.

On the other hand, the group's work was troubled with certain shortcomings. In want of an articulated theory of journalism, the ideological significance of particular micro-structures tended at times to be overstated. Perhaps a closer view into the discursive character and generic preconditions of journalism would have prevented this. It must also be asked whether or not structures interpreted by the group as ideological had ideological effects in reality. For instance, even if, in the reporting of the Rhodesia incident, the causal agency was with time deleted, the readers could easily recall it. As the old wisdom says, one cannot conclude effects from the analysis of the texts alone.

In any case, this early work of critical linguists gave much impetus to the subsequent interpretive analyses of verbal and visual texts within traditions that were later named social semiotics and critical discourse analysis (see Bell, 1991; Fairclough, 1989, 1992, 1995; Fowler, 1991; Hodge & Kress, 1988; Kress & van Leeuwen, 1996; van Dijk, 1988, 1991).

Advertising and Ideology

Williamson's (1978/1985) analyses of advertisements show certain affinities with both Screen theory and critical cultural studies. Her aim was to formulate a theory of ideology in advertising. She started her interpretive work with a view that, in order to promote its sale, a product must be signified in a way that makes it "mean something to us" (p. 12). By signifying products in certain ways, the ads produce meanings. What ads mean can only be grasped "by finding out how they mean, and analyzing the way in which they work" (p. 17). The analytic tools are provided by semiotics.

Williamson (pp. 18–19) illuminated this by interpreting an ad for tires. The ad depicted, from a bird's eye view, a car on a jetty. It was told that the car, which with its Supersteels had already done 36,000 miles, performed excellently in a braking test arranged on the jetty. The ad's verbal message is imbued with technical-numerical details indicating that "Goodyear tyres [sic] are safe and durable" (p. 18). This is reinforced by the choice of a jetty as the test place: If one could not already beforehand trust in Supersteels, the test would not have been arranged on a jetty because should the tires give way the car would dash into the sea. This charges the ad with feelings of risk and danger.

In addition to these quite apparent meanings, Williamson also found a more connotative one opposing risk and danger. Its main signifiers are the outside of the jetty, resembling that "of a tyre [sic]," and the curve of its shape: "the whole jetty is one big tyre [sic]" (p. 18). Moreover, there are some tires attached to the right side of the jetty. Because of these visual correspondences the properties of the jetty—its strength and capacity to withstand water and erosion without wearing down—are transposed to properties of the tire. Williamson noted further that the jetty encloses the car, protecting it against outer dangers. This strengthens the message that Supersteels guarantee the safety of cars.

The process of transference where a sign system (the jetty) becomes the signifier of another (the tire) or where its meaning is transposed to the other was specified by Williamson (p. 19) as follows. (a) The process is not realized by an open narrative but silently through the composition of the signifiers in the picture. (b) Because the transposition is not stated expressis verbis, the receiver must complete, with the aid of the visual cues in the composition, the juxtapositions that the transference requires. (c) The sign system whose meaning is to be transferred must have a significance (jetty's strength, durability, etc.) that fits the sign system at which it is targeted (the tire).

What Williamson ignored, in this as well as in her other analyses, is that a text often allows one to produce conflicting but equally well-grounded meanings. Of course, the ads aim at constructing a preferred meaning that affirms the advertised product, but this does not eliminate the possibility of other meanings. For instance, if the jetty in the above ad is "one big tire," it is a very deformed one. Hence, at the same time as the jetty transfers to the tire meanings of strength, durability, and so on, it transposes to it also a (joking) meaning of deformity. Moreover, the placement of the car on the jetty gives rise to connotations of the dangers of motoring regardless of what tires the car happens to have.

On the basis of Althusser's and Lacan's theories, Williamson thought that ads construct the consumers as ideological subjects by taking a position as signifiers that have the consumers as their signifieds. For instance, in a Chanel ad, Catherine Deneuve, the French film star, looks right at the consumer. In the righthand corner is the product, a perfume bottle (p. 25). For Williamson (p. 44), the ad interpellates the consumer as subject by crying out—as ideology according to Althusser (1971, pp. 170–177) does—"Hey you, you know what Catherine Deneuve means, don't you? Well, this product means the same." There are two sign processes involved. First, Deneuve becomes the signifier of the perfume: It is as elegant and chic as she. But because it is the (female) consumer who purchases the perfume, Deneuve becomes, via the perfume, the consumer's signifier.

By employing Lacan's theory of the so-called mirror phase, Williamson concluded that in this signifier/signified relationship Deneuve is a mirror image that represents the consumer's ego-ideal to which she identifies herself (pp. 61–67). Deneuve offers the consumer an image of herself that she "may aspire to," but she knows, of course, that her desire for that "Ego-Ideal can never be fulfilled" (pp. 64, 63). The consumer has, however, the perfume available to which the elegance of Deneuve has been transferred. By using it, she can appease her desire but the desire remains there as ultimately unfulfilled. In this way, the consumer becomes an ideological subject yoked in an endless pursuit of something that can never be caught up.

By becoming, through this complex identification process, a user subject of the advertised perfume, the consumer joins the Deneuve/Chanel clan and distinguishes herself from clans whose ideological subjects identify themselves with other figures by using other perfume brands. "We differentiate ourselves from other people by what we buy. In this process we become identified with the product that differentiates us; and this is a kind of totemism" (p. 46). Similar to how a clan constitutes its identity with the aid of a totem, a product is the corresponding totem to its consumers. The division of society into different clans through different consumption totems obscures real, class-based distinctions between people. For Williamson, this is the core point in the ideological working of advertising.

STUDYING MEDIA AUDIENCES

Audience research within the cultural studies of communication has often been called media or audience ethnography. For instance, Drotner (1994, p. 87) said that

> media ethnography is borne by the interest in qualitative media studies that emerged as a distinctive trend from the late 1970s on. This research interest both marks an epistemological turn towards the mediated meaning-making of audiences and a methodological turn towards qualitative methods of empirical investigation, notably in-depth interviews.

Also for Moores (1993, p. 3), the study of media consumption underwent an "ethnographic turn" in the late 1970s (see also Ang, 1989; Bird, 1982; Morley & Silverstone, 1991; Schröder; 1994). The aptness of this name has, however, been discussed. Ethnography refers to the study of cultures where the researcher lives among its members attempting, through participant observation, to understand their customs from their viewpoint (Moores, pp. 3–5). The talk of ethnography within cultural media studies has been criticized because the audience studies fulfill the requirements of a genuine ethnographic approach, at most, only to some extent (Evans, 1990; Nightingale, 1989).

Studies aiming at finding out how audiences interpret media texts usually fulfill only the requirement that the media output is looked at from the audiences' viewpoint. Participant-observation has rarely been applied in them. In contrast, studies analyzing the role of the media in people's everyday lives have often also fulfilled the criterium of participant-observation even if it has usually remained ephemeral and superficial. Consequently, Hagen and Wasko (2000, pp. 8–9) made a distinction between reception research, with its emphasis "on the process on interpretation," and ethnographic audience research, which "is more focused on media use as practice." This distinction makes the discussion analytically clearer.

The "Nationwide" Audience

Morley's (1980a) study of audience decodings of the BBC's late current affairs program Nationwide is a classic among media reception studies. Morley conducted the study as a member of the Birmingham Media Group. To test Hall's idea of the text's preferred meaning and of the three decoding positions related to it Morley (p. 26) chose such respondent groups "who might be expected to vary from 'dominant' through 'negotiated' to 'oppositional' frameworks of decoding." He assumed that different sociodemographic conditions, especially the position "in the class structure," foster specific "decoding strategies and competences," and that the actual decoding of a text takes place in the framework of the strategies one has at his or her disposal (pp. 15, 18).

The social spectrum of the respondent groups ranged from shop stewards, trade union officials, and apprentices to school children and students, to management trainees and managers from printing and banking institutions (pp. 37–38). Decodings were studied on the basis of group discussions. Morley wanted to discover "how interpretations were collectively constructed" in groups "rather than to treat individuals as the autonomous repositories of a fixed set on individual 'opinions' isolated from their social context" (p. 33). For Morley, the method succeeded because the decodings within groups varied less than between them. The inner-homogeneity in groups, however, may also be due to the pressure to conformity in group situations (Höijer, 1990, p. 34).

Before discussions, Morley showed some groups one and other groups another Nationwide program. The content of one program had been analyzed beforehand (Brunsdon & Morley, 1978) so that Morley had a point of comparison for the group decodings. He opened the discussions with general questions moving then gradually to "questions about the programme material based on earlier analysis of it" (Morley, p. 33).

The taped discussions as his material, Morley examined (a) the vocabulary and speech forms "through which interpretations are constructed," (b) "the patterns of argumentation and the manner of referring to evidence or of formulating viewpoints," and (c) "the underlying cognitive or ideological premises which structure the argument and its logic" (p. 34). He presented his results group by group by picking out from each group's speech fragments that reflected the specificities of its ways of decoding. The presentation was not based on the tripartition just described. Neither did Morley compare the speech systematically with the textual features of the programs.

The results indicated that in certain cases the decodings clearly depended on the class background. The middle-class managers tended to interpret the program according to its preferred meanings (although criticizing its mode of presentation), whereas the working-class shop stewards tended to take an oppositional position. In other cases, the influence of class background was lessened by discursive strategies alien to it. For instance, trade union officials interpreted the program from a negotiated position in the spirit of the Labour Party's right wing. Regardless of their working-class background, the apprentices interpreted it according to its preferred, especially populist meanings. For Morley (1983, p. 113), this seemed

> to be accounted for by the extent to which the lads' use of a form of populist discourse ("damn all politicians—they're as bad as each other . . . it's all down to the individual in the end, isn't it?") was quite compatible with that of the programme. Although the dominant tone of these groups' responses to Nationwide was one of cynicism, a resistance to anyone "putting one over" on them, most of the main items in the programme were, in fact, decoded by these groups within the dominant framework or preferred reading established by the programme.

The groups of Black students deviated from others by turning off the program as alien to them. They simply refused "to 'read' it at all" (p. 115). Hall's decoding positions do not offer a place for a "decoding" of this kind. Morley (1980, pp. 137–138) placed it into the oppositional position although he admitted that in so far as the Black students made any sense at all of the program, their decodings came at times "close to accepting the programme's own definitions" (p. 142). Afterward Morley (1986, p. 45) emphasized that before entering into the actual decodings of a text one should ascertain how relevant and comprehensible it is to those whose decodings are to be studied.

In addition to the theoretical shortcomings of the encoding/decoding model, which were discussed in chapter 14, the Nationwide project was troubled with some technical problems. Morley (1980a, p. 27) referred to them when regretting that the data had to be collected "in an educational or work context" instead of the "context of the family and home" where television is normally watched. In order to avoid this kind of problem Morley (1986, 1992) subsequently proceeded to study the use of television in family settings and the relevance of its output to different family members. He approached this from the point of view of the family's gendered power relations and the "politics of the living room." As a result, the study of audience decodings has been left aside in his work.

It has been claimed that in the Nationwide study "the encoding/decoding model starts to break down" (G. Turner, 1992, p. 136). According to Turner, Morley had to concede in particular that the basic assumption of a correlation between decodings and social position is untenable (p. 135). Also for Fiske (1987, p. 63), the study proved that the model "had overemphasized the role of class in producing different readings and had underestimated the variety of determinants of reading." Morley (1992, pp. 10–12) turned off such claims by stressing, on the one hand, that the model did not link the decodings directly to classes but to decoding strategies and to classes only in so far as the strategies were class specific and, on the other, that the decodings patterned, after all, quite significantly according to class positions.

Talk About News

Unlike Morley and some others (e.g. Lewis, 1985, 1991, pp. 123–157; Höijer, 1995; Jensen, 1988), Dahlgren (1988) did not study how receivers interpret particular items shown them, but how people talk and make sense of TV news in various situations. Dahlgren represented primarily the phenomenological approach. In his earlier studies he had observed that in usual decoding research settings, where people know that they are studied, they tend to speak in particular ways that have "some kind of unifying quality" determined by the situation (p. 292). In order to study this phenomenon closer, Dahlgren began to apply "more unobtrusive methods."

> I would merely make notes to myself of conversations and chats that I would have with people in a variety of settings: social gatherings like dinners and parties, on buses, trains and in stations, with neighbours, etc. I would try to steer the talk to TV news, but in a "natural" way and without adopting the role of a researcher. I was not always successful and the interactions in which I did manage to elicit talk about TV news are far from representative. But they sufficed for me to develop a preliminary typology of talk about TV news. (p. 293)

Dahlgren observed that the talk divided into official and personal forms. The former was typical in situations that "had a 'public' quality about them" (p. 293). The speakers took a role of "a citizen engaged in a form of public dialogue": the talk had "an intensity and earnestness which is not matched by, say, the general lax quality of TV news viewing" (pp. 294, 293). This talk had different forms. Incorporated discourse is "the fundamental discourse of the dutiful citizen" that takes the TV news "on its own terms: as a (for the most part) actual rendering of reality" (p. 294). Alternative decoding presents an "interpretation of society significantly at variance with the dominant view conveyed in the news" (p. 294). Media awareness "demonstrates awareness of televisual production elements"; news is seen as being "engaged in 'impression management'" (pp. 294–295).

Personal talk was prominent in situations where the speakers felt that a public role was not required. There was "a sense of 'well, now that we are alone, let me tell you what I really think. . .'" (p. 295). Also, this talk divided into the following subforms: Personal association links the news "to one's own realm of experience": the news "becomes merely an occasion for private talk"—for instance: "'Oh, I have an uncle who lives in that town. . .' (where the news story takes place)" (p. 295). Practicality "underscores the relevance of TV news for everyday life" even if such talk often admits "the limits of this practicality" (pp. 295–296). Political estrangement reflects "apathy, lack of involvement, or lack of information," but it "may also be packaged as irony" or as "gallows humour" (p. 296). Reflexivity suggests

> that things don't work, we really are powerless in relation to the centres of political, economic and administrative command as well as to the media complex itself. The discursive discomfiture seems to arise from a feeling that there is no real legitimate official discourse through which to express this degree on alienation.

Dahlgren (p. 292) stressed that none of these talk forms is more authentic or artificial than any other. They are cultural resources that people can employ in varying ways depending on situational demands. Moreover, these forms can "merge with one another in real-life talk" (p. 297). For Dahlgren (p. 297), all this referred to what he called "the dispersion of subjectivity" meaning that we present ourselves, depending on situations, now as this kind, now as that kind of a subject. Even if he fixed this dispersion here to TV news he admitted, of course, that it is a much broader phenomenon.

Mass Media in People's Everyday Life

In studying what and how people talk about TV news, Dahlgren came quite close to the question what media and their output mean to people. Hobson (1980) tackled this question directly by studying what kind of status and significance radio and television had in the everyday lives of housewives. This study, conducted within the Birmingham critical cultural studies, was ethnographic in the sense that Hobson collected her data by interviewing and observing housewives in their homes.

Hobson (p. 105) observed that radio and TV were, for these women, not "leisure activities" but "integral parts of their day." They listened to the radio during the day while "engaged in domestic labour" (p. 105). Because housework is "structureless," "the time boundaries provided by radio are important in the women's own division of their time" (p. 105). These women favored especially music that had DJs as presenters. Hobson (p. 107) interpreted this by noting that because the concentration on home life isolates women, "the disc jockey" provides them "the missing 'company' of another person." She suggested further that the DJ may also play for the women "the role of a sexual fantasy-figure" (p. 107).

For Hobson, the choices of the television programs revealed clearly how the feminine and masculine world of activities and interests differ from each other. The women chose actively

> programmes which are understood to constitute the "woman's world," coupled with a complete rejection of programmes which are presenting the "man's world." However, there is also an acceptance that the "real" or "man's world" is important, and the right of their husbands to watch these programmes is respected: but it is not a world with which the women in this study wanted to concern themselves. (p. 109)

The women's world was represented by comedy series, soap operas, and light entertainment in general, whereas the men's world came to the fore in the news, current affairs programs, and so on (pp. 109–110). Although the women regarded their own world as more important to them, it was "also seen as secondary in rank to the 'real' or 'masculine' world" (p. 111).

The women's interest in soap operas like Coronation Street or Crossroads arose, according to Hobson (p. 113), from the female characters on the shows "who themselves have to confront the 'problems' in their 'everyday' life, and the resolution or negotiation of these problems within the drama provides points of recognition and identification." On the other hand, these resolutions are not particularly "revolutionary"; what emerges is the "inevitability of the situation, without the need to change it" (p. 114). In such resolutions "the ideological basis of consensual femininity is reproduced and reinforced for women" (p. 113).

Hobson's study is one of those that broke up the conception, having lived persistently in mass communication studies, that the soaps and melodramas are trash pure and simple, offering romance-hungry women an escape from everyday cares. The inquiry into their reception indicated that they often dealt with issues and problems relevant in their spectators' everyday lives (see, e.g., Hobson, 1982). As these program types became respectable objects of study the attention was turned, among other things, to the specific interpretation competencies that their reception presupposes (see, e.g., Brunsdon, 1981). I will return to these viewpoints in the context of feminist thinking and research in chapter 17.

Lull, representing U.S. interpretive cultural studies, provided a further example of cultural research into the media in people's life. He studied, for instance, the TV program selection of families by applying mass observation as a method (Lull, 1982). Nearly 100 observers "spent most of two days with the families," selected for the study, observing "how families turn on, change channels and turn off" their television sets (pp. 803–804). The families were not told that the observers' task was to observe expressly "television-related behavior," and they "were asked to ignore the presence of the observer and carry out their routines in normal fashion" (p. 804).

The family members were also interviewed. It is surprising that in his report Lull, regardless of the study's mass observational and thereby ethnographic nature, leaned mostly on the interview data presenting the results in statistical tables. The primary issue studied was "who is responsible for control of the main television set at home" (p. 805). The result was not particularly surprising: "fathers were named most often as the person or one of the persons who controls the selection of television programs" (p. 805). This outcome from the interview data was confirmed by the observations (p. 807).

As Morley (1986, p. 36) has remarked, with the observation that fathers tend to hold the sway in program selection, "we approach the central question of power." Lull, however, did not pay theoretical notice to questions concerning the gendered power relations in families (see Moores, 1993, p. 35). He was simply content to present his findings descriptively. In any case, his early research into the TV viewing within the network of family relations, and into its social meanings

(Lull, 1980a, 1980b, 1982) spurred subsequent study to tackle these questions from theoretically more informed perspectives as, for instance, that of power inequalities in families (Morley, 1986, 1992).

DISCUSSION ABOUT CULTURAL STUDIES IN COMMUNICATION

There has been quite a lot of debate about the starting points of empirical cultural studies, as well as about the conclusions made on the basis of obtained results. These debates have been interwoven in different ways around the concept of meaning. For instance, the sign-theoretical starting point, reinforced in concrete studies, that texts can be interpreted in many different ways has led some to doom the interpretive study of texts as obsolete. Such "text-centered studies have tended to encourage," Richardson and Corner (1986, p. 486) criticized, "that meanings somehow exist as inherent properties of textual signification and are thus available there for identification and plotting, provided that a sufficiently powerful or sensitive 'reading' can be brought to bear on them."

It is a bit amusing that those rejecting textual study for audience research sometimes read the audience responses as if the meanings "somehow exist as inherent properties" in them, waiting for to be picked out. Although Schröder (1988), for one, stressed the multiple meanings of Dynasty—his respondents interpreted it differently—he remained silent of the possible ambiguity of the respondents' readings. Yet "the audience responses also constitute a representation" (Feuer, 1986, cited in Morley, 1989, p. 24). They should not be taken "at face value," but "as another text that requires 'reading'" (Nightingale, 1996, p. 99). So an audience researcher cannot get rid of textual analysis. Moreover, the analysis of audience readings of a text can often benefit from a thorough analysis of that text itself (K. Jensen, 1988).

The multiplicity of textual meanings has also led some to conclude that people are free to read the texts as they wish. Or at least the freedom of interpretation has been regarded as more interesting than the possible frameworks limiting it. Fiske (1987, 1989, 1991b, 1991c) often stressed that a text is important predominantly as an incentive that prompts people to produce various stories. For him, the television programs are "producerly texts" that delegate "the production of meaning to the viewer-producer" (Fiske, 1989, p. 63, see also 1987, pp. 95–99). This gives the receivers a possibility to resist the dominant hegemonic-ideological significations and so to rebel against their subordination. This "semiotic resistance results from the desire of the subordinated to exert control over the meanings of their life" (Fiske, 1991b, p. 10).

The construction of personal meanings from the semiotic material provided by the texts produces popular pleasure that Fiske (1991c, pp. 49–68) divided into evasive and productive forms. The former means evasion from the grip of the dominating meanings and the social control they uphold. When a person becomes "lost" in a text, he or she gets temporarily rid of his or her socially constructed ego that normally keeps the individual in good order. Productive pleasure, again, results from the production of such meanings that represent the interests and identities of the subordinated groups. For instance, an inquiry into why school children favored Prisoners, a soap opera describing a woman prison, revealed that they signified it on the basis of their own experiences drawing comical parallels between the school and the prison (Fiske, 1987, pp. 67–70).

In brief, Fiske's (1991c, pp. 20–21) program for cultural studies in communication sees

> popular culture as a site of struggle, but, while accepting the power of the forces of dominance, it focuses rather upon the popular tactics by which these forces are coped with, are evaded or are resisted. . . . Instead of concentrating on the . . . practices of dominant ideology, it attempts to understand the everyday resistances and evasions that make that ideology work so hard and insistently to maintain itself and its values. This approach sees popular culture as potentially, and often actually, progressive (though not radical), and it is essentially optimistic, for it finds in the vigor and vitality of people evidence of both the possibility of social change and of the motivation to drive it.

This program has aroused much objections. In criticizing what he called the "'don't worry, be happy' school" Morley (1992, pp. 11, 21) remarked against it that texts are not only incentives:

> The analysis of the text or message remains . . . a fundamental necessity, for the polysemy of the message is not without its own structure. . . . While the message is not an object with one real meaning, there are within it signifying mechanisms which promote certain meanings, even one privileged meaning, and suppress others: these are the directive closures encoded in the message.

For Condit (1989), the ideas of both the polysemous nature of texts and the potentialities they offer for pleasurable resistance are highly problematic. Condit's research on the reception of the Cagney & Lacey detective series led her to conclude that the different readings of the series did not result from its polysemy but from the different values that her respondents attached to meanings that they had interpreted rather similarly. "The emphasis on the polysemous quality of texts thus may be overdrawn" (p. 107). Condit observed further that to read texts against their preferred message may be quite laborious and unpleasant (pp. 108–112). Moreover, the Fiskean faith "in the capacity of audiences to resist" stays on unstable grounds as long as it remains indistinct what things are resisted and "how this resistance occurs" (pp. 116–117).

The Fiskean type of celebrating the popular texts has been criticized also on more general grounds. Some scholars see it tending to throw "the whole enterprise of a cultural critique out of the window" (Gray, 1987, p. 28). For others, its idea of a "semiotic democracy" "enthusiastically embraces the central themes of sovereign consumer pluralism" (Curran, 1990, p. 140), in which sense it would draw close to "a conservative ideology" (Morley, 1992, p. 26). Furthermore, it has been interpreted to insist "that people habitually use the content of dominant media against itself, to empower themselves" by making "their own meanings and pleasures": this would screen out the last remnants of a thought that media have any power (M. Budd, Entman, & Steinman, 1990, p. 170). As Morley (p. 31) critically summarized, "the power of viewers to reinterpret meanings is hardly equivalent to the discursive power of centralized media institutions to construct the texts which the viewers then interpret: to imagine otherwise is simply foolish."

To relativize this critique it should be noted that the Fiskean program represents a wholly legitimate limiting to particular features within communication processes. The critique, however, has not seen it as limiting but has rather given to understand that Fiske does not see anything but people who wallow in pleasures by reading texts continually in their own ways. Such a critique misses clearly the mark and obscures the fact that there indeed are situations where texts are used as devices for pleasurable resistant meaning production. By studying these moments we can learn something quite important about the relationship between the media and audiences.

17

FEMINIST VIEWS OF LANGUAGE AND MASS COMMUNICATION

In her overview of feminist mass communication studies, Kleberg (1993, p. 7) characterized women's studies as a venture aiming to find out and explain, "how women's subordination to men has been generated and how it is passed on." Of course, this state of affairs is, for feminists, not only something to be studied but something to be overcome; hence feminism "is politics directed at changing existing power relations between women and men in society" (Weedon, 1987, p. 1). In striving for "the empowerment of women," it sees "that all research is by necessity partial, not objective" (Drotner, 1994, p. 93).

FORMS OF FEMINISM

Although feminists have a common goal, the conceptions of the ways for attaining it have diverged sharply. These disagreements on strategy have dispersed feminist theory and research into different approaches. Reviewers have identified three or four such approaches. Starting with Kristeva's (1979/1986) account of the stages of feminism, Kaplan (1987a), for example, divided feminist thought into liberal, Marxist, radical, and poststructuralist feminism that came up successively from 1960s to 1980s. Roughly corresponding divisions have been presented also by others (Steeves, 1987; van Zoonen, 1991; Weedon, 1987, pp. 11–42). Of course, this kind of division results only in ideal types, because all "divisions are artificial" and "tidy up what was/is really an untidy picture" (Cameron, 1993, p. 9).

Liberal feminism has advocated equality between women and men in all respects and every realm of life, from public and working spheres to that of home (Kaplan, p. 220). In media studies, it has been particularly interested in the ways media texts represent gender roles. Using mostly quantitative content analysis, the study focused, for example, on the degree to which the texts reflect "changes in the status of women" and in their work and home roles as compared to those of men (p. 220). The aim has been to uncover biases in the representation of women to fuel the liberal project—a project whose effort to abolish the difference separating women from men means, as Kaplan (pp. 222-223) critically said, "that women 'are to become men.' The position fails to take into account that such a move demands woman's complete surrender to the patriarchy and its values, norms, and ways of being."

Marxist feminism has also aimed at total equality between women and men. But, viewing patriarchy as deriving from the economic relations of capitalism, it has regarded socialism to be the precondition of achieving equality (Kleberg, p. 14). Pre-Althusserian Marxist feminists used to approach the media as capitalist institutions and examine, among other things, how this "affects what images of women are portrayed" (Kaplan, p. 223). Are they represented in work roles, if capital needs work force, and in home roles "when that is economically beneficial" (p. 223)? Later, enriched by Althusser's views, Marxist feminists concluded that determinations are much more complex—that, for instance, representations of women in the media "cannot only be explained by the profit motive" (p. 224). This brought Marxist feminism near to poststructuralism.

Although equality has been the objective of liberal and Marxist feminism, radical feminists have been of the opinion that equality would not free women from the grip of patriarchy. For them, the only possibility is to withdraw from the patriarchy and to strive "for autonomy and wholeness through communities of women" (p. 226). From this point of view, the study of media might be focused on to what extent the "traditional family life" is depicted "as the solution for all ills" or what kind of discrepancies there are "between images of marriage in popular culture and real life" (p. 226). The implication has been that women should reject all patriarchal idealizations in the media "in order to find themselves" (p. 227).

Unlike the preceding currents, poststructuralist feminism has rejected sexual opposition "as metaphysical" and aimed to transcend "the categories of sexual difference" or at least to disclose "their cultural construction" (p. 227). Poststructuralist media scholars have particularly analyzed the symbolic systems through which "we learn to be what our culture calls 'women' as against what are called 'men'" (p. 227). I return to this research shortly.

From a more philosophical angle, women's studies have been divided into essentialism and anti-essentialism (pp. 216-218; Kleberg, pp. 17-18). For the essentialists, women can be separated from men "in terms of an essence that precedes or is outside of culture" (Kaplan, p. 217). However, under male domination, women's essence cannot be realized for which reason the patriarchy must be fought. For the anti-essentialists, the sexual difference is not reducible to some essence, but results from cultural models according to which we grow to be women and men. Therefore, anti-essentialism has been concerned with the social processes "through which sexuality and subjectivity are constructed at the same time" (p. 217). The objective is to dissolve processes reproducing traditional gendered identities.

Of the different "feminisms," radical feminism represents most clearly essentialism and poststructuralist feminism most clearly anti-essentialism. In the following, I focus especially on poststructuralist feminism—above all because it has laid particular emphasis on language, communication and media as producers and reproducers of gender. Rakow (1992, p. 10) has summarized its viewpoint as follows:

> While early research by feminists sometimes assumed . . . that gender was a pre-given biological fact that produced differences in language use and interaction, feminist researchers have come to theorize the differences between women and men as the product of language and interaction.

For this reason, "feminists do not consider language a side-issue or a luxury, but an essential part of the struggle for liberation" (Cameron, 1993, p. 1).

POSTSTRUCTURALIST FEMINISM AND LANGUAGE

The differences between the "feminisms" also appear in their views of language. For liberal feminists, language is a transparent medium for creating and conveying thoughts about reality "out there." A great drawback in language is sexism that disparages women, and that should be rooted out (Cameron, pp. 117–124). According to radical feminists, again, women have essentially a language of their own. However, because the dominating male language in the patriarchy does not give room for this language to realize itself, women cannot express themselves adequately but "fall silent" (p. 130).

The poststructuralist feminist view of language can be elucidated with Julia Kristeva's (1941–) thought. Starting with Lacan's theory, Kristeva saw that in regard to expressive activity a subject is split into semiotic and symbolic realms. The former is what Lacan spoke of as the domain of imaginary that becomes buried into unconscious. It is "a domain of drive heterogeneity" (Sivenius, 1985, p. 129). It appears, for instance, in "bodily aspects of the utterance, such as rhythms, tone of voice, metaphor, word play and gesture" (Young, 1987, p. 72). In child development, it precedes the symbolic realm. Kristeva saw, like Lacan, that a child becomes a subject first when he or she enters the symbolic world which, in distinction from the heterogenous "semiotic (drives and their articulations)," consists of the homogenous "realm of signification" (Kristeva, 1974/1984, p. 43).

Kristeva denoted with the term signifiancé the whole of expressive activity where both the semiotic and the symbolic are present:

> These two modalities are inseparable. . . . Because the subject is always both semiotic and symbolic, no signifying system he [or she] produces can be either "exclusively" semiotic or "exclusively" symbolic, and is instead necessarily marked by an indebtness to both. (p. 24)

The semiotic and the symbolic are opposite forces. Through the repression of the semiotic by the symbolic the inherently heterogenous child is constituted as a homogeneous subject. On the other hand, the semiotic always finds, despite its repression, outlets, most notably in poetry, arts, magic, and religion. In this way, it always threatens "the organization of the symbolic and the stability of its meanings" (Weedon, 1987, p. 89). This "brings about all the various transformations that are called 'creation'"; thus, "what remodels the symbolic order is always the influx of the semiotic" (Kristeva, p. 62). On the other hand, "the irruption of the semiotic within the symbolic is only relative," which accounts for the fact that the symbolic "continues to ensure the position of the subject put in process/on trial" (p. 63).

The semiotic and the symbolic become articulated differently in girls than in boys, due to the different ways in which the Oedipus and castration complexes are resolved. For Kristeva, as Cameron (p. 173) put it, "feminine subjects are not totally outside of the symbolic, but they retain stronger links than do masculine subjects to the pre-symbolic (Imaginary) stage and the pre-Oedipal mother figure." The slips of the semiotic from the grip of the symbolic "through rhythm, intonation, gaps, meaninglessness and general disruption of the rational, symbolic flow" manifest themselves "to a particularly marked degree" in women, "since for them the repression of pre-Oedipal elements is less complete" (pp. 173–174).

This view draws near to the notion of women's own language. Kristeva did not, however, emphasize this aspect but the ability of the semiotic to undermine the symbolic order. In so far as the "realist" language of the symbolic realm, being truncated as an unambiguous means for controlling and keeping order, is the sine qua non for the reproduction of patriarchal relationships, then its unsettling by the semiotic eventually undermines the whole patriarchy. Thus, the cultivation of (feminine) semiotic abilities

> is potentially subversive of the entire social order. For a Lacanian, it is the symbolic order which sustains all our social and cultural institutions. For a feminist Lacanian like Kristeva, therefore, whose interest is in changing things, it is the feminine disruption of symbolic language that has the potential to bring about a social revolution. (p. 174)

For poststructuralist feminists, then, language is not a transparent means for creating and conveying thoughts about reality, but an ambiguous and internally incongruous sign system through the use of which reality becomes signified and "produced" in this or that form. Attempts to truncate it as unambiguous cannot do away with its basic ambiguousness. These views, approaching Screen theory, have directed the poststructuralist feminists' attention to, on the one hand, how the symbolic aspect of language is constructing gendered subjects and, on the other, how its semiotic aspect always interferes with this construction offering possibilities for demolishing established subjectivities and building up new ones.

"TECHNOLOGIES OF GENDER"

From the outset, the feminist media scholars have stressed that media representations of gender have real consequences. However, the assessments of media power in this respect have varied. For Ang and Hermes (1991, p. 309), before poststructuralism this question was approached with two questionable assumptions: that the media present "unrealistic messages about women" in an unambiguous way and that girls and women absorb these messages "as (wrong) lessons about 'real life'." This implies that early feminism would have seen media as contributing directly to the constitution of gendered subjects along stereotypical lines. Influenced by cultural studies, the poststructuralist feminism has approached the question in a more sophisticated way. According to Ang and Hermes (p. 311), the

> assumption of a priori, monolithic reproduction of sexism and patriarchy has gradually made way to a view in which the media's effectivity is seen as much more conditional, contingent upon specific—and often contradictory—textual mechanisms and operations on the one hand, and upon the meanings and pleasures on the other. The latter trend, especially, has solicited a more optimistic stance towards women's role as media consumers: they are no longer seen as "cultural dupes," as passive victims of inexorably sexist media; on the contrary, media consumption can even be considered as empowering (although never unproblematically), in so far as it offers audiences an opportunity for symbolic resistance to dominant meanings and discourses and for implicit acknowledgement of their own social subordination.

A view that genres like romances and television soap operas, favored by women, are not trash manipulating them to keep to their subordination, came up during the 1980s in many studies that bestowed upon such genres appreciation as text types specifically fit to address women's psyche and their cultural abilities of interpretation (Ruoho, 1994). Modleski (1982/1990, pp. 92–93), for one, characterized the position, given by the U.S. television soap operas to their viewers, with the following affirmative albeit also problematizing words:

> The subject/spectator of soap operas . . . is constituted as a sort of ideal mother: a person who possesses greater wisdom than all her children, whose sympathy is large enough to encompass the conflicting claims of her family . . . , and who has no demands or

claims of her own. . . . It is important to notice that soap operas serve to affirm the primacy of the family not by presenting an ideal family, but by portraying a family in constant turmoil and appealing to the spectator to be understanding and tolerant of the many evils which go on within that family. The spectator/mother, identifying with each character in turn, is made to see "the larger picture" and extend her sympathy to both the sinner and the victim. . . . By constantly presenting her with the many-sidedness of any question, by never reaching a permanent conclusion, soap operas undermine her capacity to form unambiguous judgements.

Thus, for Modleski, soaps do not reflect pregiven stereotypes of women, but actively produce symbolic forms of feminine identity by inscribing specific subject positions in their "textual fabric" (Ang & Hermes, p. 309). Another question, however, is how the receivers relate themselves to such inscribed positions, stereotypical or not. For instance, a study by Seiter, Borchers, Kreutzner, and Warth (1989, p. 241) indicated that although some middle-class women adopted the textual position of the "ideal mother" described by Modleski, this position was "not easily accessible to working class women" to whose "social identity" it did not correspond. Thus, for Seiter et al. (p. 241), the "production of the (abstract and 'ideal') feminine subject" by media texts "is restricted and altered by the contradictions in women's own experiences."

During the 1980s, feminists also began to question the earlier way of taking the category of "woman" for granted as if all women were alike, similarly defined and suppressed by men as the Other. For Ang and Hermes (p. 314), such a conception "tends to naturalize sexual difference and to universalize culturally constructed and historically specific definitions of femininity and masculinity." de Lauretis (1987) questioned the same conception with her idea of the technologies of gender. With this phrase, she wanted to emphasize that gender, "both as representation and self-representation, is the product of various social technologies, such as cinema, and of institutionalized discourses, epistemologies, and critical practices, as well as practices of daily life" (p. 2).

For de Lauretis (p. 2), a naturalization of sex opposition "makes it very difficult, if not impossible, to articulate the differences of women from Woman, that is to say, the differences among women or, perhaps more exactly, the differences within women." If one starts with the view that sexual difference is produced, in addition to biological sex, by diverse cultural practices, one must conclude that the evolving subjectivity is "not unified but rather multiple, and not so much divided as contradicted" (p. 2). As van Zoonen (1994, pp. 33–34) said, gender is, for de Lauretis, not a fixed property of the individual but

> part of an ongoing process by which subjects are constituted, often in paradoxical ways. The identity that emerges is therefore fragmented and dynamic; gender does not determine or exhaust identity. In theory . . . it is even conceivable to be outside gender or to engage in a social practice in which gender discourse is relatively unimportant. Defined as such, gender is . . . subject to continuous discursive struggle and negotiation.

Thus, where early feminists saw the media as shaping fixed-gendered subjects along stereotypical lines, poststructuralist feminists have seen the issue as more complicated. If it is true, as they think it is, that there are no unified models making individuals fixed-gendered subjects—that they become gendered not in an absolute but in a relative sense—then there cannot be a unified symbolic realm in society any longer. Rather, culture must be more semiotic than even Kristeva believed it to be. This would bring the poststructuralist feminist view near to the notion of society as a postmodern one characterized by a continuous interplay of fragmentation and (new) homogenization. Indeed, for Kaplan (1987a, p. 227), for one, feminist poststructuralism is clearly indebted to "postmodern theories."

POSTSTRUCTURALIST FEMINISM AND POSTMODERN TEXT

That culture would display a continuous interplay of the homogenizing symbolic and the heterogenizing semiotic is accounted for already by the ambiguous nature of language and other sign systems. In addition, there have been conscious efforts to set the semiotic aspect of signifiancé more free—so especially in the avantgardist art whose importance in the unsettling of the symbolic has been highlighted, in particular, by Kristeva (1974/1984, pp. 165–234). Also, thoughts concerning women's language and écriture féminine have supported such efforts regardless of the fact that poststructuralist feminism has rejected "the quest for an authentic women's language" (Cameron, 1993, p. 176). These efforts have nourished the feminist study of texts violating in one or another way accustomed forms of presentation.

Such texts have been looked up not in avantgardist art but in certain forms of popular culture, especially in rock music and rock videos. For example, Bassnett and Hoskin (1986) implied that texts are traditionally composed according to a model in which Author, Text and Reader are separate and unified entities. For them, this strengthens "logo/phallocentrism" or male centrism that cannot be undone simply by changing the male sign into a female one—as the proponents of "women's language" maintained—but only by replacing the unified Author, Text and Reader triplet with "an acceptance of pluralism, of fragmentation" (pp. 238, 249, 241). A way toward this is opened by rock music: if one poses "the question 'Who speaks in rock?' the answer is both male and female, for the voice is not based in one gender" (p. 245). Thereby, rock would dissolve the sexual opposition.

Kaplan (1987b, 1988) found a corresponding text form in rock videos. Behind her approach is the view, shared by many feminists, that fundamental to the patriarchy as well as the symbolic order reproducing it is a way to see things as pairs of binary oppositions in which one term is privileged to the other. The most focal of such pairs is, of course, man/woman privileging "man" and marginalizing "woman." This opposition is accompanied with a lot of others. Yet, for Kaplan (1988, pp. 35–36), many rock videos "abandon the usual binary oppositions on which dominant culture depends": they

> forsake the usual oppositions between high and low culture; between masculine and feminine; between established film genres; between past, present and future; between the private and the public sphere; between verbal and visual hierarchies; between realism and anti-realism, etc. . . . These strategies violate the paradigm pitting a classical narrative against an avantgarde anti-narrative, the one supposedly embodying complicit, the other subversive, ideologies.

Because of their disassembling of oppositions, rock videos represent, for Kaplan (1987b, pp. 33–48), postmodern culture. Among the oppositions they unsettle is that of the genders. According to Kaplan (p. 90), typical of many rock videos is "the blurring of clear lines between genders." For her (p. 90), this indicates

> the increasing movement of rock videos into the postmodern stance, in which it is unclear what position a text is taking toward what it shows. This has implications for genders in that one often cannot tell whether a male or a female discourse dominates, and because the attitude toward sex and gender is often ambiguous.

For instance, in her video "Material Girl" Madonna represents, for Kaplan (p. 126), "the postmodern feminist heroine in that she combines unabashed seductiveness with a gutsy kind of independence." Hence, the guise of Madonna is an amalgam of typical male and female characteristics. "Material Girl" also represents postmodernism in a broader sense "in its blurring of hitherto sacrosanct boundaries and polarities": "the usual bipolar categories—male/female, high art/pop art, film/TV, fiction/reality, private/public, interior/exterior, and so on—simply no longer" apply to it (p. 126).

Even if Kaplan (1988, pp. 39, 42) thought that rock videos contain material beneficial to women—for example, "the breaking up of traditional realist forms sometimes entails a destruction of conventional sex-role representations that opens up new possibilities for female imagining"—she saw that these liberating elements remain "often superficial." Its progressive features notwithstanding, the commercial postmodernism represented by rock videos reproduces largely "male qualities" such as "violence, aggression and misogyny" (p. 42). For Kaplan (p. 42), women need to actively resist such qualities that "mark much co-opted postmodernism"—a culture, "toward which women are being drawn in the mistaken belief, perhaps, that this offers liberation from earlier 'feminine' constraints."

CONCLUDING REMARKS

According to van Zoonen (1994, pp. 2–3), feminism moved in the 1980s "from a highly visible, vital and sometimes spectacular countercultural form to a customary but at times still controversial component of established institutions." One of these institutions is academic social research. Along with the linguistic-cultural turn of this research. feminism, which had contributed to this turn, occupied in it in the 1980s an increasingly central position. Regarding this, van Zoonen (1991, p. 34) has spoken of "the successful and inspiring conjunction of feminist and cultural studies," though stressing that "not all feminist studies are cultural studies, and not all cultural studies are feminist studies."

In any case, feminism has had a clear impact on the cultural studies' research agenda. It is largely thanks to the feminists' interest in romances and television soaps that popular texts have been accepted as legitimate objects of study. Feminism has also promoted the view that such texts, being more complex than earlier believed, offer women "an opportunity for symbolic resistance to dominant meanings" (Ang & Hermes, 1991, p. 311). On the other hand, this kind of thought is vulnerable to charges already considered in the context of cultural studies—for instance, to the blame that the celebration of the multiplicity of texts and ways of their reception easily loses sight of the power that ultimately resides in the media.

Referring to the same problem, van Zoonen (1991, p. 49) has remarked critically that focusing on romances and soaps narrows feminism's "potential for articulating a comprehensive cultural criticism." Furthermore, the excessive celebration of textual ambiguity threatens to undo feminist politics, for if "one interpretation is not by definition better or more valid than another," what legitimation do feminists "have to discuss the politics of representation, to try to intervene in dominant culture" (p. 49)? Van Zoonen (1994, p. 150) also warned that the "observation that gender is a constructed and shifting subject position unstably constituted by the points of intersection of an array of radically heterogenous discourses should not lead to the conclusion that conventional forms of oppression and inequality have disappeared."

Also, the idea has been met critically that textual practices, which supposedly undermine the symbolic domain and dissolve the male/female opposition, would have something to do with an activity aimed at upsetting the inequality between the genders. Kristeva's view of women as more semiotic than men has irritated Weedon (1987, pp. 89–90) to say that to equate the feminine with the irrational "is either to concede rather a lot to masculinity or to privilege the irrational, neither of which is very helpful politically." For Moi (1985, p. 170), Kristeva's "emphasis on the semiotic as an unconscious force precludes any analysis of the conscious decision-making processes that must be part of any collective revolutionary project." Because of this, Kristeva is driven into "an anarchist and subjectivist political position" (p. 170). Moi (p. 171) crystallized her critique by stating that one cannot find in Kristeva's thought

> why it is so important to show that certain literary practices break up the structures of language when they seem to break little else. She [Kristeva] seems essentially to argue that the disruption of the subject, the sujet en procès displayed in the texts, prefigures or parallels revolutionary disruptions of society. But her argument in support of this contention is the rather lame one of comparison or homology. Nowhere are we given a specific analysis of the actual social or political structures that would produce such a homologous relationship between the subjective and the social.

18

COMMUNICATION FROM THE POSTMODERN POINT OF VIEW

The rise of feminist scholarship was one distinct feature of 1980s social science. Another was the rise of what is called postmodern discourse. At once, debates around such concepts as postmodernity and postmodernism abounded. There are reasons to think that initially the concepts were called forth by an inarticulate feeling that so far taken-for-granted certainties had fallen into crisis, that a radical change was taking place. Such a situation makes understandable why the basic terms of the postmodern discourse remained "irritatingly elusive to define" (Featherstone, 1988, p. 195) and why there emerged no "unified postmodern theory, or even a coherent set of positions" (Best & Kellner, 1991, p. 2). Unified theories or coherent positions were hardly even pursued.

The prefix post in postmodern indicates that what was seen as fallen into crisis and under change is something that has been spoken of as modern. But what does modern mean? The term has been associated with widely differing things—there has been talk of modern age, modern society, modern way of life, modern sensibility, modern art, and so on. To clarify the situation a bit, Best and Kellner (pp. 1–5), among others, have distinguished two couplets of concepts: modernity/postmodernity on the one hand, and modernism/postmodernism on the other. The first is an epochal couplet referring to historical eras; the second is an aesthetic one referring to the domain of arts. I anchor the following review on this distinction, although I am fully aware of the fact that the terms in both couplets have been heavily contested (cf. B. Turner, 1990; Smart, 1990).

MODERNITY/POSTMODERNITY

For Giddens (1990, p. 1), as for many others, "'modernity' refers to modes of social life or organization which emerged in Europe from about the seventeenth century onwards." It means not only modern society but also "the whole constellation of characteristics" that modern society gave rise to (Lyon 1999, p. 26). The most important aspect here is the mental atmosphere of modernity. It nurtured a modern mentality that viewed history as the progressive unfolding of mankind's mastery over its fate, with the ultimate

> victorious struggle of Reason against emotions or animal instincts, science against religion and magic, truth against prejudice, correct knowledge against superstition, reflection against uncritical existence, rationality against affectivity and the rule of custom. With such conceptualizations, the modern age defined itself as, above all, the kingdom of Reason and rationality. (Bauman, 1987, p. 111)

This vision was articulated especially by Enlightenment thinkers in the 18th century, and it fueled what Habermas (1980/1996) has called "the project of modernity." However, critical observers soon realized that the process of modernization did not fulfill the project's promises: reason, progress, and emancipation in one respect were offset by unreason, retrogression, and enslavement in another. Modernity has been, thus, a really "mixed blessing" (Lyon, 1999, p. 35).

The advocates of the idea of postmodernity are disposed to see that after the mid-20th century, at the latest, the project of modernity was definitely passé. It was argued that social change, which so far had taken place within the basic structure of modern society, had broken out of this structure and begun to transform it. One transforming force was found in "the introduction of new information and telecommunications technologies" (Smart, 1992, p. 142). For Poster (1990, p. 14), "the solid institutional routines that have characterized modern society for some two hundred years are being shaken by the earthquake of electronically mediated communication and recomposed into new routines whose outlines are as yet by no means clear."

For the postmodern thinkers, the disintegration of modern society's structure began also to dissolve the mental atmosphere of modernity. A new atmosphere began to spread—one that Giddens (1990, p. 46) characterized by saying that it includes

> one or more of the following: that we have discovered that nothing can be known with any certainty, since all pre-existing "foundations" of epistemology have been shown to be unreliable; that "history" is devoid of teleology and consequently no version of "progress" can plausibly be defended; and that a new social and political agenda has come into being with the increasing prominence of ecological concerns and perhaps new social movements generally.

This new atmosphere comes paradigmatically into sight in Jean-François Lyotard's (1924–) claim that the philosophical discourses, which were employed in the modern era to legitimate science and scientific knowledge—"the grand Narratives," as he called them—have died in the postmodern conditions (Lyotard, 1984, p. 15). He referred in particular to discourses that were in the heart of the project of modernity, such as the Enlightenment discourse of emancipation through reason. Discourses pursuing such grand goals have lost their "credibility" along with the postmodern "'atomization' of the social into flexible networks of language game" (pp. 17, 37). Because there circulates in society "an indeterminate number of language games, obeying different rules" (p. 40), there is no longer unity sufficient for the grand narratives to survive.

In postmodern conditions, knowledge and science can be legitimated either with a reference to performativity, to the "input/output equation" and "performance improvement," or by paralogy, with a reference to the importance of "dissensus" and contradiction as midwives of new insights (pp. 46, 47, 61). Lyotard took a stand for the "little narratives" of paralogy: They do not do "violence to the heterogeneity of language games" (p. xxv). For him, "consensus is a horizon that is never reached" (p. 61). A demand for consensus "is terrorist" (p. 63).

Although Lyotard's thoughts concern knowledge and its legitimation, they nonetheless bring out features that have been seen to be typical of the whole postmodern era. One of them is that the once centralized structures of society are becoming more and more decentralized and that, along with this process, all totalizing and grandiose visions are becoming replaced with "heterogeneity, plurality, constant innovation, and pragmatic construction of local rules and prescriptions agreed upon by the participants" (Best & Kellner, 1991, p. 165). Micropolitics is the password. Theories and theorizing are dismissed because they lead always to grand Narratives. Instead of theorizing, science is for Lyotard an activity where one intervenes in a "variety of different sorts of language games" making moves to advance his or her "own position" and to oppose "the moves and positions of other players" (Kellner, 1988, p. 255).

MODERNISM/POSTMODERNISM

Where modernity as an era traces back to the 16th or 17th century, modernism as an aesthetic current is much younger. Many regard Baudelaire as a key figure in its coming into being (Smart, 1992, p. 148). In an essay written around 1860, he described modernism to be about "the transient, the fleeting, the contingent"—a modernist attempts to "catch and perpetuate this flashing-by" (Kotkavirta & Sironen, 1986, p. 8). It is interesting that the emphasis on transitory has subsequently been viewed as a distinct aspect of the postmodern era. One could perhaps say that modernist aesthetics reflected in its way the deeply contradictory nature of modernity and, in so doing, anticipated some of the features attached by the postmodern discourse to postmodernity.

The relationship between modernism and postmodernism has been conceived in different ways. Here I follow chiefly Fredric Jameson's views. Resting on Mandel's (1978) tripartition of the development of capitalism into market, monopoly, and multinational stages, he divided culture in "the stages of realism, modernism and postmodernism" (Jameson, 1991, p. 36). He speaks of them as cultural dominants that allow "for the presence and coexistence of a range of very different, yet subordinate, features" (p. 4). There are reasons to conclude that realism was replaced as such a dominant by modernism in the latter half of the 19th century, and modernism by postmodernism around the mid-20th century, although Jameson was not particularly definite here.

These dominants can be specified with a reference to how they figured the relationship between signs and reality. For realism, the heir to "the secularization and modernization project brought about by Enlightenment philosophers" (Vainikkala 1986, p. 219), signs represented directly the outer world. By using signs according to this conception, realist texts imitated the world as it habitually appears to the senses. Such texts portrayed reality metonymically. Main realist presentation rules were "the consistency and integrity of points of view" and "dramatic showing" (p. 219). The realist presentation strategies also struck roots in mass culture that emerged at the same time with modernism as its "dialectical opposite" (Jameson, 1979, p. 134).

Where mass culture is repetitious, modernism emphasizes "innovation and novelty"—it rejects "previous styles" and strives to create "something which resists and breaks through the force of gravity of repetition" (p. 136). By utilizing signs in a way that dissolved the realist illusion of a direct correlation between signs and the outer world, modernist texts established a metaphorical relation to reality. They broke the "continuity of narration" and separated "the inner from the outer" (Vainikkala, p. 219). One can suppose that the purpose was to demonstrate that there is in the world an "inner" reality, which is the source for the outer, apparent forms. In this respect, modernism would be cognate to such scientific approaches that—as Marx's critique of capitalism and Freud's psychoanalysis—attempt to find the essential reality not directly discernible in surface forms (see Kellner, 1994, p. 11; Morley, 1996, p. 59).

As can be seen, realism and modernism related very differently to reality, but they nonetheless shared the view that the world of signs refers outside itself, to the real world. Postmodernism cut off this link of reference between signs and reality. Signs in postmodern texts and other cultural products do not refer "vertically" to what is outside or below the sign world, but "horizontally" to what is inside this world. In other words, postmodern cultural products do not imitate what appears to be "out there" or unearth what is below the appearances, but construct intertextually, with signs gleaned from other products, new sign realities.

The manner of taking all that there is as signs or sign-fragments that can be integrated into new sign constructions accounts for the central features that have been associated with postmodernist art: "the collapse of the hierarchical distinction between high and mass/popular culture; a stylistic promiscuity favouring eclecticism and the mixing of code; parody, pastiche, irony, playfulness and the celebration of surface 'depthlessness' of culture; the decline of originality/genius of the artistic producer and the assumption that art can only be repetitious" (Featherstone, 1988, p. 203). For Jameson (1985, pp. 113–118; 1991, pp. 16–18), the most typical postmodern text is pastiche, which he compared to parody, typical of modernism (1991, p. 17):

> Pastiche is, like parody, the imitation of a peculiar or unique, idiosyncratic style, the wearing of a linguistic mask, speech in a dead language. But it is a neutral practice of such mimicry, without any of parody's ulterior motives, amputated of the satiric impulses, devoid of laughter and of any conviction that alongside the abnormal tongue you have momentarily borrowed, some healthy linguistic normality still exists. Pastiche is thus blank parody, a statue with blind eyeballs.

Unlike parody's manner of commenting on the original text and of revealing its stylistic clichés, pastiche plays endogenously with a stylistic material snatched casually from here and there. Material is drawn, for example, indiscriminately from products of traditional realism, popular culture, and high modernism. This has effaced the "frontier between high culture and the so-called mass or commercial culture," with the result that "aesthetic production today has become integrated into commodity production generally" (pp. 2, 4). The mixing of styles has been typical, for example, of rock videos or such TV serials as Miami Vice (Fiske, 1991a, pp. 59–60). What this all results in is "the random cannibalization of all the styles of the past" (Jameson, 1991, p. 18).

Of the other features attached to postmodern culture by Jameson, the most interesting are superficiality and the loss of the sense of history. First, by cutting off the connection between signs and reality, postmodernism replaced the "depth models" of modernism by "a new kind of flatness or depthlessness, a new kind of supercifiality" (pp. 9, 12)—all that is left is pure surface, a "world without depth" (Morley 1996, p. 59). Second, partly as a result of the mixing of styles, the past as a historical reality "finds itself gradually bracketed, and then effaced altogether" (Jameson, p. 18). More generally, history becomes replaced by imitations or simulacra of history that, as television docudramas, do not "represent the historical past" but "only our ideas and stereotypes about that past" (p. 25).

These perspectives on postmodern aesthetics—which have been greatly debated (see, e.g., Kellner, 1989a; M. Rose 1991)—indicate two different approaches to mass communication. The first would be to focus on postmodern texts in the media or, more generally, on the postmodern features in different media fare. Kaplan's rock video study, considered in the preceding chapter, represents this approach. The second possibility would be to start with a view of a "crisis of representation" (Mumby, 1997)—that is, with the view that the media do not represent an outside reality, as realist and modernist aesthetics would have it, but that in a certain sense there is no media-independent reality to be represented, as postmodern aesthetics implies. Jean Baudrillard's (1929–) thoughts of simulation and hyperreality represent this view.

THE SIGN AS THE PRODUCER OF THE REAL:
JEAN BAUDRILLARD

Because, as one commentator (Kellner, 1994, p. 2) stated, Baudrillard "seeks to destroy modern orthodoxies" and to replace "the positions of the past with his often-novel positions," he is not an easy target for a reviewer. His thinking reflects "a transitional situation whereby new social conditions are putting into question the old orthodoxies and boundaries" (Kellner, 1989b, p. 217). Communication and the mass media have a key role in his analysis of this transition. This highly abstract analysis relies on such strange concepts as simulacrum and simulation, hyperreality, and the implosion of meaning.

Simulacrum and Simulation

The concept of simulacrum, a cornerstone of Baudrillard's whole thinking, comes from Plato and means an "identical copy for which no original has ever existed" (Jameson, 1991, p. 18). Simulation means the production of simulacra. History is, for Baudrillard, a process during which simulation strengthens and becomes autonomous. This process begins from the era of symbolic exchange, which is free from simulation, and passes the era of counterfeit, the first stage of simulation, and the era of production, the second stage of simulation, arriving in present times at the era of simulation proper, the third stage of simulation. At this stage, all bands between signs and referents have broken off: Signs have become pure simulacra, copies without the originals that they would represent (Baudrillard 1976/1988, pp. 135, 143–147).

With symbolic exchange, Baudrillard (pp. 119–124) means the exchange of gifts, an institution considered typical of premodern societies. Instead of having economic functions, this exchange expressed social relations (Baudrillard, 1972/1988, pp. 59–60). That is, social relations were the referents to which gifts as signs referred and which they helped to keep up. Alongside gifts, other appropriate objects occupied the function to signify statuses and their differences in a social hierarchy. Hence, signs had not yet begun to break off from the social constellation which they represented in a rigid one-to-one manner. In the feudal Middle Ages social prohibitions still assured that "each sign refers unequivocally to a (particular) situation and a level of status" (Baudrillard, 1976/1988, p. 136).

It was the Renaissance that destroyed "the bound sign" establishing "the reign of the emancipated sign" (p. 136). The hierarchical structure of society began to dissolve and, along with it, also its representation through a rigid system of objects as signs. Fashion and the making of an individual image of oneself—things that had had no place in previous societies—began to come to the fore. This enabled the birth of counterfeit, a sign that pretends to represent something without really doing so. A counterfeit makes the relationship of the sign to the referent problematic but does not yet break it, because a sign cannot function as a counterfeit without the illusory belief that it really represents what it seems to represent.

The era of counterfeit lasted "from the Renaissance to the industrial revolution" (p. 135). Industrial production, which enabled the manufacturing of identical products in large quantities to the wide market "out there," created "the industrial simulacrum" (p. 137), which revolutionized the relationship between the sign and the referent. While in the case of counterfeit, the referent was an original that the sign pretended to represent, an industrial commodity has no original that it as a sign would represent or pretend to represent. In fact, it gains its meaning, as it were, afterward, from its use value. Thus, the commodity, or its outlook, is a sign whose referent is its purported use. A commodity, too, can be a "counterfeit" in the sense that its outlook may give a false promise of its validity as a use value.

Because the outlook is the language for commodities to tell of themselves, there is a continuous effort to polish and make the appearance ever more attractive (about this commodity aesthetics, see Haug 1986, 1987, pp. 103–127). This increases the discrepancy between the commodity's use value and its outlook—or its sign value (Baudrillard, 1972/1988, pp. 57–97)—and accentuates the importance of the sign value at the cost of use value. Along with this, consumption moves "into the dimension of status and prestige" (Baudrillard, 1983a, p. 45). Thus, commodities as sign values become their own referents—they no longer refer outside themselves, to the reality of separate use values, but have absorbed the reality that now exists only as produced by them. In brief, although signs once represented reality, they now produce it—and not only in regard to commodities but in many other important respects, too.

Baudrillard did not insist that material reality would have disappeared in some mysterious way but that reality, which in previous times was something largely given and which was represented through signs, is in present times something largely produced—and its production is precisely simulation that takes place according to signs, that is, codes and models, for which there are no originals and which do not represent something outside them (Baudrillard 1976/1988, pp. 139–143). The idea of a social code came from biology: "it is in the genetic code that the 'genesis of simulacra' finds its most developed form" (p. 139).

For Baudrillard, then, there is something like a social DNA. But what might it be? Kellner (1989c, p. 80) illuminated it by saying that "just as our cells contain genetic codes, DNA, that structure how we experience and behave, so too society contains codes and models of social organization and control which structure the environment and human life." An example of the functioning of "the society of coded simulation" is the work of urban planners who "modulate codes of city planning and architecture in creating urban systems" (p. 80). Models functioning according to the logic of codes have begun to replace reality ever more extensively—this is

> exemplified in such phenomena as the ideal home in women's or lifestyle magazines, ideal sex as portrayed in sex manuals or relationship books, ideal fashion as exemplified in ads or fashion shows, ideal computer skills as set forth in computer manuals, and so on. In these cases, the model becomes a determinant of the real, and the boundary between hyperreality and everyday life is erased. (Best & Kellner, 1991, pp. 119–120)

Hyperreality and Mass Communication

Along with its breaking off from its bonds to outside referents, simulation begins to construct a hyperreality. The mass media play a prominent role in this work. According to Kellner (1989c, p. 68), Baudrillard interpreted "the media as key simulation machines." They reproduce signs and codes

> which in turn come to constitute an autonomous realm of (hyper)reality. . . . This process constitutes a significant reversal of the relation between representation and reality. Previously the media were believed to mirror, reflect or represent reality, whereas now they are coming to constitute a (hyper)reality, a new media reality, "more real than the real", where "the real" is subordinate to representation thus leading ultimately to a dissolving of the real. (p. 68)

Because the media are an essential part of the machinery turning reality into hyperreality, what they present does not imitate reality, but reality imitates what they present—reality becomes, therefore, merged in media presentations and inseparable from them. That reality sometimes twists itself into a form suited to the media had been observed before Baudrillard. For example, the politicians' eagerness to take up an image that is particularly appealing for television, is no news. On the other hand, talk of an image implies a distinction between an imaginary, polished appearance and the real unpolished person who puts up this false appearance. Baudrillard rejected such a distinction. For him, the appearance is all there is—there is nothing behind it.

An example utilized by Baudrillard (1983b, pp. 49–58) in this context is a TV program portraying the life of an American family "authentically," as if the TV apparatus would not have been present. But of course the presence of cameras transformed the family members' behaviors from what they normally would have been. Nonetheless, this did not mean for Baudrillard the turning of authenticity into unauthenticity, but simply that the family began to live according to television codes—the codes produced the family reality and there was no other for that time. What happened was "the dissolution of TV into life, the dissolution of life into TV" (p. 55). In this way, the difference between the genuine and the illusory disappears in hyperreality. In such a situation, we no longer look at television but television looks at us—that is, we start to behave as if we were permanently in the focus of television cameras.

There are many examples that have been interpreted to show that the media—especially television—produce hyperreality with their codes. Think, for example, of the way in which the actors in television merge, in the eyes of some viewers, into those characters they play. Best and Kellner (1991, p. 119) tell that Robert Young, who played Dr. Welby in a TV serial in the 1970s, "received thousands of letters asking for medical advice." Raymond Burr, who successively played lawyer Perry Mason and detective Ironside, received first letters asking for legal advice and then letters asking for detective aid. Some actors playing soap opera villains and villainesses can not manage without hiring bodyguards to protect them "from the irate fans angered by their shenanigans in television world" (p. 119).

As can be seen, Baudrillard radicalized the culturalist thesis that the media take part in the construction of reality. According to the culturalists, the media construct reality by signifying it in this or that way, and by influencing people's activity in so far as they accept the significations as valid. Baudrillard went a step further—for him, there is no signification but transformation: The media literally construct (hyper)reality with their codes. Metaphorically speaking, the media are for him a part of a huge computer, whose digital codes spring up as undetermined mutations. Although radically undetermined by their birth—remember, there are no originals for them—the codes exert very determined influence: They dictate what is possible and what impossible to do.

The Implosion of Meaning in the Media

Baudrillard (1980, 1983a) must reject the talk of the signifying media also for the reason that, for him, the media do not constitute meanings but implode them, imploding, at the same time, the social in the masses. To clarify this thought, we must return to his view of symbolic exchange. As a transaction, it is mutual and maintains social relations. Meaning is like such a transaction: It is generated in mutual social relationships. Also, communication as communication, not as mere transmission of information, takes place in mutual relations—mutuality and interactivity seem to be characteristics that Baudrillard attaches to meaning constituting communication.

Along with the growth of simulation, however, symbolic exchange and the mutual sociality it sustained began to get ruined. An important aspect in the history of simulation is the shift from symbolic exchange to commodity exchange aimed at economic utility. This utility pushed sociality aside. And when, at the second stage of simulation, commodities began to be produced for a market, anonymous to the producers, the relationship between the exchangers—producers and purchasers—was no longer mutual and social, because purchasers had a direct relationship only to the commodities on sale. This process, thus, turned a two-way social relationship of symbolic exchange into a one-way relationship between commodities and customers.

This is the background of Baudrillard's (1980, pp. 137, 138) paradoxical point that "we live in a world of proliferating information and shrinking sense"—in a world where "information destroys or at least neutralizes sense and meaning." He placed information abreast with commodities: Like the industry produces commodities, the media produce information to an anonymous market. The audiences have necessarily a one-way, receptive relationship to it, comparable to the customers' relationship to commodities. Because information runs from the media to the receivers, there is no mutuality and, consequently, no meaning constructing communication. It is exactly this that gives rise to the paradox: The more information, the less meaning.

This must, however, be specified on the basis of the following point (pp. 142–143):

> Whatever its content, be it political, pedagogical, cultural, the objective of information is always to circulate meaning, to subjugate the masses to meaning. This imperative to produce meaning translates itself into an impulse to moralize: to inform better, to socialize better, to raise the cultural level of the masses, etc. What nonsense! The masses remain scandalously resistant to this imperative of rational communication. They are offered meaning when what they want is entertainment.

It is not so that the media would not offer meaning—on the contrary, they are swelling with it—but it is so that this meaning has no sense for the receivers, because they have no such mutual relationship to it that would render it meaningful. It is precisely this that gets the meaning to implode in the media: What is meaning from the standpoint of the media, is signs without meaning from the standpoint of receivers. But it is just this, signs without meaning, under whose spell the audience falls. Signs without meaning offer pure entertainment. This is again an example of the transformation of reality into hyperreality.

The replacement of meaning by information accelerates the implosion of the social in the masses. Because information is one-way bombardment, cut off from social relationships, and because the meanings offered by it are rejected, information is incapable of "intensifying or even creating the 'social relationship'" (p. 140), that is, of organizing the germs of joint action that possibly exist among the crowds. Unable to release the energy smoldering among the masses, information "simply produces more and more mass" (p. 140). This has put "an end to revolutionary expectations," because it is no longer possible to appeal "to 'class' or to the 'people'" (p. 145). Today, masses do not even speak but are silent. However, again paradoxically, the silence is, for Baudrillard, the force with which the masses resist the system.

But is not silence a sign of impotence rather than a resisting force? Perhaps, but for Baudrillard an attempt to resist the system through the empowerment of the masses corresponds to

> an anterior phase of the system. . . . The current strategy of the system is to inflate utterance to produce the maximum of mean-

ing. Thus the appropriate strategic resistance is to refuse meaning and utterance, to simulate in a hyper-conformist manner the very mechanisms of the system, itself a form of refusal and non-reception. This is the resistance strategy of the masses. It amounts to turning the system's logic back on itself by duplicating it, reflecting meaning, as in a mirror, without absorbing it. (p. 148)

The strategy of silence drives at ruining the aims of the system by rejecting the meaning it presses on and/or by rejecting the system through assenting to its logic—but not to its efforts—in an excessive manner. The masses "know that there is no liberation, and that a system is abolished only by pushing it into hyperlogic, by forcing it into an excessive practice which is equivalent to a brutal amortization" (Baudrillard, 1983a, p. 46). What is at issue is "a destructive hypersimulation, a destructive hyperconformity" which in the end destroys the system's "whole edifice" (p. 46). A sort of catastrophe mystique! But what after the catastrophe, when or if it comes? According to Kellner (1994, p. 10), Baudrillard hovers "between nostalgia and nihilism": a return to the sociality of symbolic exchange might take place—or perhaps not.

DEBATE OVER THE POSTMODERN DISCOURSE

There are many who have taken a repudiating stand to the postmodern views, in particular to "the claim that we are currently experiencing an epochal change in our social life" (Callinicos, 1989, p. ix). Some dismissed it outright arguing that we simply do not live in "a 'postmodern' epoch fundamentally different from the industrial capitalism of the nineteenth and twentieth centuries" (p. 4). Others have been more hesitant. Frisby (1985, p. 272) remarked that to talk of an ever-new postmodernity is "premature" because this talk ignores "the ever-same reproduction of the social relations necessary for the ever-new to appear." Also Best and Kellner (1991, p. 280) said that it is "premature to claim that we are fully in a new postmodern scene," even though they regarded "postmodern culture and society as new emergent tendencies."

Perhaps the most notable critic of the postmodern discourse is Habermas (1980/1996; see also 1987). For Habermas, modernity is by no means over but its project is still unfinished. Thus, "we should learn" from the mistakes "which have accompanied the project of modernity," rather "than abandoning modernity and its project"

(1980/1996, p. 51). The refusal of modernity by celebrating post-modernity would mean, for him, the abandonment of the irreplaceable values bequeathed by the Enlightenment: aspirations of cognitive rationality, moral autonomy, and social-political self-determination. The result would be irrational nihilism. Such horror visions have inspired Habermas to label the advocates of the postmodern discourse sometimes as conservatives (pp. 53–54), sometimes as irrationalists and anarchists (Best & Kellner, 1991, p. 245).

Where Habermas' criticism moved on a philosophical terrain, some other critics have attacked postmodern discourse from a social theoretical perspective by blaming it for a naive belief that new information technology would have displaced the capitalist mode of production as the structuring force of society. Callinicos (1989, p. 121) dismissed such a view as pure "nonsense." Best and Kellner (1991, p. 276) said that by stressing technological development as "the motor of social change," postmodern discourse has occluded the extent to which "economic imperatives" continue "to structure contemporary societies." Those few postmodern theorists—as Jameson, for one—who have acknowledged the role of economy have received criticism from the opposite direction—more extreme postmodernists have accused them for "economic reductionism" (McRobbie, 1994, p. 29) or for other totalizing sins (Horne, 1989; Radhakrishnan, 1989).

Also the aesthetic tenets of the postmodern discourse has been met with criticism. Even the postmodern theorists themselves have debated much over how to distinguish postmodernism from modernism (cf. M. Rose, 1991). In light of this, it is not surprising that critics of postmodernism have tended to deny the whole existence of postmodern art, separable from modernism. Callinicos (1989, pp. 9–28), for example, could not find any difference between modernism and postmodernism. The manner of ascribing allegedly postmodern features to art products has aroused criticism, too. For example, Kellner (1989b, p. 29) doubted whether the so-called postmodern cultural texts "really manifest the lack of depth and flatness which Jameson attributes to them."

The critics have found postmodern discourse as self-contradictory in many respects. As observed, Lyotard rejects grand narratives and totalizing views but, as Kellner (1988, p. 253) asked, does not his talk of a break from modernity to postmodernity "presuppose a Master Narrative, a totalizing perspective, which envisages the transition from a previous stage of society to a new one?" Moreover, Lyotard is inconsistent "in calling for a plurality and heterogeneity of language games, and then excluding from his kingdom of discourse" terroristically the "grand narratives" (p. 254). In this respect, Lyotard's discourse would be no better than those he criticizes. Best and Kellner (1991, p. 174) remarked, in addition, that Lyotard's cele-bration of little narratives brings him close to "liberal pluralism and empiricism"—a stance that characterized, for example, the classical behavioral mass communication research.

Baudrillard has also been criticized quite harshly. For Callinicos (1989, p. 6), his views represent "a vulgar caricature" of the ideas with which the postmodern discourse started. Kellner (1989c, pp. 60–84), for his part, accused Baudrillard, especially, for technological determinism. Furthermore, like Lyotard, Baudrillard also violated the postmodern tenets with his totalizing approach: He "tends to take tendencies in the current social situation for finalities, trends for finished states" (Kellner, 1988, p. 248). And finally, although signs, for Baudrillard, do not have referents, he wrote as if what he said would correspond straight away to the social reality outside the signs (cf. Callinicos, 1989, pp. 146–148; Kellner, 1989c, p. 90). Or is his purpose to produce with his writings new hyperreality? Then, what would be the code working in him? Be it as it may, Kellner's (1988, p. 248) judgment is that Baudrillard has produced "good science fiction but poor social theory."

Despite all the objectionable points, the postmodern discourse includes important insights into contemporary society and culture. Thus, Best and Kellner (1991, p. 143), for example, have balanced their Baudrillard critique by stating that his work has captured often pertinently "the turn toward simulation and hyperreality in contem-porary capitalist societies." Communication studies, in particular, should take seriously the view that, along with the development of the means of communication, reality and its representations have begun to intermix in ever more complicated ways. Our life is mediat-ed by signs to an ever-growing extent. Therefore, the Baudrillardian view, to mention only one, that our conception of nature is based "on photographs and TV documents rather than on authentic experience in the midst of nature" (Aro, 1990, p. 46), appears truer today than it did yesterday.

19

THE CHANGING MEDIA SCENE

New Challenges
to Communication Studies

For some time, one of the greatest challenges to communication studies has been the rapid development of information and communication technologies (ICTs). Starting with the microelectronics revolution of the 1970s, this development has enabled the digitalization of information and the convergence of computers and telecommunications (Forester, 1987; Lyon, 1990, pp. 22–41). There has been much discussion of the impact of this development on societies and people's everyday life. This topic, condensed often into the concept of the information society, has been the focus of widely differing discourses and theories. Webster (1995) found as many as seven theoretical perspectives on it, ranging from the theory of postindustrial society to postmodern discourse.

In this respect, the discussion around the ICTs and the new media is reminiscent of the theoretical discussion around the press in the 19th century, which also was conducted from multiple points of view. There are even further affinities. Many of the 19th century's theorists saw the press, above all, as a great connector binding a vast society together. Similarly—as book titles like Wired Cities (Dutton, Blumler, & Kraemer, 1987) or The Rise of the Network Society (Castells, 1996) suggest—a major theme in today's discussion is the power of ICTs to link society and the whole world even more densely and effectively together. Furthermore, where the press aroused both optimistic and pessimistic prophecies in the 19th century, the debate on ICTs, too, has oscillated "between utopian and dystopian perspectives" (Dutton, 1999, p. 7; see also Lyon, 1990, pp. 7–21; Mosco, 1982, pp. 1–7).

From this perspective, the discussion around ICTs closes the circle started in this book with the early press theories. What is more, it recapitulates certain major stretches of the route we have been travelling. It has, for example, turned repeatedly to the Innisian and McLuhanian views of communication technologies as preconditions for the shapes societies may take on. In particular, McLuhan's notion of the global village has become widely popular. Furthermore, some visions of the capacity of the ICTs to increase people's possibilities for participation bring to mind Dewey's utopia of the Great Community (e.g., Aikens, 1998; Hague & Loader, 1999a; Tsagarousianou, Tambini, & Bryan, 1998). Indeed, one might argue that the discussion necessarily repeats, in strategic points, the past of communication studies because many questions asked about traditional mass communication unavoidably recur, albeit possibly in new guises, in regard to the new media.

So far, the discussion has been somewhat fuzzy, especially in regard to the new media. Communication scholars seem not to have been able to keep abreast with the rapid change of the media scene. In fact, they have been charged with overlooking the area "altogether" (Slevin, 2000, p. 4). There are many unsettled issues. Even the familiar notions of the media have become obscure as the media have blended together in complex ways, blurring the formerly clear boundaries in the media field. This makes the review of the new media discussion problematic. Before entering this difficult topic, however, I survey briefly the general debate over the information society, introducing this theme with a glance at an important source for that debate, the theory of postindustrial society.

THE THEORY OF POSTINDUSTRIAL SOCIETY

The development of societies is often depicted as a progress through certain phases. Daniel Bell's (1919–) theory of postindustrial society represents such a stage theory (Bell, 1973). He said "it is possible to trace a movement from preindustrial, through industrial, to postindustrial societies" (Webster, 1995, p. 32). Similar stage models also have been presented by other writers, for example, by Toffler (1971, 1980) and Allardt (1988, 1989). It should be noted, however, that Bell was not interested in the earlier phases as such but only as a backdrop against which he could emphasize those characteristics he saw as typical of the postindustrial society.

Bell's (1973, p. 9) theory rests on a view of society as "a web of many different kinds of relations," a complex formation whose parts may develop very discordantly. This heterogeneity allows society to be described with diverse conceptual schemata, each of which "selects particular attributes from a complex reality." The tripartition into preindustrial, industrial, and postindustrial stages is one such conceptual schema. Another important schema is the analytic division of society into social structure, polity, and culture (p. 12). For Bell, each of these has its own logic of development; they do not causally influence one another. Formerly, they were connected through a "common value system," but in the postindustrial phase there has emerged "an increasing disjunction" between them (pp. 12–13).

For Bell (pp. 9–12), the purpose of a conceptual schema is to specify the axial principle and the axial structure of society or some part of it. In regard to the parts he singled out in society, he described the axes as follows:

> The axial principle of the social structure is economizing—a way of allocating resources according to principles of the least cost, substitutability, optimization, maximization and the like. The axial principle of the modern polity is participation, sometimes mobilized or controlled, sometimes demanded from below. The axial principle of the culture is the fulfillment and enhancement of the self. (p. 12)

"The axial principle of the postindustrial society," Bell (1980, p. 501) stated, "is the centrality of theoretical knowledge." And he continued (p. 506): "just as capital and labor have been the central variables in industrial society, so information and knowledge are the crucial variables of postindustrial society." For Bell, this is testified by the fact that production is based increasingly on the discoveries of theoretical natural science, instead of the insights of talented amateurs. Likewise, governments tend to ground their policies on theoretical models of economy. Because theoretical knowledge is produced by universities and research institutes, they become "the axial structures of the emergent society" (Bell, 1973, p. 26).

The coming of the postindustrial society is aided especially by the diffusion of new intellectual technologies, above all computers that enable the utilization of calculated decision models and procedures for planning. The growth of technologies turns from a haphazard process to a controlled development. The dominant economic sector has moved from agriculture to the industry, and now moves to the production of services. Occupational structure is transformed as well—jobs demanding high professional skill and technical know-how increase their proportion at the cost of other jobs. For Bell (p. 17), scientists and engineers "form the key group in the postindustrial society."

What moves societies from one stage to the next is their increasing productivity which, again, is propelled by technological innovations. Such innovations enable people "to get 'more for less' and to choose the more 'rational' course of action" (p. 76). This development has allowed the bulk of the workforce to shift first from agriculture to industry and then from industry to services. From such a perspective, it is quite natural to see technically relevant theoretical knowledge as the most prominent feature of the postindustrial society, or knowledge society, as Bell also called it (see pp. 212–262). Only after the microelectronics revolution did Bell (1980) take the term information society in a more permanent use.

Bell's view of postindustrial development may be to the point with respect to the United States but not necessarily regarding all advanced societies (Castells, 1996, pp. 202–231). Critics have doubted, in addition, whether this development has brought about, as Bell is disposed to see, a new form of society. For Kumar (1978, p. 232), the trends singled out by Bell "are extrapolations, intensifications, and clarifications of tendencies which were apparent from the very birth of industrialism" (see also M. Rose, 1991, pp. 31–37; Smart, 1992, pp. 38–42; Webster, 1995, pp. 40–50). Poster (1990, p. 24), again, argued critically that, contrary to his aspirations, Bell remains trapped in technological determinism since he attributes the cause of the postindustrial society "to a technical innovation," the computer. Anyway, Bell's theory and the criticism aroused by it have anticipated many characteristics of the subsequent debate over the information society.

DEBATING THE INFORMATION SOCIETY

There is "little doubt that the spread of computers and new communication systems is one of the most striking phenomena within the advanced societies of the late twentieth century" (Lyon, 1990, p. 22). This "informatisation" process has put its mark everywhere. Thus, what has been under dispute is not the presence of the new ICTs but what their presence means for people and for societies. Are they beneficial, for the most, or do they lead to harmful consequences? Do they bring about such fundamental changes that we must speak of "information society" as a new mode of society, qualitatively different from the preceding ones? Or are the changes only a sequel to tendencies already discernible in societies before the introduction of the ICTs in which case we could not talk of a qualitatively new mode of society?

The debate around these issues has been quite cacophonous—at least up to the beginning of the 1990s to which its consideration is limited here. Yet, certain camps and front lines can be identified. Those who see the ICTs generally as a blessing have been inclined to regard the information society as a radically new social formation, whereas those critical of the ICTs have taken mostly the stand that "we have only had the 'informatisation' of established relationships" (Webster, 1995, p. 4). The debate, so far conducted mainly from such positions, has concentrated on certain focal points. These points, as they are singled out by Lyon (1990), provide the frame of reference for the following description of the discussion.

Economy and Occupational Structure

The view that we have entered a new, information-based society has often been argued for by referring to changes that have taken place in the realm of economy and occupations. At the beginning of the 1960s, Machlup (1962) calculated that at those times a little less than one third of the U.S. gross national product (GNP) came from economic activities around the production and distribution of information and that this sector had grown faster than the others, thus increasing its share of the growing economy. Porat (1977) examined the situation some 10 years later. His more nuanced calculations pointed at the same direction as Machlup's: The "information economy" had continually increased its significance, yielding at the end of the 1960s 46% of the U.S. GNP.

The growth of the information economy has also been examined by computing the distribution of the workforce in different employment sectors at different points of time. Where Bell's theory of postindustrial society paid attention only to the traditional sectors of agriculture, industry, and services, Machlup and Porat placed the information sector at the side of the these three. According to Machlup (1962), in 1900 only 13% of the U.S. labor force was employed in the information sector, whereas in 1959 that share was already 43%. Porat's (1977) figures show that this proportion had approached 50% by the latter half of the 1970s.

These impressive figures are not without problems, however. For Webster (1995, p. 12), "there is a great deal of hidden interpretation and value judgement as to how to construct categories and what to include and exclude from the information sector." Machlup's and Porat's calculations, for example, were based on dissimilar grounds. A further problem is that occupations included in the information sector are quite heterogenous. Lyon (1990, p. 50) wondered whether or not one can "usefully mix, as for example OECD figures do, diverse categories of 'information work' from telecommunication researchers to television repairers." Such questions are pertinent because a sector's share of the workforce depends on the criteria with which occupations are included in or excluded from it.

It is obvious, however, that the significance of the information sector has grown, although the quantity of this growth cannot be assessed for sure. But does this growth warrant the conclusion that there has emerged a new form of society? Was, for instance, the United States transformed into an information society in 1956, as Naisbitt (1984, pp. 11–14) contended on the basis that the information sector exceeded the other sectors as an employer at that time? Such a view has been contested by the argument that information work is nothing new and that it predominantly serves the needs of industrial production. Thus, the emphasis laid on information in Western societies may stem from their development as industrial societies rather than from the surpassing of that form of society (Schement & Lievrouw, 1987, p. 43).

On the other hand, some have prophesied that the ICTs will lead to a new economic order. Masuda (1980/1990, 1985) spoke of a synergetic economy that will replace today's relentless, competitive pursuit for profit with a system where "individuals and groups cooperate in complementary efforts to achieve the common goals set by the society as a whole" (1980/1990, p. 135). In such an economy, people will "voluntarily participate in the synergetic construction of public facilities," and there will be an "autonomous restraint of consumption by the people" (pp. 78–79), whatever that might mean. Expressive of this paradise vision is that its "final goal" will be "the theological synergism of man and the supreme being" (p. 139).

Working Conditions

The ICTs have changed drastically the working conditions: Factories are increasingly robotized and offices are filled with computerized technology. The consequences of these changes, however, have been assessed quite contradictorily. The following questions belong to the most contested ones: (a) What is the effect of the ICTs on employment and on the nature of jobs? (b) Will ICTs change the industrial relations and if so, in what way? (c) Will they "decentralize" work and release it from its bounds to specific working places—that is, will the so-called telecommuting from home be the future form of work?

It is generally agreed that the new technology will reduce industrial jobs. For optimistic commentators, the jobs lost will be replaced with new jobs in the service and information sectors whereas pessimists believe the automatization of offices will cause subsequent unemployment in those sectors. Furthermore, the optimists believe the new technology will release workers from routine tasks enabling them to do more creative ones, whereas the pessimists warn that it will only create new monotonous tasks. For most commentators, the informatization has put employees with different qualifications in unequal positions in the competition for jobs (Lyon, 1990, pp. 66–77; see also Clement, 1988; Douglas & Guback, 1984; Kumar, 1995, pp. 15–27).

According to Lyon (pp. 77–78), the debate over the impact of the ICTs on industrial relations has ranged "from the optimism of those who see the future in the apparent egalitarianism of 'Silicon Valley' shirtsleeves and common canteen" to the pessimism of those for whom computerisation is simply "a means to capitalist oppression and worker degradation." There are cases in which the new technology has diminished control and enabled workers to steer their work more autonomously, but in other cases, the control has only become invisible. If the benefits and inconveniences of the ICTs have been distributed unevenly in the working community, this has easily led to controversies and frictions.

"A major theme in the 'information society' literature is that of work decentralization" (p. 82). The most manifest form of this decentralization is telecommuting (working from home). The vision of telecommuting as work form of the future was popularized especially by Toffler (1980, pp. 210–223) with his view of the "electronic cottage." In principle, working from home might bring about many advantages—as, for example, the reduction of the air pollution from travel to work (pp. 216–220). On the other hand, there are many obstacles in its way, which is why its expansion has lagged clearly behind the prognoses (see J. Becker, 1988). It may also have negative effects, such as the transformation of the home into a living place of people estranged from one another (Kumar, 1995, pp. 154–163) or the privatization of workers as a result of their "separation from workmates and colleagues" (Lyon, 1990, p. 84).

Despite the divergent assessments, a factum is that working conditions have undergone a huge transformation. But does this entitle us to conclude that we have entered a brave new information society? In 1990, Lyon (p. 84) assessed that the arrival of the ICTs was not "taking the advanced societies beyond industrial capitalism"—in fact, "many familiar features of the old system are still present, albeit with some new variations." His conclusion was that changes taking place in the realm of work are better thought of as a restructuring of industrial capitalism than as the coming of a new society. This view still seems valid today.

Politics, Administration, and Surveillance

In politics, the new catchword has been electronic democracy (London, 1994)—or teledemocracy, cyberdemocracy, or digital democracy (Hague & Loader, 1999b; London, 1995; Tsagarousianou et al., 1998). These words express the hope that the ICTs might radically alter the relationship between citizens and their elected representatives, on one hand, and provide citizens real opportunities to participate in public affairs, on the other. Interactive media have been expected to bring about "electronic referenda and polls" and enable the voters to be continually in touch with their representatives (Marien, 1985, p. 654). For Masuda (1980/1990, p. 81), the information society will replace the representative democracy by a participatory one "in which policy decisions both for the state and for the local self-government bodies will be made through the participation of ordinary citizens." This will be "a classless society, free of overruling power" (p. 136). Although there has been some development in the expected direction, these utopias are, as yet, far from being realized.

The inertia in the realm of politics is more than offset by the activity of state administration as an user and promoter of the ICTs. The role of the military sector has been especially pronounced here. In fact, much of the ICTs were developed to meet military needs (Kumar, 1995, pp. 7–8, 27–29; Lyon, 1990, pp. 26–30; Webster, 1995, pp. 61–66). The promoting role of state administration is testified by the fact that, in the 1980s, the British government funded more than half of the research and development in information technology and purchased half of the total output of the British electronics industry—the Ministry of Defense alone more than 20% (Kumar, pp. 27–29). Governments have also eagerly marketed "the idea of an information society—including vigorous attempts to encourage a 'computer culture' in schools and universities" (p. 27).

If an electronic participatory democracy is still a dream, an electronically supervised "Big Brother" society is, for many commentators, already there (Lyon, pp. 93–104; Webster, pp. 52–73). In Western societies, there are diverse electronic systems—reaching from direct camera monitoring to huge data archives—that different agencies of control have installed to monitor citizens. In itself, the surveillance of people by official and private agencies "is no novel phenomenon" (Lyon, p. 97). In fact, Beniger (1986) stressed that information society is but a sequel to the control revolution that already started in the 19th century. What is new is that the ICTs have vastly increased capacity "for different databases to be 'interfaced' with one another" (Lyon, p. 95). In front of all this, data-protection legislation is not superfluous.

Global Networking

For many commentators, McLuhan's vision of a global village has begun to come true in tandem with the spreading of information networks all over the globe. For example, there are prophecies that nationalism, characteristic of industrial societies, will lose its significance as the Internet opens possibilities for limitless interaction between people with different cultural backgrounds. But does the possible reduction of nationalism testify that the ICTs are producing a new multicultural world community, an information universe for all?

Those critical of the information society have remarked that global networking is not taking place for the needs of intercultural communication but for those of transnational business. From a historical point of view, today's World Wide Web is "a creation of the capitalist industrial system" (Lyon, 1990, p. 109). Modern

> corporations which range the globe in pursuit of their business require a sophisticated computer communications infrastructure in their daily activities. It is unthinkable that a company with headquarters in New York could co-ordinate and control activities in perhaps fifty or sixty other countries . . . without a reliable and sophisticated information network. (Webster, 1995, p. 78)

Besides corporations, governments also have had their part to play in this game. For example, the "United States needs a strong world communications network to support its overseas interests" (Dizard, 1989, p. 184). What has been largely ruled out of this networking game is the interest of the citizens and the publics (D. Schiller, 1982).

This networking has enabled transnational corporations (TNCs) to take advantage of a flexible "international division of labour" (Lyon, p. 114). For example, production can be flexibly distributed among countries according to the fluctuation of profitability. Moreover, the ICTs allow TNCs "to conduct their businesses with minimum concern for restrictions imposed by nation states" (Webster, p. 93). We have also witnessed a "global integration of financial markets" (Castells, 1996, p. 2). Networks enable the brokers "to buy and sell at any time" which is why a kind of stateless currency "circulates around the globe, twenty-four hours a day" (Lyon, p. 115).

Due to the dominance of business, global networking is "far from symmetrical," but the cards—or, in this case, the semiconductor chips—are stacked "overwhelmingly in favour" of advanced nations (Lyon, p. 105). The developing countries have received only crumbs (Rada, 1985). Some futurologists, like Toffler (1980, pp. 345–365), have considered it possible that the developing nations can jump, with the aid of the ICTs, right into the stage of information society. Lyon (p. 109), however, believes such a view displays "ethnocentric Western bias"—among other things, it "conveniently forgets the connection between imperialism and technological development" underestimating thus "the difficulties of 'closing the information gap'."

The following assessment, formulated by Lyon (p. 121) in the late 1980s, is still quite valid:

> Any concept of information society must be global in scope; informatization is nowhere a merely local process. The notion of a "global village," however, should be treated with caution. The international telecommunications web . . . seems far from producing the "one world" hinted at by that phrase. Indeed, given the inter-connections between states, TNCs and military interests involved in the I[C]Ts, the "global village" is a pathetically hollow concept.

Everyday Life: Leisure and Consumption

Kumar (1995, p. 155) said it "is in the sphere of leisure and consumption, rather than work and production, that we see the most direct and dramatic impact of the revolution of information technology." Directed by big business interests, the ICT

> has been increasingly put at the service of home-based consumption. Entertainment is the most obvious example. "Going out" has been replaced by "staying in." Instead of visits to the pub or the

> cinema, families . . . watch video-cassettes at home or choose from
> around thirty channels of broadcast, satellite or cable television.
> Home computers supply the facility for an endless arrays of elec-
> tronic games. (pp. 155–156)

"Other services apart from entertainment are equally seeking
the home as their base" (p. 156). Telebanking and teleshopping are
the most striking examples. Yet, home-centeredness does not necessarily lead to family-centeredness. A. Tomlinson (1990, pp. 67–68)
believes this development is turning the home into a "site for an
unprecedentedly privatized and atomized leisure and consumer
lifestyle." Kumar (p. 158) sees the reason for this in the making of
information equipment to fit an individual use, with the result that
there will no longer be need "for collective or group activities," a
development that strengthens "the individual, not the family."
However, as Morley (1992, pp. 221–222) remarked, we still do not
know much about how the equipment is used at homes and what
meanings are attached to them (see also Mackay, 1997).

One should also note that not all have equal opportunities to
retire to the privatized world of home ICTs even if they would want
to do so. Although information technology has with time become
cheaper, differences in incomes have all the while divided people into
"information-rich" and "information-poor" (Lyon, pp. 125–129;
Morley, pp. 217–218). Thus, not all can similarly take advantage of
the supposedly increased choices opened through "the huge new
array of cultural commodities" (Lyon, p. 125).

But has the range of choices really expanded? Instead of
increased choices one might speak, as Kumar (p. 155) does, of the
"reshaping of consumption" where "ever more areas of social and cultural life" are brought "within the purview of capitalist activity and
market rationality." As "choice is increasingly circumscribed by commercial culture," it seems, for Lyon (p. 129), "that the expanding
diversity of channels and commodities within the 'electronic culture'
is leading, paradoxically, to less rather than more choice."

THE NEW MEDIA

Problems of Definition

In the discussion of the 1990s, a specific subtheme within the overall
theme of information society, that of the new media, arose to the fore.
But what are the new media? Although the term has been among us

for some time, its meaning is still unclear. In fact, the task of defining it has been judged as "almost impossible" (Jankowski & Hanssen, 1996, p. 2), because the technological landscape, which the term wishes to circumscribe, is under continuous change. Consequently, "no sooner has the ink dried than the words already written need revision" (Feldman, 1997, p. ix). Therefore, every account of the subject is doomed to remain transitory, at least for the time being.

In light of this, it is understandable that the term new media has been employed in quite different ways. For some, it has served as a catch-all phrase for communication technologies that have appeared after broadcast television. Such innovations include, among other things,

> high-definition television, digital radio broadcasting, multimedia computers, handheld data banks, wireless cable systems, CD-ROM (compact disc-read-only memory) laser discs, direct broadcast satellites, advanced facsimile machines, intelligent telephones, consumer computer networks, portable electronic newspapers and national videotext services. (Dizard, 1997, pp. 3–4)

Pavlik (1996, pp. 1–4) compiled a more systematic list by dividing innovations of this kind into technologies of production, distribution, display, and storage. Some others refer to the term new media in a more focused manner, for example, referring to multimedia or, what for many seems to amount to quite the same, to digital media or hypermedia (Hansen, 1999, p. 161). For Feldman (p. 24), multimedia "is the seamless integration of data, text, sound and images of all kinds within a single, digital information environment." There are still others according to whom the category new media includes only computer-based communication networks and the cyberspace grounded on them (Hintikka, 1996, pp. 2–3). Among the networks, the most renowned is of course the Internet.

Characterizations of this kind look at the new media from a technical point of view (Leeuwis, 1996). Another way to approach this phenomenon is to look for features that distinguish the modus operandi of the new media from that of the traditional mass media. The main distinctive characteristics can be summarized as follows (see Hintikka, 1996).

First, the traditional media are typically one-way channels from one sender to many receivers, whereas the new media allow a two-way many-to-many communication where senders and receivers can exchange roles. The new media have thus a higher interaction potential than the traditional media. Second, the traditional media hardly give the audience more choices than to pay or not to pay attention to their supply, whereas the new media enable users to choose "what services they receive, when they get them, and in what form" (Dizard, p. 4). And third, where the traditional media tend to position the receivers as passive onlookers of what is presented to them, the new media create a virtual environment, a cyberspace, and invite the users to enter in it and to wander therein.

This distinction between the traditional and new media is, however, highly ideal-typical—in reality the dividing line between them "is being smudged every day" (Dizard, p. 4). The difference between the two, then, is relative, not absolute. However, there is a difference that perhaps can most aptly be crystallized with the concept of interactivity. This notion has played "a prominent role in virtually all definitions and descriptions of new media" (Jankowski & Hanssen, 1996, p. 9). Interactivity has been seen, for example, as "the very aspect of the Internet that has supplanted the first media-age culture industry of radiated communication" (Holmes, 1997, p. 13).

What is Interactivity?

Unfortunately, the meaning of interactivity is hardly any clearer than that of the new media. Much of the literature, "both popular and scholarly," uses the term "with few or no attempts to define it" (Downes & McMillan, 2000, p. 158). For some scholars, "the attraction and familiarity" of the term have been "at the same time barriers for fundamental consideration of its meaning" (Hanssen, Jankowski, & Etienne, 1996, p. 61). Be that as it may, interactivity has been used in different senses depending of the context of its use (Goertz, 1995; Jäckel, 1995). Of this plethora of senses, relevant here are only those that include human beings at least as one partner of interaction.

Within social sciences, interaction usually refers to a mutual, communicative process between human actors (Jäckel, 1995). It has been defined, for example, as "the reciprocal action and communication between two or more individuals, or two or more social groups" (Watson & Hill, 1987, p. 88). However, with the development of computer networks there has emerged a new view, according to which the term "refers to the relationship between people and machines" (J. Jensen, 1999, p. 169). From such a view, interaction is "reciprocal communication between a user and a playback device or digital media system" (Hansen, 1999, p. 158). Sticking to the technical human–computer interaction (HCI), this view tends to ignore the more social computer-mediated communication (CMC) between people (Jensen, p. 169).

There are, however, formal approaches to interaction that offer perspectives on both HCI and CMC. One comes from Rafaeli (1988) who, equalizing responsiveness and interaction, distinguished between three levels. Messages flowing bilaterally compose the first level of two-way communication, but this case does not as such represent interaction. When each subsequent message relates to the preceding one in the process, we move onto the second level of reactive or quasi-interactive communication. The third level of full interaction is reached first when messages refer not only to the preceding ones but "to even earlier messages" as well as "to the way previous messages are related to those preceding them" (pp. 119–120).

It is best to see these levels as ideal types from which real cases may deviate more or less. Anyway, it is clear that human–machine processes reach the third level only in specific cases. An action–reaction process where the user makes a move, the computer responds, and the user makes a new move on the basis of this response—as in reading a hypertext or in interrogating databases for information—remains quasi-interactive, at the most. On the other hand, CMC can easily reach the third level, even if it does not need to do so. Actually, all discussions, be they computer-mediated or face to face, may fluctuate between quasi-interactive and full interactive modes of communication (Rafaeli & Sudweeks, 1998, p. 176).

The cases of HCI may take on two opposite forms. In the case of consultation, information is produced by a central agency but utilized by the individual user; in the case of registration, again, information is produced by the individual user but utilized by a central agency (Bordewijk & van Kaam, 1986, pp. 18–19; see Jensen, 1999). In both cases, the interaction is asymmetrical as the options open to users are predetermined by computer software applications (Hanssen et al., 1996, pp. 63–64). The interaction becomes symmetrical first in CMC, that is, in the case of conversation where information is both produced and utilized by the users (Bordewijk & van Kaam, 1986, pp. 17–18). As an example, one can think of an Internet discussion group where "someone posts an initial query or comment, and other members reply, still others reply to the replies, and so the 'discussion' goes" (Freedman & Grossbrenner, 1998, p. 271).

Virtual Communities, Virtual Publics?

Conversations "held simultaneously or asynchronously" by numbers of people living physically far apart from one another compose one of the most interesting phenomena made possible by computer networks (Rafaeli & Sudweeks, 1998, p. 174). Electronic bulletin boards (BBSs), e-mail mailing lists, Usenet newsgroups, and Internet Relay Chat are examples of spaces for such interaction. On these fora, discussion is conducted by way of electronic messaging. The emergence of Internet discussion groups of this kind has given rise to the notion of virtual communities. Rheingold (1995, p. 5) defined these communities as "social aggregations that emerge from the Net when enough people carry on those public discussions long enough, with sufficient human feeling, to form webs of personal relationships in cyberspace."

Whether "what comes out of all this virtual talk can be properly termed 'community' is," however, "a complicated question" (Porter, 1997, p. xii). The sheer multiplicity of virtual discussion groups makes understandable that "so far the question of what constitutes an 'electronic community' has remained largely unresolved" (Höflich, 1995, p. 528). Groups of this kind differ in many respects from such offline or real-life collectives that are usually termed communities—admitting that this term "is infinitely complex and amorphous" (Fernback, 1997, p. 39; see also Slevin 2000, pp. 90–117). Above all, virtual discussion groups are not bound by place, and people do not live in them as they do in offline communities. As Doheny-Farina (1996, p. 37) expressed, "you don't subscribe to a community as you subscribe to a discussion group on the net." A "connection does not inherently make for community" (Jones, 1998, p. 5).

On the other hand, Internet discussion groups also display characteristics usually associated with offline communities. One is the emergence of a certain kind of tradition. That is, like offline communities, online discussion groups, too, develop specific customs and shared norms of interaction "the observance of which is required for the participation in a 'community'" (Höflich, 1995, p. 531). Baym (1998, pp. 38, 51) said that when there emerges, within CMC, "group-specific forms of expression, identities, relationships and normative conventions" and when they "develop into stable group-specific understandings, the group gains the potential to be imagined as a community." The adherence to such customs will "distinguish group insiders from outsiders" (p. 53). Insiders "continually reinforce the norms by creating structural and social sanctions against those who abuse the groups' systems of meanings" (p. 60). The "standards of conduct" are "aimed toward the goal of preserving the group" (McLaughlin, Osborne, & Ellison, 1997, p. 147).

Perhaps such groups represent a wholly new species of community, instead of replicating real-life communities (see Jones, 1998, pp. 8-9). One problem is, however, that the fora on which these groups act have been equated with public places like cafés or squares where people in the old days gathered to argue about public affairs (Höflich, pp. 522–523). Despite the fact that such gatherings followed certain rules of conduct, they cannot be termed communities without totally sacrificing the sense of this term. Instead, they must be termed publics (see Blumer, 1946/1961; Carey, 1987; Habermas, 1962/1989). Aren't Internet discussion groups, then, more like publics than like communities? The safest answer is that these groups represent different kinds of collectives—some communities, some publics, and some maybe still other species.

Images of cafés and squares imply a view of the Internet as a public sphere. In fact, many explicitly expect the new media to provide "a new public sphere that can replace the old one now crippled by commodification and fragmentation" (Bryan, Tsagarousianou, & Tambini, 1998, p. 8). This expectation is usually based on a belief that these media have the "capacity to challenge the existing political hierarchy's monopoly" and to "revitalize citizen-based democracy" as citizens begin to debate and deliberate about matters of public concern online (Rheingold, 1995, p. 14). This is an essential part of what has been called variously "electronic democracy," "cyberdemocracy," or "digital democracy" (Hague & Loader, 1999b).

In an extreme view, the Internet "is conceived as an electronic forum comprising a vast network of liberated and equal citizens of the world capable of debating all facets of their existence without fear of control from national sovereign authorities" (Hague & Loader, p. 6). While taking generally a more cautious view, Poster (1997, p. 213) sees Internet discussion groups serving "the function of a Habermasian public sphere without intentionally being one." Tabbi (1997, p. 237) believes the fate of the Internet as a public sphere "depends largely on the ability of its numerous constituencies to use it critically, and with some awareness of each other's existence."

Although it is impressive to learn that in the last years of the 1990s "tens of thousands" of discussion groups were carried over the Usenet, "each containing from a few dozen to tens of thousands of messages" (Kollock & Smith, 1999, p. 6), the online discussions themselves seemed to leave much to be desired in regard to what one might expect from a rational public debate. Schwartz (1996, p. 64) said these discussions "aren't so disciplined" but "move from topic to topic at the whim of participants." Empirical analyses, few in number it is true, seem to confirm such assessments. A content analysis of some Usenet newsgroups indicated that Usenet "possesses certain disadvantages as a forum for public discussion of political issues. These include opinion reinforcement, flaming, and unrepresentativeness" (Davis, 1999, pp. 161–162). Wilhelm (1999, p. 175; see also 2000, pp. 86–104) drew the following conclusion from his corresponding content analysis:

> The sorts of virtual political forum that were analyzed do not provide viable sounding boards for signalling and thematizing issues to be processed by the political system. They neither cultivate nor iterate a public opinion that is the considered judgment of persons whose preferences have been contested in the course of a public gathering; at least there is insufficient evidence to support such a salubrious picture of the political public sphere in cyberspace.

Beyond such points, those doubting the Internet's capacity to function as a public sphere refer also to the fact that the "renaissance of open public discussion," enabled by the net, has "been experienced by a relatively tiny minority of the world's population" (Moore, 1999, p. 48). For Lockard (1997, p. 220), a hard fact is "that access capital is the poll tax for would-be virtual citizens." Moreover, the germ of an Internet public sphere, nurtured by a noncommercial ethos, may "not survive the commercial onslaught" (Moore, p. 48). Bryan et al. (1998, pp. 8-16) said that this survival cannot be secured without at least some public regulation. Moreover, it is questionable, whether there is such a germ, as initial research has suggested

> that information traffic flow on high-bandwidth networks is skewed toward downstream movement. Trade Unions, voluntary organisations and political parties use the Internet to send information, rather than receive it, implying that it is a monologue not a dialogue which is facilitated by technological developments. (p. 12; see also Hale, Musso, & Weare, 1999)

Concluding Remarks

The questions dealt with here represent only a fraction of the overall discussion about the new media. There are many other important themes. Much of the discussion has been concerned with the technological developments and especially with the convergence of the different media into integrated broadband, full service networks (see Baldwin, McVoy, & Steinfeld, 1996). As there are strong commercial interests bound with this undertaking, it is very likely that "most of the actual construction of the new system focuses on 'video-on-demand,' tele-gambling and VR [virtual reality] theme parks" instead of "wiring classrooms, doing surgery at a distance and tele-consulting the Encyclopaedia Britannica" as governments and futurologists have speculated (Castells, 1996, p. 366).

Another theme, important from the viewpoint of mass communication studies, involves Net journalism or, in general, online publishing. This activity has increased very rapidly. Newspaper enterprises, in particular, have been eager to set up Web versions, mostly to offset troubles hanging over the traditional printed press (Dizard, 1997, pp. 165-180; Reddick & King, 1997, pp. 221–238). Often the newspapers' rush to the Internet has happened, however, "with rather vague ideas of the cost-effectiveness of the exercise, or even a clear idea of what is the purpose of the action" (Heinonen, 1999, p. 43). In many cases, material appearing on the printed pages has simply been shoveled onto the online versions, even though the Net technology offers rich possibilities to make the news differently: The stories "may consist of real-time flashes, background stories may be linked to them from archives, comments and new background stories may be added as the event unfolds and the whole issue can be contextualised by means of hypertext throughout the Internet information space" (p. 72).

An online newspaper is a mass medium on the Net. On the other hand, Internet technology has begun to challenge familiar ideas of the mass media and their mass audience. There are expectations, for example, that in the near future everyone can make a personal newspaper issue for him or herself instead of receiving a copy of a ready-made issue. Viewing the development of such an electronic newspaper in a very rosy light, Negroponte (1995, p. 153) suggested one to imagine "a future in which your interface agent can read every newswire and newspaper and catch every TV and radio broadcast on the planet, and then construct a personalized summary. This kind of newspaper is printed in an edition of one." What is more, the Internet enables people to bypass journalists altogether by using alternative information sources. Thereby "the audience is in a position to seriously challenge journalists as information (and entertainment) disseminators" (Heinonen, p. 82).

Also within the theme of virtual interaction discussed above there are aspects that I did not take up. An absorbing question concerns the identity construction of the interactants. Usually, one's correspondents in cyberspace "have no bodies, no faces, no histories beyond what they may choose to reveal" (Porter, 1997, p. xi). This enables them to "have multiple identities"; moreover, they "can shift identities rather easily, taking on characteristics of others' identities" (Jones, 1998, p. 28). For Thu Nguyen and Alexander (1996, p. 116), people "are proving perilously willing" to play with identities online. Some scholars consider this as a sign of "a postmodern condition, in which identities have become more fragmented and flexible" (Baym, 1998, p. 54). Turkle (1995, p. 20), for example, sees that the play with identities indicates "a postmodern culture of simulation."

But even if the Internet allows for a play with identities, it is another question to what extent people are actually doing so—at least with a conscious intent to deceive. Although "many varieties of identity deception can be found within the Usenet," "many individual identity deceptions are acts of omission, rather than commission" (Donath, 1999, pp. 44, 52). In other words, what is at issue is often not faking but only "hiding one's identity" (p. 52). It has also been pointed out that if Internet users were permanently engaged in identity plays, there would be "only a very limited range of opportunities for human association" (Slevin, 2000, p. 106). Be that as it may, "the work on on-line identity demonstrates a scholarly fascination with how anonymity can be used to invent alternative versions of one's self and to engage in untried forms of interaction, theoretically problematizing the notion of 'real self'" (Baym, p. 54).

The themes discussed in the context of the new media are no novelties in mass communication studies. As the earlier pages of this book demonstrate, even interaction has been a long-standing subject matter in the field notwithstanding the fact that traditional mass media are not particularly interactive. On the other hand, the differences of the new media from the traditional media give the old themes new accents or situate them in novel contexts. What these accents and contexts will be is far from clear for the time being. Therefore, an exciting new disciplinary history is in store for us—a history to which the history of thinking and research on the traditional media will offer an important and interesting point of comparison.

20

*FROM INCOHERENCE
TO MULTIPLICITY*

Wilbur Schramm (1959/1964, p. 511) once said that communication studies is, in the world of human and social sciences,

> one of the great crossroads where many pass but few tarry. Scholars come into it from their own disciplines, bringing valuable tools and insights, and later go back . . . to the more central concerns of their disciplines.

Schramm spoke naturally of the classical behavioral form of mass communication studies. Nonetheless, as can easily be discerned from this book, his parable still preserves its actuality in the sense that, during its whole history, mass communication studies has attracted influences and ingredients from many different directions.

Initially, in the first phase of scattered openings, there was no crossroads, no specific field of mass communication research, but the problems of mass communication were discussed quite separately within the then established disciplines—Dewey discussed them within social philosophy, Park within sociology, and so on. Furthermore, when the specific field of mass communication studies emerged during the second period of consolidation, it was, and has been ever since, a multidisciplinary compound of different discourses. Also, many of the discourses have themselves been mixtures of ingredients received or taken from different disciplines although often some parent disciplines have given them the most definite shape.

The field's multidisciplinarity has put it in a dependent position in regard to the surrounding disciplines proper, such as psychology or sociology. The discourses, operative in the field at each particular time, have received or taken from other disciplines theories, concepts, and viewpoints, and applied them to the study of mass communication. Political economists have applied views of political economy, cultural scholars semiotic and linguistic insights, effect researchers psychological learning theories or theories of cognitive consistency, to give only a few examples. Further, the struggles between different discourses in the field can often be traced back to controversies between or within surrounding disciplines. The often strained relation between social sciences and humanities, for instance, has fueled some of the field's central schisms, as that between social-structurally oriented political economy and humanistically oriented cultural studies (see Garnham, 1995; Grossberg, 1995; see also Ferguson & Golding, 1997).

A metaphor like crossroads is expressive of the field's heterogeneity. As indicated earlier, this heterogeneity is partly a consequence of cross-pressures coming from surrounding disciplines. But it also results partly from interests coming from outside the scholarly world and nourishing different discourses in the field. The close relationship of the behavioral tradition to media industry and administrative agencies is but one example. The issue driving Marxism was to untie the field from the commercial-administrative bonds to which the behavioralists had bound it, and to turn it into an activity directed against social inequality and repression. And the way in which cultural studies celebrates the audience's freedom of choice and interpretation is—intentionally or not—in accord with the interests of a deregulated and increasingly commercial media industry.

In the context of his crossroads-simile, Schramm (1959/1964, p. 511) emphasized that "communication research is a field, not a discipline" and continued: "Therefore, we must not look for the unique theory in communication which we are accustomed to see in disciplines, or the kind of career in communication research which we are accustomed to see within disciplines." With these words, he conceded the fact that even the behavioral tradition was far from a unified discipline. Nevertheless, he cherished a secret hope that in some day there will emerge "an integrated social science of human communication" (Chaffee & Rogers, 1997, p. 156). This hope did not come true—the field, which for Schramm was tantamount to the behavioral tradition, was continually lacking a unifying theory and did not, for this reason, qualify as the hoped-for science, as Schramm (1983) ruefully admitted late in his life.

The problem of the field's unity or connectedness has naturally also preoccupied minds outside the behavioral tradition. In fact, according to an analysis by Monahan and Collins-Jarvis (1993), connectedness is one of the central values that communication scholars have proposed as guiding principles for the activity in the field. As a value, it obliges the field to pursue "a shared core of knowledge" (p. 151). Another important value is pluralism, which is, in a sense, opposite to connectedness since it obliges the field to "encourage theoretical diversity" (p. 151). Monahan and Collins-Jarvis observed that while pluralism was cherished more than connectedness in the scholarly discourses of the 1980s, connectedness generated "considerable debate" in the 1990s while pluralism took on "less significance" (p. 154). In this way, the distinctiveness of the field, which in the years dominated by pluralism was not considered particularly important, was emerging "as a highly salient issue" (p. 154).

It may very well be that voices advocating connectedness and distinctiveness have increased in the 1990s. For example, in the same issue of the Journal of Communication in which Monahan and Collins-Jarvis published their analysis, many writers emphasized these values, sometimes with an edifying purpose in mind (Beniger, 1993; Craig, 1993; Dervin, 1993; Krippendorff, 1993; Rosengren, 1993), even though some others spoke against coherence and for a greater diversity (O'Keefe, 1993; Rothenbuhler, 1993). Another question is whether or not the field has in reality become more coherent. I'm afraid that it has not—if by coherence is meant that there would have emerged a set of shared principles. From this perspective it seems, on the contrary, that the field has become even more pluralist than before. During its historical trajectory the field, then, would have moved from incoherence, not to coherence, but to multiplicity.

There are various reasons for this multiplication. The mere fact that the field has for a long time included "scholars from a multiplicity of theoretical perspectives, using disparate methodological means to achieve diverse intellectual ends," has brought along an increasing divergency, though Monahan and Collins-Jarvis (p. 153) see here a reason for "a yearning for connections." Furthermore, the multiplication of the means of communication through the introduction of the new media and other ICTs has had multiplying effect on media theory and research, too. There is also the simple reason that new discourses do not necessarily annihilate the old ones, rather these usually survive, even if often in changed guises and/or in more marginal positions than before. The cross-breeding of discourses makes the field ever more like a jungle.

In front of all this, it is no surprise that suggestions for rendering the field more coherent abound. Unfortunately—or perhaps fortunately—the suggestions tend to start with premises that are incompatible or at least difficult to accommodate to one another. Therefore, it is not likely that there could be brought forth an agreement as to what would be the best way to attain a greater coherence in the above sense. On the contrary, the suggestions may lead to an intensifying fragmentation of the field. In fact, it is not uncommon to hear laments that the field has been caught in a process of ever deepening fragmentation. Rosengren (1993, p. 9) expressed this view by stating acidly that it "is as if the field of communication research were punctuated by a number of isolated frog ponds—with no friendly croaking between the ponds, very little productive intercourse at all, few cases of successful cross-fertilization."

This assessment was written at a time when the field's most pronounced controversies and debates had already calmed down. Such a point of "quiet waters" after a hectic process, during which disparate standpoints proliferated in the field, easily leads to a pessimistic prognosis of the field's capacity to cohere, all the more so if one defines a coherent field as one that is built on widely shared premises. But coherence might be understood in a more modest way that presumes, instead of a common sharing of basic premises, only that the field's different discourses are capable of interacting meaningfully with one another. In this modest sense a field could be regarded as coherent regardless of the multiplicity and disparity of the discourses of which it consists at each particular time.

In his assessment, Rosengren was doubtful of such a capacity, but in my view the many disputes considered in this book show at least that that the field's discourses have not been "isolated frog ponds" taking, at the most, only scant cognizance of each other. On the other hand, the debates have not been particularly constructive, above all for the reason that the disputants have not usually had patience enough to listen to the other but have resorted headlong to their prejudices and portrayed the other as a "straw man." Thus, what would be desirable is a more ecumenic leaning, a willingness to listen to the other even in a case in which one would see no need to compromise with his or her specific premises. But even if the debates would not come up to this ideal, they are significant because they shed light on the principles with which the disputing discourses start, and on the metatheoretical points that they consider important.

What is often debated is the direction in which mass communication studies should be going. Reviews of the field's history are also sometimes written with the intent to promote a certain line of development and to downplay other possibilities, or at least there is a tendency to close the reviews with some programmatic remarks of what would be the desirable course for the field. A debate between different scenarios of the future is important, of course—not least because it would foster the field's self-understanding by keeping the representatives of the contending discourses aware of what goals each of them is pursuing and for what reasons. However, to intervene here in such a discussion by outlining a specific vision of the future would be contrary to the book's purpose which is to describe the field's development as a multidisciplinary undertaking, not to advocate certain trends at the cost of others.

Thus, instead of taking a position on where the field should be going and why, I will close this exposition with a few lines from T.S. Eliot's poem Little Gidding. What the meaning of these lines is, in the specific context of this review over the trajectory of mass communication studies, remains for the reader to decide:

> We shall not cease from exploration
> And the end of all our exploring
> Will be to arrive where we started
> And know the place for the first time.

REFERENCES

Abercrombie, N., & Longhurst, B. (1998). Audiences: A sociological theory of performance and imagination. London: Sage.

Adatto, K. (1990). Sound bite democracy: Network evening news presidential campaign coverage, 1968 and 1988 (Research paper R-2). Cambridge, MA: Harvard University, Joan Shorenstein Barone Center.

Adorno, Th.W. (1953). A social critique of radio music. In B. Berelson & M. Janowitz (Eds.), Reader in public opinion and communication (enlarged ed., pp. 309–316). Glencoe: IL: The Free Press. (Original work published 1940)

Adorno, Th.W. (1957). Television and patterns of mass culture. In B. Rosenberg & D.M. White (Eds.), Mass culture: The popular arts in America (pp. 474–488). Glencoe, IL: The Free Press. (Original work published 1953)

Adorno, Th.W. (1975). The psychological technique of Martin Luther Thomas' radio addresses. In Th.W. Adorno, Gesammelte Schriften, Band 9.1: Soziologische Schriften II (pp. 7–141). Frankfurt am Main, Germany: Suhrkamp. (Original work written 1943)

Adorno, Th.W. (1976). Sociology and empirical research. In Th.W. Adorno et al., The positivist dispute in German sociology (pp. 68–86). London: Heinemann. (Original work published 1957)

Adorno, Th.W. (1977). Kulturkritik und Gesellschaft. In Th.W. Adorno Gesammelte Schriften, Band 10.1: Kulturkritik und Gesellschaft I (pp. 11–30). Frankfurt am Main, Germany: Suhrkamp. (Original work published 1955)

Adorno, Th.W. (1984). Zur gesellschaftlichen Lage der Musik. In Th.W. Adorno, Gesammelte Schriften, Band 18: Musikalische Schriften V (pp. 729–777). Frankfurt am Main, Germany: Suhrkamp. (Original work published 1932)

Adorno, Th.W. (1991). On the fetish character in music and the regression of listening. In Th.W. Adorno, The culture industry: Selected essays on mass culture (pp. 26–52). London: Routledge. (Original work published 1938)

Adorno, Th.W. (1991). Culture industry reconsidered. In Th.W. Adorno, The culture industry: Selected essays on mass culture (pp. 85–92). London: Routledge. (Original work published 1963)

Adorno, Th.W. (1994). The stars down to earth and other essays (S. Crook, Ed.). London: Routledge. (Original work published 1953)

Adorno, Th.W., Frenkel-Brunswik, E., Levinson, D.J., & Sanford, R.N. (1969). The authoritarian personality. New York: Norton. (Original work published 1950)

Adorno, Th.W., & Horkheimer M. (1986). The culture industry: Enlightenment as mass deception. In Th.W. Adorno & M. Horkheimer, Dialectic of enlightenment (pp. 120–167). London: Verso. (Original work published 1944)

Aikens, G.S. (1998). American democracy and computer-mediated communication: A case study in Minnesota. http://www.aikens.org/phd/(6.4.00).

Allardt, E. (1988). Yhteiskuntamuoto ja kansallisvaltio [Form of society and the national state]. In E. Allardt, S. Hall, & I. Wallerstein, Maailmankulttuurien äärellä (pp. 15–33). Publication of the University of Jyväskylä's Research Unit of Contemporary Culture, 11.

Allardt, E. (1989). Yhteiskuntamuoto ja yhdenmukaisuuden paine [Form of society and pressure towards conformity]. In P. Suhonen (Ed.), Suomi—muutosten yhteiskunta (pp. 13–25). Helsinki: WSOY.

Almond, C.A. (1990). A discipline divided: Schools and sects in political science. Newbury Park, CA: Sage.

Altheide, D. (1977). Creating reality: How TV news distorts reality. Beverly Hills: CA: Sage.

Althusser, L. (1971). Lenin and philosophy and other essays. New York: Monthly Review Press.

Altschull, J.H. (1990). From Milton to McLuhan: Ideas behind American journalism. New York: Longman.

Anderson, J.A., & Meyer, T.P. (1975). Functionalism and the mass media. Journal of Broadcasting, 19(1) 11-22.

Ang, I. (1989). Wanted: audiences. On the politics of empirical audience studies. In E. Seiter, H. Borchers, G., Kreutzner, & E-M. Warth (Eds.), Remote control (pp. 96–115). London: Sage.

Ang, I., & Hermes, J. (1991). Gender and/in media consumption. In J. Curran & M. Gurevitch (Eds.), Mass media and society (pp. 307–328). London: Edward Arnold.

Arens, K. (1971). Manipulation. Berlin: Volker Spiess.

Arnold, M. (1965). Culture and anarchy with friendship's garland and some literary essays. The complete works of Matthew Arnold (R.H. Super, Ed.). Ann Arbor: The University of Michigan Press. (Original work published 1869)

Aro, J. (1990). Jean Baudrillard ja modernin kulttuurin patologiat [Jean Baudrillard and the pathologies of modern culture]. Sosiologia, 27(1), 42–51.

Asch, S. (1963). Effects of group pressure upon the modification and distortion of judgments. In H. Guetzkow (Ed.), Groups, leadership and men (pp. 177–190). New York: Russell & Russell.

Asp, K. (1986). Mäktiga massmedier [Powerful mass media]. Stockholm, Sweden: Akademilitteratur.

Astala, E. (1989). Katsaus elokuvasosiologian teoriaan [An overview of the theory in film sociology]. In R. Kinisjärvi, M. Lukkarila, & T. Malmberg (Eds.), Elokuvateorian historia (pp. 262–279). Helsinki: Like.

Atteslander, P. (1980). Ist Medieneinfluss bei Wahlen messbar? Media Perspektiven, Heft 9, 597–604.

Baldwin, T.S., McVoy, D.S., & Steinfeld, C. (1996). Convergence: Interacting media, information, and communication. Thousand Oaks, CA: Sage.

Bargh, J. (1988). Automatic information processing: Implications for communication and affect. In L. Donohew, H.E. Sypher & T. Higgins (Eds.), Communication, social cognition, and affect (pp. 9–32). Hillsdale, NJ: Erlbaum.

Barnlund, D.C. (1970). A transactional model for communication. In K. Sereno & C.D. Mortensen (Eds.), Foundations of communication theory (pp. 83–102). New York: Harper & Row.

Barthes, R. (1983). Elemente der Semiologie. Frankfurt am Main, Germany: Suhrkamp. (Original work published 1964)

Bartlett, F.C. (1954). Remembering: A study in experimental and social psychology. Cambridge, UK: Cambridge University Press. (Original work published 1932)

Bassnett, S., & Hoskin, K. (1986). Textuality/sexuality. In D. Punter (Ed.), Introduction to contemporary cultural studies (pp. 327–351). London: Edward Arnold.

Baudrillard, J. (1980). The implosion of meaning in the media and the implosion of the social in the masses. In K. Woodward (Ed.), The myths of information: Technology and postindustrial culture (pp. 137–148). London: Routledge & Kegan Paul.

Baudrillard, J. (1983a). In the shadow of silent majorities . . . or the end of the social. New York: Semiotext(e).

Baudrillard, J. (1983b). Simulacra and simulations. New York: Semiotext(e).

Baudrillard, J. (1988). For a critique of the political economy of the sign. In J. Baudrillard, Selected writings (M. Poster, Ed., pp. 57–97). Cambridge, UK: Polity Press. (Original work published 1972)

Baudrillard, J. (1988). Symbolic exchange and death. In J. Baudrillard, Selected writings, (M. Poster, Ed., pp. 119–148). Cambridge, UK: Polity Press. (Original work published 1976)

Bauer, R.A., & Bauer, A.H. (1960). America, "mass society" and mass media. Journal of Social Issues, 16(3), 3–66.

Bauman, Z. (1987). Legislators and interpreters: On modernity, post-modernity and intellectuals. Cambridge, UK: Polity Press.

Baym, N. (1998). The emergence of on-line community. In S.G. Jones (Ed.), Cybersociety 2.0: Revisiting computer-mediated communication and community (pp. 35–68). Thousand Oaks, CA: Sage.

Becker, J. (1988). Electronic homework in West Germany: A critical appraisal. In V. Mosco & J. Wasko (Eds.), The political economy of information (pp. 247–273). Madison: The University of Wisconsin Press.

Becker, L.B. (1982). The mass media and citizen assessment of issue importance: A reflection of agenda-setting research. In D.C. Whitney, E. Wartella, & S. Windahl (Eds.), Mass communication review yearbook (Vol. 3, pp. 521–536). Newbury Park; CA: Sage.

Becker, S.L. (1975). Viewpoint: McLuhan as Rorschach. Journal of Broadcasting, 19(2), 235–240.

Bell, A. (1991). The language of news media. Oxford, UK: Basil Blackwell.

Bell, D. (1973). The coming of post-industrial society: A venture in social forecasting. New York: Basic Books.

Bell, D. (1980). The social framework of information society. In T. Forester (Ed.), The microelectronic revolution (pp. 500–549). Oxford, UK: Basil Blackwell.

Belman, L.S. (1977). John Dewey's concept of communication. Journal of Communication, 27(1), 29–37.

Belsey, C. (1980). Critical practice. London: Methuen.

Beniger, J.R. (1978). Media content as social indicators: The Greenfield index of agenda-setting. Communication Research, 5(4), 437–453.

Beniger, J.R. (1986). The control revolution: Technological and economic origins of the information society. Cambridge, MA: Harvard University Press.

Beniger, J.R. (1993). Communication—embrace the subject, not the field. Journal of Communication, 43(3), 18–25.

Benjamin, W. (1977). Das Kunswerk im Zeitalter seiner technischen Reproduzierbarkeit. In W. Benjamin, Das Kunstwerk im Zeitalter seiner technischen Reproduzierbarkeit: Drei Studien zur Kunstsoziologie (H. Schweppenhäuser & R. Tiedemann, Eds., pp. 7–44). Frankfurt am Main, Germany: Suhrkamp. (Original work published 1936)

Benjamin, W. (1978). The author as producer. In A. Arato & E. Gebhardt (Eds.), The essential Frankfurt School reader (pp. 254–269). Oxford, UK: Basil Blackwell. (Original work published 1937)

Bennett, T. (1982). Theories of the media, theories of society. In M. Gurevitch, T. Bennett, J. Curran, & J. Woollacott (Eds.), Culture, society and the media (pp. 30–55). London: Methuen.

Bennett, T., & Woollacott, J. (1987). Bond and beyond: The political career of a popular hero. Houndmills, UK: Macmillan Education.

Bentele, G. (1985). Wissenskluft-Konzeption und Theorie der Massenkommunikation. In U. Saxer (Ed.), Gleichheit oder Ungleichheit der Massenmedien? (pp. 87–104). Munich, Germany: Ölschläger.

Berelson, B. (1949). What "missing the newspaper" means? In P.F. Lazarsfeld & F.N. Stanton (Eds.), Communications research 1948-49 (pp. 111–129). New York: Harper & Brothers.

Berelson, B. (1952). Content analysis in communication research. Glencoe, IL: The Free Press.

Berelson, B. (1964). The state of mass communication research. In L.A. Dexter & D.M. White (Eds.), People, society, and mass communications (pp. 503–509). New York: The Free Press.

Berelson, B. (1968). Behavioral sciences. In D.L. Sills (Ed.), International encyclopedia of the social sciences (Vol. 2, pp. 41–45). New York: Crowell, Collier & Macmillan.

Berelson, B., Lazarsfeld, P.F., & McPhee, W.N. (1954). Voting: A study of opinion formation in a presidential campaign. Chicago: The University of Chicago Press.

Berlo, D.K. (1960). The process of communication. New York: Holt, Rinehart & Winston.

Best, S., & Kellner, D. (1991). Postmodern theory: Critical interrogations. Houndmills, UK: Macmillan Education.

Bineham, J.L. (1988). A historical account of the hypodermic model in mass communication. Communication Monographs, 55(3), 230–249.

Bird, S.E. (1992). Travels in nowhere land: Ethnography and the "impossible" audience. Critical Studies in Mass Communication, 9(3), 250–260.

Blank, D.M. (1977). The Gerbner violence profile. Journal of Broadcasting, 21(3), 273–279.

Blumer, H. (1956). Sociological analysis and the "variable." American Sociological Review, 21(6), 683–690.

Blumer, H. (1961). The crowd, the mass, and the public. In W. Schramm (Ed.), The process and effects of mass communication (pp. 363–379). Urbana: University of Illinois Press. (Original work published 1946)

Blumer, H. (1965). Public opinion and public opinion polling. In D. Katz, D. Cartwright, S. Eldersweld, & A. McClung Lee (Eds.), Public opinion and propaganda: A book of readings (pp. 70–78). New York: Holt, Rinehart & Winston. (Original work published 1947)

Blumer, H. (1970). Movies and conduct. New York: Arno Press & New York Times. (Original work published 1933)

Blumer, H. (1974). Symbolic interactionism: An approach to human communication. In R.W. Budd & B.D. Ruben (Eds.), Approaches to human communication (pp. 401–419). Rochelle Park, NJ: Hayden.

Blumer, H. (1986). Suggestions for the study of mass-media effects. In H. Blumer, Symbolic interactionism: Perspective and method (pp. 183–194). Berkeley: University of California Press. (Original work published 1959)

Blumer, H. (1986). Symbolic interactionism: Perspective and method. Berkeley: University of California Press. (Original work published 1969)

Blumler, J.G. (1964). British television: The outlines of a research strategy. The British Journal of Sociology, 15(3), 223–233.

Blumler, J.G. (1979). The role of theory in uses and gratifications studies. Communication Research, 6(1), 9–36.

Blumler, J.G. (1980). Purposes of mass communication research: A transatlantic perspective. In G.C. Wilhoit & H. de Bock (Eds.), Mass communication review yearbook (Vol. 1, pp. 33–44). Beverly Hills, CA: Sage.

Blumler, J.G. (1983). Communication and democracy: The crisis beyond and the ferment within. Journal of Communication, 33(3), 166–173.

Blumler, J.G., & Gurevitch, M. (1982). The political effects of mass communication. In M. Gurevitch, T. Bennett, J. Curran, & J. Woollacott (Eds.), Culture, society and the media (pp. 236–267). London: Methuen.

Blumler, J.G., Gurevitch, M., & Katz, E. (1985). Reaching out: A future for gratifications research. In K.E. Rosengren, L.A.Wenner, & P. Palmgreen (Eds.), Media gratifications research: Current perspectives (pp. 255–273). Beverly Hills, CA: Sage.

Blumler, J.G., & Katz, E. (1974). Foreword. In J.G. Blumler & E. Katz (Eds.), The uses of mass communications: Current perspectives on gratifications research (pp. 13–16). Beverly Hills, CA: Sage.

Blumler, J.G., & McQuail, D. (1968). Television in politics: Its uses & influences. London: Faber and Faber.

Boguschewsky-Kube, S. (1990). Der Theorienstreit zwischen Publizistik und Zeitungswissenschaft: Ein Paradigmenproblem. Munich, Germany: tuduv-Verlag.

Bohrmann, H. (1986). Grenzüberschreitung? Zur Beziehung von Soziologie und Zeitungswissenschaft 1900-1960. In S. Papcke (Ed.), Ordnung und Theorie: Beiträge zur Geschichte der Soziologie in Deutschland (pp. 93–112). Darmstadt, Germany: Wissenschaftliche Buchgesellschaft.

Bohrmann, H., & Sülzer, R. (1973). Massenkommunikationsforschung in der BRD. In J. Aufermann, H. Bohrmann, & R. Sülzer (Eds.), Gesellschaftliche Kommunikation und Information, Band 1 (pp. 83–120). Frankfurt am Main, Germany: Fischer Athenäum.

Bömer, K. (1929). Bibliographisches Handbuch der Zeitungswissenschaft. Leipzig, Germany: Otto Harassowitz.

Bordewijk, J.L., & van Kaam, B. (1986). Towards a new classification of tele-information services. Inter Media, 14(1), 16-21.

Bottomore, T., & Nisbet, R. (Eds.). (1979). A history of sociological analysis. London: Heinemann.

Bower, G.H., & Hilgard, E.R. (1981). Theories of learning. Englewood Cliffs, NJ: Prentice-Hall.

Boyd-Barrett, O. (1982). Cultural dependency and the mass media. In M. Gurevitch, T. Bennett, J. Curran, & J. Woollacott (Eds.), Culture, society and the media (pp. 174–195). London: Methuen.

Bramson, L. (1961). The political context of sociology. Princeton, NJ: Princeton University Press.

Bransford, J.D., & Johnson, M.K. (1972). Contextual prerequisites for understanding: Some investigations of comprehension and recall. Journal of Verbal Learning and Verbal Behavior, 11(6), 717–726.

Brecht, B. (1983). Radio as a means of communication: A talk of the function of radio. In A. Mattelart & S. Siegelaub (Eds.), Communication and class struggle (Vol. 2, pp. 169–171). New York: International General. (Original work published 1930)

Bredemeier, H. (1955). The methodology of functionalism. American Sociological Review, 20(2), 173–180.

Brosius, H-B. (1991). Schema-Theorie—ein brauchbarer Ansatz in der Wirkungsforschung? Publizistik, 36(3), 285–297.

Brosius, H-B., & Kepplinger, H.M. (1990). The agenda-setting function of television news: Static and dynamic views. Communication Research, 17(2), 183–211.

Bross, M. (1992). McLuhan's theory of sensory functions: A critique and analysis. Journal of Communication Inquiry, 16(1), 91–107.

Brown, R.L. (1970). Approaches to the historical development of mass media studies. In J. Tunstall (Ed.), Media sociology: A reader (pp. 41–57). Urbana: University of Illinois Press.

vom Bruch, R. (1980). Zeitungswissenschaft zwischen Historie und Nationalökonomie: Ein Beitrag zur Vorgeschichte der Publizistik als Wissenschaft im späten deutschen Kaiserreich. Publizistik, 25(4), 579–600.

vom Bruch, R. (1986). Einleitung. In R. vom Bruch & O.B. Roegele (Eds.), Von der Zeitungskunde zur Publizistik (pp. 1–30). Frankfurt am Main, Germany: Haag+Herchen.

Brunhuber, R. (1907). Das moderne Zeitungswesen. Leipzig, Germany: G.J. Göschen'sche Verlagshandlung.

Brunsdon, C. (1981). "Crossroads": Notes on a soap opera. Screen, 22(4), 32–37.

Brundson, C., & Morley, D. (1978). Everyday television: Nationwide. London: BFI.

Bryan, C., Tsagarousianou, R., & Tambini, D. (1998). Electronic democracy and the civic networking movement in context. In R. Tsagarousianou, D. Tambini, & C. Bryan (Eds.), Cyberdemocracy: Technology, cities and civic networks (pp. 1–17). London: Routledge.

Bücher, K. (1922). Zur Frage der Pressereform. Tübingen, Germany: J.C. Mohr (Paul Siebeck).

Bücher, K. (1980). Akademische Berufsbildung für Zeitungskunde. Publizistik, 25(4), 606–607. (Original work published 1915)

Bücher, K. (1981). Entstehung und Evolution des Zeitungswesens. In K. Bücher, Auswahl der publizistikwissenschaftlichen Schriften (H.D. Fischer & H. Minte, Eds., pp. 117–146). Bochum, Germany: Brockmeyer. (Original work published 1892)

Budd, M., Entman, R. M., & Steinman, C. (1990). The affirmative character of U.S. cultural studies. Critical Studies in Mass Communication, 7(2), 169–184.

Budd, R.W., McLean, M.S., & Barnes, A.M. (1966). Regularities in the diffusion of two major news events. Journalism Quarterly, 43(2), 221–230.

Budd, R.W., & Ruben, B.D. (Eds.). (1979). Beyond media: New approaches to mass communication. Rochelle Park, NJ: Hayden.

Bulmer, M. (1984). The Chicago School of sociology: Institutionalization, diversity and the rise of sociological research. Chicago: Chicago University Press.

Burke, K. (1968). Medium as "message." In R. Rosenthal (Ed.), McLuhan: Pro & con (pp. 165–177). New York: Funk & Wagnalls.

Buxton, W.J. (1998). Harold Innis' excavation of modernity: The newspaper industry, communications, and the decline of public life. Canadian Journal of Communication, 23(3), 321–339.

Bybee, C. (1999). Can democracy survive in the post-factual age?: A return to the Lippmann-Dewey debate about the politics of news. Journalism & Communication Monographs, 1(1).

Callinicos, A. (1989). Against postmodernism: A Marxist critique. Cambridge, UK: Polity Press.

Cameron, D. (1993). Feminism and linguistic theory (2nd ed.). Basingstoke, UK: Macmillan.

Cancian, F.M. (1968). Varieties of functional analysis. In D.L. Sills (Ed.), International encyclopedia of the social sciences (Vol. 6, pp. 29–41). New York: Crowell, Collier & Macmillan.

Cantril, H., Gaudet, H., & Herzog, H. (1940). The invasion from Mars. Princeton, NJ: Princeton University Press.

Carey, J.W. (1968). Harold Adams Innis and Marshall McLuhan. In R. Rosenthal (Ed.), McLuhan: Pro & con (pp. 270–308). New York: Funk & Wagnalls.

Carey, J.W. (1975). A cultural approach to communication. Communication, 2(1), 1–22.

Carey, J.W. (1977). Mass communication research and cultural studies: An American view. In J. Curran, M. Gurevitch, & J. Woollacott (Eds.), Mass communication and society (pp. 409–425). London: Edward Arnold.

Carey, J.W. (1979). Foreword. In H. Hardt, Social theories of the press: Early German & American perspectives (pp. 9–14). Beverly Hills, CA: Sage.

Carey, J.W. (1981). McLuhan and Mumford: The roots of modern media analysis. Journal of Communication, 31(3), 162–187.

Carey, J.W. (1987). The press and the public discussion. The Center Magazine, 20(2), 4–16.

Carey, J.W. (1989). Communication as culture. Boston, MA: Unwin Hyman.

Carey, J.W. (1991). Communication and the Progressives. In R.K. Avery & D. Eason (Eds.), Critical perspectives on media and society (pp. 28–48). New York: Guilford Press.

Carey, J.W. (1997). The Chicago School and the history of mass communication research. In E.S. Munson & C.A. Warren (Eds.), James Carey: A critical reader (pp. 14–33). Minneapolis: University of Minnesota Press.

Carey, J.W. (1998). Marshall McLuhan: Genealogy and legacy. Canadian Journal of Communication, 23(3), 293–306.

Carey, J.W., & Kreiling, A.L. (1974). Popular culture and uses and gratifications: Notes toward an accommodation. In J.G. Blumler & E. Katz (Eds.), The uses of mass communications: Current perspectives on gratifications research (pp. 225–248). Beverly Hills, CA: Sage.

Carragee, K.M. (1990). Interpretive media study and interpretive social science. Critical Studies in Mass Communication, 7(2), 81–96.

Carragee, K., Rosenblatt, M., & Michaud, G. (1987). Agenda-setting research: A critique and theoretical alternative. In S. Thomas (Ed.),

Culture and communication: Studies in communication (Vol. 3, pp. 35–49). Norwood, NJ: Ablex.

Castells, M. (1996). The rise of the network society. Oxford, UK: Blackwell.

Chaffee, S.H., & Hochheimer, J.L. (1985). The beginnings of political communication research in the United States. In E.M. Rogers & F. Balle (Eds.), The media revolution in America and in western Europe (pp. 267–296). Norwood, NJ: Ablex.

Chaffee, S.H., & Rogers, E.M. (1997). The establishment of communication study in America. In W. Schramm, The beginnings of communication study in America: A personal memoir (S.H. Chaffee & E.M. Rogers, Eds., pp. 125–180). Thousand Oaks, CA: Sage.

Chambers, I., Clarke, J., Curti, L., Hall, S., & Jefferson, T. (1977–1978). Marxism and culture. Screen, 18(4), 109–119.

Charters, W.W. (1953). Motion pictures and youth. In B. Berelson & M. Janowitz (Eds.), Reader in public opinion and communication (enlarged ed., pp. 397–406). Glencoe, IL: The Free Press. (Original work published 1933)

Cheesman, R., & Kyhn, C. (1975). Masskommunikation och medvetandeproduktion: En antologi [Mass communication and the production of consciousness: An anthology]. Nordisk sommeruniversitetes skriftserie nr. 7. Copenhagen: Nordisk sommeruniversitet.

Clausen, L. (1997). International news on Japanese television: A reception analysis. Keio Communication Review, 19, 39–66.

Clement, A. (1988). Office automation and the technical control of information workers. In V. Mosco & J. Wasko (Eds.), The political economy of information (pp. 217–246). Madison: The University of Wisconsin Press.

Coffin, T.E., & Tuchman, S. (1972–1973). Rating television programs for violence: A comparison of five surveys. Journal of Broadcasting, 17(1), 3–20.

Cohen, B. (1963). The press and foreign policy. Princeton, NJ: Princeton University Press.

Coleman, R. (1997). The intellectual antecedents of public journalism. Journal of Communication Inquiry, 21(1), 60–76.

Compton, N. (1968). The paradox of Marshall McLuhan. In R. Rosenthal (Ed.), McLuhan: Pro & con (pp. 106–124). New York: Funk & Wagnalls.

Condit, C.M. (1989). The rhetorical limits of polysemy. Critical Studies in Mass Communication, 6(2), 103–122.

Connell, I. (1980). Television news and the social contract. In S. Hall, D. Hobson, A. Lowe, & P. Willis (Eds.), Culture, media, language (pp. 139–156). London: Hutchinson.

Conter, C. D. (1999). Zu Besuch bei Kaspar Stieler: "Zeitungs Lust und Nutz"—ein Beitrag zur historischen Kommunikationsforschung. Publizistik, 44(1), 75–93.

Cook, D. (1996). The culture industry revisited: Theodor W. Adorno on mass culture. Lanham, MD: Rowman & Littlefield.

Cooley, C.H. (1967). Social organization. New York: Schocken Books. (Original work published 1909)

Cooper, T.W. (1981). McLuhan and Innis: The Canadian theme of boundless exploration. Journal of Communication, 31(3), 153–161.

Corrigan, P., & Willis, P. (1980). Cultural forms and class mediations. Media, Culture & Society, 2(3), 297–312.

Coser, L.A. (1977). Masters of sociological thought (2nd ed.). New York: Harcourt, Brace & Jovanovich.

Coward, R. (1977). Class, "culture," and the social formation. Screen, 18(1), 75–105.

Coward, R., & Ellis, J. (1978). Language and materialism. London: Routledge & Kegan Paul.

Craig, R.T. (1993). Why there are so many communication theories? Journal of Communication, 43(3), 26–33.

Creighton, D. (1981). Harold Adams Innis—an appraisal. In W.H. Melody, L. Salter, & P. Heyer (Eds.), Culture, communication, and dependency (pp. 13–25). Norwood, NJ: Ablex.

Crook, S. (1994). Introduction: Adorno and authoritarian irrationalism. In Th.W. Adorno, The stars down to earth and other essays (S. Crook, Ed., pp. 1–33). London: Routledge.

Curran, J. (1990). The new revisionism in mass communication research: A reappraisal. European Journal of Communication, 5(2-3), 135–164

Curran, J., Gurevitch, M., & Woollacott, J. (1982). The study of the media: Theoretical approaches. In M. Gurevitch, T. Bennett, J. Curran, & J. Woollacott (Eds.), Culture, society and the media (pp. 11–29). London: Methuen.

Curran, J., & Seaton, J. (1985). Power without responsibility (2nd ed.). London: Methuen.

Curtis, J.M. (1981). McLuhan: The aesthete as historian. Journal of Communication, 31(3), 144–152.

Czitrom, D. (1982). Media and the American mind. Chapel Hill: University of North Carolina Press.

Dahlgren, P. (1985). Beyond information: TV news as a cultural discourse. In L. Furhoff & P. Hemánus (Eds.), New directions in journalism research (pp. 80-95). Publications of the Department of Journalism and Mass Communication at the University of Tampere, B:17.

Dahlgren, P. (1988). What's the meaning of this: Viewers plural sense-making of TV news. Media, Culture & Society, 10(3), 285–301.

Dahlmüller, G., Hund, W.D., & Kommer, H. (1974). Politische Fernsehfibel: Materialen zur Klassenkommunikation. Reinbek bei Hamburg, Germany: Rowohlt Taschenbuch Verlag.

Davis, R. (1999). The web of politics: The Internet's impact on the American political system. New York: Oxford University Press.

Dearing, J.W., & Rogers, E.M. (1996). Communication concepts 6: Agenda-setting. Thousand Oaks, CA: Sage.

DeFleur, M.L. (1966). Theories of mass communication. New York: David McKay.

DeFleur, M.L., & Ball-Rokeach, S.J. (1975). Theories of mass communication (3rd ed.). New York: Longman.

De Lauretis, T. (1987). Technologies of gender: Essays on theory, film and fiction. Bloomington & Indianapolis: Indiana University Press.

Delia, J.G. (1987). Communication research: A history. In R.C. Berger & S.H. Chaffee (Eds.), Handbook of communication science (pp. 20–98). Newbury Park, CA: Sage.

Demers, D.P., Craft, D., Choi, Y.H., & Bessin, B.M. (1989). Issue obtrusiveness and the agenda-setting effects of national network news. Communication Research, 16(6), 793–812.

DeMott, B. (1968). Against McLuhan. In A. Casty (Ed.), Mass media and mass man (pp. 55–62). New York: Holt, Rinehart & Winston.

Dennis, E.E., & Wartella, E. (Eds.). (1996). American communication research: The remembered history. Mahwah, NJ: Erlbaum.

Denzin, N.K. (1992). Symbolic interaction and cultural studies. Oxford, UK: Basil Blackwell.

Dervin, B. (1980). Communication gaps and inequities: Moving toward reconceptualization. In. B. Dervin & M.J. Voigt (Eds.), Progress in communication sciences (Vol. II, pp. 73–112). Norwood, NJ: Ablex.

Dervin, B. (1989a). Audience as listener and learner, teacher and confidante: The sense-making approach. In R. Rice & C. Atkins (Eds.), Public communication campaigns (2nd ed., pp. 67–86). Newbury Park, CA: Sage.

Dervin, B. (1989b). Users as research inventions: How research categories perpetuate inequities. Journal of Communication, 39(3), 216–232.

Dervin, B. (1993). Verbing communication: Mandate for disciplinary invention. Journal of Communication, 43(3), 45–54.

Dervin, B., Grossberg, L., O'Keefe, B.J., & Wartella, E. (Eds.). (1989). Rethinking communication (Vol. 1: Paradigm issues & Vol. 2: Paradigm exemplars). Newbury Park, CA: Sage.

d'Ester, K. (1928). Zeitungswesen. Breslau, Germany: Ferdinand Hirt.

Dewey, J. (1916). Democracy and education. New York: Macmillan

Dewey, J. (1925). Experience and nature. Chicago: Open Court.

Dewey, J. (1954). The public and its problems. Denver: Alan Swallow. (Original work published 1927)

Dizard, W.P. (1989). The coming information age: An overview of technology, economics and politics (3rd ed.). New York: Longman.

Dizard, W.P. (1997). Old media, new media: Mass communication in the information age (2nd ed.). New York: Longman.

Doheny-Farina, S. (1996). The wired neighborhood. New Haven, CT: Yale University Press.

Donath, J.S. (1999). Identity and deception in the virtual community. In M.A. Smith & P. Kollock (Eds.), Communities in cyberspace (pp. 29–59). London: Routledge.

Donohew, L., & Tipton, L. (1974). A conceptual model for information seeking, avoiding and processing. In P. Clarke (Ed.), New models for mass communication research (pp. 243–268). Beverly Hills, CA: Sage.

Donohue, G.A., Tichenor, P.J., & Olien, C.N. (1973). Mass media functions, knowledge and social control. Journalism Quarterly, 50(4), 652–659.

Donohue, G.A., Tichenor, P.J., & Olien, C.N. (1975). Mass media and knowledge gap: A hypothesis reconsidered. Communication Research, 2(1), 3–23.

Donsbach, W. (1987). Die Theorie der Schweigespirale. In M. Schenk, Medienwirkungsforschung (pp. 324–343). Tübingen, Germany: J.C.B. Mohr (Paul Siebeck).

Donsbach, W., & Stevenson, R.L. (1986). Herausforderungen, Probleme und empirische Evidenzen der Theorie der Schweigespirale. Publizistik, 31(1-2), 7–34.

Doob, A.N., & Macdonald, G.E. (1980). Television viewing and fear of victimization: Is the relationship causal? In G. C. Wilhoit & H. deBock (Eds.), Mass communication review yearbook (Vol. 1, pp. 479–488). Beverly Hills, CA: Sage.

Douglas, S., & Guback, T. (1984). Production and technology in the communication/information revolution. Media, Culture & Society, 6(3), 233–245.

Dovifat, E. (1929). Wege und Ziele der Zeitungswissenschaftlichen Arbeiit. Berlin: Walter de Gruyter.

Downes, E.J., & McMillan, S.J. (2000). Defining interactivity: Identification of key dimensions. New Media & Society, 2(2), 157–179.

Dröge, F. (1972). Wissen ohne Bewusstsein: Materialen zur Medienanalyse. Frankfurt am Main, Germany: Fischer Athenäum.

Dröge, F. (1973). Wissensvermittlung in der bürgerlichen Gesellschaft. In J. Aufermann, H. Bohrmann, & R. Sülzer (Eds.), Gesellschaftliche Kommunikation und Information, Band 1 (pp. 174–189). Frankfurt am Main, Germany: Fischer Athenäum.

Dröge, F., & Lerg, W.B. (1965). Kritik der Kommunikationswissenschaf. Publizistik, 10(3), 251–266.

Drotner, K. (1994). Media ethnography: An other story? Communications, 19(1), 87–103.

Dubiel, H. (1988). Kritische Theorie der Gesellschaft. Weinheim, Germany: Juventa Verlag.

Dutton, W.H. (1999). Society on the line: Information politics in the digital age. Oxford, UK: Oxford University Press.

Dutton, W.H., Blumler, J.G., &. Kraemer, K.L. (1987). Wired cities: Shaping the future of communication. London: Cassel.

Dworkin, D. (1997). Cultural Marxism in postwar Britain: History, the New Left and the origins of cultural studies. Durham, NC: Duke University Press.

Dyson, K., & Humphreys, P. (Eds.). (1990). The political economy of communications: International and European dimensions. London: Routledge.

Eberhard, F. (1961). Thesen zur Publizistikwissenschaft. Publizistik, 6(5–6), 259–266.

Eberhard, F. (1964). Grenzen der Publizistikwissenschaft. Publizistik, 9(4), 348–350.

Eberhard, F. (1965). Würdigung nach fünfzig Jahren: Otto Groths Dissertation "Die politische Presse Württenbergs." Publizistik, 10(3), 196–205.

Ehlers, R. (1983). Themenstrukturierung durch Massenmedien: Zum Stand der empirischen Agenda-Setting-Forschung. Publizistik, 28(2), 167–186.

Eleey, M.F., Gerbner, G., & Tedesco, N. (1972–1973). Apples, oranges, and the kitchen sink: An analysis and guide to the comparison of "violence ratings". Journal of Broadcasting, 17(1), 21–31.

Elliott, P. (1974). Uses and gratifications research: A critique and a sociological alternative. In J.G. Blumler & E. Katz (Eds.), The uses of mass communications: Current perspectives on gratifications research (pp. 249–268). Beverly Hills, CA: Sage.

Epstein, E.J. (1974). News from nowhere. New York. Vintage Books.

Ettema, J.S., & Kline, G. (1977). Deficits, differences and ceilings: Contingent conditions for understanding the knowledge gap. Communication Research, 4(2), 179–202.

Evans, W.A. (1990). The interpretive turn in media research: Innovation, iteration or illusion? Critical Studies in Mass Communication, 7(2), 147–168.

Everth, E. (1927). Zeitungskunde und Universität. Jena, Germany: Verlag von Gustav Fischer.

Fairclough, N. (1989). Language and power. London: Longman.

Fairclough, N. (1992). Discourse and social change. Oxford, UK: Polity Press.

Fairclough, N. (1995). Media discourse. London: Edward Arnold.

Featherstone, M. (1988). In pursuit of the postmodern: An introduction. Theory, Culture & Society, 5(2–3), 195–215.

Fejes, F. (1981). Media imperialism: An assessment. Media, Culture & Society, 3(3), 281–289.

Fekete, J. (1977). The critical twilight. Explorations in the ideology of Anglo-American literary theory from Eliot to McLuhan. London: Routledge & Kegan Paul.

Feldman, T. (1997). An introduction to digital media. London: Routledge.

Ferguson, M. (1991). Marshall McLuhan revisited: 1960s Zeitgeist or pioneer postmodernist? Media, Culture & Society, 13(1), 71–90.

Ferguson, M., & Golding, P. (Eds.). (1997). Cultural studies in question. London: Sage.

Fernback, J. (1997). The individual within the collective: Virtual ideology and the realization of collective principles. In S.G. Jones (Ed.), Virtual culture: Identity and communication in cybersociety (pp. 36–54). London: Sage

Festinger, L. (1957). A theory of cognitive dissonance. Evanston, IL: Row, Peterson and Company.

Fischer, B.A. (1978). Perspectives on human communication. New York: Macmillan.

Fischer, B.M., & Strauss, A.L. (1979). Interactionism. In T. Bottomore & R. Nisbet (Eds.), A history of sociological analysis (pp. 457–498). London: Heinemann.

Fishman, M. (1980). Manufacturing the news. Austin: University of Texas Press.

Fiske, J. (1982). Introduction to communication studies. London: Methuen.

Fiske, J. (1987). Television culture. London: Methuen.

Fiske, J. (1989). Moments of television: Neither the text nor the audience. In E. Seiter, H. Borchers, G. Kreutzner, & E-M. Warth (Eds.), Remote control (pp. 56–78). London: Routledge.

Fiske, J. (1991a). Postmodernism and television. In J. Curran & M. Gurevitch (Eds.), Mass media and society (pp. 55–67). London: Edward Arnold.

Fiske, J. (1991b). Reading the popular. London: Routledge.

Fiske, J. (1991c). Understanding popular culture. London: Routledge.

Fiske, J. (1998). Television: Polysemy and popularity. In R. Dickinson, R. Harindranath, & O. Linne (Eds.), Approaches to audiences: A reader (pp. 194–204). London: Arnold. (Original work published 1986)

Forester, T. (1987). High-tech society: The story of the information technology revolution. Oxford, UK: Basil Blackwell.

Fowler, R. (1991). Language in the news. London: Routledge.

Fowler, R., Kress, G., Trew, A.A., & Hodge, R. (1979). Language and control. London: Routledge & Kegan Paul.

Fredin, E.S., Monnet, T.H., & Kosicki, G.M. (1994). Knowledge gaps, social locators, and media schemata: Gaps, reverse gaps and gaps of disaffection. Journalism Quarterly, 71(1), 176–190.

Freedman, A., & Grossbrenner, E. (1998). The Internet glossary and quick reference guide. New York: Amacom.

Freidson, E. (1971). Communication research and the concept of the mass. In W. Schramm & D.F. Roberts (Eds.), The process and effects of mass communication (rev. ed., pp. 197–208). Urbana: University of Illinois Press. (Original work published 1953)

Friedrichs, R.W. (1970). A sociology of sociology. New York: The Free Press.

Frisby, D. (1985). Fragments of modernity: Theories of modernity in the work of Simmel, Kracauer and Benjamin. Cambridge, UK: Polity Press.

Fuchs, D., Gerhards, J., & Neidhardt, F. (1992). Öffentliche Kommunikationsbereitschaft: Ein Test zentraler Bestandteile der Theorie der Schweigespirale. Zeitschrift für Soziologie, 21(4), 284–295.

Funkhouser, G.R. (1973). The issues of the sixties: An exploratory study in the dynamics of public opinion. Public Opinion Quarterly, 37(1), 62–75.

Gamson, W.A., & Modigliani, A. (1989). Media discourse and public opinion on nuclear power: A constructionist approach. American Journal of Sociology, 95(1), 1–37.

Gans, H.J. (1980). Deciding what's news. London: Constable.

Garnham, N. (1979). Contribution to a political economy of mass communication. Media, Culture & Society, 1(2), 123–146.

Garnham, N. (1995). Political economy and cultural studies: Reconciliation or divorce? Critical Studies in Mass Communication, 12(1), 62–71.

Gary, B. (1996). Communication research, the Rockefeller Foundation, and mobilization for the war of words, 1938–1944. Journal of Communication, 46(3), 124–148.

Gaziano, C. (1983). The knowledge gap: An analytical review of media effects. Communication Research, 10(4), 447–486.

Gaziano, C. (1997). Forecast 2000: Widening knowledge gaps. Journalism & Mass Communication Quarterly, 74(2), 237–264.

Genova, B.K.L., & Greenberg, B.S. (1979). Interest in news and the knowledge gap. Public Opinion Quarterly, 43(1), 79–91.

Geras, N. (1972). Marx and the critique of political economy. In R. Blackburn (Ed.), Ideology in social science (pp. 284–305). Glasgow: Fontana/Collins.

Gerbner, G. (1964). On content analysis and critical research in mass communication. In L.A. Dexter & D.M. White (Eds.), People, society, and mass communications (pp. 476–500). New York: The Free Press. (Original work published 1958)

Gerbner, G. (1967). An institutional approach to mass communication research. In L. Thayer (Ed.), Communication: Theory and research (pp. 429–445). Springfield, IL: Charles C. Taylor.

Gerbner, G. (1973). Cultural indicators: The third voice. In G. Gerbner, L.P. Gross, & W.H. Melody (Eds.), Communications technology and social policy (pp. 555–573). New York: Wiley.

Gerbner, G. (1983). Elämä television mukaan: George Gerbnerin haastattelu [Living with television: An interview with George Gerbner]. Tiedotustutkimus, 6(4), 55–63.

Gerbner, G. (1994). Toimijana Historiassa: George Gerbnerin haastattelu [As an actor in history: An interview with George Gerbner]. Tiedotustutkimus, 17(2), 106–112.

Gerbner, G., & Gross, L. (1976). Living with television: The violence profile. Journal of Communication, 26(2), 173–199.

Gerbner, G., & Gross, L. (1980). Editorial response: A reply to Newcomb's "humanistic critique." In G.C. Wilhoit & H. de Bock (Eds.), Mass communication review yearbook (Vol. 1, pp. 451–477). Beverly Hills, CA: Sage.

Gerbner, G., Gross, L., Eleey, M.F., Jackson-Beech, M., Jeffries-Fox, S., & Signorielli, N. (1977). "The Gerbner violence profile": An analysis of the CBS report. Journals of Broadcasting, 21(3), 280–286.

Gerbner, G., Gross, L., Morgan, M., & Signorielli, N. (1980b). The "mainstreaming" of America: Violence profile no. 11. Journal of Communication, 30(3), 10–29.

Gerbner, G., Gross, L., Morgan, M., & Signorielli, N. (1981a). A curious journey into the scary world of Paul Hirsch. Communication Research, 8(1), 39–71.

Gerbner, G., Gross, L., Morgan, M., & Signorielli, N. (1981b). Final reply to Hirsch. Communication Research, 8(3), 259–280.

Gerbner, G., Gross, L., Signorielli, N., Morgan, M., & Jackson-Beech, M. (1980a). The demonstration of power: Violence profile no. 10. In G.C. Wilhoit & H. de Bock (Eds.), Mass communication review yearbook (Vol. 1, pp. 403–422). Beverly Hills, CA: Sage.

Gerhards, J. (1996). Reder, Schweiger, Anpasser und Missionare: Eine Typologie öffentlicher Kommunikationsbereitschaft und ein Beitrag zur Theorie der Schweigespirale. Publizistik, 41(1), 1–14.

Giddens, A. (1990). The consequences of modernity. Cambridge, UK: Polity Press.

Giner, S. (1976). Mass society. New York: Academic Press.

Gitlin, T. (1980). The whole world is watching. Berkeley: University of California Press.

Gitlin, T. (1981). Media sociology: The dominant paradigm. In G. C. Wilhoit & H. de Bock (Eds.), Mass communication review yearbook (Vol. 2, pp. 73–121). Beverly Hills, CA: Sage.

Glynn, C.J., & McLeod, J.M. (1985). Implications of the spiral of silence theory for communication and public opinion research. In K.R. Sanders, L.L. Kaid, & D. Nimmo (Eds.), Political communication yearbook 1984 (pp. 43–65). Carbondale: Southern Illinois University Press.

Glynn, C.J., Hayes, A.F., & Shanahan J. (1997). Perceived support for one's opinion and willingness to speak out: A meta-analysis of survey studies on the "spiral of silence." Public Opinion Quarterly, 61(3), 452–463.

Godelier, M. (1972). Structure and contradiction in "Capital". In R. Blackburn (Ed.), Ideology in social science (pp. 334–368). Glasgow: Fontana/Collins.

Goertz, L. (1995). Wie interaktiv sind Medien? Auf dem Weg zu einer Definition von Interaktivität. Rundfunk und Fernsehen, 43(4), 477-493.

Goffman, E. (1974). Frame analysis. New York: Harper & Row.

Golding, P., & Elliott, P. (1979). Making the news. London: Longman.

Golding, P., & Murdock, G. (1979). Ideology and the mass media: The question of determination. In M. Barrett, P. Corrigan, A. Kuhn, & J. Wolff (Eds.), Ideology and cultural production (pp. 198–224). London: Croom Helm.

Golding, P., & Harris, P. (1997). Introduction. In P. Golding & P. Harris (Eds.), Beyond cultural imperialism: Globalization, communication and the new international order (pp. 1–9). London: Sage.

Gonzenbach, W.J. (1992). The conformity hypothesis: Empirical considerations for the spiral of silence's first link. Journalism Quarterly, 69(3), 633–645.

Gordon, W.T. (1997). Marshall McLuhan, escape into understanding: A biography. New York: Basic Books.

Gouldner, A.W. (1970). The coming crisis of western sociology. New York: Basic Books.

Gouldner, A.W. (1976). The dialectic of ideology and technology. London: Macmillan.

Graber, D. (1988). Processing the news: How people tame the information tide (2nd ed.). New York: Longman.

Gray, A. (1987). Reading the audience. Screen, 28(3), 24–35.

Greenberg, B.S. (1974). Gratifications of television viewing and their correlates for British children. In J.G. Blumler & E. Katz (Eds.), The uses of mass communications: Current perspectives on gratifications research (pp. 71–92). Beverly Hills, CA: Sage.

Gripsrud, J. (1995). The Dynasty years: Hollywood television and critical media studies. London: Routledge.

Gross, L., & Morgan, M. (1985). Television and enculturation. In J.R. Dominick & J.E. Fletcher (Eds.), Broadcasting research methods (pp. 221–234). Boston, MA: Allyn & Bacon.

Grossberg, L. (1983). Cultural studies revisited and revised. In M.S. Mander (Ed.), Communications in transition (pp. 39–71). New York: Praeger.

Grossberg, L. (1991). Strategies of Marxist cultural interpretation. In R.K. Avery & D. Eason (Eds.), Critical perspectives on media and society (pp. 126–159). New York: Guilford Press.

Grossberg, L. (1995). Cultural studies vs. political economy: Is anybody else bored with this debate? Critical Studies in Mass Communication, 12(1), 72–81.

Groth, O. (1928). Die Zeitung (1. Band). Mannheim, Germany: J. Bensheimer.

Groth, O. (1948). Die Geschichte der deutschen Zeitungswissenschaft Munich, Germany: Weinmayer.

Groth, O. (1960). Die unerkannte Kulturmacht (1. Band). Berlin: Walter de Gruyter.

Groth, O. (1962). Die unerkannte Kulturmacht (4. Band). Berlin: Walter de Gruyter.

Groth, O. (1972). Die unerkannte Kulturmacht (7. Band). Berlin: Walter de Gruyter.

Haacke, W. (1970). Publizistik und Gesellschaft. Stuttgart, Germany: K.F. Koehlers Verlag.

Habermas, J. (1987). The philosophical discourse of modernity: Twelve lectures. Cambridge, UK: Polity Press.

Habermas, J. (1989). The structural transformation of the public sphere: An inquiry into a category of bourgeois society. Cambridge, MA: The MIT Press. (Original work published 1962)

Habermas, J. (1996). Modernity: An unfinished project. In M.P. d'Entreves & S. Benhabib (Eds.), Habermas and the unfinished project of modernity (pp. 38–55). Cambridge, UK: Polity Press. (Original work published 1980)

Hachmeister, L. (1987). Theoretische Publizistik: Studien zur Geschichte der Kommunikationswissenschaft in Deutschland. Berlin: Volker Spiess

Hachmeister, L., Baum, A., & Schuppe, M. (1983). Praktizismus und kommunikationswissenschaftliches Studium. Publizistik, 28(2), 187–203.

Hagen I., & Wasko, J. (2000). Introduction: Consuming audiences? In I. Hagen & J. Wasko (Eds.), Consuming audiences? Production and reception in media research (pp. 1–28). Cresskill, NJ: Hampton Press.

Hague, B.N., & Loader, B.D. (Eds.). (1999a). Digital democracy: Discourse and decision making in the information age. London: Routledge.

Hague, B.N., & Loader, B.D. (1999b). Digital democracy: An introduction. In B.N. Hague & B.D. Loader (Eds.), Digital democracy: Discourse and decision making in the information age (pp. 3–22). London: Routledge.

Hale, M., Musso, J., & Weare, C. (1999). Developing digital democracy: Evidence from Californian municipal web pages. In B.N. Hague & B.D. Loader (Eds.), Digital democracy: Discourse and decision making in the information age (pp. 96–115). London: Routledge.

Hall, S. (1972). External influences on broadcasting. Stencilled occasional papers (Media series: SP no. 4). Birmingham: Centre for Contemporary Cultural Studies.

Hall, S. (1975). The "structured communication" of events. In Getting the message across (pp. 115–145). Paris: The Unesco Press.

Hall, S. (1977). Culture, media and the "ideological effect". In J. Curran, M. Gurevitch, & J. Woollacott (Eds.), Mass communication and society (pp. 315–348). London: Edward Arnold.

Hall, S. (1980a). Cultural studies and the centre: Some problematics and problems. In S. Hall, D. Hobson, A. Lowe, & P. Willis (Eds.), Culture, media, language (pp. 15–47). London: Hutchinson.

Hall, S. (1980b). Encoding/decoding. In S. Hall, D. Hobson, A. Lowe, & P. Willis (Eds.), Culture, media, language (pp. 128–138). London: Hutchinson.

Hall, S. (1980c). Introduction to media studies at the Centre. In S. Hall, D. Hobson, A. Lowe, & P. Willis (Eds.), Culture, media, language (pp. 117–121). London: Hutchinson.

Hall, S. (1981). The whites of their eyes: Racist ideologies and the media. In G. Bridges & R. Brunt (Eds.), Silver linings: Some strategies for the eighties (pp. 28–52). London: Lawrence & Wishart.

Hall, S. (1982). The rediscovery of "ideology": Return of the repressed in media studies. In M. Gurevitch, T. Bennett, J. Curran, & J. Woollacott (Eds.), Culture, society and the media (pp. 56–90). London: Methuen.

Hall, S. (1983). The problem of ideology: Marxism without guarantees. In B. Matthews (Ed.), Marx: A hundred years on (pp. 57–85). London: Lawrence & Wishart.

Hall, S. (1989). Ideology and communication theory. In B. Dervin, L. Grossberg, B. J. O'Keefe, & E. Wartella (Eds.), Rethinking communication: Paradigm issues (Vol. 1, pp. 40–52). Newbury Park, CA: Sage.

Hall, S. (1992). Intellektuaalisen elämän kutsumus [The calling of intellectual life]. In S. Hall, Kulttuurin ja politiikan murroksia (J. Koivisto, M. Lehtonen, T. Uusitupa, & L. Grossberg, Eds., pp. 11–21). Tampere: Vastapaino. (Original work published 1989)

Hall, S., Connelly, I., & Curti, L. (1981). The "unity" of current affairs television. In T. Bennett, S. Boyd-Bowman, C. Mercer, & J. Woollacott (Eds.), Popular television and film (pp. 88–117). London: BFI.

Hall, S., Crichter, C., Jefferson, T., Clarke, J., & Roberts, B. (1978). Policing the crisis: Mugging, the state, and law and order. Basingstoke, UK: Macmillan.

Hallin, D.C. (1992). Sound bite news: Television coverage of elections, 1968–1988. Journal of Communication, 42(2), 5–24.

Halloran, J., Elliott, P., & Murdock, G. (1970). Demonstrations and communication; A case study. Harmondsworth, UK: Penguin.

Hansen, B. (1999). The dictionary of multimedia: Terms & acronyms. Chicago: Fitzroy Dearborn.

Hanssen, L., Jankowski, N.W., & Etienne, R. (1996). Interactivity from the perspective of communication studies. In N.W. Jankowski & L. Hanssen (Eds.), The contours of multimedia: Recent technological, theoretical and empirical developments (pp. 61–73). Luton, UK: The University of Luton Press.

Hardt, H. (1979). Social theories of the press: Early German & American perspectives. Beverly Hills, CA: Sage.

Hardt, H. (1992). Critical communication studies: Communication, history and theory in America. New York: Routledge.

Hartley, J. (1982). Understanding news. London: Methuen.

Harvey, L. (1987). Myths of the Chicago School of sociology. Aldershot, UK: Avebury.

Haug, W.F. (1986). Critique of commodity aesthetics. Cambridge, UK: Polity Press.

Haug, W.F. (1987). Commodity aesthetics, ideology and culture. New York: International General.

Heider, F. (1946). Attitudes and cognitive organization. Journal of Psychology, 21, 107–112.

Heider, F. (1958). Social perception and phenomenal causality. In R. Tagiuri & L. Petrullo (Eds.), Person perception and interpersonal behavior (pp. 1–21). Stanford, CA: Stanford University Press. (Original work published 1944)

Heikkilä, H., & Kunelius, R. (1996). Public journalism and its problems: A theoretical perspective. Javnost/The Public, 3(3), 81–95.

Heinonen, A. (1999). Journalism in the age of the net. Acta Universitatis Tamperensis, vol. 685.

Held, D. (1980). Introduction to critical theory: Horkheimer to Habermas. London: Hutchinson.

Hellman, H. (1981). Ajatusten Marshall–suunnitelma [A Marshall plan of thoughts]. Publications of the Department of Journalism and Mass Communication at the University of Tampere, B:4.

Hemánus, P. (1966). Helsingin sanomalehtien rikosaineisto [Crime material in the newspapers of Helsinki]. Acta Universitatis Tamperensis, ser. A., 6.

Herman, E., & Chomsky, N. (1988). Manufacturing consent: The political economy of mass media. New York: Pantheon Books.

Herzog, H. (1961). Motivations and gratifications of daily serial listeners. In W. Schramm (Ed.), The process and effects of mass communication (pp. 50–55). Urbana: University of Illinois Press. (Original work published 1944)

Heyer, P. (1981). Innis and the history of communication. In W.H. Melody, L. Salter, & P. Heyer (Eds.), Culture, communication, and dependency (pp. 247–259). Norwood, NJ: Ablex.

Heyer, P. (1988). Communication and history: Theories of media, knowledge and civilization. Westport, CT: Greenwood Press.

Hill, J. (1979). Ideology, economy and the British cinema. In M. Barrett, P. Corrigan, A. Kuhn, & J. Wolff (Eds.), Ideology and cultural production (pp. 112–134). London: Croom Helm.

Hill, R.J., & Bonjean, C.M. (1964). News diffusion: A test of the regularity hypothesis. Journalism Quarterly, 41(3), 336–342.

Hintikka, K.A. (1996). Uusi media–viestintäkanava ja elinympäristö [New media—new communication channel and living environment]. In M. Tarkka, K.A. Hintikka, & A. Mäkelä (Eds.), Johdatus uuteen mediaan (pp. 2–18). Helsinki: Edita.

Hirsch, P.M. (1980). The "scary world" of the nonviewer and other anomalies: A reanalysis of Gerbner et al.'s findings on cultivation analysis, part I. Communication Research, 7(4), 403–456.

Hirsch, P.M. (1981a). On not learning from one's own mistakes: A reanalysis of Gerbner et al.'s findings on cultivation analysis, part II. Communication Research, 8(1), 3–37.

Hirsch, P.M. (1981b). Distinguishing good speculation from bad theory: Rejoinder to Gerbner et al. Communication Research, 8(1), 73–95.

Hobson, D. (1980). Housewives and the mass media. In S. Hall, D. Hobson, A. Lowe, & P. Willis (Eds.), Culture, media, language (pp. 105–114). London: Hutchinson.

Hobson, D. (1982). "Crossroads": Drama of a soap opera. London: Methuen.

Hoch, P. (1974). The newspaper game. London: Galder & Boyans.

Hodge, R., & Kress, G. (1988). Social semiotics. Oxford, UK: Polity Press.

Hoffmann, B. (1973). Zur Problem der Entwicklung einer materialistischen Kommunikationstheorie. In J. Aufermann, H. Bohrmann, & R. Sülzer (Eds.), Gesellschaftliche Kommunikation und Information, Band 1 (pp. 190–206). Frankfurt am Main, Germany: Fischer Athenäum.

Hoffmann, B. (1983). On the development of a materialist theory of communication in West Germany. Media, Culture & Society, 5(1), 7–24.

Hofmann, W. (1983). Springer als symptom: Ten theses. Media, Culture & Society, 5(1), 25–27. (Original work published 1968)

Höflich, J.R. (1995). Vom dispersen Publikum zu "elektronischen Gemeinschaften." Rundfunk und Fernsehen, 43(4), 518–537.

Höijer, B. (1990). Studying viewers' reception of television programmes: Theoretical and methodological considerations. European Journal of Communication, 5(1), 29–56.

Höijer, B. (1995). Genreföreställningar och tolkningar av berättande i tv [Views of genre and interpretations of narration in TV]. Publications of the JMK at the University of Stockholm, 1995: 1.

Höijer, B. (1998). Cognitive and psychodynamic perspectives on reception of television narration. In B. Höijer & A. Werner (Eds.), Cultural cognition: New perspectives in audience theory (pp. 73–84). Publications of the Nordicom-Sverige at the University of Gothenburg, no. 12.

Höijer, B., & Findahl, O. (1984). Nyheter, förståelse och minne [News, comprehension and memory]. Lund, Sweden: Studentlitteratur.

Holmes, D. (1997). Introduction: Virtual politics—identity and community in cyberspace. In D. Holmes (Ed.), Virtual politics: Identity and community in cyberspace (pp. 1–25). London: Sage.

Holzer, H. (1973). Kommunikationssoziologie. Reinbek bei Hamburg, Germany: Rowohlt Taschenbuch Verlag.

Honneth, A. (1985). Kritik der Macht: Reflexionstufen einer kritischen Gesellschaftstheorie. Frankfurt am Main, Germany: Suhrkamp.

Horkheimer, M. (1972). Traditional and critical theory. In M. Horkheimer, Critical theory: Selected essays (pp. 188–243). New York: Seabury Press. (Original work published 1937)

Horne, H. (1989). Jameson's strategies of containment. In D. Kellner (Ed.), Postmodernism, Jameson, critique (pp. 268–300). Washington, DC: Maisonneuve Press.

Hovland, C.I., Lumsdaine, A.A., & Sheffield, F.D. (1949). Experiments on mass communication. Princeton, NJ: Princeton University Press.

Hovland, C.I, Janis, I.L., & Kelley, H.H. (1953). Communication and persuasion. New Haven, CT: Yale University Press.

Hovland, C.I., & Weiss, W. (1954). The influence of source credibility on communication effectiveness. In D. Cartwright, D. Katz, S. Eldersweld, & A. McClung Lee (Eds.), Public opinion and propaganda (pp. 337–347). New York: Holt, Rinehart & Winston.

Hsia, H.J. (1988). Mass communication research methods: A step-by-step approach. Hillsdale, NJ: Erlbaum.

Hughes, M. (1980). The fruits of cultivation analysis: A reexamination of some effects of television viewing. Public Opinion Quarterly, 44(3), 287–302.

Huhtiniemi, J. (1986). Otto Groth—kadonneen tutkimusesineen metsästäjä [Otto Groth—raider of the lost object of study]. M.A. thesis, The University of Tampere.

Hund, W.D. (1976). Ware Nachricht und Informationsfetisch: Zur Theorie der gesellschaftlichen Kommunikation. Darmstadt, Germany: Luchterhand.

Hurwitz, D. (1988). Market research and the study of U.S. radio audience. Communication, 10(2), 223–241.

Hyman, H.H. (1955). Survey design and analysis. Glencoe, IL: The Free Press.

Hyman, H.H., & Sheatsley, P.B. (1947). Some reasons why information campaigns fail. Public Opinion Quarterly, 11(3), 412–423.

Innis, H.A. (1978). The press: A neglected factor in the economic history of the 20th century. New York: AMS Press. (Original work published 1949)

Innis, H.A. (1980). Empire and communications. Toronto: University of Toronto Press. (Original work published 1950)

Innis, H.A. (1982). The bias of communication. Toronto: University of Toronto Press. (Original work published 1951)

Isajiw, W. (1968). Causation and functionalism in sociology. London: Routledge & Kegan Paul.

Iyengar, S., & Kinder, D.R. (1987). News that matters. Chicago: The University of Chicago Press.

Jäckel, M. (1995). Interaktion: Soziologische Anmerkungen zu einem Begriff. Rundfunk und Fernsehen, 43(4), 463–473.

Jaeger, K. (1926). Von der Zeitungskunde zur publizistischen Wissenschaft. Jena, Germany: Verlag von Gustav Fischer.

Jahoda, M., Lazarsfeld, P.F., & Zeisel, H. (1933). Die Arbeitslosen von Marienthal. Leipzig, Germany: Hirzel.

Jameson, F. (1979). Reification and utopia in mass culture. Social Text, Winter, 130–148.

Jameson, F. (1985). Postmodernism and consumer society. In H. Foster (Ed.), Postmodern culture (pp. 111–125). London: Pluto Press.

Jameson, F. (1991). Postmodernism, or, the cultural logic of late capitalism. London: Verso.

Janowitz, M. (1968). The study of mass communication. In D.L. Sills (Ed.), International encyclopedia of the social sciences (Vol. 3, pp. 41–55). New York: Crowell, Collier & Macmillan.

Jankowski, N.W., & Hanssen, L. (1996). Introduction: Multimedia come of age. In N.W. Jankowski & L. Hanssen (Eds.), The contours of multimedia: Recent technological, theoretical and empirical developments (pp. 1–21). Luton, UK: The University of Luton Press.

Jansen, B., & Klönne, A. (Eds.). (1968). Imperium Springer: Macht & Manipulation. Cologne, Germany: Pahl–Rugestein Verlag.

Jarvie, I.C. (1970). Movies and society. New York: Basic Books.

Jarvis, A. Jr. (1991). The Payne Fund reports: A discussion of their content, public reaction, and affect on motion picture industry, 1930–1940. Journal of Popular Culture, 25(2), 127–140.

Jay, M. (1974). The dialectical imagination: A history of the Frankfurt School and the Institute of Social Research, 1923–1950. London: Heinemann.

Jay, M. (1984). Adorno. Cambridge, MA: Harvard University Press.

Jeffrey, L. (1989). The heat and the light: Towards a reassessment of the contribution of H. Marshall McLuhan. Canadian Journal of Communication, 14(4–5), 1–26.

Jensen, J.F. (1999). "Interactivity"—tracking a new concept in media and communication studies. In P.A. Mayer (Ed.), Computer media and communication: A reader (pp. 160–187). Oxford, UK: Oxford University Press.

Jensen, K.B. (1988). News as social resource: A qualitative empirical study of the reception of Danish television news. European Journal of Communication, 3(3), 275–301.

Jones, S.G. (1998). Information, Internet and community: Notes toward an understanding of community in the information age. In S.G. Jones (Ed.), Cybersociety 2.0: Revisiting computer-mediated communication and community (pp. 1–34). Thousand Oaks, CA: Sage.

Journal of Communication (1983). Special issue: Ferment in the Field, 33(3).

Journal of Communication (1984). World forum: The U.S. Decision to Withdraw from Unesco, 34(4).

Jowett, G.S. (1991). Propaganda critique: The forgotten history of American communication studies. In J. A. Anderson (Ed.), Communication Yearbook (Vol. 14, pp. 239–248). Newbury Park, CA: Sage.

Jowett, G.S. (1992). Social science as a weapon: The origins of Payne Fund studies, 1926–1929. Communication, 13(3), 211–225.

Jowett, G.S., Jarvie, I.C., & Fuller, K.H. (1996). Children and the movies: Media influence and the Payne Fund controversy. Cambridge, UK: Cambridge University Press.

Juntunen, M., & Mehtonen, L. (1977). Ihmistieteiden filosofiset perusteet [The philosophical foundations of human sciences]. Jyväskylä, Finland: Gummerus.

Kaplan, E.A. (1987a). Feminist critics and television. In R.C. Allen (Ed.), Channels of discourse: Television and contemporary criticism (pp. 211–253). London: Routledge.

Kaplan, E.A. (1987b). Rocking around the clock: Music television, postmodernism and consumer culture. New York: Methuen.

Kaplan. E.A. (1988). Feminism/Oedipus/postmodernism: The case of MTV. In E.A. Kaplan (Ed.), Postmodernism and its discontents (pp. 30–44). London: Verso.

Käsler, D. (1979). Einführung in das Studium Max Webers. Munich, Germany: Verlag C.H. Beck.

Käsler, D. (1981). Der Streit um die Bestimmung der Soziologie auf den deutschen Soziologentagen 1910 bis 1930. In R. Lepsius (Ed.), Soziologie in Deutschland und Österreich 1918–1945. Kölner Zeitschrift für Soziologie und Sozialpsychologie, Sonderheft 23 (pp. 159–199). Opladen, Germany: Westdeutscher Verlag.

Katz, E. (1959). Mass communication research and the study of popular culture. Studies in Public Communication, 2, 1–6.

Katz, E. (1979). The uses of Becker, Blumler, and Swanson. Communication Research, 6(1), 74–83.

Katz, E. (1981). Publicity and pluralistic ignorance: Notes on "the spiral of silence." In H. Baier, H.M. Kepplinger, & K. Reumann (Eds.), Öffentliche Meinung und sozialer Wandel: Für Elisabeth Noelle-Neumann (pp. 28–38). Opladen, Germany: Westdeutscher Verlag.

Katz, E. (1987). Communication research since Lazarsfeld. Public Opinion Quarterly, 51(4), S25–S45.

Katz, E., Blumler, J.G., & Gurevitch, M. (1974). Utilization of mass communication by the individual. In J.G. Blumler & E. Katz (Eds.), The uses of mass communications: Current perspectives on gratifications research (pp. 19–32). Beverly Hills, CA: Sage.

Katz, E., & Foulkes, D. (1962). On the use of mass communication as "escape": Clarification of a concept. Public Opinion Quarterly, 26(3), 377–388.

Katz, E., Gurevitch, M., & Haas, H. (1973). On the use of mass media for important things. American Sociological Review, 38(2), 164–181.

Katz, E., & Lazarsfeld, P.F. (1955). Personal influence: The part played by people in the flow of mass communications. Glencoe, IL: The Free Press.

Katz, E., & Liebes, T. (1985). Mutual aid in the decoding of Dallas: Preliminary notes from a cross-cultural study. In P. Drummond & R. Paterson (Eds.), Television in transition (pp. 187–198). London: BFI Publishing.

Kausch, M. (1988). Kulturindustrie und Popularkultur: Kritische Theorie der Massenmedien. Frankfurt am Main, Germany: Fischer Verlag

Keane, J. (1984). Public life and late capitalism. Cambridge, UK: Cambridge University Press.

Kellner, D. (1982). Kulturindustrie und Massenkommunikation. In W. Bonss & A. Honneth (Eds.), Sozialforschung als Kritik (pp. 482–515). Frankfurt am Main, Germany: Suhrkamp.

Kellner, D. (1988). Postmodernism as social theory: Some challenges and problems. Theory, Culture & Society, 5(2–3), 239–269.

Kellner, D. (1989a). Critical theory, Marxism and modernity. Cambridge, UK: Polity Press.

Kellner, D. (1989b). Jameson, Marxism and postmodernism. In D. Kellner (Ed.), Postmodernism, Jameson, critique (pp. 1–42). Washington, DC: Maisonneuve Press.

Kellner, D. (1989c). Jean Baudrillard: From Marxism to postmodernism and beyond. Cambridge, UK: Polity Press.

Kellner, D. (1994). Introduction: Jean Baudrillard in the fin-de-millennium. In D. Kellner (Ed.), Baudrillard: A critical reader (pp. 1–23). Oxford, UK: Basil Blackwell.

Kennamer, J.D. (1990). Self-serving biases in perceiving the opinion of others: Implications for the spiral of silence. Communication Research, 17(3), 393–404.

Kepplinger, H.M. (1979). Ausgewogen bis zur Selbstaufgabe? Media Perspektiven, Heft 11, 750–755.

Kepplinger, H.M. (1982). Visual biases in television campaign coverage. Communication Research, 9(3), 432–446.

Kepplinger, H.M., & Daschmann, G. (1997). Today's news—tomorrow's context: A dynamic model of news processing. Journal of Broadcasting & Electronic Media, 41(4), 548–565.

Kepplinger, H.M., & Roth, H. (1978). Kommunikation in der Ölkrise des Winters 1973/74: Ein Paradigma für Wirkungsstudien. Publizistik, 23(4), 337–356.

Kiefer, M-L. (1977). Rundfunkjournalisten als Wahlhelfer? Zur Diskussion über die Wahlniederlage von CDU/CSU und ihre möglichen Ursachen. Media Perspektiven, Heft 1, 1–10.

Klapper, J.T. (1960). The effects of mass communication. New York: The Free Press.

Klapper, J.T. (1963). Mass communication research: An old road resurveyed. Public Opinion Quarterly, 27(4), 515–527.

Kleberg, M. (1993). Feminisk teoribildning och mediaforskning [Feminist theory building and the study of the media]. In U. Carlsson (Ed.), Norsisk forskning om kvinnor och medier (pp. 7-24). Publications of the Nordicom-Sverige at the University of Gothenburg, no. 3.

Kleinpaul, J. (1927). Zeitungskunde. Leipzig, Germany: Verlag Julius Mäser.

Klose, H–G. (1989). Zeitungswissenschaft in Köln. Dortmunder Beiträge zur Zeitungsforschung, Band 45. Munich, Germany: K.G. Saur.

Koivisto, J., & Pietilä, V. (1993). W.F. Haugs Theorie des Ideologischen im Vergleich. In W.F. Haug, Elemente einer Theorie des Ideologischen (pp. 233–246). Hamburg, Germany: Argument Verlag.

Koivisto, J., & Väliverronen, E. (1987). Julkisuuden valta [The power of the publicness]. Publications of the Department of Journalism and Mass Communication at the University of Tampere, A:57.

Kollock, P., & Smith, M.A. (1999). Introduction: Communities in cyberspace. In M.A. Smith & P. Kollock (Eds.), Communities in cyberspace (pp. 3–25). London: Routledge.

Kornhauser, W. (1960). The politics of mass society. London: Routledge & Kegan Paul.

Kosicki, G.M. (1993). Problems and opportunities in agenda-setting research. Journal of Communication, 43(2), 100–127.

Kostelanetz, R. (1968). A hot apostle in a cool culture. In R. Rosenthal (Ed.), McLuhan: Pro & con (pp. 207–228). New York: Funk & Wagnalls.

Kotkavirta, J. (1991). Jälkisanat [Afterword]. In J. Kotkavirta (Ed.), Järjen kritiükki (pp. 169–203). Tampere: Vastapaino.

Kotkavirta, J., & Sironen, E. (1986). Modernin maailman tuleminen [The coming of the modern world]. In J. Kotkavirta & E. Sironen (Eds.), Moderni/postmoderni (pp. 7–34). Publications of the Finnish Union of Researchers, no. 44.

Kress, G. (1983). Linguistic and ideological transformations in news reporting. In H. Davis & P. Walton (Eds.), Language, image, media (pp. 120–138). Oxford, UK: Basil Blackwell.

Kress, G., & Hodge, R. (1979). Language as ideology. London: Routledge & Kegan Paul.

Kress, G., & Trew, A.A. (1978). Ideological transformation of discourse. Sociological Review, 26(4), 755–776.

Kress, G., & van Leeuwen, T. (1996). Reading images: The grammar of visual design. London: Routledge.

Krippendorff, K. (1993). The past of communication's hoped-for future. Journal of Communication 43(3), 34–44.

Kristeva, J. (1984). Revolution in poetic language. New York: Columbia University Press. (Original work published 1974)

Kristeva, J. (1986). Women's time. In J. Kristeva, The Kristeva reader (pp. 187–213). Oxford, UK: Basil Blackwell.

Kroker, A. (1984). Technology and the Canadian mind: Innis/McLuhan/Grant. New York: St. Martin's Press.

Kumar, K. (1978). Prophecy and progress: The sociology of industrial and postindustrial society. Harmondsworth, UK: Penguin.

Kumar, K. (1995). From post-industrial to post-modern society. Oxford, UK: Blackwell.

Kunelius, R. (1996). The news, textually speaking. Acta Universitatis Tamperensis, ser. A, vol. 520.

Kutsch, A. (1984). Karl Oswin Kurth (1910–1981). In A. Kutsch (Ed.), Zeitungswissenschaftler im Dritten Reich: Sieben biographische Studien (pp. 215–243). Cologne, Germany: Studienverlag Hayit.

Kutsch, A. (1988). Max Webers Anregung zu einer "Zeitungsenquête". Publizistik, 33(1), 5–31.

Laclau, E. (1977). Politics and ideology in Marxist theory. London: Verso.

Lang, G.E., & Lang, K. (1983). The battle for public opinion: The president, the press and the polls during Watergate. New York: Columbia University Press.

Lang, K. (1980). The critical functions of empirical communication research. In G.C. Wilhoit & H. de Bock (Eds.), Mass communication review yearbook (Vol. 1, pp. 45–58). Beverly Hills, CA: Sage.

Lang, K. (1996). The European roots. In E.E. Dennis & E. Wartella (Eds.), American communication research: The remembered history (pp. 1–20). Mahwah, NJ: Erlbaum.

Lang, K., & Lang, G.E. (1983). The "new" rhetoric of mass communication research: A longer view. Journal of Communication, 33(3), 128–140.

Lang, K., & Lang, G.E. (1993). Perspectives on communication. Journal of Communication, 43(3), 92–99.

Larrain, J. (1979). The concept of ideology. London: Hutchinson.

Larrain, J. (1983). Marxism and ideology. London: Macmillan.

Larsen, O.N. (1962). Innovators and early adopters of television. Sociological Inquiry, 32(1), 16–33.

Lasswell. H.D. (1927). The theory of political propaganda. American Political Science Review, 21(3), 627–631.

Lasswell, H.D. (1938). Propaganda technique in the World War. London: Kegan Paul, Trench, Trubner. (Original work published 1927)

Lasswell, H.D. (1960). The structure and function of communication in society. In W. Schramm (Ed.), Mass communications (pp. 117–130). Urbana: University of Illinois Press. (Original work published 1948)

Lasswell, H.D. (1968). Why be quantitative? In H.D. Lasswell, & N. Leites (Eds.), The language of politics: Studies in quantitative semantics (pp. 40–52). Cambridge, MA: The MIT Press. (Original work published 1949)

Lasswell. H.D. (1971). A pre-view of policy sciences. New York: American Elsevier.

Lawrence, D.H., & Festinger, L. (1962). Deterrents and reinforcement. Stanford, CA: Stanford University Press.

Lazarsfeld, P.F. (1941). Remarks on administrative and critical communications research. Studies in Philosophy and Social Sciences, 9(1), 2–16.

Lazarsfeld, P.F. (1955). Interpretation of statistical relations as a research operation. In P.F. Lazarsfeld & M. Rosenberg (Eds.), The language of social research (pp. 115–125). Glencoe, IL: The Free Press.

Lazarsfeld, P.F., Berelson, B., & Gaudet, H. (1968). The people's choice (3rd ed.). New York: Columbia University Press. (Original work published 1944)

Lazarsfeld, P.F., & Merton, R.K. (1960). Mass communication, popular taste and organized social action. In W. Schramm (Ed.), Mass communications (pp. 492–512). Urbana: University of Illinois Press. (Original work published 1948)

Lazarsfeld, P.F., & Stanton, F.N. (Eds.) (1949). Communications research 1948–1949. New York: Harper & Brothers.

Le Bon, G. (1960). The crowd: A study of the popular mind. New York: The Viking Press. (Original work published 1895)

Leeuwis, C. (1996). Communication technologies for information-based services: Experiments and implications. In N.W. Jankowski & L. Hanssen (Eds.), The contours of multimedia: Recent technological, theoretical and empirical developments (pp. 86–102). Luton, UK: The University of Luton Press.

Lenin, V.I. (1983). The work of the People's Commissariat for Education. In A. Mattelart & S. Siegelaub (Eds.), Communication and class struggle (Vol. 2, pp. 245–248). New York: International General. (Original work published 1921)

Lent, J.A. (Ed.) (1995). A different road taken: Profiles in critical communication. Boulder, CO: Westview Press.

Lerner, D. (1958). The passing of traditional society: Modernizing the Middle East. New York: The Free Press.

Lerner, D. (1967). International cooperation and communication in national development. In D. Lerner & W. Schramm (Eds.), Communication and change in developing countries (pp. 103–125). Honolulu: East-West Center Press.

Lerner, D. (1968). Lasswell, Harold D. In D.L. Sills (Ed.), International encyclopedia of the social sciences, biographical supplement (pp. 405–411). New York: Crowell, Collier & Macmillan.

Lerner, D., & Nelson, L.M. (1977). Communication research: A half-century appraisal. Honolulu: The University Press of Hawaii.

Lewis, J. (1985). Decoding television news. In P. Drummond & R. Paterson (Eds.), Television in transition (pp. 205–234). London: BFI Publishing.

Lewis, J. (1991). The ideological octopus. An exploration of television and its audience. New York: Routledge.

Lewis, J. (1997). What counts in cultural studies? Media, Culture & Society, 19(1), 83–97.

Liebes, T., & Katz, E. (1990). The export of meaning: Cross-cultural readings of Dallas. New York: Oxford University Press.

Lincourt, J.M. (1978). Communication as semiotic. Communication, 3(1), 3–20.

Lindlof, T.R., & Meyer, T.P. (1987). Mediated communication as ways of seeing, acting and constructing culture. In T.R. Lindlof (Ed.), Natural audiences: Qualitative research of media use and effects (pp. 1–30). Norwood, NJ: Ablex.

Lippmann, W. (1965). Public opinion. New York: The Free Press. (Original work published 1922)

Löbl, E. (1903). Kultur und Presse. Leipzig, Germany: Duncker & Humblot.

Lockard, J. (1997). Progressive politics, electronic individualism and the myth of virtual community. In D. Porter (Ed.), Internet culture (pp. 219–231). New York: Routledge.

London, S. (1994). Electronic democracy: A literature survey. http://www.scottlondon.com/reports/Ed.html (5.1.01)

London, S. (1995). Teledemocracy vs. deliberative democracy: A comparative look at two models of public talk. Journal of Interpersonal Computing and Technology, 3(2), 33–55.

Lovrich, N.P., & Pierce, J.C. (1984). "Knowledge gap" phenomena: Effect of situation-specific and transsituational factors. Communication Research, 11(3), 415–434.

Lowenthal, L. (1968). The triumph of mass idols. In L. Lowenthal, Literature, popular culture, and society (pp. 109–140). Palo Alto, CA: Pacific Books. (Original work published 1944)

Lowenthal, L. (1968). The debate over art and popular culture: A synopsis. In L. Lowenthal, Literature, popular culture, and society (pp. 14–51). Palo Alto, CA: Pacific Books. (Original work published 1960)

Lowery, S., & DeFleur, M.L. (1983, 1988, 1995). Milestones in mass communication research: Media effects (1st, 2nd, and 3rd eds.). New York & White Plains, NY: Longman.

Lull, J. (1980a). Family communication patterns and the social use of television. Communication Research, 6(3), 198–209.

Lull, J. (1980b). The social uses of television. Human Communication Research, 6(3), 198–209.

Lull, J. (1982). How families select television programs: A mass-observational study. Journal of Broadcasting, 26(4), 801–811.

Lull, J. (1985). The naturalistic study of media use and youth culture. In K.E. Rosengren, L.A. Wenner, & P. Palmgreen (Eds.), Media gratifications research: Current perspectives (pp. 209–224). Beverly Hills, CA: Sage.

Lundberg, D., & Hultén, O. (1968). Individen och massmedia [The individual and the mass media]. Stockholm, Sweden: P.A. Norstedt & Söners Förlag.

Luskin, J. (1972). Lippmann, liberty, and the press. Tuscaloosa: The University of Alabama Press.

Lyon, D. (1990). The information society: Issues and illusions. Cambridge, UK: Polity Press.

Lyon, D. (1999). Postmodernity (2nd ed.). Buckingham, UK: Open University Press.

Lyotard, J-F. (1984). The postmodern condition: A report of knowledge. Manchester: Manchester University Press.

MacCabe, C. (1974). Realism and the cinema: Notes on some Brechtian theses. Screen, 15(2), 7–27.

MacCabe, C. (1979). James Joyce and the Revolution of the Word. London: Macmillan.

Macdonald, D. (1968). Running it up the totem pole. In R. Rosenthal (Ed.), McLuhan: Pro & con (pp. 29–37). New York: Funk & Wagnalls.

Machlup, F. (1962). The production and distribution of knowledge in the United States. Princeton, NJ: Princeton University Press.

Mackay, H. (1997). Consuming communication technologies at home. In H. Mackay (Ed.), Consumption and everyday life (pp. 259–297). Thousand Oaks, CA: Sage.

MacKuen, M.B. (1981). Social communication and the mass policy agenda. In M.B. MacKuen & S.L. Coombs, More than news: Media power in public affairs (pp. 19–114). Beverly Hills, CA: Sage.

Mandel, E. (1987). Late capitalism. London: Verso.

Mandler, J.M. (1978). A code in the node: The use of story schema in retrieval. Discourse Processes, 1(1), 14–35.

Mandler, J.M. (1984). Stories, scripts and scenes: Aspects of schema theory. Hillsdale, NJ: Erlbaum.

Mandler, J.M., & DeForest, M. (1979). Is there more than one way to recall a story? Child Development, 50(3), 886–889.

Maoro, B. (1987). Die Zeitungswissenschaft in Westfalen 1914–1945. Dortmunder Beiträge zur Zeitungsforschung, Band 43. Munich, Germany: K.G. Saur.

Marcuse, H. (1964). One-dimensional man. London: Routledge & Kegan Paul.

Marcuse, H. (1979). Philosophie und kritische Theorie. In H. Marcuse, Schriften, Band 3 (pp. 227–249). Frankfurt am Main, Germany: Suhrkamp. (Original work published 1937)

Marien, M. (1985). Some questions for the information society. In T. Forester (Ed.), The information technology revolution (pp. 648–660). Oxford, UK: Basil Blackwell.

Markus, H., & Zajonc, R.B. (1985). The cognitive perspective in social psychology. In G. Lindzey & E. Aronson (Eds.), The handbook of social psychology (Vol. 1, 3rd ed., pp. 137–230). New York: Random House.

Martindale, D. (1981). The nature and types of sociological theory (2nd ed.). Boston: MA: Houghton Mifflin.

Marx, K. (1990). Capital, vol. 1. Harmondsworth, UK: Penguin Books. (Original work published 1867)

Marx, K., & Engels, F. (1970). The German ideology, part one with selections from part two and three. London: Lawrence & Wishart. (Original work written 1846)

Masterman, L. (1985). Teaching the media. London: Comedia.

Masuda, Y. (1985). Computopia. In T. Forester (Ed.), The information technology revolution (pp. 620–634). Oxford, UK: Basil Blackwell.

Masuda, Y. (1990). Managing in the information society: Releasing synergy Japanese style. Oxford, UK: Basil Blackwell. (Original work published 1980)

Mattelart, A. (1979). Multinational corporations and control of culture. Brighton, UK: The Harvester Press.

Mattelart, A., & Mattelart, M. (1998). Theories of communication: A short introduction. London: Sage.

Matthews, F.H. (1977). Quest for an American sociology: Robert Ezra Park and the Chicago School. Montreal, Canada: McGill-Queen's University Press.

Mayer, J.P. (1946). Sociology of film. London: Faber and Faber.

McCombs, M.E. (1981). The agenda-setting approach. In D. Nimmo & K.R. Sanders (Eds.), Handbook of political communication (pp. 121–140). Beverly Hills, CA: Sage.

McCombs, M.E. (1994). News influence on our pictures of the world. In J. Bryant & D. Zillmann (Eds.), Media effects: Advances in theory and research (pp. 1–16). Hillsdale, NJ: Erlbaum.

McCombs, M.E., & Shaw, D. (1972, The agenda-setting function of mass media. Public Opinion Quarterly, 34(2), 176–187.

McDougall, D. (1984). Harold D. Lasswell and the study of international relations. Lanham, MD: University Press of America.

McGuire, W.J. (1966). The current status of cognitive consistency theories. In S. Feldman (Ed.), Cognitive consistency (pp. 1–46). New York: Academic Press.

McGuire, W.J. (1996). The Yale communication and attitude-change program in the 1950s. In E.E. Dennis & E. Wartella (Eds.), American communication research: The remembered history (pp. 39–59). Mahwah, NJ: Erlbaum.

McLaughlin, M.L., Osborne, K.K., & Ellison, N.B. (1997). Virtual culture in a telepresence environment. In S.G. Jones (Ed.), Virtual culture: Identity and communication in cyberspace (pp. 146–168). London: Sage.

McLeod, D.M. (1995). Communicating deviance: The effects of television news coverage of social protest. Journal of Broadcasting & Electronic Media, 39(1), 4–19.

McLeod, D.M., & Detenber, B.H. (1999). Framing effects on television news coverage of social protest. Journal of Communication, 49(3), 3–23.

McLeod, D.M., & Perse, E.M. (1994). Direct and indirect effects of socioeconomic status in public affairs knowledge. Journalism Quarterly, 71(2), 433–442.

McLeod, J., Ward, S., & Tancill, K. (1965). Alienation and uses of the mass media. Public Opinion Quarterly, 29(4), 583–594.

McLuhan, M. (1962). The Gutenberg galaxy: The making of typographic man. Toronto: University of Toronto Press.

McLuhan, M. (1965). Understanding media: The extensions of man. New York: McGraw-Hill.

McLuhan, M. (1967). The mechanical bride: Folklore of industrial man. Boston, MA: Beacon Press. (Original work published 1951)

McLuhan, M. (1980). Foreword. In H.A. Innis, Empire and communications (pp. v–xii). Toronto: University of Toronto Press.

McLuhan, M. (1982). Introduction. In H.A. Innis, The bias of communication (pp. vii–xvi). Toronto: University of Toronto Press.

McQuail, D. (1977). The influence and effects of mass media. In J. Curran, M. Gurevitch, & J. Woollacott (Eds.), Mass communication and society (pp. 70–94). London: Edward Arnold.

McQuail, D. (1985). With the benefit of hindsight: Reflections on uses and gratifications research. In M. Gurevitch & M.R. Levy (Eds.), Mass communication review yearbook (Vol. 5, pp. 125–141). Beverly Hills, CA: Sage.

McQuail, D. (1987). Mass communication theory (2nd ed.). London: Sage.

McQuail, D., & Windahl, S. (1981). Communication models. London: Longman.

McRobbie, A. (1994). Postmodernism and popular culture. London: Routledge.

Meehan, E. (1993). Commodity audience, actual audience: The blindspot debate. In J. Wasko, V. Mosco, & M. Pendakur (Eds.), Illuminating the blindspots: Essays honoring Dallas W. Smythe (pp. 378–397). Norwood, NJ: Ablex.

Melody, W.H. (1981). Introduction. In W.H. Melody, L. Salter, & P. Heyer (Eds.), Culture, communication, and dependency (pp. 3–11). Norwood, NJ: Ablex.

Melody, W.H., & Mansell, R.E. (1983). The debate over critical vs. administrative research: Circularity of challenge? Journal of Communication, 33(3), 103–116.

Mepham, J. (1979). The theory of ideology in "Capital". In J. Mepham & D-H. Ruben (Eds.), Issues in Marxist philosophy (Vol. 3, pp. 141–173). Atlantic Highlands, NJ: Humanities Press.

Merten, K. (1973). Aktualität und Publizität: Zur Kritik der Publizistikwissenschaft. Publizistik, 18(3), 216–235.

Merten, K. (1985). Some silences in the spiral of silence. In K.R. Sanders, L.L. Kaid, & D. Nimmo (Eds.), Political communication yearbook 1984 (pp. 31–42). Carbondale: Southern Illinois University Press.

Merton, R.K. (1946). Mass persuasion. New York: The Free Press.

Merton, R.K. (1949). Patterns of influence: A study of interpersonal influence and of communication behavior in a local community. In P.F. Lazarsfeld & F.N. Stanton (Eds.), Communications research 1948–1949 (pp. 180–219). New York: Harper & Row.

Merton, R.K. (1968). Social theory and social structure. New York: The Free Press. (Original work published 1949)

Mill, J. (1992). Liberty of the press. In J. Mill, Political writings (T. Ball, Ed., pp. 97–135). Cambridge, UK: Cambridge University Press. (Original work published 1825)

Mill, J.St. (1948). On liberty. In J.St. Mill, On liberty and considerations on representative government (R.B. McCallum, Ed., pp. 1–104). Oxford, UK: Basil Blackwell. (Original work published 1859)

Mills, C.W. (1995). The mass society. In R. Jackall (Ed.), Propaganda (pp. 74–101). Houndmills, UK: Macmillan Press. (Original work published 1956)

Modleski, T. (1990). Loving with vengeance: Mass-produced fantasies for women. New York: Routledge. (Original work published 1982)

Moi, T. (1985). Sexual/textual politics: Feminist literary theory. London: Methuen.

Monahan, J.L., & Collins-Jarvis, L. (1993). The hierarchy of institutional values in the communication discipline. Journal of Communication, 43(3), 150–157.

Moore, D.W. (1987). Political campaign and the knowledge-gap hypothesis. Public Opinion Quarterly, 51(2), 186–200.

Moore, R.K. (1999). Democracy and cyberspace. In B.N. Hague & B.D. Loader (Eds.), Digital democracy: Discourse and decision making in the information age (pp. 39–59). London: Routledge.

Moores, S. (1993). Interpreting audiences: The ethnography of media consumption. London: Sage.

Morgan, M. (1995). The critical contribution of George Gerbner. In J.A. Lent (Ed.), A different road taken: Profiles in critical communication (pp. 99–117). Boulder, CO: Westview Press.

Morgan, M., & Signorielli, N. (1990). Cultivation analysis: Conceptualization and methodology. In N. Signorielli & M. Morgan (Eds.), Cultivation analysis (pp. 13–34). Newbury Park, CA: Sage.

Morley, D. (1980a). The "Nationwide" audience. London: BFI.

Morley, D. (1980b). Texts, readers, subjects. In S. Hall, D. Hobson, A. Lowe, & P. Willis (Eds.), Culture, media, language (pp. 163–173). London: Hutchinson.

Morley, D. (1981). The "Nationwide" audience: A critical postscript. Screen Education, 39, 3–14.

Morley, D. (1983). Cultural transformations: The politics of resistance. In H. Davis & P. Walton (Eds.), Language, image, media (pp. 104–117). Oxford, UK: Basil Blackwell.

Morley, D. (1986). Family television: Cultural power and domestic leisure. London: Comedia.

Morley, D. (1989). Changing paradigms in audience studies. In E. Seiter, H. Borchers, G. Kreutzner, & E-M. Warth (Eds.), Remote control (pp. 16–43). London: Routledge.

Morley, D. (1992). Television, audiences & cultural studies. London: Routledge.

Morley, D. (1996). Postmodernism: The rough guide. In J. Curran, D. Morley, & V. Walkerdine (Eds.), Cultural studies and communication (pp. 50–65). London: Arnold.

Morley, D., & Silverstone, R. (1991). Communication and context: Ethnographic perspectives on the media audience. In K.B. Jensen & N.W. Jankowski (Eds.), A handbook of qualitative methodologies for mass communication research (pp. 149–162). London: Routledge.

Morrison, D. (1978). Kultur & culture: The case of Theodor W. Adorno and Paul F. Lazarsfeld. Social Research, 45(2), 331–355.

Morrison, D. (1988). The transference of experience and the impact of ideas: Paul F. Lazarsfeld and mass communication research. Communication, 10(2), 185–209.

Mosco, V. (1982). Pushbutton fantasies: Critical perspectives on videotex and information technology. Norwood, NJ: Ablex.

Mosco, V. (1983). Critical research and the role of labor. Journal of Communication, 33(3), 237–248.

Mosco, V. (1996). The political economy of communication: Rethinking and renewal. London: Sage.

Moscovici, S. (1985). The age of crowd: A historical treatise on mass psychology. Cambridge, UK: Cambridge University Press.

Mullins, N.C., & Mullins, C.J. (1973). Theories and theory groups in contemporary American sociology. New York: Harper & Row.

Mumby, D. (1997). Modernism, postmodernism, and communication studies: A rereading of an ongoing debate. Communication Theory, 7(1), 1–28.

Murdock, G. (1982). Large corporations and the control of communication industries. In M. Gurevitch, T. Bennett, J. Curran, & J. Woollacott (Eds.), Culture, society and the media (pp. 118–150). London: Methuen.

Murdock, G. (2000). Peculiar commodities: Audiences at large in the world of goods. In I. Hagen & J. Wasko (Eds.), Consuming audiences? Production and reception in media studies (pp. 47–70). Cresskill, NJ: Hampton Press.

Murdock, G., & Golding, P. (1974). For a political economy of mass communications. In R. Miliband & J. Saville (Eds.), Socialist register (pp. 205–234). London: Merlin Press.

Murdock, G., & Golding, P. (1977). Capitalism, communication and class relations. In J. Curran, M. Gurevitch, & J. Woollacott (Eds.), Mass communication and society (pp. 12–43). London: Edward Arnold.

Naisbitt, J. (1984). Megatrends: Ten new directions transforming our lives. London: Macdonald & Co.

Naschold, F. (1973). Kommunikationstheorien. In J. Aufermann, H. Bohrmann, & R. Sülzer (Eds.), Gesellschaftliche Kommunikation und Information, Band 1 (pp. 11–48). Frankfurt am Main, Germany: Fischer Athenäum.

Nedzynski, S. (1973). Inequalities in access to communication facilities for working-class organizations. In G. Gerbner, L.P. Gross, & W.H. Melody (Eds.), Communications technology and social policy (pp. 413–423). New York: Wiley.

Negroponte, N. (1995). Being digital. London: Hodder and Stoughton.

Neff, B. (1986). Aspekte zur öffentlichen Diskussion um die akademische Journalistenbildung im ersten Drittel des 20. Jahrhunderts in Deutschland. In R. vom Bruch & O.B. Roegele (Eds.), Von der Zeitungskunde zur Publizistik (pp. 63–74). Frankfurt am Main, Germany: Haag+Herchen.

Negt, O., & Kluge, A. (1972). Öffentlichkeit und Erfahrung: Zur Organizationsanalyse von bürgerlicher und proletarischer Öffentlichkeit. Frankfurt am Main, Germany: Suhrkamp.

Nelson, C., Treichler, P.A., & Grossberg, L. (1992). Cultural studies: An introduction. In L. Grossberg, C. Nelson, & P.A. Treichler (Eds.), Cultural studies (pp. 1–22). New York: Routledge.

Neurath, P. (1983). Paul F. Lazarsfeld and the institutionalization of empirical social research. In B. Holzner, K.D. Knorr, & H. Strasser (Eds.), Realizing social science knowledge (pp. 13–26). Wien: Physica-Verlag.

Newcomb, H. (1980). Assessing the violence profile studies of Gerbner and Gross: A humanist critique and suggestion. In G.C. Wilhoit & H. de Bock (Eds.), Mass communication review yearbook (Vol. 1, pp. 451–469). Beverly Hills, CA: Sage.

Nguyen, D.T., & Alexander, J. (1996). The coming of cyberspacetime and the end of the polity. In R. Shields (Ed.), Cultures of Internet: Virtual spaces, real histories, living bodies (pp. 99–124). London: Sage.

Nightingale, V. (1989). What's "ethnographic" about ethnographic audience research? Australian Journal of Communication, 16, 50–63.

Nightingale, V. (1996). Studying audience: The shock of the real. London: Sage.

Noelle-Neumann, E. (1973). Kumulation, Konsonanz und Öffentlichkeitseffekt: Ein neuer Ansatz zur Analyse der Wirkung der Massenmedien. Publizistik, 18(1), 26–55.

Noelle-Neumann, E. (1980). Die Schweigespirale: Öffentliche Meinung— unsere soziale Haut. Munich, Germany: R. Piper.

Noelle-Neumann, E. (1982). Der Konflikt zwischen Wirkungsforschung und Journalisten: Ein wissenschaftsgeschichtliches Kapitel. Publizistik, 27(1–2), 114–128.

Noelle-Neumann, E. (1985). The spiral of silence: A response. In K.R. Sanders, L.L. Kaid, & D. Nimmo (Eds.), Political communication yearbook 1984 (pp. 66–94). Carbondale: Southern Illinois University Press.

Noelle-Neumann, E. (1989). Die Theorie der Schweigespirale als Instrument der Medienwirkungsforschung. In M. Kaase & W. Schultz (Eds.), Massenkommunikation: Theorien, Methoden, Befunde. Kölner Zeitschrift für Soziologie und Sozialpsychologie, Sonderheft 30 (pp. 418–440). Opladen, Germany: Westdeutscher Verlag.

Noelle-Neumann, E. (1990). Die öffentliche Meinung und die Wirkung der Massenmedien. In J. Willke (Ed.), Fortschritte der Publizistikwissenschaft (pp. 11–23). Freiburg, Germany: Verlag Karl Alber.

Noelle-Neumann, E. (1991). The theory of public opinion: The concept of spiral of silence. In J.A. Anderson (Ed.), Communication yearbook (Vol. 14, pp. 256–287). Newbury Park, CA: Sage.

Noelle-Neumann, E. (1992). Manifeste und latente Funktionen öffentlicher Meinung. Publizistik, 37(3), 283–297.

Noelle-Neumann, E. (1993). The spiral of silence: Public opinion—our social skin (2nd ed.). Chicago: The University of Chicago Press. (Original work published 1980)

Nordenstreng, K. (1968). Communication research in the United States: A critical perspective. Gazette, 14(3), 207–216.

Nordenstreng, K. (1977). From mass media to mass consciousness. In G. Gerbner (Ed.), Mass media policies in changing cultures (pp. 269–283). New York: Wiley.

Nordenstreng, K. (1993). New information order and communication scholarship: Reflections on a delicate relationship. In J. Wasko, V. Mosco, & M. Pendakur (Eds.), Illuminating the blindspots: Essays honoring Dallas W. Smythe (pp. 251–273). Norwood, NJ: Ablex.

Nordenstreng, K. (1994). The Unesco expert panel with the benefit of hindsight. In C.J. Hamelink & O. Linné (Eds.), Mass communication research: On problems and policies (pp. 3–19). Norwood, NJ: Ablex.

Nordenstreng, K. (1999). The context: Great media debate. In R.C. Vincent, K. Nordenstreng, & M. Traber (Eds.), Towards equity in global communication: MacBride update (pp. 235–268). Cresskill, NJ: Hampton Press.

Nye, R.A. (1975). The origins of crowd psychology: Gustave LeBon and the crisis of mass democracy in the third republic. London: Sage.

Obst, B. (1986). Die Ende der Presse-Enquete Max Webers: Professorenprozess von 1912 und seine Auswirkungen auf die deutsche Zeitungswissenschaft. In R. vom Bruch & O.B. Roegele (Eds.), Von der Zeitungskunde zur Publizistik (pp. 45–62). Frankfurt am Main, Germany: Haag+Herchen.

O'Keefe, B. (1993). Against theory. Journal of Communication, 43(3), 75–82.

Olien, C.N., Donohue, G.A., & Tichenor, P.J. (1983). Structure, communication and social power: Evolution of the knowledge gap hypothesis. In E. Wartella, D. C. Whitney, & S. Windahl (Eds.), Mass communication review yearbook (Vol. 4, pp. 455–461). Beverly Hills, CA: Sage.

Olson, D.R. (1981). McLuhan: Preface to literacy. Journal of Communication, 31(3), 136–143.

Paech, J., Borchers, D., Donnerberg, G., Hartweg, I., & Hohenberger, E. (Eds.). (1985). Screen-Theory: Zehn Jahre Filmtheorie in England von 1971 bis 1981. Osnabrück: Selbsverlag Universität Osnabrück.

Palmgreen, P. (1984). Uses and gratifications: A theoretical perspective. In R. N. Bostrom (Ed.), Communication yearbook (Vol. 8, pp. 20–55). Beverly Hills: Sage.

Palmgreen, P., & Clarke, P. (1977). Agenda-setting with local and national issues. Communication Research, 4(4), 435–452.

Palmgreen, P., & Rayburn II, J.D. (1985). An expectancy-value approach to media gratifications. In K.E. Rosengren, L.A. Wenner & P. Palmgreen (Eds.), Media gratifications research: Current perspectives (pp. 61–72). Beverly Hills, CA: Sage.

Palmgreen, P., Wenner, L.A., & Rosengren, K.E. (1985). Uses and gratifications research: The past ten years. In K.E. Rosengren, L.A. Wenner, & P. Palmgreen (Eds.), Media gratifications research: Current perspectives (pp. 11–37). Beverly Hills, CA: Sage.

Park, R.E. (1925). The city: Suggestions for the investigation of human behavior in the urban environment. In R.E. Park, E.W. Burgess, & R.D. McKenzie (Eds.), The city (pp. 1–46). Chicago: University of Chicago Press.

Park, R.E. (1950). Our racial frontier on the Pacific. In R.E. Park, Race and culture: The collected papers of Robert Ezra Park (Vol. I, pp. 138-151). Glencoe, IL: The Free Press. (Original work published 1926)

Park, R.E. (1953). Reflections on communication and culture. In B. Berelson & M. Janowitz (Eds.), Reader in public opinion and communication (enlarged ed., pp. 165–175). Glencoe, IL: The Free Press. (Original work published 1939)

Park, R.E. (1955). Sociology and the social sciences. In R.E. Park, Society: The collected papers of Robert Ezra Park (Vol. II pp. 187–242). Glencoe, IL: The Free Press. (Original work published 1921)

Park, R.E. (1955). The natural history of the newspaper. In R.E. Park, Society: The collected papers of Robert Ezra Park (Vol. III, pp. 89–104). Glencoe, IL: The Free Press. (Original work published 1923)

Park, R.E. (1955). News as a form of knowledge. In R.E. Park, Society: The collected papers of Robert Ezra Park (Vol. III, pp. 71–88). Glencoe, IL: The Free Press. (Original work published 1940a)

Park, R.E. (1955). Physics and society. In R.E. Park, Society: The collected papers of Robert Ezra Park (Vol. III, pp. 301–321). Glencoe, IL: The Free Press. (Original work published 1940b)

Park, R.E. (1955). Morale and the news. In R.E. Park, Society, The collected papers of Robert Ezra Park (Vol. III, pp. 126–142). Glencoe, IL: The Free Press. (Original work published 1941)

Park, R.E. (1955). Modern society. In R.E. Park, Society: The collected papers of Robert Ezra Park (Vol. III, pp. 322–341). Glencoe, IL: The Free Press. (Original work published 1942)

Park, R.E. (1967). Human ecology. In R.E. Park, On social control and collective behavior (R.H.Turner, Ed., pp. 64–84). Chicago: The University of Chicago Press. (Original work published 1936a)

Park, R.E. (1967). Succession, an ecological concept. In R.E. Park, On social control and collective behavior (R.H. Turner, Ed., pp. 85–94). Chicago: The University of Chicago Press. (Original work published 1936b)

Park, R.E. (1972). The crowd and the public and other essays (H. Elsner, Jr., Ed.). Chicago: The University of Chicago Press. (Original work published 1904)

Parker, I. (1981). Innis, Marx, and the economics of communication. In W.H. Melody, L. Salter, & P. Heyer (Eds.), Culture, communication, and dependency (pp. 127–143). Norwood, NJ: Ablex.

Parkin, F. (1971). Class inequality and political order. London: MacGibbon & Kee.

Parsons, T., Bales, R.F., & Shils, E.A. (1953). Working papers in the theory of action. Glencoe, IL: The Free Press.

Parsons, T., & Smelser, N.J. (1956). Economy and society: A study in the integration of economic and social theory. Glencoe, IL: The Free Press.

Parsons, T., & White, W. (1960). The mass media and the structure of American society. Journal of Social Issues, 16(3), 67–77.

Patterson, G. (1990). History and communication: Harold Innis, Marshall McLuhan, the interpretation of history. Toronto: University of Toronto Press.

Patterson, T.E. (1980). The mass media election: How Americans choose their president. New York: Praeger.

Patterson, T.E. (1994). Out of order. New York: Vintage Books.

Pavlik, J.V. (1996). New media technology and the information superhighway. Boston, MA: Allyn and Bacon.

Pepitone, A. (1966). Some conceptual and empirical problems of consistency models. In S. Feldman (Ed.), Cognitive consistency (pp. 257–297). New York: Academic Press.

Peters, A. (1930). Die Zeitung und ihr Publikum. Dortmund, Germany: Verlag Fr. Wilh. Ruhfus.

Peters, J.D. (1986). Reconstructing mass communication theory. Doctoral dissertation. Stanford, CA: Stanford University.

Peters, J.D. (1989a). Democracy and American mass communication theory. Communication, 11(3), 199–220.

Peters, J.D. (1989b). Satan and savior: Mass communication in progressive throught. Critical Studies in Mass Communication, 6(3), 247–263.

Philo, G. (1990). Seeing & believing: The influence of television. London: Routledge.

Picard, R. (1989). Media economics: Concepts and issues. Newbury Park, CA: Sage.

Pietilä, K. (1978). Yleisradiotutkimuksen metodista [On the method of broadcasting studies]. In Y. Littunen, P. Rautio, & A. Saarinen (Eds.), Tieto, tiede, yhteiskunta (pp. 221–252). Publications of the Research Institute of Social Sciences at the University of Tampere, E:6.

Pietilä, K. (1980). Formation of the newspaper: A theory. Acta Universitatis Tamperensis, ser. A., 119.

Pietilä, K. (1985). Saksalaisesta sanomalehtitieteestä [On the German newspaper science]. Tiedotustutkimus, 8(2), 2-6.

Pietilä, V. (1974). Gratifications and content choices in mass media use. Publications of the Research Institute of Social Sciences at the University of Tampere, B:22.

Pietilä, V. (1977). On the effects of mass media: Some conceptual viewpoints. In M. Berg, P. Hemánus, J. Ekecrantz, F. Mortensen, & P. Sepstrup (Eds.), Current theories in Scandinavian mass communication research (pp. 116–146). Grenaa, Denmark: GMT.

Pietilä, V. (1978). On the scientific status and position of communication research (2nd ed.). Publications of the Department of Journalism and Mass Communication at the University of Tampere, 35.

Pietilä, V. (1979). Yhteiskuntatieteen tieteenfilosofisia lähtökohtia [Science philosophical starting points of the social sciences]. Publications of the Research Institute of the Social Sciences at the University of Tampere, C:26.

Pietilä, V. (1980). Selittämisestä yhteiskuntatieteessa [Explanation in the social sciences]. Publications of the Research Institute of the Social Sciences at the University of Tampere, C:27.

Pietilä, V. (1982). Tiedotustutkimus: teitä ja tienviittoja [Mass communication research: Roads and signposts]. Publications of the Department of Journalism and Mass Communication at the University of Tampere, C:3.

Playboy (1989). Marschall McLuhan: A candid conversation with the high priest of popcult and metaphysician of the media. Canadian Journal of Communication, 14(4–5), 101–137. (Original work published 1969)

Pope, W. (1986). Alexis de Tocqueville: His social and political theory. Beverly Hills: CA: Sage.

Popper, K.R. (1952). The open society and its enemies (Vol. 1). London: Routledge & Kegan Paul.

Porat, M.U. (1977). The information economy: Definition and measurement. U.S. Department of Commerce, OT special publication (77–12[1]). Washington DC: U.S. Government Printing Office.

Porter, D. (1997). Introduction. In D. Porter (Ed.), Internet culture (pp. xi–xviii). New York: Routledge.

Poster, M. (1990). The mode of information: Poststructuralism and social context. Cambridge, UK: Polity Press.

Poster, M. (1997). Cyberdemocracy: Internet and the public sphere. In D. Porter (Ed.), Internet culture (pp. 201–217). New York: Routledge.

Potter, W.J. (1993). Cultivation theory and research: A conceptual critique. Human Communication Research, 19(4), 564–601.

Poulantzas, N. (1977). Den moderna kapitalismens klassstruktur [The class structure of modern capitalism]. Lund, Sweden: Zenit/Rabén & Sjögren.

Preston, W., Jr., Herman, E. S., & Schiller, H. I. (1989). Hope & folly: The United States and Unesco 1945-1985. Minneapolis: University of Minnesota Press.

Price, V., & Allen, S. (1990). Opinion spirals, silent and otherwise: Applying small-group research to public opinion phenomena. Communication Research, 17(3), 369–392.

Prince, G. (1973). A grammar of stories. The Hague: Mouton.

Pryluck, C. (1975). Functions of functional analysis: Comments on Anderson-Meyer. Journal of Broadcasting, 19(4), 413–420.

Pye, L.W. (1963). Introduction. In L.W. Pye (Ed.), Communications and political development (pp. 3–23). Princeton, NJ: Princeton University Press.

Rada, J. (1985). Information technology and the third world. In T. Forester (Ed.), The information technology revolution (pp. 571–589). Oxford, UK: Basil Blackwell.

Radhakrishnan, R. (1989). Poststructural politics: Towards a theory of coalition. In D. Kellner (Ed.), Postmodernism, Jameson, critique (pp. 301–332). Washington, DC: Maisonneuve Press.

Rafaeli, S. (1988). Interactivity: From new media to communication. In R.P. Hawkins, J.M. Wiemann, & S. Pingree (Eds.), Advancing communication science: Merging mass and interpersonal processes (pp. 110–134). Newbury Park: CA: Sage.

Rafaeli, S., & Sudweeks, F. (1998). Interactivity in the nets. In F. Sudweeks, M. McLaughlin, & S. Rafaeli (Eds.), Network & netplay: Virtual groups on the Internet (pp. 172–189). Menlo Park, CA: AAAI Press.

Rakow, L.F. (1992). The field reconsidered. In L.F. Rakow (Ed.), Women making meaning: New feminist directions in communication (pp. 3–17). New York: Routledge.

Rantanen, T. (1997). "Maailman ihmeellisin asia": Johdatus viestinnän oppihistoriaan ["The most wonderful thing in the world": An introduction to the disciplinary history of communication]. Lahti: Helsingin yliopiston tutheimus-ja koulutuskestus.

Rauschenbush, W. (1979). Robert E. Park: Biography of a sociologist. Durham, NC: Duke University Press.

Real, M. (1984). The debate on critical theory and the study of communication. Journal of Communication, 34(4), 72–80.

Reddick, R., & King, E. (1997). The online journalist (2nd ed.). Fort Worth, TX: Harcourt Brace College Publishers.

Rhee, J.W. (1997). Strategy and issue frames in election coverage: A social cognitive account of framing effects. Journal of Communication, 47(3), 26–48.

Rheingold, H. (1995). The virtual community: Finding connection in a computerized world. London: Minerva.

Richardson, K., & Corner, J. (1986). Reading reception: Mediation and transparency in viewers' accounts of a TV programme. Media, Culture & Society, 8(4), 485–508.

Ridell, S. (1994). Kaikki tiet vievät genreen [All roads lead to genre]. Publications of the Department of Journalism and Mass Communication at the University of Tampere, A:82.

Riedel, M. (1978). Verstehen oder Erklären? Zur Theorie und Geschichte der hermeneutischen. Wissenschaften. Stuttgart, Germany: Klett-Cotta.

Riesman, D. (1950). The lonely crowd. New Haven: Yale University Press.

Roach, C. (1990). The movement for a new world information and communication order: A second wave? Media, Culture & Society, 12(3), 283–308.

Roach, C. (1997). Cultural imperialism and resistance in media theory and literary theory. Media, Culture & Society, 19(1), 47–66.

Robes, J. (1990). Die vergessene Theorie: Historischer Materialismus und gesellschaftliche Kommunikation. Stuttgart, Germany: Silberburg-Verlag.

Robinson, G.J. (1973). 25 Jahre 'Gatekeeper'-Forschung: Eine kritische Rückshau und Bewertung. In J. Aufermann, H. Bohrmann, & R. Sülzer (Eds.), Gesellschaftliche Kommunikation und Information, Band 1 (pp. 344–355). Frankfurt am Main, Germany: Fischer Athenäum.

Robinson, J.P., & Davis, D.K. (1986). Comprehension of a single evening's news. In J.P. Robinson & M.R. Levy (Eds.), The main source: Learning from television news (pp. 107–132). Beverly Hills, CA: Sage.

Rogers, E.M. (1962). Diffusion of innovations. New York: The Free Press.

Rogers, E.M. (1994). A history of communication study: A biographical approach. New York: The Free Press.

Rogers, E.M., & Dearing, J.W. (1988). Agenda-setting research: Where has it been, where is it going? In J.A. Anderson (Ed.), Communication yearbook (Vol. 11, pp. 555–594). Newbury Park, CA: Sage.

Rogers, E.M., Dearing, J.W., & Bregman, D. (1993). The anatomy of agenda-setting research. Journal of Communication, 43(2), 68–84.

Rogers, E.M., & Schement, J.R. (1984). Introduction: Media flows in Latin America. Communication Research, 11(2), 159–162.

Rose, A.M. (1962). A systematic summary of symbolic interaction theory. In A.M. Rose (Ed.), Human behavior and social processes (pp. 3–19). Boston, MA: Houghton Mifflin Company.

Rose, M.A. (1991). The post-modern and the post-industrial: A critical analysis. Cambridge, UK: Cambridge University Press.

Rosen, J. (1994). Making things more public: On the political responsibility of the media intellectual. Critical Studies in Mass Communication, 11(4), 362–388.

Rosenberg, B., & White, D.M. (Eds.). (1957). Mass culture: Popular arts in America. Glencoe, IL: The Free Press.

Rosengren, K.E. (1974). Uses and gratifications: A paradigm outline. In J.G. Blumler & E. Katz (Eds.), The uses of mass communications: Current perspectives on gratifications research (pp. 269–286). Beverly Hills, CA: Sage.

Rosengren, K.E. (1985). Growth of a research tradition: Some concluding remarks. In K.E. Rosengren, L.A. Wenner, & P. Palmgreen (Eds.), Media gratifications research: Current perspectives (pp. 275–284). Beverly Hills, CA: Sage.

Rosengren, K.E. (1993). From field to frog ponds. Journal of Communication, 43(3), 6–17.

Rosengren, K.E., & Windahl, S. (1972). Mass media consumption as a functional alternative. In D. McQuail (Ed.), Sociology of mass communications (pp. 166–194). Harmondsworth, UK: Penguin Books.

Roshco, B. (1975). Newsmaking. Chicago: The University of Chicago Press.

Roszak, T. (1968). The Summa Popologica of Marshall McLuhan. In R. Rosenthal (Ed.), McLuhan: Pro & con (pp. 257–269). New York: Funk & Wagnalls.

Rothenbuhler, E.W. (1993). Argument for a Durkheimian theory of the communicative. Journal of Communication, 43(3), 158–163.

Rowland, W.D., Jr. (1983). The politics of TV violence: Policy uses of communication research. Beverly Hills, CA: Sage.

Rowland, W.D., Jr. (1988). Recreating the past: Dilemmas in rewriting the history of communication research. Communication, 10(2), 121–140.

Rubin, A.M. (1994). Media uses and effects: A uses-and-gratifications perspective. In J. Bryant & D. Zillmann (Eds.), Media effects: Advances in theory and research (pp. 417–436). Hillsdale, NJ: Erlbaum.

Rubin, A.M., & Windahl, S. (1986). The uses and dependency model of mass communication. Critical Studies in Mass Communication, 3(2), 184–199.

Rumelhart, D.E. (1976). Notes on a schema for stories. In D.G. Bobrow & A. Collins (Eds.), Representation and understanding (pp. 211–236). New York: Academic Press.

Ruoho, I. (1992). Saippuoiden feministinen kritiikki: Naideuden ja saippuoiden yhteydestä eron politisointiin [The feminist critique of soaps: From the association of the feminine and soaps to the politicizing of difference]. Tiedotustutkimus, 17(2), 42-55.

Rühl, M. (1969). Die Zeitungsredaktion als organisiertes soziales System. Bielefield, Germany: Bertelsmann Universitätsverlag.

Rühl, M. (1980). Journalismus und Gesellschaft: Bestandsaufnahme und Theorieentwurf. Mainz, Germany: v. Hase & Koehler Verlag.

Salmon, C.T., & Kline, G. (1985). The spiral of silence ten years later: An examination and evaluation. In K.R. Sanders, L.L. Kaid, & D. Nimmo (Eds.), Political communication yearbook 1984 (pp. 3–30). Carbondale: Southern Illinois University Press.

Salter, L. (1981). "Public" and mass media in Canada: Dialectics in Innis' communication analysis. In W.H. Melody, L. Salter, & P. Heyer (Eds.), Culture, communication, and dependency (pp. 193–207). Norwood, NJ: Ablex.

de Saussure, F. (1974). Course in general linguistics. Glasgow: Fontana/Collins. (Original work published 1916)

Sayer, D. (1979). Marx's method: Ideology, science and critique in "Capital". Brighton, UK: The Harvester Press.

Schank, R.C., & Abelson, R.P. (1977). Scripts, plans, goals and understanding. Hillsdale, NJ: Erlbaum.

Schement, J.R., & Liewrouw, L. (1987). A third vision: Capitalism and the industrial origins of the information society. In J.R. Schement & L. Liewrouw (Eds.), Competing visions, complex realities: Social aspects of the information society (pp. 33–45). Norwood, NJ: Ablex.

Schenk, M. (1987). Medienwirkungsforschung. Tübingen, Germany: J.C.B. Mohr (Paul Siebeck).

Scheufele, D.A. (1999). Framing as a theory of media effects. Journal of Communication, 49(1), 103–122.

Schiller, D. (1982). Telematics and government. Norwood, NJ: Ablex.

Schiller, D. (1996). Theorizing communication: A history. New York: Oxford University Press.

Schiller, H.I. (1969). Mass communications and the American empire. New York: Augustus M. Kelley.

Schiller, H.I. (1976). Communication and cultural domination. White Plains, NY: International Arts and Sciences Press.

Schiller, H.I. (2000). Social context of research and theory. In I. Hagen & J. Wasko (Eds.), Consuming audiences? Production and reception in media research (pp. 111–122). Cresskill, NJ: Hampton Press.

Schlesinger, P. (1978). Putting "reality" together: BBC news. London: Constable.

Schöne, W. (1928). Die Zeitung und ihre Wissenchaft. Leipzig, Germany: Verlag Heinrich F.A. Timm.

Schramm, W. (1949). The nature of news. Journalism Quarterly, 26(3), 259–269.

Schramm, W. (Ed.). (1960). Mass communications. Urbana: University of Illinois Press.

Schramm, W. (1963). Communication research in the United States. In W. Schramm (Ed.), Science of human communication (pp. 1–16). New York: Basic Books.

Schramm, W. (1964). Comments on Berelson. In L.A. Dexter & D.M. White (Eds.), People, society, and mass communications (pp. 509–512). New York: The Free Press. (Original work published 1959)

Schramm, W. (1967). Communication and change. In D. Lerner & W. Schramm (Eds.), Communication and change in developing countries (pp. 5–32). Honolulu: East-West Center Press.

Schramm, W. (1971). The nature of communication between humans. In W. Schramm & D.F. Roberts (Eds.), The process and effects of mass communication (rev. ed., pp. 3–53). Urbana: University of Illinois Press.

Schramm, W. (1974). World distribution of the mass media. In H-D. Fischer & J.C. Merrill (Eds.), International and intercultural communication (pp. 179–185). New York: Hastings House Publishers. (Original work published 1964)

Schramm, W. (1983). The unique perspective of communication: A retrospective view. Journal of Communication, 33(3), 6-17.

Schramm, W. (1997). The beginnings of communication study in America: A personal memoir (S.H. Chaffee & E.M Rogers, Eds.). Thousand Oaks, CA: Sage.

Schramm, W., Lyle, J., & Parker, E.B. (1961). Television in the lives of our children. Stanford, CA: Stanford University Press.

Schröder, K. (1988). The pleasure of "Dynasty": The weekly reconstruction of self-confidence. In P. Drummond & R. Paterson (Eds.), Television and its audience (pp. 61–82). London: BFI.

Schröder, K. (1994). Audience semiotics, interpretive communities and the "ethnographic" turn in media research. Media, Culture & Society, 16(2), 337-347.

Schröder, K. (1999). The best of both worlds? Media audience research between rival paradigms. In P. Alasuutari (Ed.), Rethinking the media audience: The new agenda (pp. 38–68). London: Sage.

Schudson, M. (1992). Was there ever a public sphere? If so, when? Reflections on the American case. In C. Calhoun (Ed.), Habermas and the public sphere (pp. 143-163). Cambridge, MA: The MIT Press.

Schwartz, E. (1996). NetActivism: How citizens use the Internet. Sebastopol, CA: Songline Studios.

Seiter, E., Borchers, H., Kreutzner, G., & Warth, E-M. (1989). "Don't treat us like we're so stupid and naive": Towards an ethnographic study of soap opera viewers. In E. Seiter, H. Borchers, G. Kreutzner, & E-M. Warth (Eds.), Remote control (pp. 223–247). London: Routledge.

Selucky, K. (1984, August-September). News, narrative and the Quebec referendum. Paper presented at the IAMCR Congress, Prague.

Servaes, J. (1999). Communication for development: One world, multiple cultures. Cresskill, NJ: Hampton Press.

Shannon, C.E., & Weaver, W. (1949). The mathematical theory of communication. Urbana: University of Illinois Press.

Shils, E.A. (1951). The study of the primary group. In D. Lerner & H. D. Lasswell (Eds.), The policy sciences (pp. 44–69). Stanford, CA: Stanford University Press.

Shils, E.A. (1978). Daydreams and nightmares: Reflections on the criticism of mass culture. In P. Davison, R. Meyersohn, & E. Shils (Eds.), Literary taste, culture, and mass communication (Vol. 13: The cultural debate, part I, pp. 17–38). Cambridge, UK: Chadwyck-Healey. (Original work published 1957)

Signorielli, N., & Morgan, M. (Eds.). (1990). Cultivation analysis: New directions in media effects research. Newbury Park, CA: Sage.

Silbermann, A. (1973). Schwächen und Marotten der Massenmedienforschung. In H. Koschwitz & G. Pötter (Eds.), Publizistik als Gesellschaftswissenschaft: Internationale Beiträge (pp. 3–18). Konstanz, Germany: Konstanz Universitätsverlag.

Sills, D.L. (1996). Stanton, Lazarsfeld, and Merton: Pioneers in communication research. In E.E. Dennis & E. Wartella (Eds.), American communication research: The remembered history (pp. 105–116). Mahwah, NJ: Erlbaum.

Simonson, P. (1996). Dreams of democratic togetherness: Communication hope from Cooley to Katz. Critical Studies in Mass Communication, 13(4), 324–342.

Simpson, C. (1993). U.S. mass communication research, counterinsurgency and scientific "reality". In W.S. Solomon & R.W. McChesney (Eds.), Ruthless criticism: New perspectives in U.S. communication history (pp. 313–348). Minneapolis: University of Minnesota Press.

Simpson, C. (1996). Elisabeth Noelle-Neumann's "spiral of silence" and the historical context of communication theory. Journal of Communication, 46(3), 149–173.

Sivenius, P. (1985). Kieli keskellä kämmentä [Tongues all as thumbs]. Politiikka, 27(2), 126–133.

Sklar, R. (1976). Movie-made America: A cultural history of American movies. New York: Vintage Books.

Slack, J.D. (1984). Communication technologies and society. Norwood, NJ: Ablex.

Slack, J.D., & Allor, M. (1983). The political and epistemological constituents of critical communication research. Journal of Communication, 33(3), 208–218.

Slater, P. (1977). Origin and significance of the Frankfurt School: A Marxist perspective. London: Routledge & Kegan Paul.

Slevin, J. (2000). The internet and society. Cambridge, UK: Polity Press.

Smart, B. (1990). Modernity, postmodernity and the present. In B.S. Turner (Ed.), Theories of modernity and postmodernity (pp. 14–30). London: Sage

Smart, B. (1992). Modern conditions, postmodern controversies. London: Routledge.

Smith, D. (1988). The Chicago School: A liberal critique of capitalism. Houndmills, UK: Macmillan Education.

Smythe, D. (1977). Communications: Blindspot of western Marxism. Canadian Journal of Political and Social Theory, 3(1), 1–27.

Smythe, D. (1981). Dependency road: Communication, capitalism, consciousness, and Canada. Norwood, NJ: Ablex.

Smythe, D., & Dinh, T.V. (1983). On critical and administrative research: New critical analysis. Journal of Communication, 33(3), 117–127.

de Sola Pool, I. (1983). What ferment? A challenge for empirical research. Journal of Communication, 33(3), 258–261

Son, J., Reese, S.D., & Davie, W.R. (1987). Effects of visual-verbal redundancy and recaps of television news learning. Journal of Broadcasting & Electronic Media, 31(2), 207–216.

Spitzer, S.P., & Denzin, N.K. (1965). Levels of knowledge in an emergent crisis. Social Forces, 44(2), 234–237.

Sproule, J.M. (1987). Propaganda studies in American social science. Quarterly Journal of Speech, 73(1), 60–78.

Sproule, J.M. (1989). Progressive propaganda critics and the magic bullet myth. Critical Studies in Mass Communication, 6(3), 225–246.

Sproule, J.M. (1991). Propaganda and American ideological critique. In J.A. Anderson (Ed.), Communication yearbook (Vol. 14, pp. 211–238). Newbury Park, CA: Sage.

Stamps, J. (1995). Unthinking modernity: Innis, McLuhan, and the Frankfurt School. Montreal: McGill-Queens University Press.

Star, S.A., & Hughes, H.M. (1950). Report on an education campaign: The Cincinnati plan for the United Nations. American Journal of Sociology, 55(4), 389–400.

Steel, R. (1980). Walter Lippmann and the American century. Boston, MA: Little, Brown & Company.

Steeves, H. (1987). Feminist theories and media studies. Critical Studies in Mass Communication, 4(2), 95–135.

Stevenson, R.L. (1983). A critical look at critical analysis. Journal of Communication, 33(3), 262–269.

Straetz, S. (1986). Das Institut für Zeitungskunde in Leipzig bis 1945. In R. vom Bruch & O.B. Roegele (Eds.), Von der Zeitungskunde zur Publizistik (pp. 75–103). Frankfurt am Main, Germany: Haag+Herchen.

Streeter, T. (1984). An alternative approach to television analysis: Developments in British cultural studies in Birmingham. In W.D. Rowland, Jr. & B. Watkins (Eds.), Interpreting television (pp. 74–97). Beverly Hills, CA: Sage

Swanson, D.L. (1977). The uses and misuses of uses and gratifications. Human Communication Research, 3(3), 214–221.

Swanson, D.L. (1979). Political communication research and the uses and gratifications: A critique. Communication Research, 6(1), 37–53.

Swanson, D.L. (1988). Feeling the elephant: Some observations on agenda-setting research. In J.A. Anderson (Ed.), Communication yearbook (Vol. 11, pp. 603–619). Newbury Park, CA: Sage.

Swingewood, A. (1977). The myth of mass culture. London: The Macmillan Press.

Swingewood, A. (1984). A short history of sociological thought. London: Macmillan.

Tabbi, J. (1997). Reading, writing, hypertext: Democratic politics in the virtual classroom. In D. Porter (Ed.), Internet culture (pp. 233–252). New York: Routledge.

Tannenbaum, P.H. (1963). Experimental method in communication research. In R.O. Nafziger & D.M. White (Eds.), Introduction to mass communication research (pp. 51–77). Baton Rouge: Louisiana State University Press.

Tarde, G. (1969). Opinion and conversation. In G. Tarde, On communication and social influence (T. N. Clark, Ed., pp. 297–318). Chicago: The University of Chicago Press. (Original work published 1898)

Tarde, G. (1969). The public and the crowd. In G. Tarde, On communication and social influence (T. N. Clark, Ed., pp. 277–294). Chicago: The University of Chicago Press. (Original work published 1901)

Taylor, D.G. (1983). Pluralistic ignorance and the spiral of silence: A formal analysis. In E. Wartella, D.C. Whitney, & S. Windahl (Eds.), Mass communication review yearbook (Vol. 4, pp. 101–125). Beverly Hills, CA: Sage.

Thayer, L. (1962). Administrative communication. Homewood, IL: Irwin.

Thayer, L. (1974). Journal Editor's introduction. Communication, 1(1), 1–4.

Thayer, L. (1979). On the mass media and mass communication: Notes toward a theory. In R.W. Budd & B.D. Ruben (Eds.), Beyond media: New approaches to mass communication (pp. 52–83). Rochelle Park, NJ: Hayden Book Company.

Thompson, E.P. (1978). The poverty of theory and other essays. London: Merlin Press.

Thompson, J.B. (1995). The media and modernity: A social theory of the media. Cambridge, UK: Polity Press.

Tichenor, P.J., Donohue, G.A., & Olien, C.N. (1970). Mass media flow and the differential growth of knowledge. Public Opinion Quarterly, 34(2), 159–170.

Tichenor, P.J., Donohue, G.A., & Olien, C.N. (1980). Community conflicts and the press. Beverly Hills, CA: Sage

Tichenor, P.J., Rodenkirehen, J. H., Olien, C.N., & Donohue, G.A. (1973). Community issues, conflict, and public affairs knowledge. In P. Clarke (Ed.), New models for mass communication research (pp. 45–79). Beverly Hills, CA: Sage.

Tipton, L., Haney, R.D., & Baseheart, J. (1975). Media agenda-setting in city and state election campaigns. Journalism Quarterly, 52(1), 15–22.

de Tocqueville, A. (1990). Democracy in America (Vols 1 & 2). New York: Vintage Books. (Original work published 1835, 1840)

Toffler, A. (1971). Future shock. London: Pan.

Toffler, A. (1980). The third wave. London: Collins.

Tomlinson, A. (1990). Home fixtures: Doing-it-yourself in a privatized world. In A. Tomlinson (Ed.), Consumption, identity and style (pp. 57–73). London: Routledge.

Tomlinson, J. (1991). Cultural imperialism: A critical introduction. London: Pinter Publishers.

Tönnies, F. (1935). Gemeinschaft und Gesellschaft. Leipzig, Germany: Buske. (Original work published 1887)

Traub, H. (1933). Grundbegriffe des Zeitungswesens. Stuttgart, Germany: C.E. Poeschel Verlag.

Tsagarousianou, R., Tambini, D., & Bryan, C. (Eds.) (1998). Cyberdemocracy: Technology, cities and civic networks. London: Routledge.

Tuchman, G. (1972). Objectivity as strategic ritual. American Journal of Sociology, 77(4), 660–679.

Tuchman, G. (1973). Making news by doing work: Routinizing the unexpected. American Journal of Sociology, 79(1), 110–131.

Tuchman, G. (1978). Making news: A study in the construction of reality. New York: The Free Press.

Turkle, S. (1995). Life on the screen: Identity in the age of the Internet. New York: Simon & Schuster.

Turner, B.S. (1990). Periodization and politics in the postmodern. In B.S. Turner (Ed.), Theories of modernity and postmodernity (pp. 1–13). London: Sage.

Turner, G. (1992). British cultural studies: An introduction. New York: Routledge.

Turner, R.H. (1967). Introduction. In R.E. Park, On social control and collective behavior (R.H. Turner, Ed., pp. ix-xlvi). Chicago: The University of Chicago Press.

Unger, I. (1974). The movement: A history of the American new left 1959–1972. New York: Harper & Row.

Vainikkala, E. (1986). Fredric Jameson: Esittely [Introduction to Fredric Jameson]. In J. Kotkavirta & E. Sironen (Eds.), Moderni/postmoderni (pp. 207-225). Publications of the Finnish Union of Researchers, no. 44.

Van Dijk, T.A. (1983). Discourse analysis: Its development and application to the structure of news. Journal of Communication, 33(2), 20–43.

Van Dijk, T.A. (1985). Structures of news in the press. In T.A. van Dijk (Ed.), Discourse and communication (pp. 69–93). Berlin: Walter de Gruyter.

Van Dijk, T.A. (1986). News schemata. In C.R. Cooper & S. Greenbaum (Eds.), Studying writing: Linguistic approaches. Written communication annual, 1 (pp. 155–185). Beverly Hills, CA: Sage.

Van Dijk, T.A. (1988). News as discourse. Hillsdale, NJ: Erlbaum.

Van Dijk, T.A. (1991). Racism and the press. London: Routledge.

Van Zoonen, L. (1991). Feminist perspectives on the media. In J. Curran & M. Gurevitch (Eds.), Mass media and society (pp. 33–54). London: Edward Arnold.

Van Zoonen, L. (1994). Feminist media studies. London: Sage.

Vehmas, R. (1964). Lehdistö- ja tiedotusopin tavoitteista [On the objectives of journalism and mass communication studies]. Suomalainen Suomi, 8, 462–468.

Vehmas, R. (1985). Lehdistö- ja tiedotusopin kehitysnäkymät [The perspectives of development of journalism and mass communication studies]. In K. Nordenstreng (Ed.), 60 vuotta toimittajakoulutusta (appendix 7). Publications of the Department of Journalism and Mass Communications at the University of Tampere, C:7. (Original work published 1967)

Viswanath, K., & Finnegan, J.R. Jr. (1996). The knowledge gap hypothesis: Twenty-five years later. In B.R. Burleson (Ed.), Communication yearbook (Vol. 19, pp. 186–227). Thousand Oaks, CA: Sage.

Viswanath, K., Kahn, E., Finnegan, J.R., Jr., Hertog, J., & Potter, J.D. (1993). Motivation and the knowledge gap: Effects of campaign to reduce diet-related cancer risk. Communication Research, 20(4), 546–563.

Wagner, G. (1968). Misunderstanding media: Obscurity as authority. In R. Rosenthal (Ed.), McLuhan: Pro & con (pp. 153–164). New York: Funk & Wagnalls.

Wagner, H. (1993). Kommunikationswissenschaft—ein Fach auf den Weg zur Sozialwissenschaft: Eine wissenschaftsgeschichtliche Besinnungspause. Publizistik, 38(4), 491–526.

Wanta, W., & Wu, Y-C. (1992). Interpersonal communication and agenda-setting process. Journalism Quarterly, 69(4), 847–855.

Wartella, E., & Reeves, B. (1985). Historical trends in research on children and the media. In M. Gurevitch & M.R. Levy (Eds.), Mass communication review yearbook (Vol. 6, pp. 160–175). Newbury Park, CA: Sage.

Watson, J., & Hill, A. (1987). A dictionary of communication and media studies. London: Edward Arnold.

Watzlawick, P., Beavin, J.H., & Jackson, D.D. (1967). Pragmatics of human communication. New York: Norton.

Webster, F. (1995). Theories of the information society. London: Routledge.

Weedon, C. (1987). Feminist practice and poststructuralist theory. Oxford, UK: Blackwell Publishers.

Westbrook, R.B. (1991). John Dewey and American democracy. Ithaca, NY: Cornell University Press.

White, D.M. (1964). Mass-communication research: A view in perspective. In L.A. Dexter & D.M. White (Eds.), People, society, and mass communications (pp. 521–546). New York: The Free Press.

Wicks, R.H. (1992). Schema theory and measurement in mass communication research: Theoretical and methodological issues in news information processing. In S. A. Deetz (Ed.), Communication yearbook (Vol. 15, pp. 115–145). Newbury Park, CA: Sage

Wiggershaus, R. (1994). The Frankfurt School: Its history, theory and political significance. Cambridge, UK: Polity Press.

Wiio, O.A. (1974). Viestinnän perusteet [The elements of communication]. Tapiola, Finland: Weilin+Göös.

Wiio, O.A. (1981). Information and communication: A conceptual analysis. Department of Communication, publication, 1F/6/81. Helsinki, Finland: University of Helsinki.

Wilder, C. (1979). The Palo Alto group: Difficulties and directions of the interactional view for human communication research. Human Communication Research, 5(2), 171–186.

Wilensky, R. (1982). Points: A theory of the structure of stories in memory. In W.G. Lehnert & M.H. Ringle (Eds.), Strategies for natural language processing (pp. 345–374). Hillsdale, NJ: Erlbaum.

Wilhelm, A.G. (1999). Virtual sounding boards: How deliberative is online political discussion. In B.N. Hague & B.D. Loader (Eds.), Digital democracy: Discourse and decision making in the information age (pp. 154–178). London: Routledge.

Wilhelm, A.G. (2000). Democracy in the digital age: Challenges to political life in cyberspace. New York: Routledge.

Willey, M.M. (1926). The country newspaper. Chapel Hill: University of North Carolina Press.

Williams, R. (1976). Keywords. London: Fontana Books.

Williams, R. (1980). A hundred years of culture and anarchy. In R. Williams, Problems in materialism and culture (pp. 3–8). London: Verso.

Williamson, J. (1985). Decoding advertisements: Ideology and meaning in advertising. London: Marion Boyars. (Original work published in 1978)

Wilson, T.P. (1970). Concepts of interaction and forms of sociological explanation. American Sociological Review, 35(4), 697–707.

Windahl, S. (1981). Uses and gratifications at the crossroads. In G.C. Wilhoit & H.de Bock (Eds.), Mass communication review yearbook (Vol. 2, pp. 174-185). Beverly Hills, CA: Sage.

Winter J.P. (1981). Contingent conditions in the agenda-setting process. In G.C. Wilhoit & H. de Bock (Eds.), Mass communication review yearbook (Vol. 2, pp. 235–243). Beverly Hills, CA: Sage.

Winter, J.P., & Eyal, C.H. (1981). Agenda setting for the civil rights issue. Public Opinion Quarterly, 45(3), 376–383.

Winter, J., & Goldman, I. (1989). Comparing the early and late McLuhan to Innis's political discourse. Canadian Journal of Communication, 14(4–5), 92–100.

Wirth, W. (1997). Von der Information zum Wissen: Die Rolle der Rezeption für die Entstehung von Wissensunterschieden. Opladen, Germany: Westdeutscher Verlag.

Woodall, W.G. (1986). Information processing theory and television news. In J.P. Robinson & M.R. Levy, The main source: Learning from television news (pp. 133–158). Beverly Hills, CA: Sage.

Woodall, W.G., Davis, D.K. & Sahin, H. (1983). From the boob tube to the black box: TV news comprehension from an information processing perspective. In E. Wartella, D.C. Whitney, & S. Windahl (Eds.), Mass communication review yearbook (Vol. 4, pp. 173–194). Beverly Hills, CA: Sage.

Woodward, J.R. (1930). Foreign news in American morning newspapers: A study in public opinion. New York: Columbia University Press.

Wren-Lewis, J. (1983). The encoding/decoding model: Criticisms and redevelopments for research on decoding media. Media, Culture & Society, 5(2), 179–197.

Wright, B.F. (1973). Five public philosophies of Walter Lippmann. Austin: University of Texas Press.

Wright, C.R. (1972). Mass communication: A sociological perspective (2nd ed.). New York: Random House. (Original work published 1959)

Wright, C.R. (1964). Functional analysis and mass communication. In L.A. Dexter & D.M. White (Eds.), People, society, and mass communications (pp. 91–109). New York: The Free Press. (Original work published 1960)

Wright, C.R. (1986). Mass communication rediscovered. In S.J. Ball-Rokeach & M.G. Cantor (Eds.), Media, audience, and social structure (pp. 22–33). Newbury Park, CA: Sage.

Young, I.M. (1987). Impartiality and the civic public: Some implications of feminist critiques of moral and political theory. In S. Benhabib & D. Corner (Eds.), Feminism as critique: Essays on the politics of gender in late-capitalist societies (pp. 57–76). Cambridge, UK: Polity Press.

Zhu, J-H., Watt, J. H., Snyder, L. B., Yan, J., & Jiang, Y. (1993). Public issue priority formation: Media agenda-setting and social interaction. Journal of Communication, 43(1), 8–29.

Zingrone, F., & McLuhan, E. (1995). Introduction. In E. McLuhan & F. Zingrone (Eds.), Essential McLuhan (pp. 1–10). London: Routledge.

Zoll, R. (Ed.). (1971). Manipulation der Meinungsbildung. Opladen, Germany: Westdeutscher Verlag.

Zucker, H.G. (1978). The variable nature of news media influence. In B.D. Ruben (Ed.), Communication yearbook (Vol. 2, pp. 225–240). New Brunswick, NJ: Transaction Books.

AUTHOR INDEX

SUBJECT INDEX

385

Printed in the United States
34036LVS00006B/198